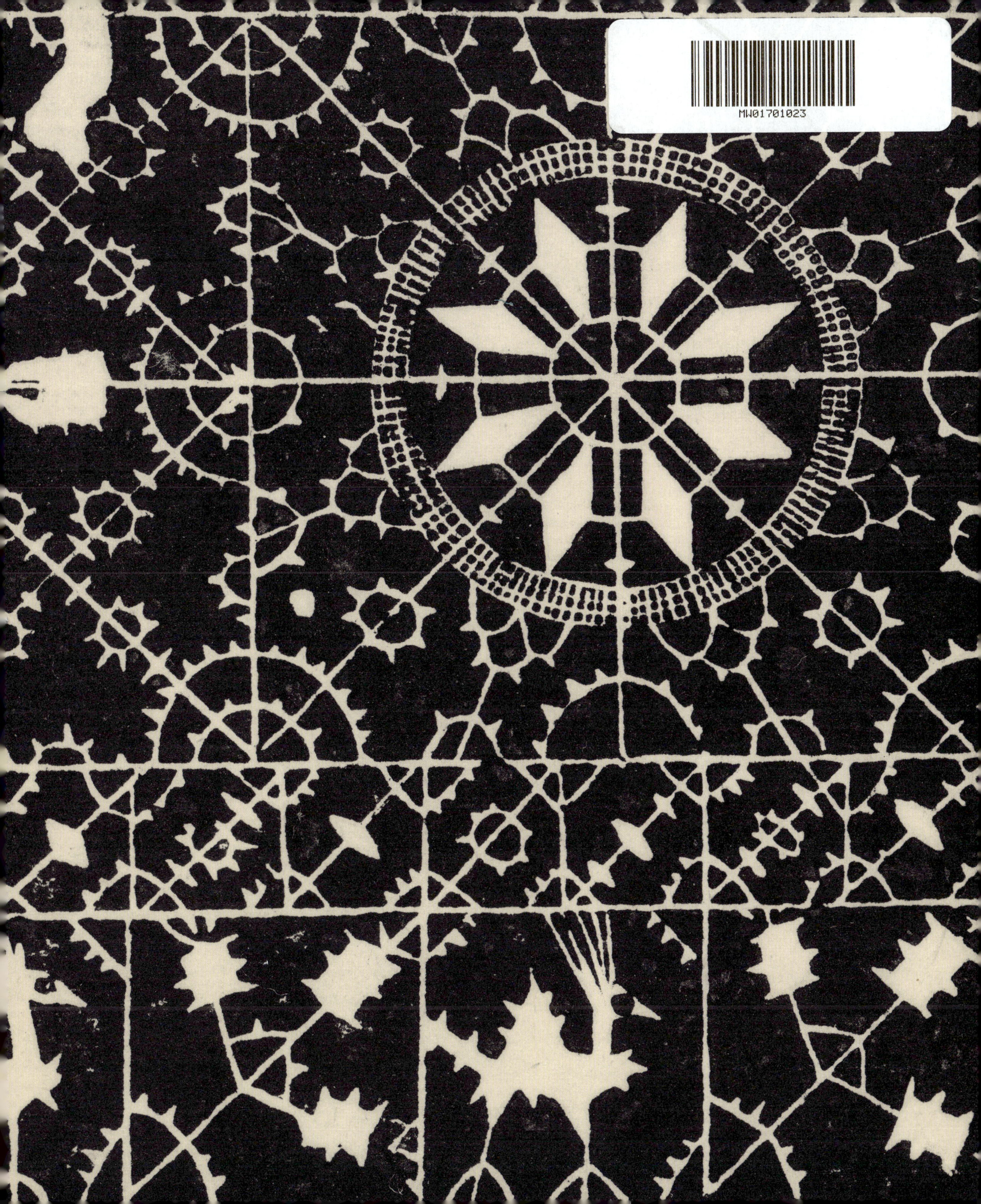

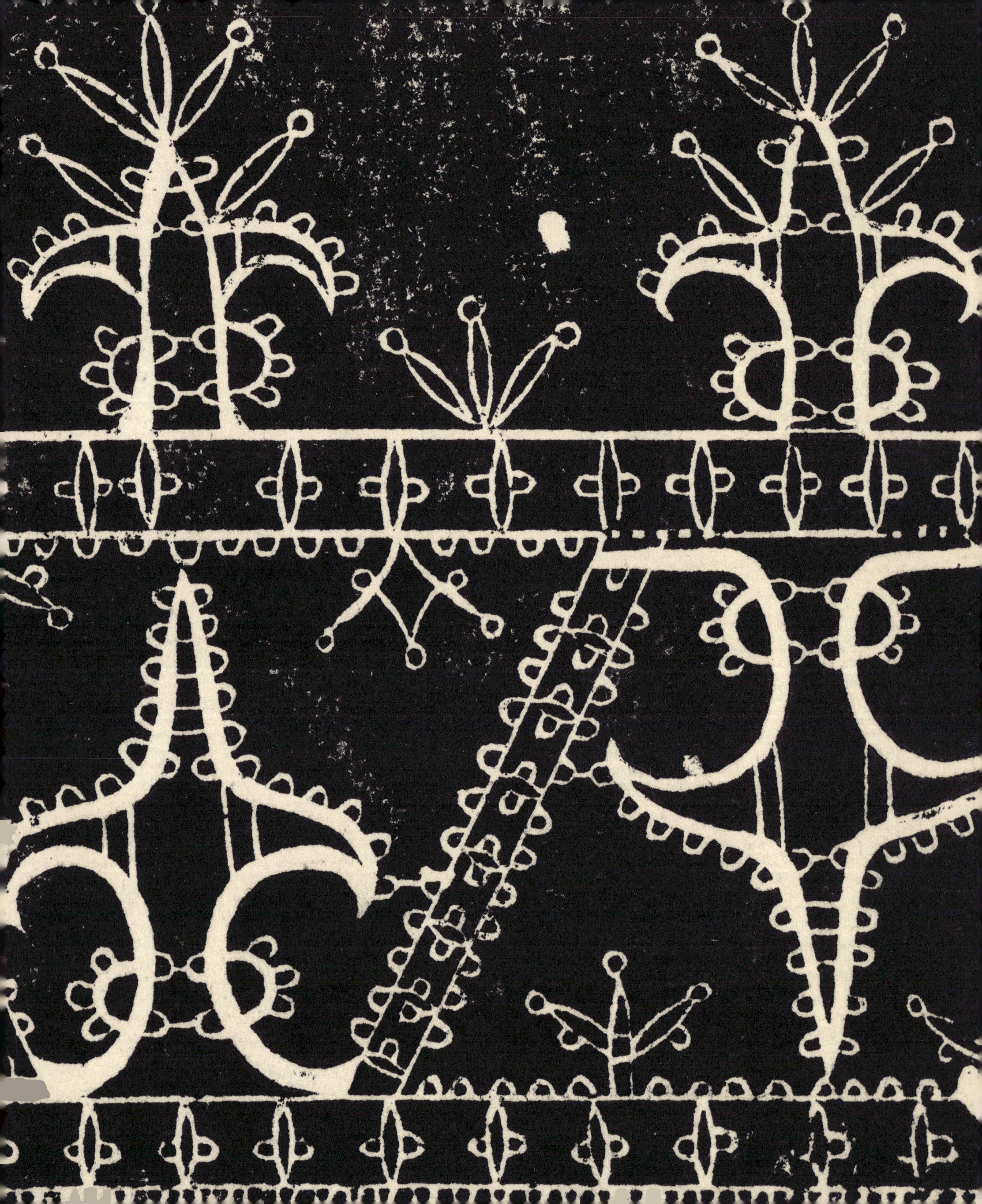

Strong Women in Renaissance Italy

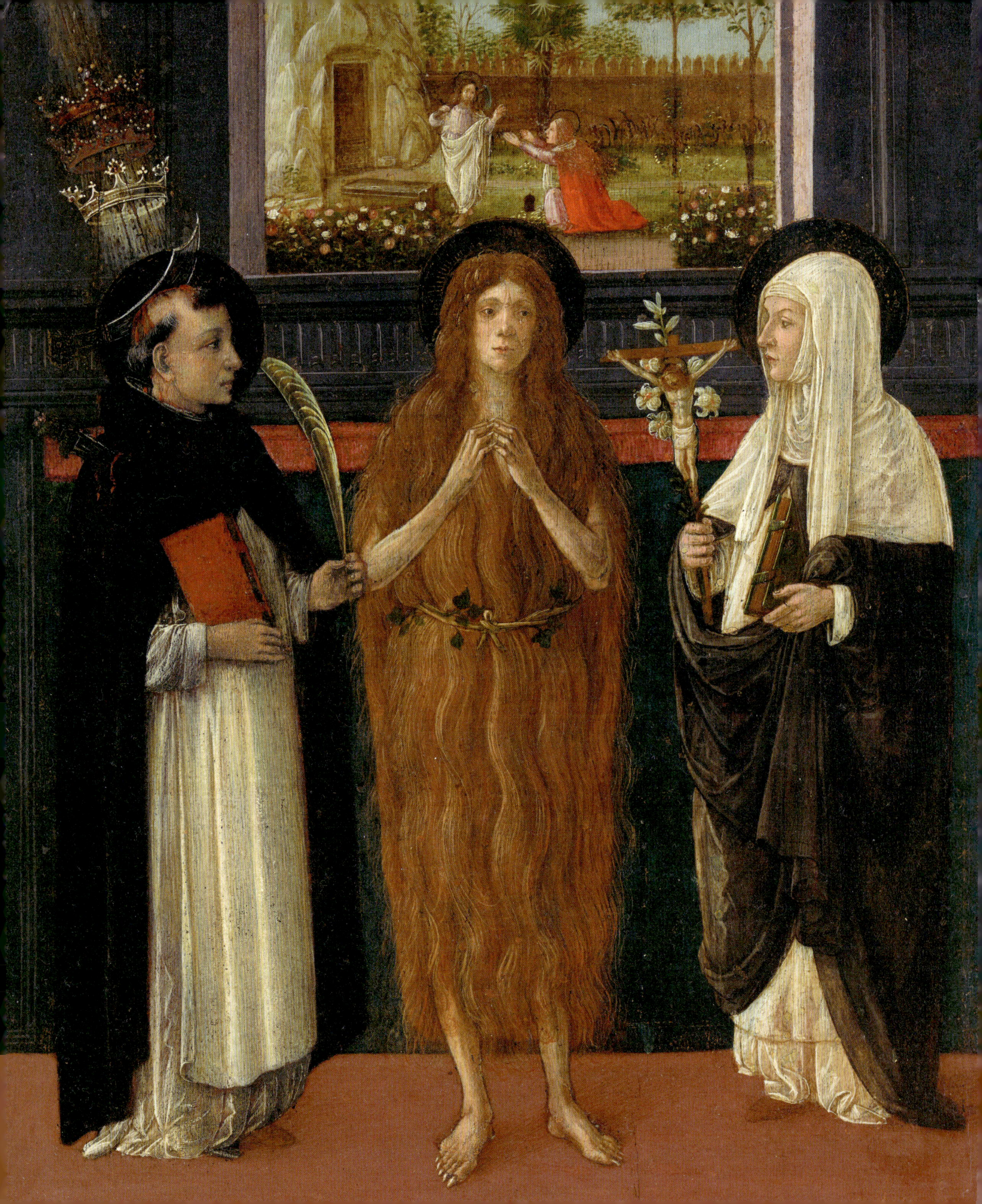

Strong Women in Renaissance Italy

Marietta Cambareri

MFA Publications
Museum of Fine Arts, Boston

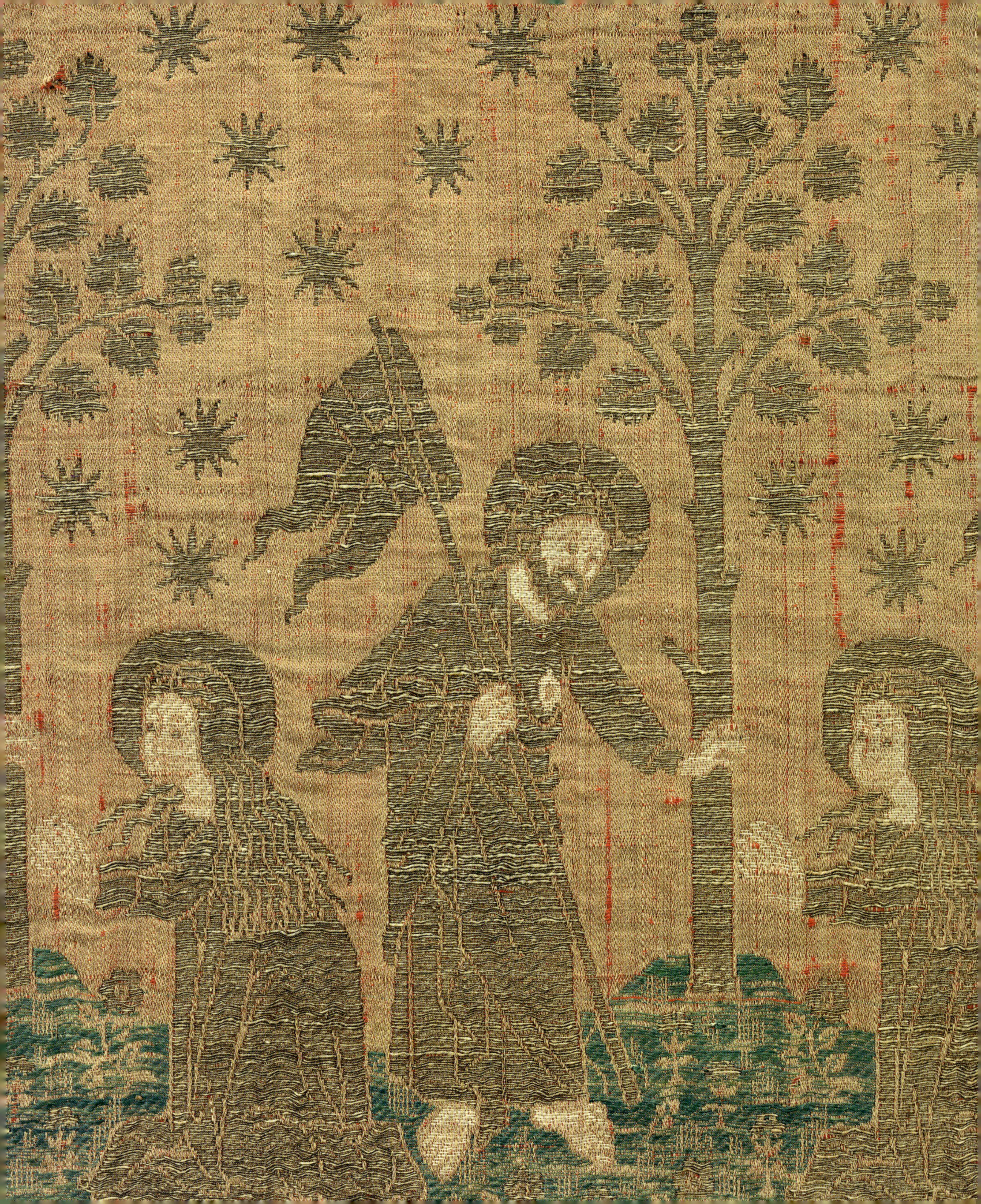

Contents

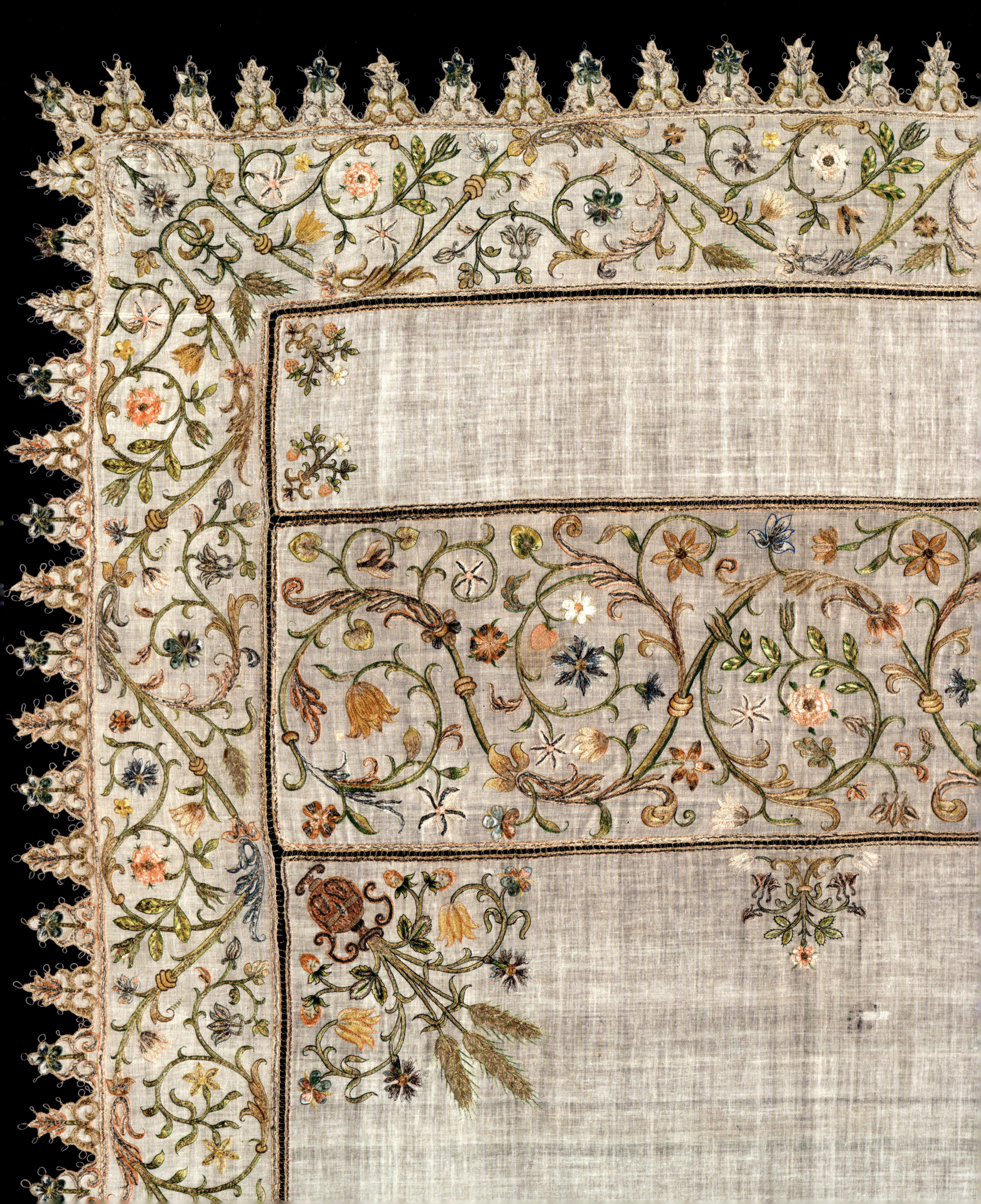

Director's Foreword

Strong Women in Renaissance Italy explores women's lives from the fourteenth to early seventeenth centuries by drawing on a wide range of artworks: paintings, prints, and sculptures, as well as velvet panels, illustrated books, embroideries, woven narrative images, and even a box decorated with cut straw that emulates gold. By asking new questions and reflecting on new approaches to the study of the Italian Renaissance, this book and the exhibition it accompanies use the stories these objects tell to illuminate how Italian Renaissance women forged paths to creativity as well as found ways to exert power and influence, even in the face of great challenges. This broad view encompasses works made by women, including the many women whose names are lost to history; works commissioned or influenced by women; works made for women's use; and images of female exemplars of power, strength, and wisdom. The material culture of Renaissance Italy evokes timeless and timely issues of health, intellect, education, family, creativity, spirituality, joy, sorrow, and hope. Beyond being witnesses to history, these works of art delight, charm, and speak to us today, offering ways of considering our own lives and suggesting our connections to past and future.

We are proud that the artworks presented here are drawn almost exclusively from our own rich collections, with a handful of enriching loans from institutions and private collectors. Generous support for this publication was provided by the Andrew W. Mellon Publications Fund, with additional support from Tamara Petrosian Davis and Charles Howard Davis II. We are especially pleased to show many textiles, books, and works on paper that are being published for the first time, many of which can be exhibited only rarely, for the sake of their own preservation. Their appearance here can be seen as a metaphor for the stories we seek to tell: we invite you to experience the ways they shed light on lives and works long hidden away.

Matthew Teitelbaum
Ann and Graham Gund Director
Museum of Fine Arts, Boston

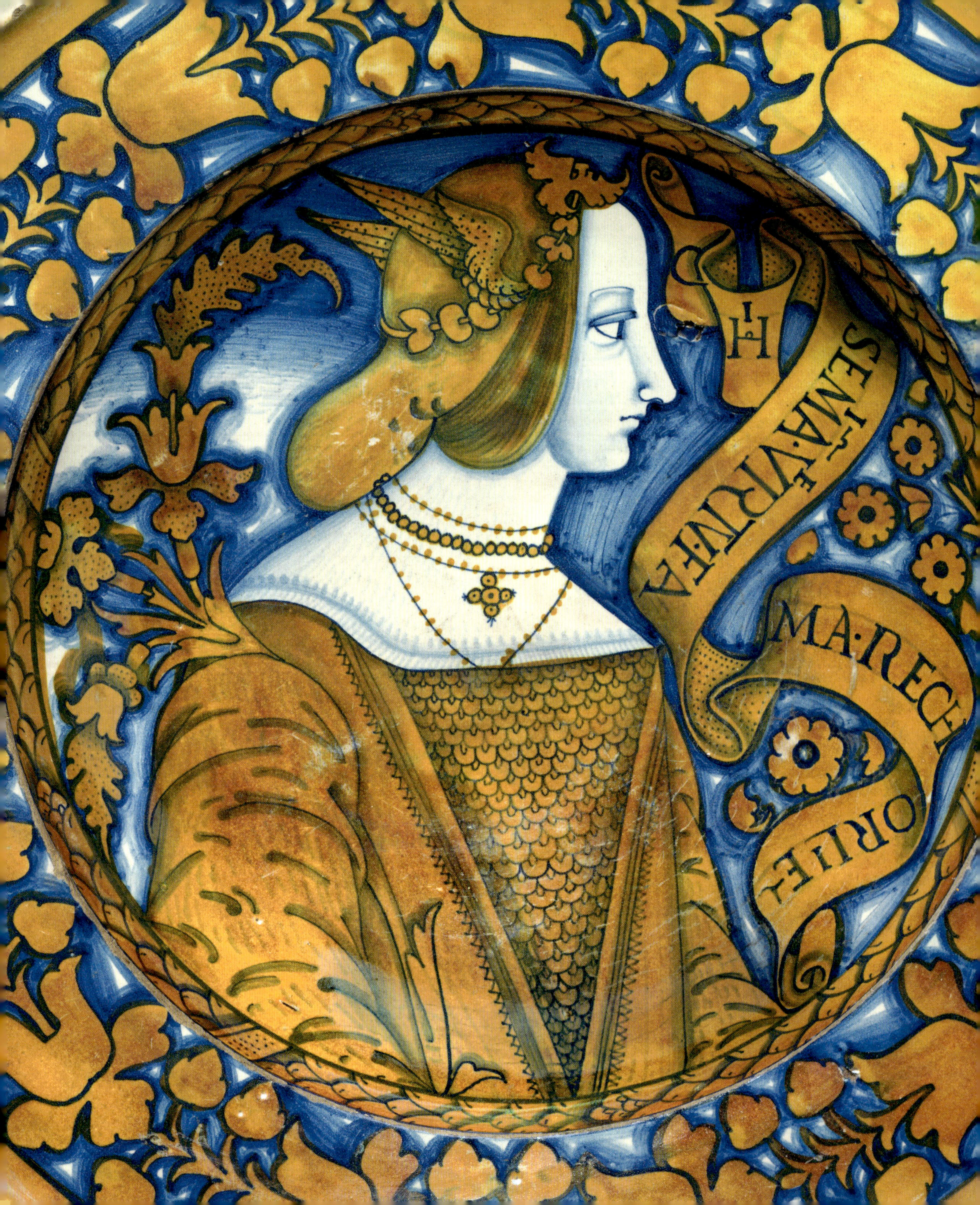
I·H
SEMA·VIRTV·A
MA·RECH
ORIE

Preface

The collection of Italian Renaissance art at the Museum of Fine Arts, Boston, includes sculptures, paintings, ceramics, furniture, furnishings, books, works on paper, textiles, and clothing accessories. There are works created by women, including artists whose names we know and artists whose names we are likely never to discover; works commissioned by women; and works made for women. In this book, nearly one hundred objects from the MFA's collections, along with a small group of works from other collections, are brought together around themes and ideas that spur conversation and inquiry, with these objects at the center of the discussion.

In recent decades, ever-expanding scholarly research into women's lives in Renaissance Italy has revealed a much richer, more nuanced picture than previously understood. Scholarship has uncovered a wealth of documentary and written sources on women's lives, for example, in convent settings and in professions including pharmacy, textile production, and sex work. Books and exhibitions focusing on works by women artists have proliferated in recent years, some organized thematically with multiple artists and others monographic. These projects have encouraged scholars, curators, and audiences to refine their understanding of individual oeuvres and their significance, as well as to formulate more accurate views of the professional lives of women artists: How did they learn their crafts, how did they shape their personae, and how did they manage the finances of producing and selling their works while supporting themselves and their families? Recently, museums have also begun to collect works by women in a purposeful and focused way. Patronage studies have explored ways in which women impacted the commissioning of works of art through influence and interests beyond the information contained in contracts and account books. Focused attention on the lives of those outside the upper classes has shed light on women's work in towns and the countryside. Growing awareness and questioning of how history is shaped make it clear that it is time to reevaluate the ways Italian Renaissance art is presented in museum settings, not just in temporary exhibitions, but in collection galleries as well. Doing so reveals a much richer sense of how Renaissance women shaped and experienced their lives and impacted the lives of those around them.

Presenting this wide range of objects is a goal that sets an example. It encourages readers, scholars, and curators to take the time to search out works that can help fill out stories of women's lives. Works of art can provide new information, just as written sources do. Refusing to see creative women as "exceptional," but rather as embedded in the broader context of the period, can shed light on women's ingenuity and talents. Identifying the strategies Renaissance women used to achieve agency illuminates the realities, accomplishments, and extraordinary abilities of women across social and economic spheres. In seeking a fuller sense of women's experience in Renaissance Italy, it is important to look beyond the standards, established in the period itself, of painting and sculpture by famous men to works often sidelined as craft or set lower on a constructed hierarchical scale. By examining the material world of Renaissance art, women's lives and accomplishments shine through.

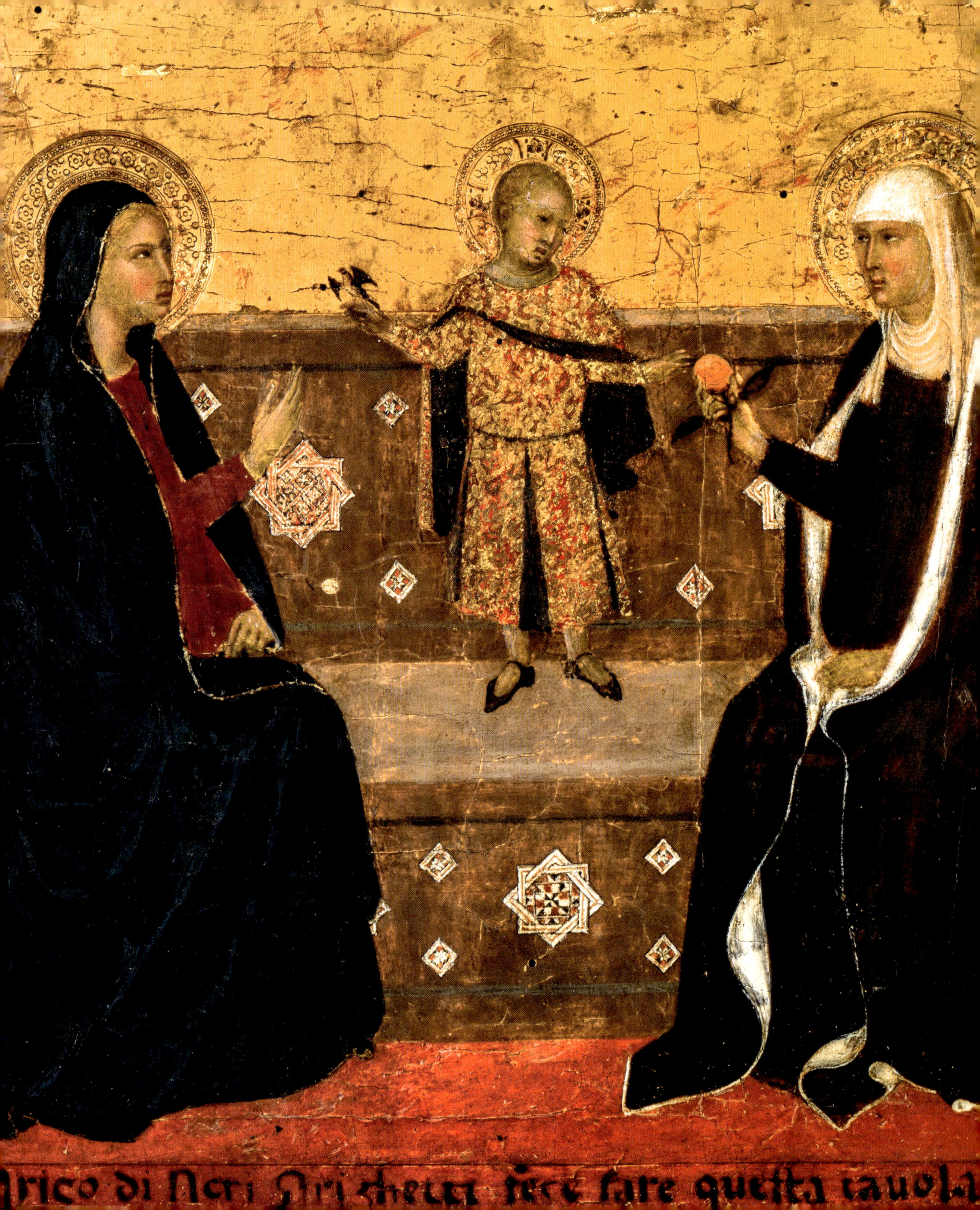
rrico di Neri Arrighetti fece fare questa tavola

Hidden Gold

In her 1582 epic poem *Floridoro*, Venetian writer Moderata Fonte described gold buried in mines, waiting to be unearthed, shaped, and polished, as a metaphor for women's intelligence, talents, and strength: "Gold which stays hidden in the mines is no less gold, though buried, and when it is drawn out and worked, it is as rich and beautiful as other gold."[1] The search for hidden gold can be a guiding principle in considering women of the Renaissance through art: What riches can be found among objects from the Italian Renaissance that tell the stories of women's lives, if only one looked for them? What previously effaced stories can be recovered? What do Renaissance objects offer the contemporary viewer, and how might they illuminate women's lives, creativity, aspirations, challenges, and realities?

The Renaissance in Italy—broadly considered here as the fourteenth through the early seventeenth centuries to acknowledge continuity, tradition, innovation, and change across these centuries—was a period of flourishing creativity in art, architecture, poetry, science, and religion. Art was pervasive in civic, religious, and domestic settings, almost always serving specific functions that make it a window into the life of Renaissance Italy. Artistic production included sculpture, painting, furnishings, textiles, books, music, and poetry.

Italy was not yet a unified country in this period, but a sense of shared Italian culture did exist. Individual states were centered around cities like Florence and Venice; courts such as Milan, Naples, Ferrara, and Mantua; and the papacy, the seat of the Catholic Church as well as a political, secular power with lands known as the Papal States. Alliances and boundaries shifted as foreign powers sought to influence if not rule over parts of the peninsula via diplomacy or war. Italy thus played an important political role across the Mediterranean region and Europe as a whole. Italian economic strength, driven by banking and commerce, the textile industry, and artistic production, encouraged international trade and travel. The era was fueled by innovative technologies and artistic practices inspired by ancient and foreign cultures, as well as local civic and religious traditions. Interest in recovering, reading, translating, and studying ancient texts drove the intellectual and cultural program of humanism, which impacted philosophy, civic life, and education. Though the word *Renaissance*, meaning rebirth, was not used in the period itself, there was a sense that Italians were living in a period of renewal and transformation. When the French term *Renaissance* was applied to the epoch in the nineteenth century, it had a resonance that still engages imaginations today.

Recent scholarship has expanded ways of looking at the Renaissance, challenging the history that was already taking shape during the period. Writers like Francesco Petrarca (Petrarch), Leon Battista Alberti, and Giorgio Vasari, among others, developed and codified ideas about artistic progress inspired by antiquity. This narrative championed the creativity of great men of genius, a creativity supported by the enlightened patronage of elite society as well as civic and religious institutions. However, more recently, scholars have challenged the long-dominant historiographical framework by tracing the histories of people of lower social and economic status, and by seeking out different kinds of sources that reveal women's lives and experiences, as well as the stories of other marginalized groups including people of color and those practicing faiths other than the dominant Catholic religion, such as Jews, Muslims, and Eastern Orthodox Christians.

Looking at the Italian Renaissance from the point of view of women has become a flourishing field of study.[2] First encouraged by feminist scholars who called for a rethinking of the artistic and literary canons, this work is supported by careful, thoughtful, and innovative archival work, including the reading and publication of women's writings.[3] These sources, including letters, poetry, and personal narratives, often remained hidden away in archives and libraries in manuscript form. A broader approach to the written sources has been accompanied by a reevaluation of the material and artistic culture of the period. Renaissance ideas about women were often expressed through works of art made or commissioned by men, but women might view and understand these images in different ways. Works made by women, works commissioned or influenced by women, works made for use by women, and works representing women all reveal aspects of female experience in Renaissance Italy.

Women's lives were generally restricted to the home and to roles as daughter, wife, mother, and widow. Women could not become priests or clerics or participate in civic government, nor could they become part of guilds except in rare cases.[4] If, however, a woman needed to earn a living or contribute to her family's support, there were possibilities: poorer women could work as farmers, gardeners, embroiderers, and sex workers. Women from households of artisans could work in the family business, learn trades and crafts, and sometimes branch out as professionals in their own right.[5] Women might enter convents, either by choice or by necessity, and take vows as nuns. Convents were places where many skills, crafts, and arts could be learned, and they were primary centers of education for young women and girls.[6] Women were healers in family, convent, and hospital settings and produced medicines, remedies, and cosmetics.[7] They were deeply involved in the textile trade as lace makers, embroiderers, weavers, and makers of metal threads.[8] In leading families and in court settings, wives often took over for husbands who were away from home on diplomatic missions or military assignments, or as exiles; they also might take over responsibilities as widows and as regents for young sons. Widows often became heads of households and looked after family businesses.[9] Women acted as patrons, commissioning works of art, supporting poets and musicians, and influencing commissions made by other family members.[10] Particular groups of women, including nuns and courtesans, had different experiences beyond the norms of traditional family life, allowing for other possibilities of creative expression.

Women, in addition to being daughters, wives, mothers, and widows in relatively restricted home lives, were also artists, poets, healers, apothecaries, rulers, patrons, nuns, laity, singers, actors, composers, musicians, dancers, lace designers, lace makers, embroiderers, farmers, vendors, scribes, scholars, courtesans, prostitutes, and teachers. The list goes on, and in such roles, women often emerged into civic and public life and impacted culture in various ways that are not necessarily evident in institutional and economic records. By changing perspective, by asking new questions, and by considering women within their own spheres of influence and creativity, new stories can be told.

The challenges and restrictions that were imposed on women in the period should not be minimized. The metaphor of worked and burnished gold described by Moderata Fonte also appeared in Christine de Pizan's groundbreaking treatise on women, *La livre de la cité des dames* (The Book of the City of Ladies) of 1405. Early in the book, the narrator, Christine herself, laments the challenges and injustices of being a woman and is scolded by the character of Lady Reason: "My dear girl, what has happened to your common sense? Have you forgotten that gold proves itself in the furnace? It does not change its quality but increases in value the more it is beaten and fashioned in various ways."[11] In the book, Christine goes on to tell the stories of women's lives across history, reveal avenues to power and creativity, and find meaning even in the mundane, often restrictive female experience of home and family life. Christine wrote because she had to: widowed at the age of twenty-five, she found herself responsible for the support of three children and her widowed mother. Her works were dedicated to or commissioned by members of the ruling elite and were published and translated in her own lifetime. She wrote about women, religious devotion, and politics, in hopes of improving the lives of women and the state of her world.

Christine de Pizan and Moderata Fonte, professional writers who contributed to the literature about women's lives—both its challenges and opportunities—illustrate why it is especially appropriate to focus on Renaissance Italy, where considerable numbers of women were educated and literate. Though she moved to France at an early age, Christine de Pizan was born in Italy, and her Italian father oversaw her education; this kind of encouragement was essential for permitting women to develop their talents. In addition to writing *Floridoro*, Moderata Fonte wrote *Il merito delle donne* (The Worth of Women: Wherein is Clearly Revealed Their Nobility and Their Superiority to Men) in 1600, a book that took up the theme of women's natural, innate value. This treatise passionately and sometimes humorously calls for the elevation of the status and education of women given the severe limitations of men. In the almost two centuries between Christine de Pizan's *The Book of the City of Ladies* and Moderata Fonte's *The Worth of Women*, many Italian women became professional artists and writers, took on roles of cultural and religious leadership, and served as role models for other women across Europe. Indeed, many of the issues, joys, and challenges that faced Italian women in the Renaissance remain central to women's lives today: access to education and professional accomplishment; control over women's bodies and health; the constrictions and possibilities offered by marriage and family life; and economic parity, independence, and agency. These are just a few of the issues that Renaissance women faced that still resonate today.

The Mystic Marriage of Saint Catherine, possibly painted around 1340 by the so-called Barna da Siena, can be seen almost as a protofeminist manifesto in the ways it references women's lives as brides,

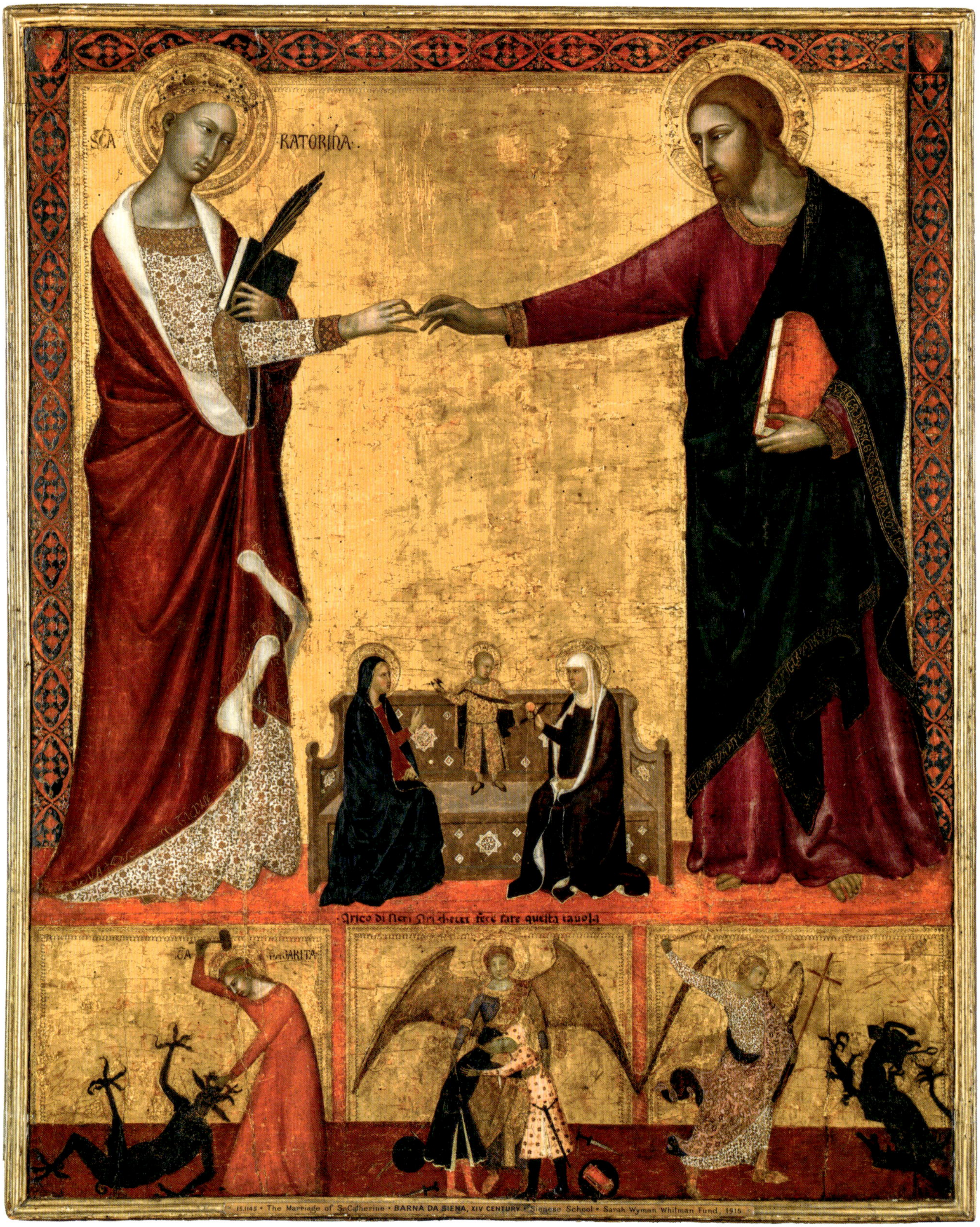

1 Barna da Siena, *The Mystic Marriage of Saint Catherine*, about 1340, 138.7 x 111.1 cm (54⅝ x 43¾ in.)

mothers, grandmothers, educated women, and mystic visionaries (fig. 1). Catherine of Alexandria was one of the saints most frequently represented in Italian art from the late thirteenth century through the seventeenth centuries.[12] Her legend places her in Alexandria, Egypt, in the early fourth century and is likely a composite of the stories of several women. Of noble status, she was renowned for her intellect, wisdom, and skill as a speaker. When her Christian beliefs were challenged by a council of scholars and philosophers gathered for that purpose by the Roman emperor Maxentius, she not only defended her faith but also persuaded her listeners to convert, as she herself had done. Maxentius also tried to convince her to marry him, but upon her conversion and mystical vision of her marriage to Jesus Christ, she had vowed to remain a virgin. She survived torture on a wheel and was subsequently beheaded. Her common attributes are books, the wheel, and the palm of martyrdom, as well as her elegant dress.

The Mystic Marriage of Saint Catherine presents the sumptuously attired Catherine, holding a book and a palm. She is identified by her name KATORINA, and stands across from Jesus as he places a ring on her finger. This scene recounts Catherine's vision of her mystical union with Christ, which is described for the first time in surviving written sources in 1337, though the story probably emerged in the later thirteenth century.[13] An early representation of the scene, the painting evokes an actual wedding, as the joining of hands and exchange of rings were part of the legal ritual of marriage at this time, and shows the adult Jesus and Catherine on an equal footing. Representations of this scene typically show Catherine with an infant Jesus, usually held by his mother, Mary.[14] Truer to written versions of the tale, such representations of the scene focus on a more tender display of affection and love shown to the baby, making it a vision that would guide meditative devotion to the Christ child, with the intercession of Mary. In another version showing the much rarer depiction of Jesus as a grown man, attributed to Jacopo di Cione and dated to around 1375–80, Catherine kneels before Jesus, with the Virgin Mary acting as intermediary by holding their wrists (fig. 2). Saint Louis of Toulouse and a Franciscan nun, both smaller in scale, are placed to either side; the presence of the nun suggests a commission for a convent. In Barna's painting, Catherine stands on her own, face to face with Jesus, and without the intercession of Mary.

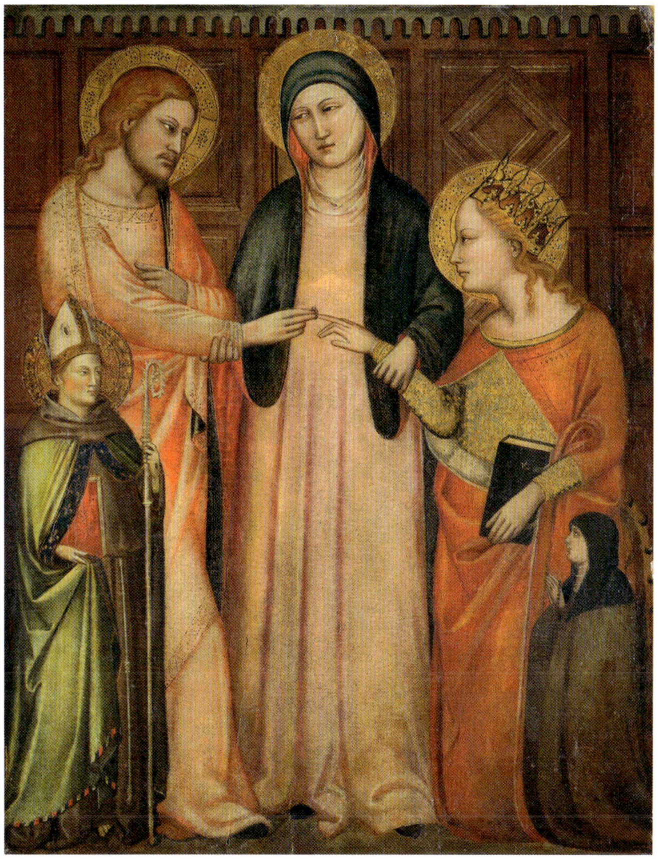

2 Jacopo di Cione, *The Mystic Marriage of Saint Catherine of Alexandria, with Saint Louis of Toulouse and a Franciscan Nun Donor*, about 1375–80, 81.1 x 62.2 cm (31⅞ x 24½ in.)

The child Jesus is also present in Barna's painting. On the same plane as the figures of the mystical marriage but smaller in scale, he stands between his mother, Mary, and his grandmother Anne on a high-backed bench. Here, Jesus holds a bird in his right hand and reaches with his left hand for a rose offered to him by Anne. He wears an elegant brocaded tunic and cape and is the focus of the two women charged with raising him. Jesus's interaction with his mother and grandmother indicates a domestic setting for

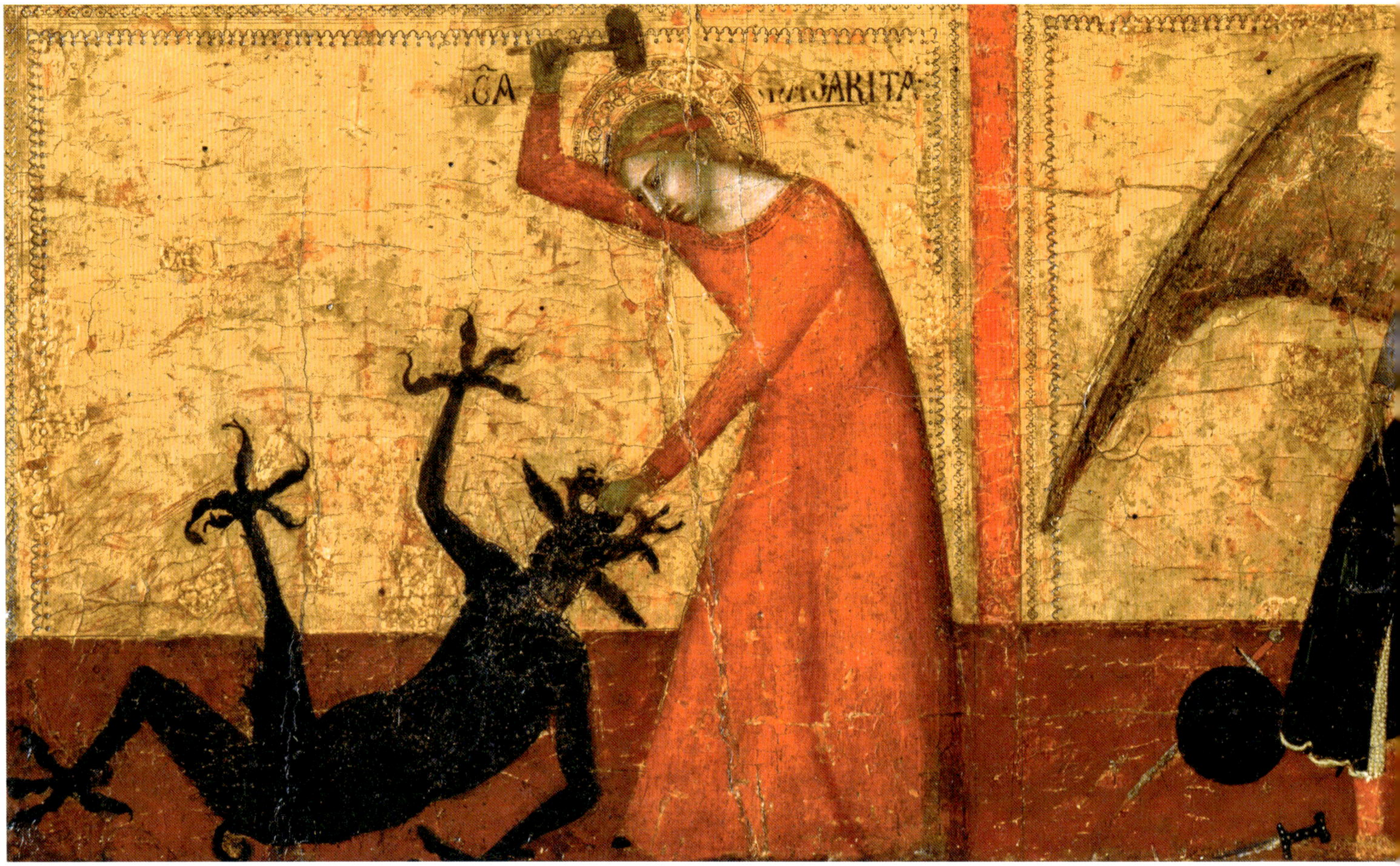

3 Detail of Barna da Siena, *The Mystic Marriage of Saint Catherine*, about 1340

this scene, as does the wooden bench decorated with intarsia inlays, which recalls daybeds (*lettucci*), high-backed benches often found in bedrooms.[15] The scene can be interpreted on one level as the domestic life of the young Jesus, looked after by the women of his household, which would resonate with female viewers who helped instill faith and devotion in their children from a young age. But the bench with its curving arms also recalls the throne-like seats that accommodate the Virtues in Ambrogio Lorenzetti's frescoes of Good Government in the Sala della Pace (Hall of Peace) in Siena's Palazzo Pubblico, or Town Hall, the most famous public example of the importance of virtue for civic harmony. If considered in a civic context, the *Mystic Marriage* speaks to family life underlying peace and stability for a town, with the holy family as role models, and the child Jesus standing in a position of virtuous power between the two women.

This link to civic life is reinforced by the scene set directly below. Overseen by an angel, two men have thrown down their arms and embrace to exchange the kiss of peace (fig. 3). Like the exchange of rings above, this is a ritual act, marking the legal institution of a peace.[16] The contrasting colors of their clothing suggest their allegiances to their respective families, possibly representing the resolution not just of a quarrel between two men but of strife between warring factions. The central spine of the painting, from the evocation of an actual marriage above in the exchange of a ring, through the domestic scene of child rearing, to this act of peace

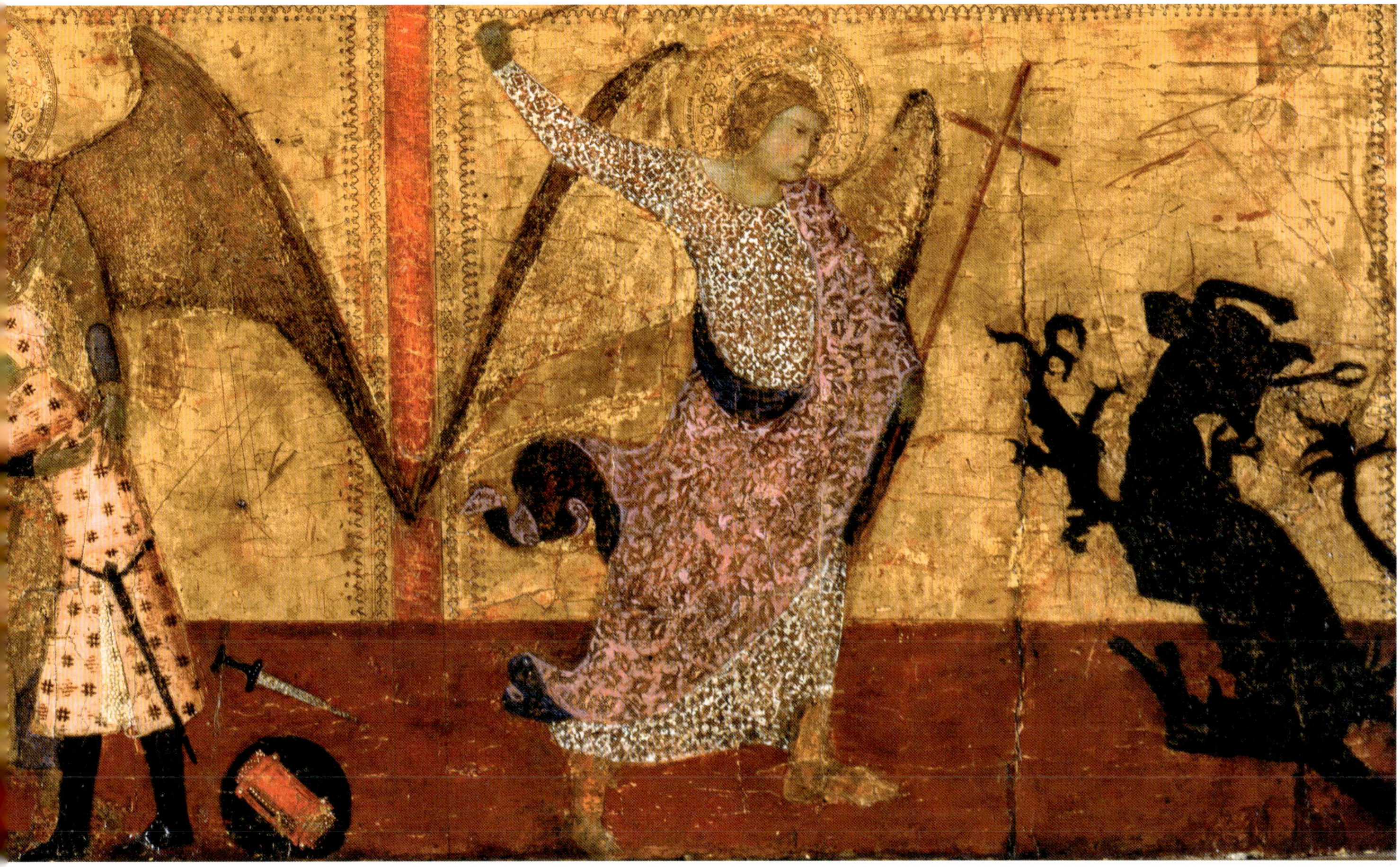

and reconciliation, demonstrates the ways that women's roles as wives, teachers, grandmothers, and mothers contribute in fundamental ways to the stability and peace of civic life.

To the left and right of the scene of peace, Saint Margaret of Antioch, like Catherine an early Christian saint of the Eastern church, is paired with Saint Michael the Archangel, showing female power as comparable to that of angels in supporting peace and harmony. Margaret, her name written beside her, is shown beating down a horned demonic figure with a hammer.[17] It is an act of extreme violence carried out, unusually, by a woman, and is part of her legend. Jailed for her beliefs, Margaret had a vision of being visited by a devil, whom she attacked and subdued. To the right, Michael repels a demon with raised sword and cross. With the devil and the demon pressed to the far ends of the panel, the two heroic figures block the evil that might disrupt peace. The composition of Margaret beating down the devil is based, like many scenes in Sienese art of the period, on icons, a connection that is reinforced by the shimmering gold ground of the painting. The narratives of such icons had a strong impact on Italian art, providing models for scenes with long-standing authority and traditions. Indeed, the overall format is reminiscent of Byzantine *vita* (life) icons, which in Italy were popular sources for images of saints like Francis.[18] In such paintings, central standing figures fill much of the height of the panel, and smaller narrative scenes from their lives are set below and/or vertically along the sides

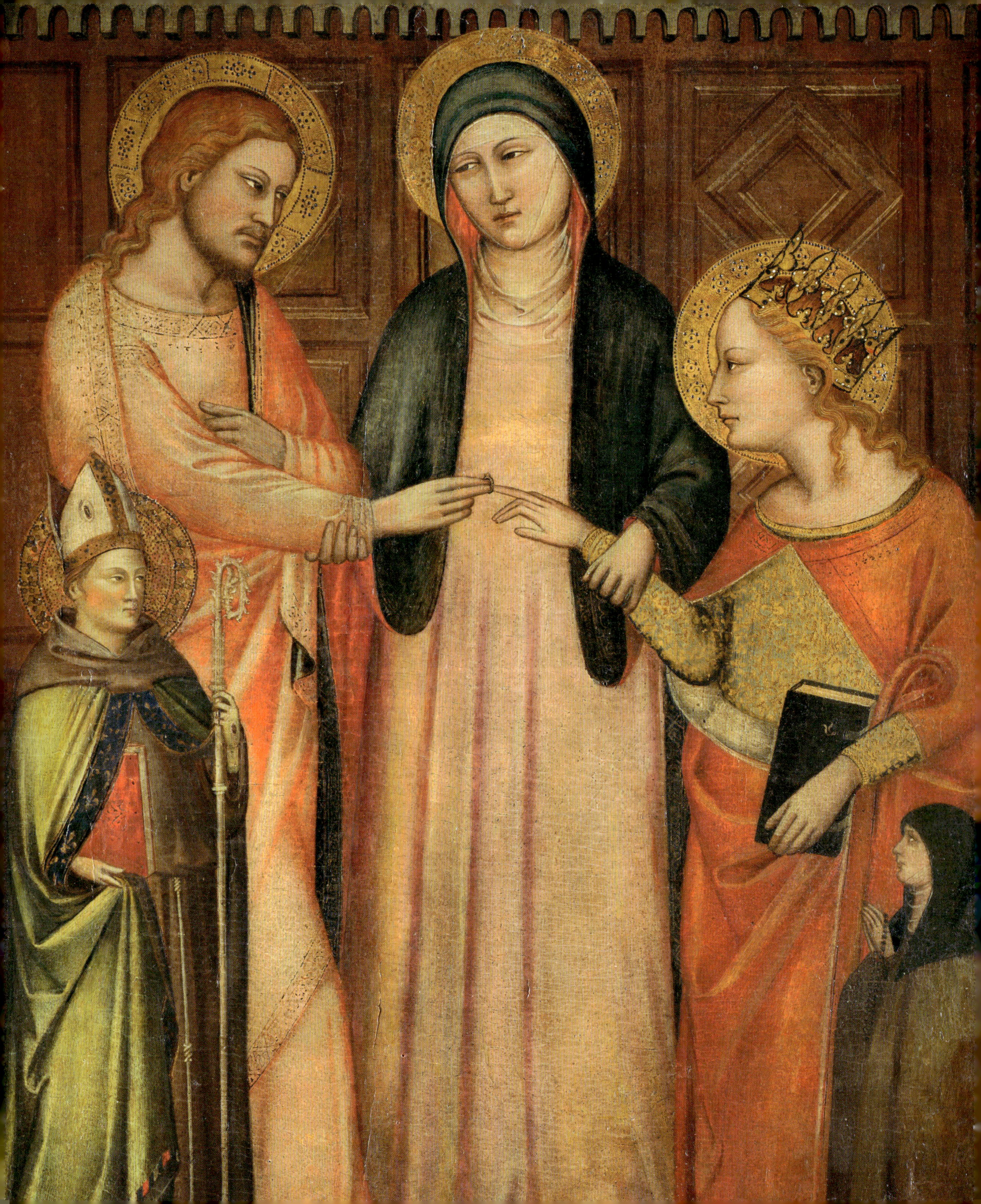

in compartmented fields. Perhaps the fact that both Catherine and Margaret were early Christian Eastern Orthodox saints encouraged the adaptation of Byzantine models. Here, the three scenes innovatively present narratives that are not part of the life of the saint, and the placement of the Virgin, young Jesus, and Saint Anne as if under the canopy of the larger marriage scene is both compositionally unusual and an early representation of the three figures together.

The original function and placement of this painting are unknown.[19] The inscription just below Jesus, Mary, and Anne on the bench translates to "Arigo di Neri Arighetti had this painting made," and given the subject matter, it was likely made to commemorate the end of a feud. The artist who painted it is also uncertain, since "Barna da Siena" is a constructed figure, with stylistically similar works of art grouped around a name. It is likely that the viewers of the painting included women, given the saints depicted here. Saint Catherine was considered a model of wisdom and chastity for women, either in their own marriages or as part of the symbolic marriage to Christ that was included in the vows taken by nuns.[20] Saint Margaret was seen as an intercessor for women who hoped to become pregnant and to guide them safely through childbirth. Both are represented by their mystical visions, and their names are written near their figures in the work, suggesting there was a reason to emphasize their identities. Anne and Mary are shown in their roles as caregivers to the young Jesus. All of these aspects come together to imply a particular setting, audience, and function that all still elude viewers and scholars today. The painting may have been offered as an ex-voto to a church or oratory to commemorate the reconciliation represented at the bottom. The focus on two specific legal acts, marriage and peace, suggests that it was seen in a public setting, where it might assert the importance of marriage, harmony, child bearing, and child rearing to peaceful civic life. Not long after the painting's creation, such ideas would be given voice by Christine de Pizan in *The Book of the City of Ladies*, where she considers the roles of women in family life and presents stories that cast them as peacemakers. For example, in her discussion of the Sabine women, who were abducted as part of the foundation of the city of Rome, Christine tells the story of how they accepted their fate and "made peace among their loved ones" by preventing their kinsmen from exacting revenge upon the Romans. All threw down their arms and peace reigned.[21]

The powerful role of women in this painting cannot be denied, though so much about its creation and history remains unknown. In *The Mystic Marriage of Saint Catherine*, women are encouraged to develop their intellects to prepare to meet Jesus in a mystical marriage; to be fierce and courageous when battling evil; to care for their children as Mary and Anne did with Jesus; and to consider these acts as on a par with the efforts of angels battling evil and overseeing peace. Many of the threads that come together in this painting are evident in the objects that follow in this book: images of women as exemplars in civic, personal, and religious life; works that speak to the material culture of Renaissance marriage and home life; women as scholars and intellectuals; works that reveal the ways that religious, civic, and domestic life interweave in Renaissance Italy, making women's roles more complex than the simpler idea that they were generally confined to the home or a convent. Even the fact that the painting's history, which may have had its origins in female experience, has been lost over time alludes to the fate of so many women's stories. By looking closely at many objects and asking new questions, hidden gold can be revealed.

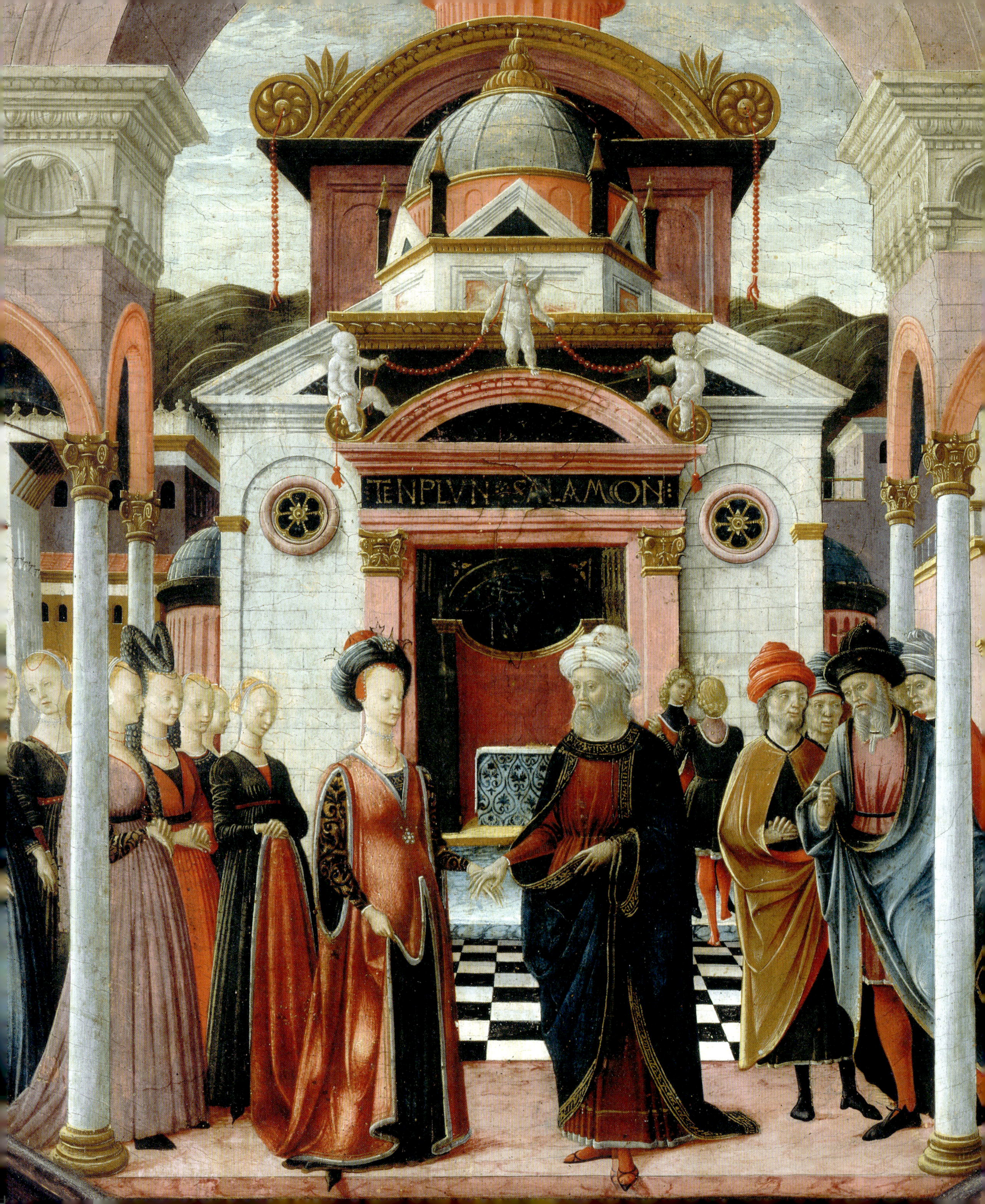
TENPLVN SALAMON

Exemplary Women

One of the functions of art in Renaissance Italy was to present values and ideas that might help shape behaviors and beliefs. Images of saints, biblical figures, and allegories could be seen in religious, civic, and domestic settings, serving as role models of virtue, piety, and civic identity for men, women, and even children. In fifteenth-century Florence, Dominican friar Giovanni Dominici advised parents to provide children with images of saints in the home, such as the young John the Baptist, patron saint of Florence, so that they could emulate his devotion to Jesus and see themselves in him.[1] Florentines were socialized to their faith in this way from a young age. Throughout Italy, saints and other exemplary figures were represented often enough that they became familiar characters in Renaissance life, almost like friends, and that familiarity made their virtues seem attainable. By considering female saints, biblical heroines, female allegories, and wise women as represented in works of art, it is possible to distinguish virtues and strengths that women were seen to embody and that women and men alike might emulate. These images, in turn, provide insights into civic values, religious beliefs, as well as personal fears and aspirations.

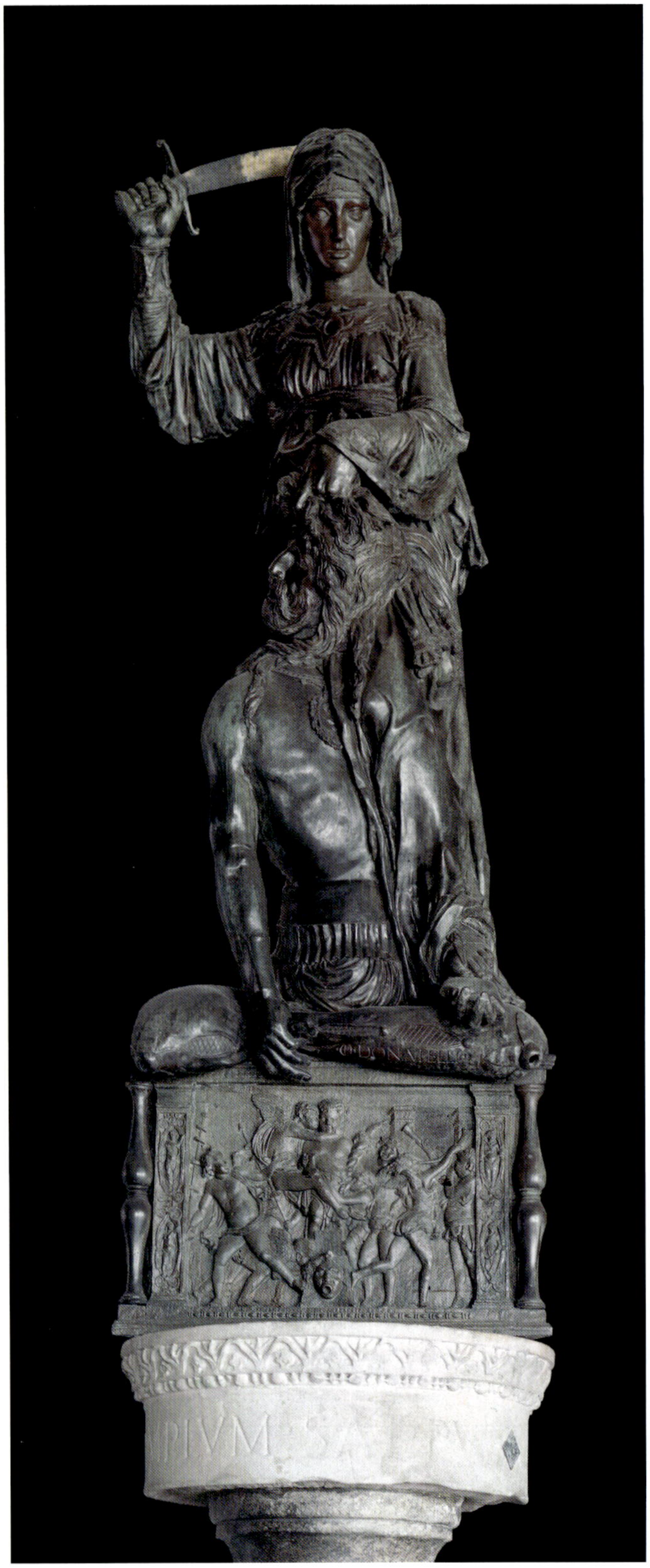

4 Donatello, *Judith and Holofernes*, 1457–64, H. 236 cm (93 in.)

In the fifteenth century, Florentine sculptor Donatello creatively rethought the presentation of well-known subjects, producing images of women that stood as exemplars of civic virtue and religious piety for both women and men. His *Judith and Holofernes*, a monumental two-figured group in bronze, presents the Bethulian widow Judith as a powerful warrior in the act of slaying the evil Holofernes (fig. 4).[2] According to the biblical tale, in an effort to save her people from defeat and destruction, Judith infiltrated the enemy camp and visited the general Holofernes in his tent after a meal that left him weakened and drowsy from drink. When he fell asleep, she beheaded him. A woman much weaker and smaller than her enemy, Judith overcame Holofernes through her ingenuity, courage, and cunning.[3] Donatello's Judith stands tall with her sword raised, holding the head of Holofernes by his hair as he straddles the triangular base that supports both figures. A pillow sets the scene in Holofernes's tent. This sculpture was commissioned probably around 1456 by the Medici family, the de facto rulers of Florence. In 1495, the Medici were overthrown and expelled, and the leaders of the republic of Florence removed the sculpture from the Medici palace to the city's central civic square. Placed on the *ringhiera* (platform) in front of the town hall, this powerful sculpture of a weak but brave woman overcoming tyranny made a strong statement about civic values and independence for the population of Florence, and Judith thus became an icon for the city. In 1504, Michelangelo's marble *David*, originally commissioned for the cathedral, replaced Donatello's *Judith* on the ringhiera, again as a representation of Florence as a small but strong republic.[4] The figure of the young David overcoming the enemy giant Goliath was a long-standing civic image for the city. Replacing Judith with David was seen to have "corrected" the image of a woman overcoming a man, considered a brave but unnatural act for a female protagonist. "It is not fitting that the woman should slay the man," as one member of

OPPOSITE
5 Giovanni della Robbia, *Judith*, about 1520, H. 71.1 cm (28 in.)

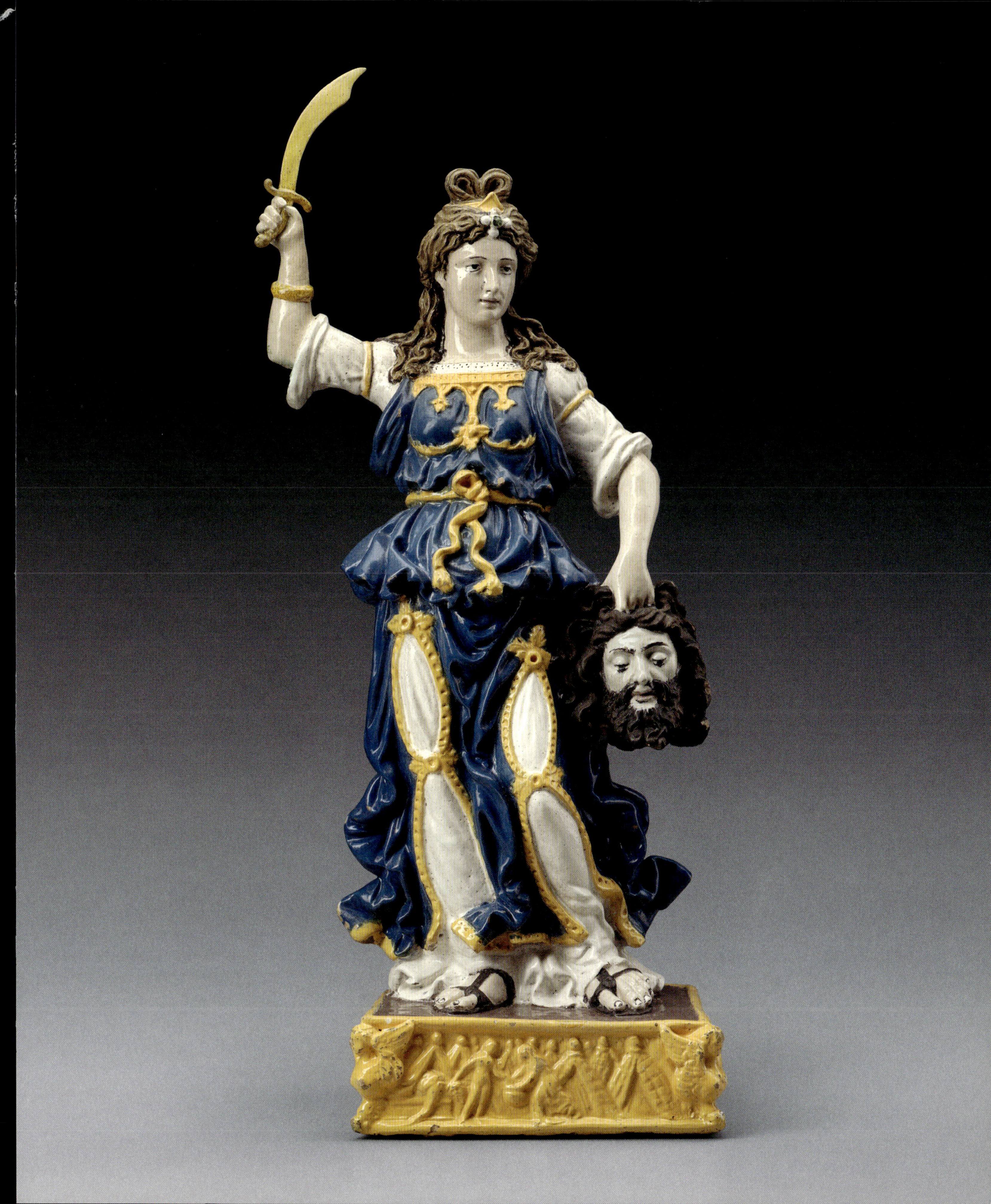

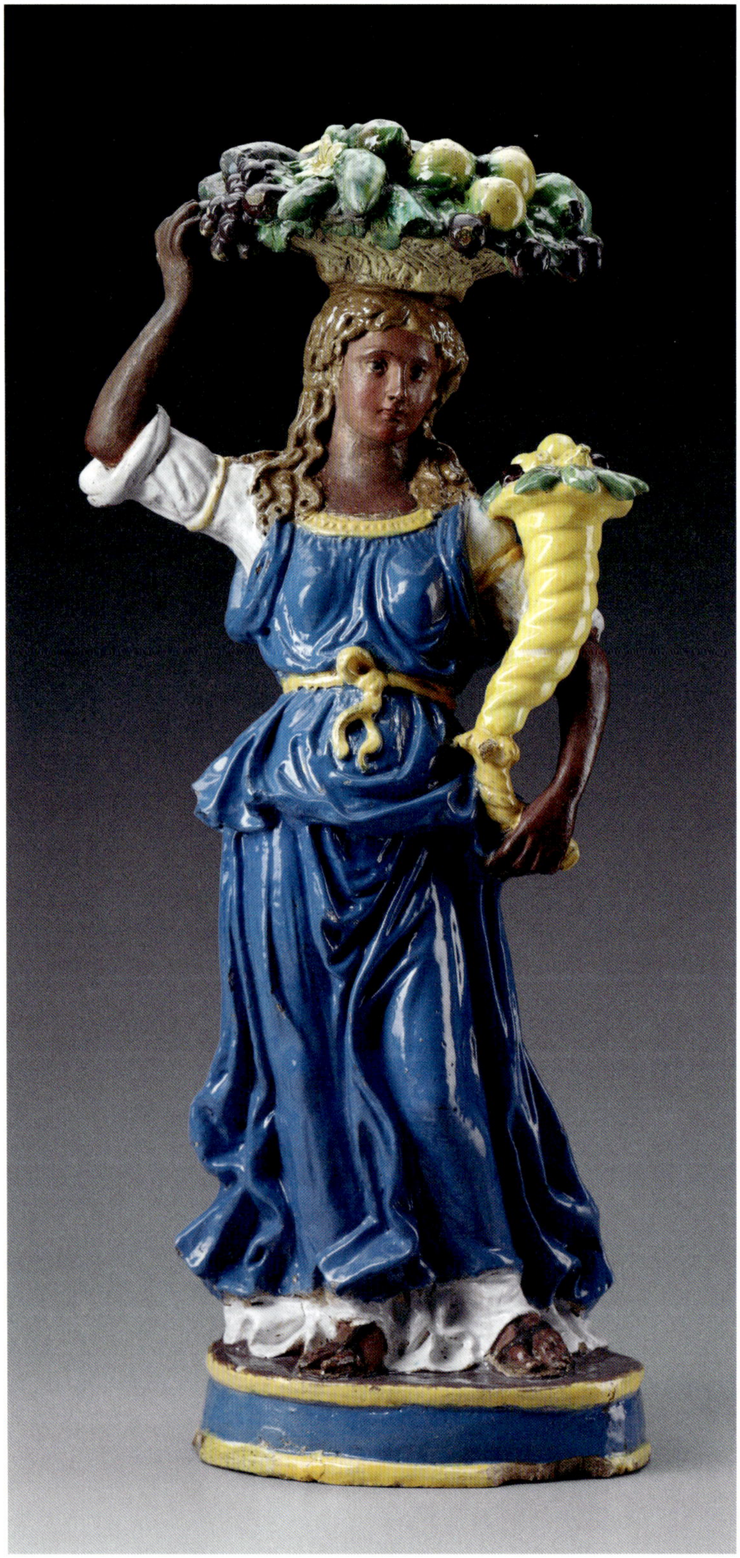

6 Giovanni della Robbia, *Abundance*, about 1520, H. 65.8 cm (25⅞ in.)

the committee that gathered to discuss the placement of the *David* put it.[5] A powerful female heroine was seen as dangerous and threatening, and the *Judith* was placed inside the palace; two years later, in 1506, she was once again brought out into the square and set in the Loggia dei Lanzi.

Giovanni della Robbia's *Judith with the Head of Holofernes* exemplifies the way private citizens in the early decades of the sixteenth century could bring civic virtue and identity into the home (fig. 5).[6] By the time this sculpture was made, around 1520, the Medici had been restored to power, but Donatello's *Judith* and Michelangelo's *David* both stood in the piazza as witnesses to the short-lived republic and were now firmly established as civic icons. This small-scale reworking of the theme clearly references Donatello's model, with her raised sword and suggestion of military costume in her cuirass-like bodice, but here the focus is on her triumphant presentation of the head of Holofernes. With his head in her left hand, she is the war hero returned to the people she has saved from peril. The scene of the beheading takes place in a narrative relief on the base, in a bright yellow glaze that would have suggested gold or gilded bronze to the viewer, and she stands on a floor that emulates rich porphyry. By bringing a work with such strong civic messages into the home, owners would be able to look at it from their own points of view. If they were Medici supporters, they might see it as a celebration of the family's return, given the origins of Donatello's sculpture as a Medici commission. If they were not adherents of the leading family, they might view it as a statement of their discontent, expressed privately. Other Florentines might have seen it not in political terms at all, but instead as a way to consider the biblical heroine as a role model for courage, wisdom, and justice. Once in the private sphere, this representation of Judith could mean different things to different viewers.

Several statuettes of Judith on this scale by the Della Robbia shop survive, along with another variation on the same sculptural model: a standing female figure in lively draperies with her right arm raised. The allegorical figure of *Dovizia,* or Abundance, usually carries fruits and flowers in a symbolic cornucopia of plenty and in a basket supported on her head (fig. 6).[7] She is sometimes accompanied by one or two little boys, or a dog or other creature. She, like *Judith*, also refers directly to a civic sculpture made by Donatello. His *Dovizia*, now lost, was placed on a high column in the central market square of Florence, celebrating the plentiful goods available to the city from its fertile countryside. In its domestic reworking by the Della Robbia shop, *Dovizia* became associated with marriage, prosperity, and healthy children. These statuettes of Judith and Dovizia were made in a quintessential Florentine technique from local Arno clay and glazed in brilliant, opaque, colorful glazes that were considered an invention of the Della Robbia family. Therefore, in both materials and subject matter, the sculptures could serve to remind viewers of their own identities as Florentines, the artistic excellence of their town, and the importance of educating children about civic responsibilities.

Mary Magdalen is another figure whose representations can offer multiple messages depending on the setting and audience. Her life and legend are complex, and she is associated with various women in the Gospels, always as a close disciple of Jesus. These stories, where she is not named or she is called only Mary, include that of the fallen woman whom Jesus pardoned for her sins, the story that gave rise to Magdalen being seen as a repentant sinner. She was specifically mentioned by name in the Gospels as a witness to Jesus's crucifixion, the first to see him after his resurrection, and the first to spread the word of this event. As her legend developed, she was said to have retreated after Christ's resurrection to a cave in France to fast and atone for her sins, linked to her identification as a penitent.[8] Donatello's gilded wood sculpture of the saint was probably made about 1453 to 1455 (fig. 7). In his moving representation, Mary Magdalen's body becomes the message of her repentance. Donatello presents her wasted body, transformed by her acts of repentance, with the protruding bones of her rib cage and her sunken cheeks evidence of long fasting. With her hands held in prayer, her mouth open as if speaking, and her eyes imploring, she also shows great strength.

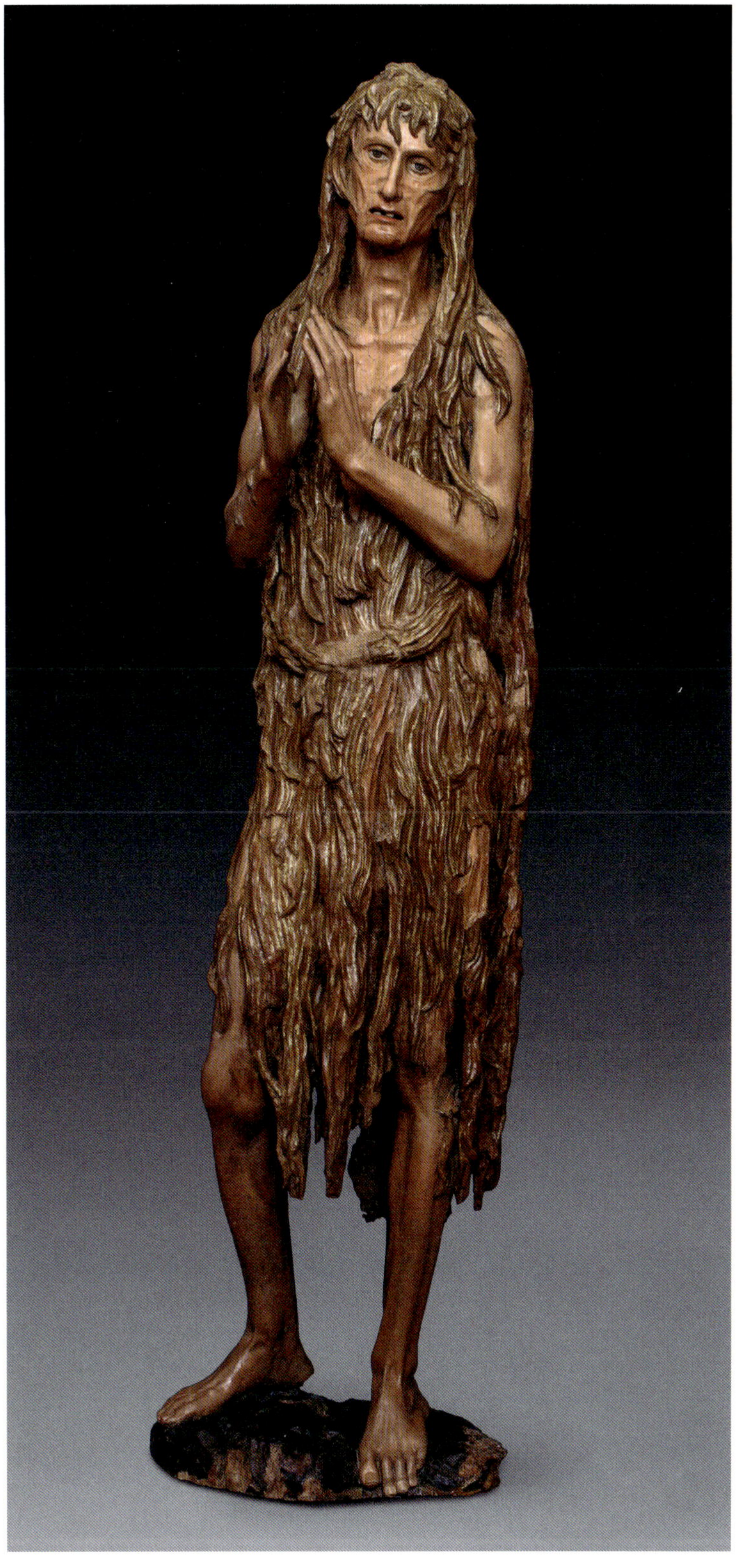

7 Donatello, *Penitent Magdalen*, about 1453–55, H. 188 cm (74 in.)

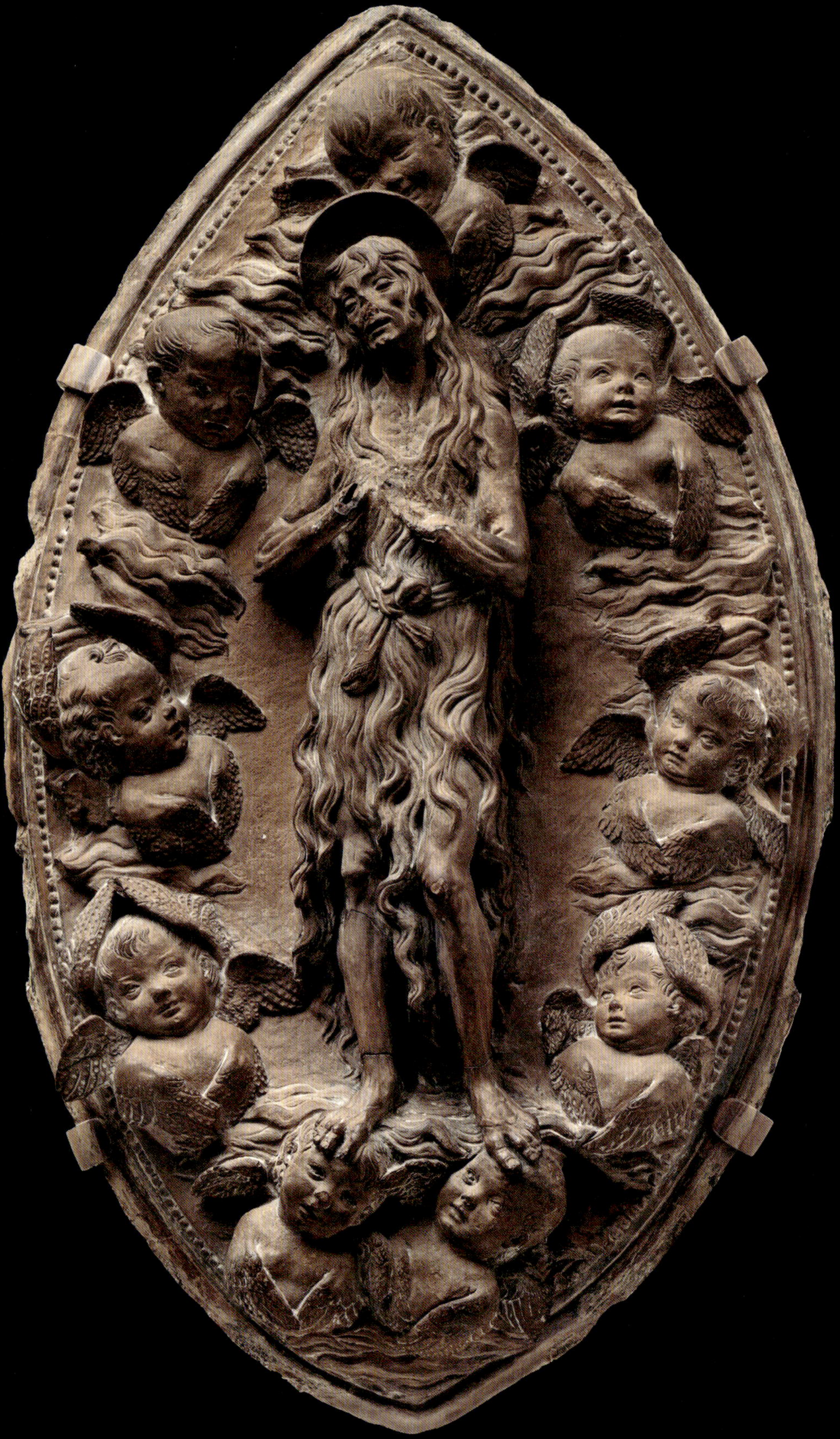

Her muscular arms and legs and powerful feet express the idea that self-denial exemplified fortitude.[9] Working in the soft material of wood, which allowed for detailed carving of her body, face, and hair, Donatello seems to have been inspired by the natural color of the material to emphasize simplicity. Traces of gilding remain, which originally would have added the illusion of glowing light on the figure, calling attention to her radiant holiness even in her extreme humility.

It is not known who commissioned Donatello's *Mary Magdalen*, but by at least the later 1490s, and probably well before that date, the statue was in Florence's baptistery, the church in which all Florentines were baptized and the titular church of the patron saint of Florence. The sculpture's presence there meant that it would bridge religious and civic experience in its meanings for viewers, amplifying its power as a role model for devotees.[10]

Directly related to Donatello's *Magdalen* is a sculpture representing the saint in a similar pose and wearing a similar garment of her own long hair, surrounded by angels in an aureole of glory, modeled in terracotta by an unidentified Florentine artist (fig. 8). It was likely made in the 1490s, a period of spiritual crisis when reforming voices, especially that of the Dominican preacher Girolamo Savonarola, called for Florentines to abandon their luxurious and worldly lifestyles and return to a purer form of Christianity embodied in the lives of ascetic saints like Mary Magdalen. Made from humble clay, which furthered its message of repentance, it may have been painted or gilded, like Donatello's wood sculpture. The work is one of several versions, indicating its popularity as a devotional image.[11] The relief may have been made for private devotion or for placement in a church, monastery, or convent. Wherever it was placed, its purpose was to inspire devotees to prayer, meditation, and repentance.

Mary Magdalen was an especially popular saint because of her devotion to Jesus and her closeness to him as a disciple. In addition to being known for her repentance, she was present at Jesus's crucifixion and was the first to see him after his resurrection. Jesus instructed her to tell others about this miracle, which is why she is considered the apostle to the apostles and the first apostle. Mary Magdalen visited Christ's tomb, and finding it empty, walked away and came across a man she mistook for a gardener but who was instead the resurrected Jesus Christ, whom she recognized only once he called her by name. Jesus told her not to touch him, or "Noli me tangere" in Latin. A small painting by Gherardo di Giovanni del Fora brings these two aspects of her story together (fig. 9). Mary Magdalen is presented in her penitential form in the foreground of this painting, flanked by Saint Peter and Saint Catherine of Siena, two Dominican saints suggesting that this image was painted for a Dominican setting, probably a convent. The scene of the Noli me tangere takes place in the background, with Mary Magdalen kneeling before Jesus in a garden. Devotion to the penitent saint was common in convents that housed reformed prostitutes because the story of the fallen woman who was forgiven by Jesus was seen as emblematic of the power of conversion and repentance. In addition, the Noli me tangere story resonated more generally for nuns in a convent setting, where the garden is a metaphor for their enclosed lives. Just as Mary Magdalen was a role model of repentance for all, the garden was seen as a metaphor for the soul and spiritual life of every believer. A 1495 devotional manual, *Monte della Oratione* (The Mountain of Prayer), for example, includes a woodcut showing monks as gardeners (fig. 10). They are overseen by God as they tend to the garden of their own souls and the souls of their community.[12]

Gherardo di Giovanni del Fora's painting puts the garden of the Noli me tangere scene squarely at the center of the painting, just above the image of the penitent Magdalen in the foreground, over an altar, as if seen through a window.[13] Mary in the garden is shown on

OPPOSITE
8 *Mary Magdalen Surrounded by Angels*, about 1480–1500, 64.5 x 40 cm (25⅜ x 15¾ in.)

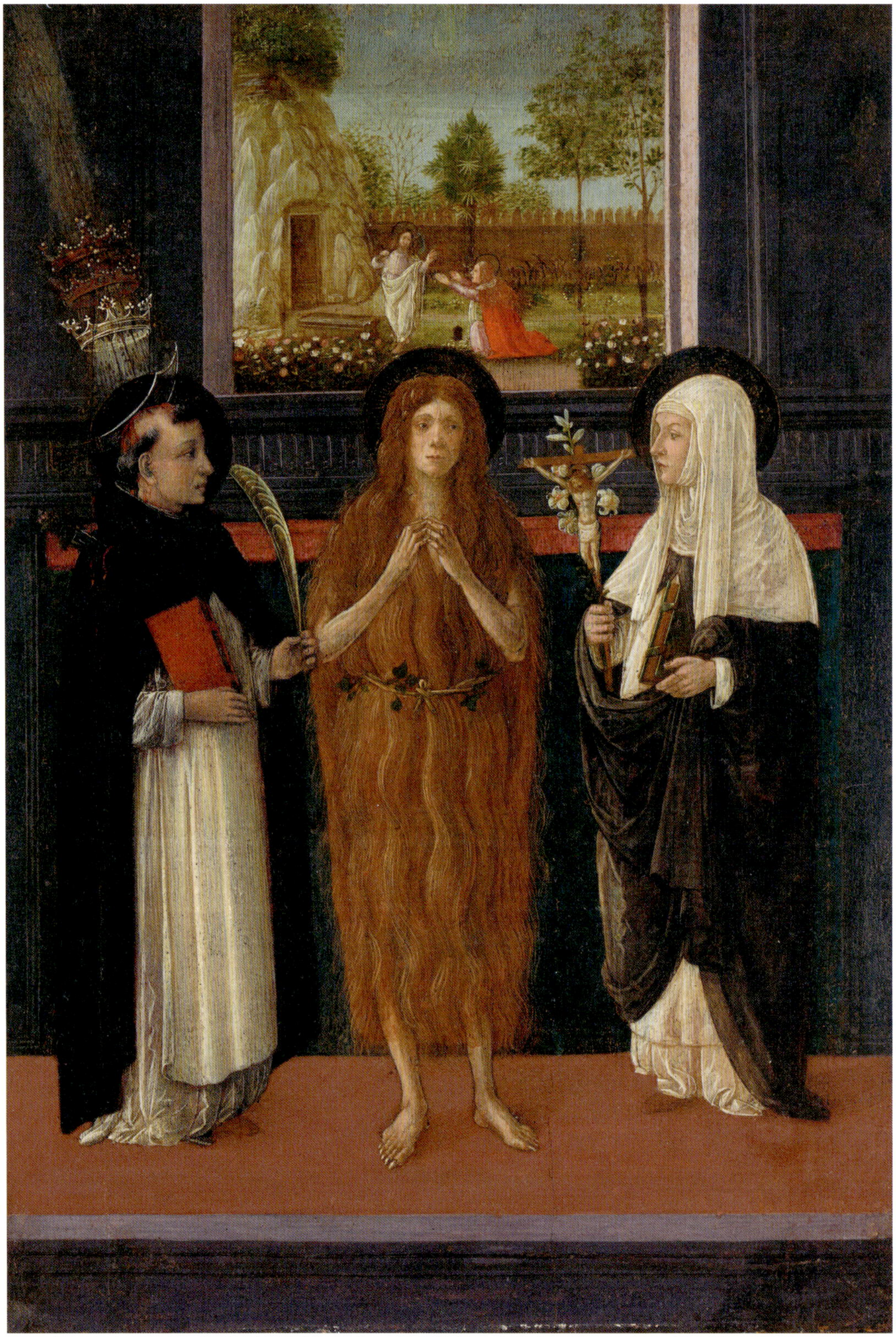

9 Gherardo del Fora, *Saint Mary Magdalen between Saint Peter Martyr and Saint Catherine of Siena*, about 1475, 42.5 x 28.5 cm (16¾ x 11¼ in.)

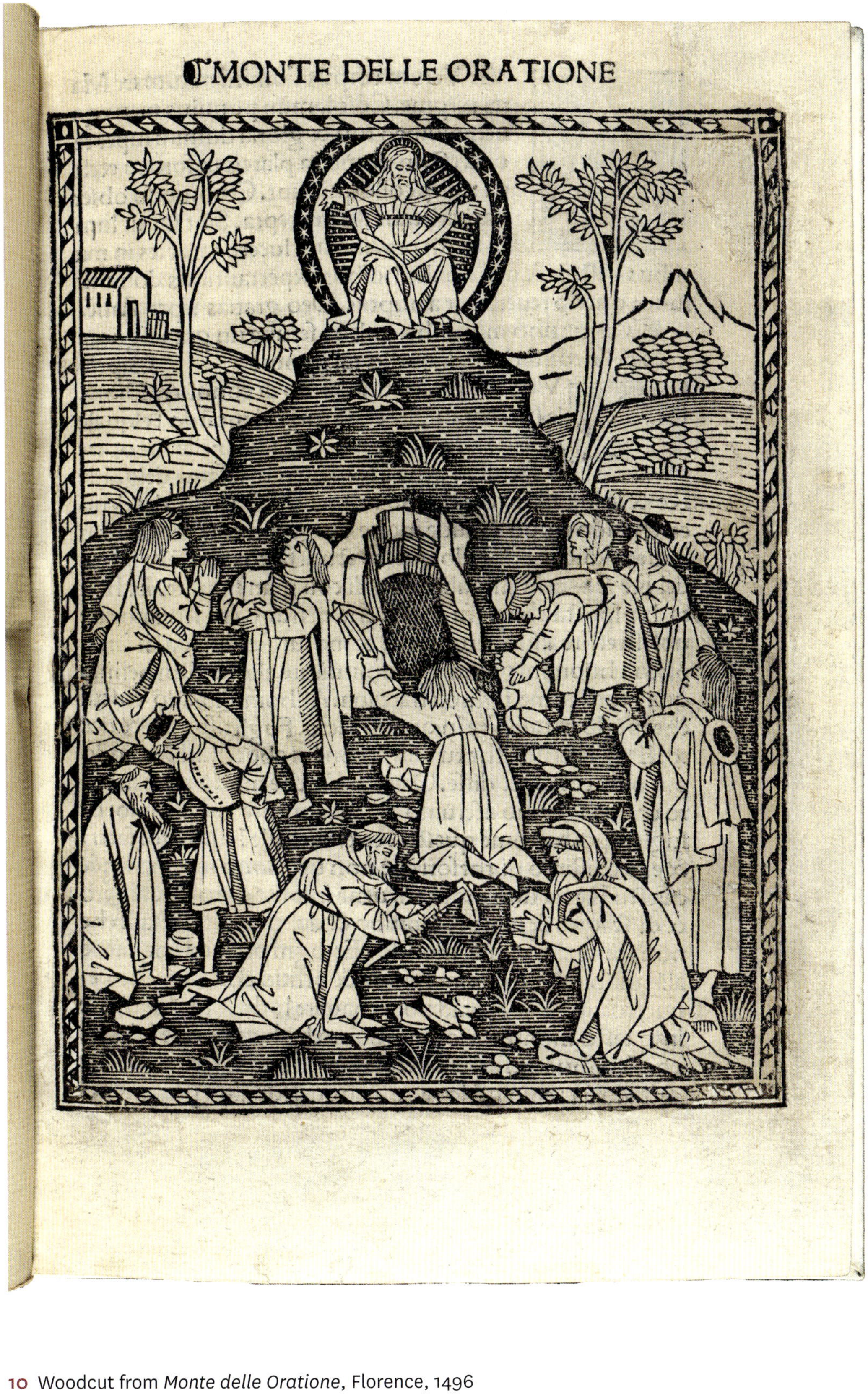

10 Woodcut from *Monte delle Oratione*, Florence, 1496

her knees and stretching out both arms as if to embrace Jesus. She wears white with a red cloak, her long hair flowing and her ointment jar on the ground. Mary Magdalen's story held so many possibilities to shape and transform Christian lives, yet over time her status as first apostle was diminished and instead her association with the fallen woman who repents was emphasized, an illustration of how often female power could be, and was, minimized across history. The painting redresses this by emphasizing the Noli me tangere scene as well as the penitent saint in the foreground. That the Noli me tangere became a popular scene in Florentine convents, not just those for reformed prostitutes, suggests the ways that communities of women may have sought to reassert Mary Magdalen's primary place in the history of Jesus's life, death, and resurrection.[14]

The Noli me tangere appears in a fragment of a woven textile whose maker and original function are unknown (fig. 11). Set in a garden with trees, this textile shows Mary Magdalen kneeling on a flowery field, her arms reaching out for Jesus. His gesture is both a greeting and a warning not to touch him. The metallic threads that would have made the textile shimmer in candlelight have darkened, but the repeated motif encourages extended meditation and prayer, allowing the viewer to become part of the story through the kneeling figure of Mary Magdalen. This is just a small fragment of a larger piece, possibly made as an altar cloth. It is tempting to place it into a convent setting or to consider whether it might have been made by a nun. A number of convents in Italy in this period produced textiles, which served not only to decorate convent spaces, but also were made for sale or on commission to support the community.[15] This textile confirms that there were many ways in which such an important biblical narrative could be placed before people's eyes.

Biblical narratives about wise and heroic women also became part of works associated with marriage and childbirth, setting them firmly in women's experience. One such subject was the Queen of Sheba, a learned woman who had heard about the wisdom of King Solomon and undertook a voyage to Jerusalem to meet him.[16] They each were impressed with the other's intelligence and exchanged precious gifts marking the encounter. The scene of their meeting became popular in fifteenth-century Italy, and one of its earliest appearances was on the second set of bronze doors made by Lorenzo Ghiberti for Florence's baptistery. There the two figures stand at the center of a large crowd of spectators, joining hands in greeting. Scholars have associated interest in this scene, especially in such a public religious setting, with councils seeking to reunite the Eastern and Western churches, held in Ferrara and Florence in the years around 1440. The joining of hands could also be misinterpreted as a wedding, as it recalls the legal ceremony of marriage.[17] The meeting was also sometimes interpreted in allegorical ways, with the idea that it alluded to the marriage of Christ to his church. This may have led to the scene's representation on objects associated with marriage and childbirth rituals. Although not a wedding, perhaps this scene might assert the hope for a marriage of like-minded individuals, guided by great wisdom, and marked by prosperity and fertility.

Scenes from their story also appear on cassoni, the large chests that held the material goods of a woman's dowry.[18] These chests played a role in rituals of marriage in Renaissance Florence, as the transfer of goods from the home of the bride's family to that of her husband's marked the vital economic aspect of the union. These processions through the city also stressed the civic import of marriage, demonstrating alliances and status. A mid-fifteenth-century cassone panel by Apollonio di Giovanni shows the journey of the Queen of Sheba, a scene that might recall wedding processions for its contemporary viewers (fig. 12). Glittering with costly gold leaf decoration, the scene speaks of wealth and status, with the queen's large entourage filling the length of the panel. At center, the queen, riding in an elaborate carriage, is presented as a beautiful woman wearing a tall hat with a long pointed brim, a sign of her power and royalty. This sort of hat would have signaled her foreign origins for contemporary viewers in Renaissance Florence. For example, the Byzantine emperor John VIII Paleologos is shown wearing a similarly styled helmet on a medal by Italian artist Pisanello.[19]

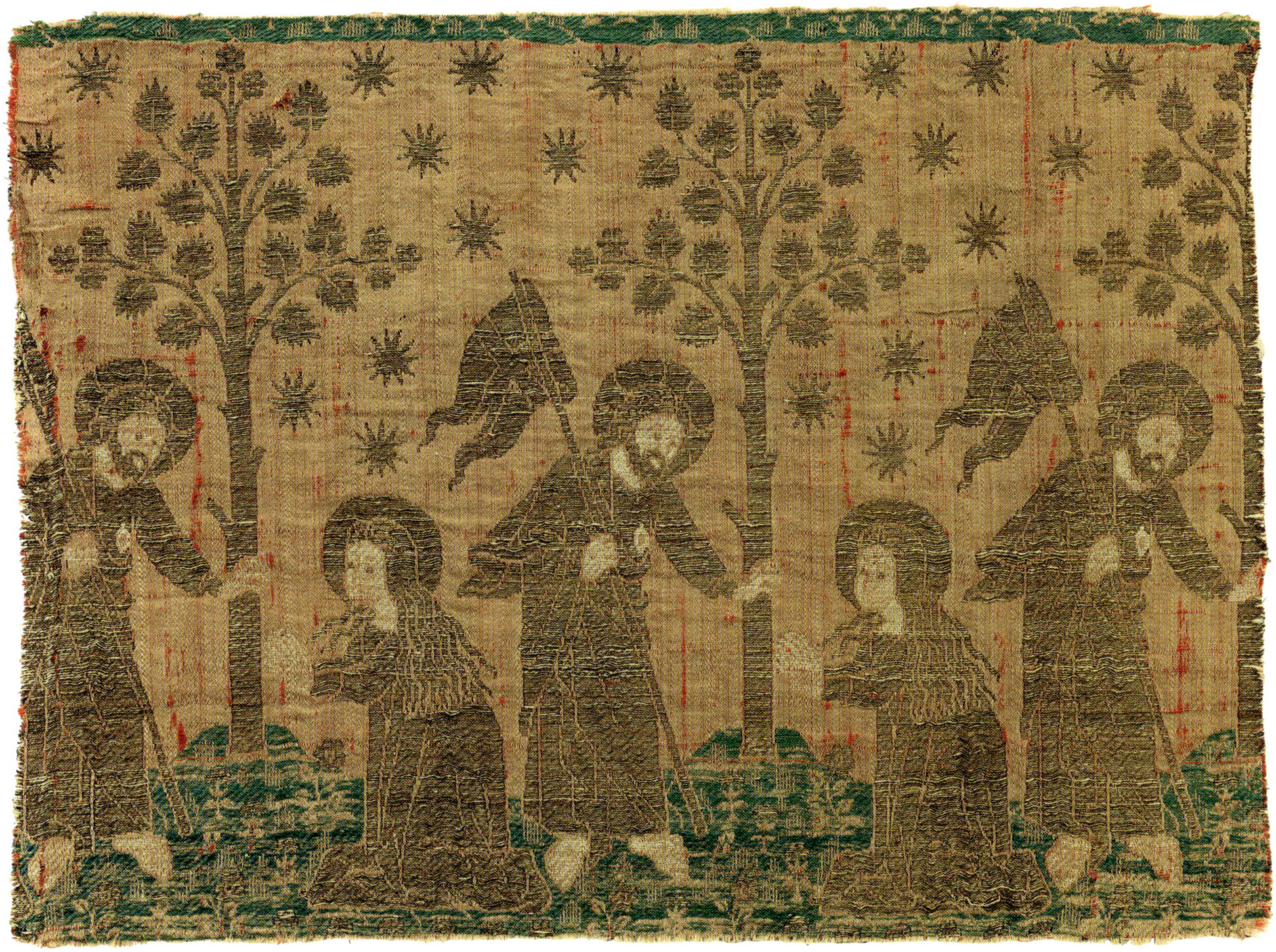

11 Fragment of a textile with the Noli Me Tangere, 14th–15th century

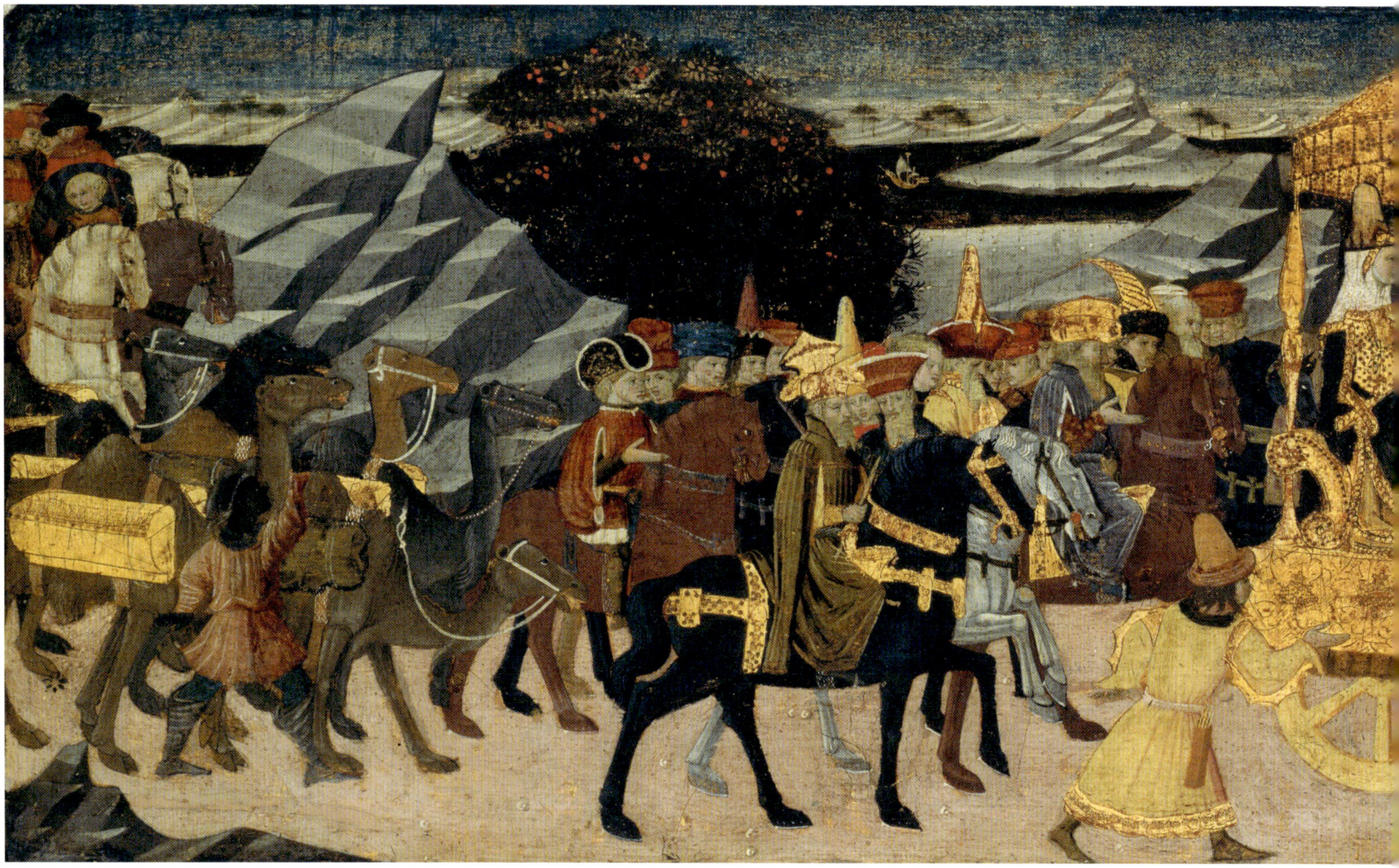

12 Apollonio di Giovanni di Tomaso, *Journey of the Queen of Sheba*, 39.1 x 133.4 cm (15⅜ x 52½ in.)

It is not clear where the Queen of Sheba came from; she is described in the Bible as coming from the east and traveling across Ethiopia and Arabia to arrive in Jerusalem, and today she is thought to have come from Africa or Yemen.[20] The possibility that she was a woman of color, which might have been inferred from the biblical descriptions, does not seem to have been taken into account in Renaissance depictions, though here three Black men are part of her retinue. The wealth, luxury, and exoticism depicted in this panel would have served to elevate the status of the couple whose wedding was being celebrated.[21] Once the cassone became part of the furnishings of a woman's new home, might she look to this image for messages of empowerment? Might she seek out the story of the Queen of Sheba, learn about this female leader, and teach her children about her? Could this image of a woman of wisdom exert power in the lives of the family and especially the women of the household who would live with it over time?

The story of the meeting of the Queen of Sheba and King Solomon also appears on *deschi da parto*, or birth trays, including one attributed to Francesco del Cossa and thought to have been made in Ferrara in the third quarter of the fifteenth century (fig. 13).[22] Birth trays were commissioned and used as part of the rituals of childbirth in Renaissance Italy. Often painted on both sides with scenes that could be seen to encourage safe childbirth and healthy offspring, they were used to bring gifts of food, sweets, and drinks to the mother in bed, to offer her sustenance before or after a birth.

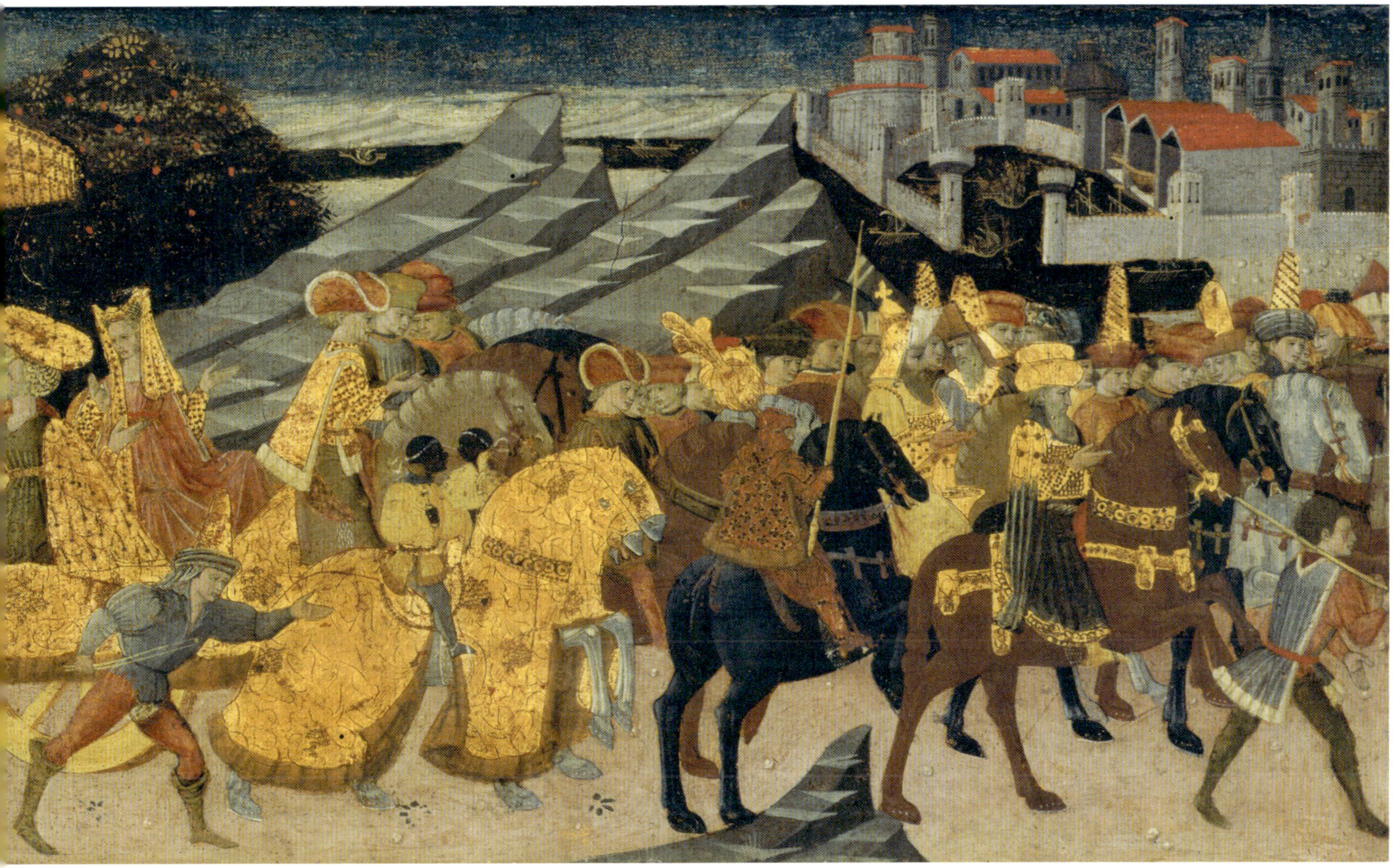

Covered with a cloth during use, these trays would later serve as decorative objects in the home, moving from functional object to family keepsake. Here, the queen and king join hands, again recalling the idea of an exchange of marriage vows. In contrast to the cassone panel, the queen is presented as an ideal Italian Renaissance woman. Dressed in fine clothing, with her blond hair tweezed back to emphasize her high forehead in the contemporary fashion, she might easily be mistaken for a Renaissance bride. Any notion of her foreignness is eschewed. The scene takes place in an idealized Italian square before a centralized building, an architectural form that viewers would have understood to represent the destroyed Temple of Solomon in Jerusalem.[23] Centralized churches with domes became popular in Italian architecture in emulation of this idea of the Temple of Jerusalem. Inside is an altar-like structure that once held an impressive golden vessel, now abraded. The queen and king come together in front of the temple, flanked by large groups of men on the right and of women on the left. At the far-left edge of the group of women is a figure wearing a dark veil; she may be the matriarch of the family for whom this tray was made, likely a widow, supporting this birth and the future of her family. She may have participated in the commission, perhaps choosing the subject or paying for the work and presenting it to her younger kinswoman. The ornamented architecture of the temple is draped in talismanic coral held by little angels, to encourage an easy childbirth and healthy offspring.[24] The gathering of women on

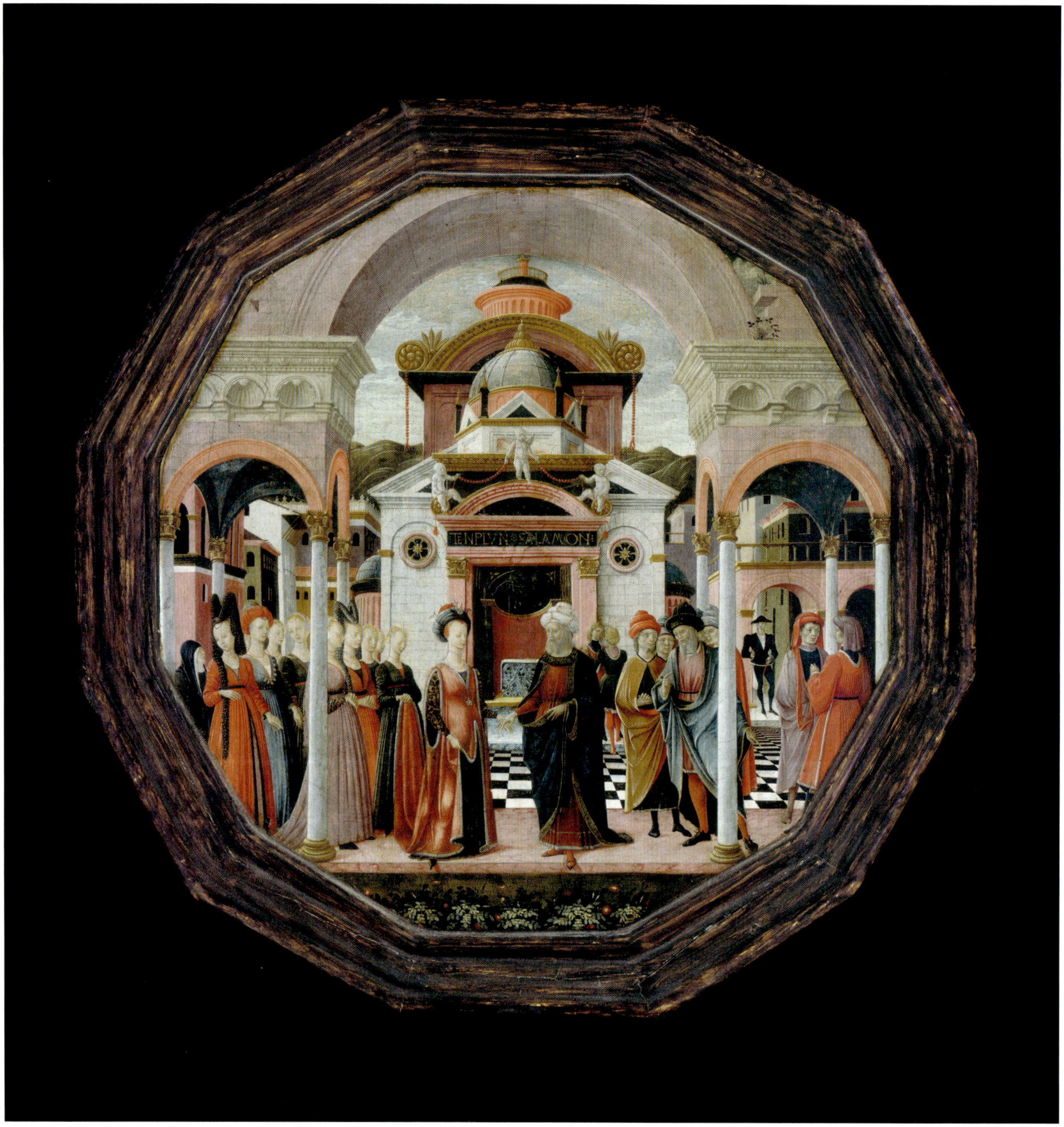

13 Francesco del Cossa, *The Meeting of the Queen of Sheba and Solomon*, third quarter of the 15th century, 61 x 61 cm (24 x 24 in.)

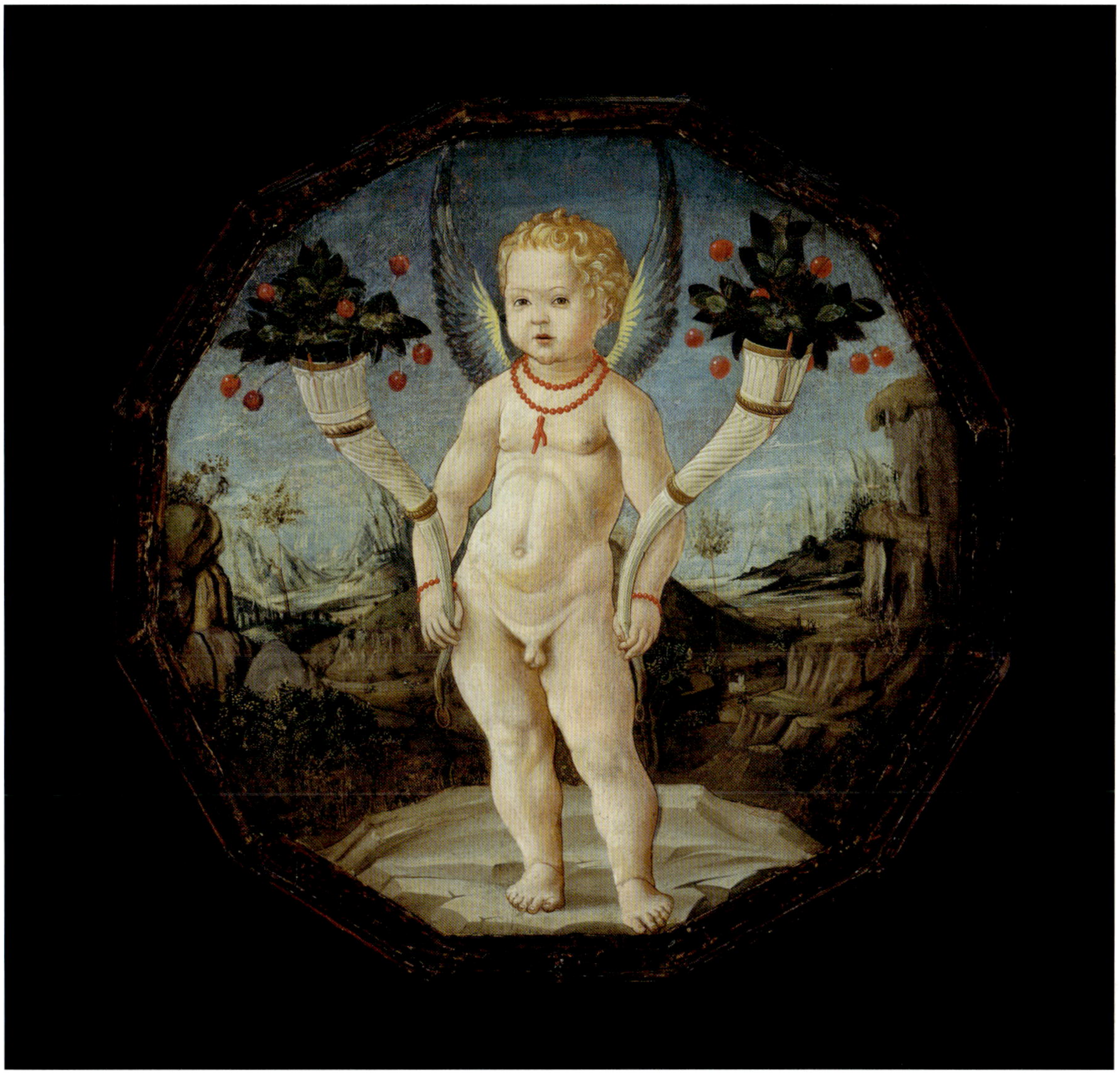

14 Francesco del Cossa, *Cherub Holding Cornucopias of Cherries*, third quarter of the 15th century, 61 x 61 cm (24 x 24 in.)

the side of the queen brings forward the women's world of the bedchamber, where this object would have been used and kept. Childbirth served to continue a family line, but also meant women coming together around a mother in multiple roles: as family, midwives, wet-nurses, servants, and other members of the household. That this scene takes place outside in a civic setting underscores how important birth rituals were beyond the home. The winged putto on the underside of the tray, also wearing coral, made the message clear that the best outcome of any birth would be a healthy male child (fig. 14).

Judith, Mary Magdalen, and the Queen of Sheba are just some of the female figures depicted during the Renaissance as role models for all viewers in their strength, piety, and wisdom. Whether in public or private, representations of these women also offer a look at the perception of and potential in women's civic, private, intellectual, and religious lives during the Renaissance.

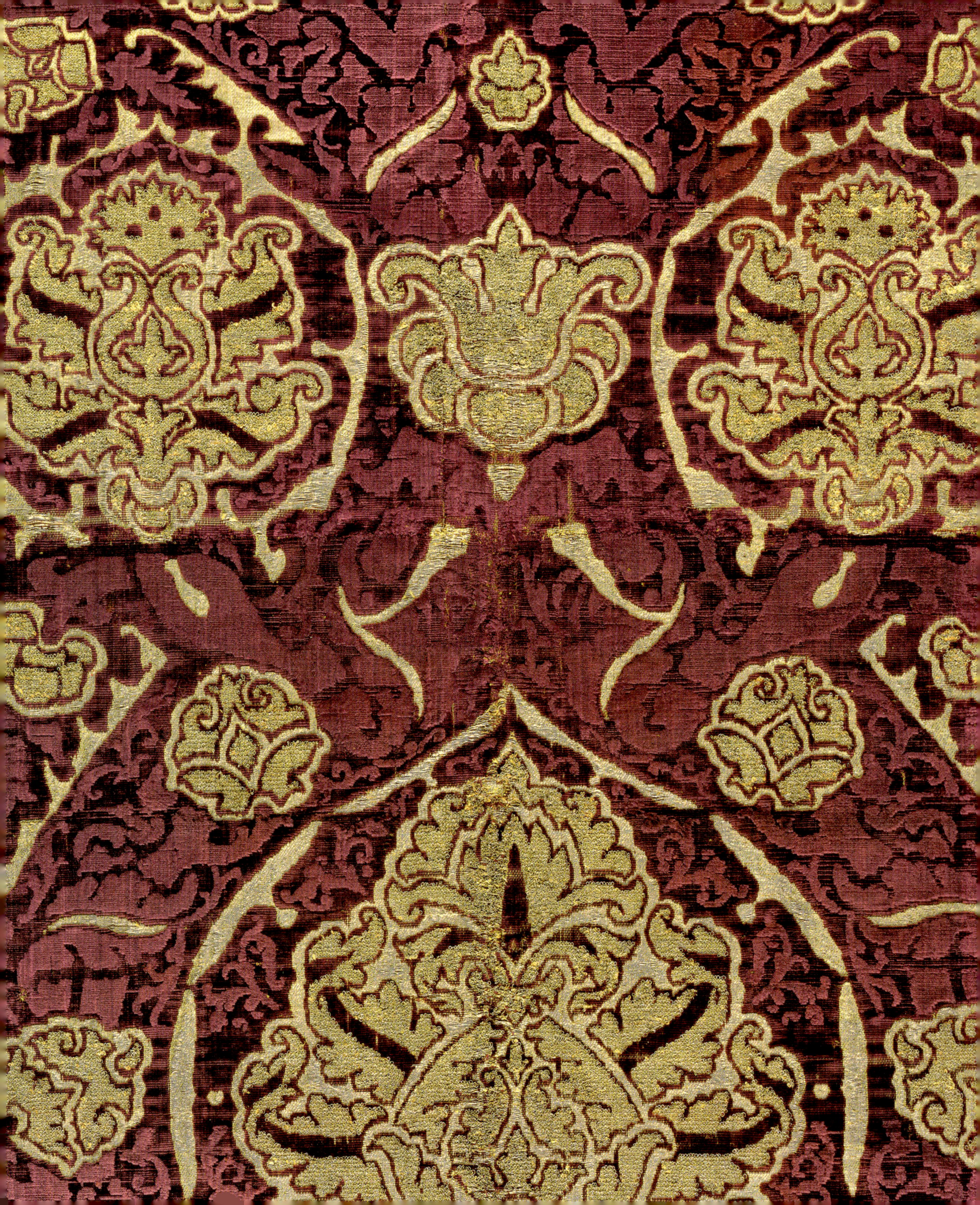

The Materials of Marriage

Marriage marked one of the central milestones in people's lives at all levels of society. For women, it was the single most important passage, leading to a new family and, ideally, to the birth of children. Since marriage required a dowry for the woman and resources among even wealthy families might be limited, not all women could be married. Poorer women whose families were unable to gather together dowries for them might rely on charity. Another alternative for women who were not to be married was to enter a convent, which often required some sort of payment by the woman's family or from charitable donations. Unmarried women without family support would have had to find other means, sometimes in trades like the textile industry and other times in more precarious situations like sex work. It was a societal goal to make suitable marriages for as many women as possible.

Marriage in Renaissance Italy took place in stages, each marked by certain rituals.[1] Among elite families, for whom most of the objects in this book were likely made, planning began early in the lives of children in order to ensure advantageous alliances that might serve political, social, or economic

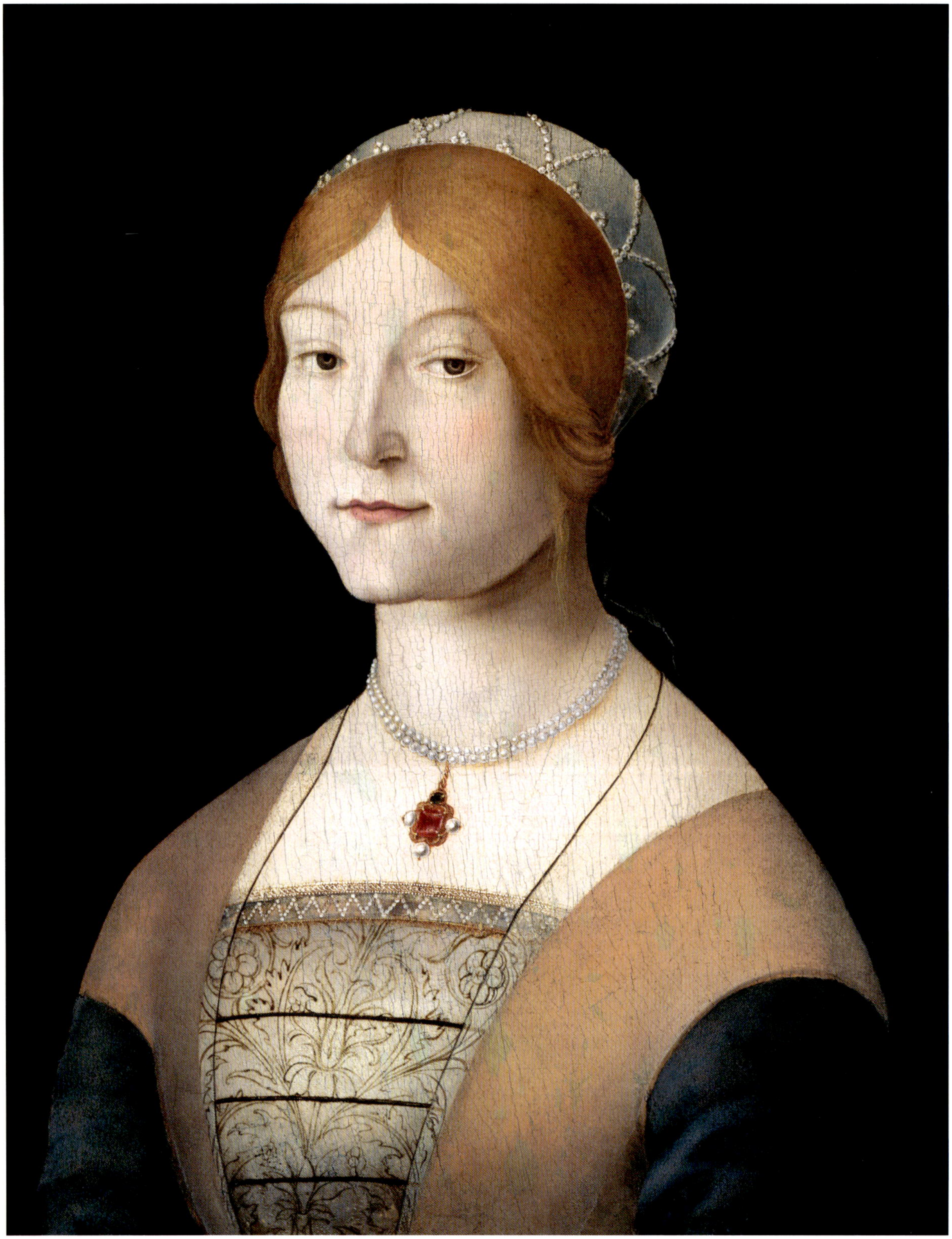

15 Lorenzo Costa, *Portrait of a Woman with a Pearl Necklace*, probably 1485–95, 44.1 x 33.9 cm (17⅜ x 13⅜ in.)

purposes. Betrothals could sometimes be arranged years before the actual marriage. Agreements were negotiated for dowries offered by the woman's family and counter-dowries by that of the man, and these dowries usually included money as well as material goods like expensive textiles, jewels, and other luxury items. Marriage contracts were drawn up. Ceremonial legal acts included the *annellamento*, or the exchange of rings, and the *impalmamento*, the joining of hands. Portraits of both men and women were produced at various stages of the process and might be sent as part of the negotiations for betrothal, or as markers of the marriage itself. Profile and three-quarter-length portraits of bride and groom were sometimes made singly or in pairs. Portrait-like images, joined hands, and hearts sometimes decorate other functional objects almost like emblems, helping to elucidate the ways in which material goods supported marriage.

Luxury items associated with marriage were sometimes made in materials that resonate with meaning, including, for example, pearls, which because of their whiteness, smoothness, and shine were seen as symbols of purity and chastity, in addition to being rare and expensive objects in their own right.[2] Gold also was an important material in the context of marriage: as coins or jewelry, woven or embroidered into valuable textiles, and as gilded decoration on paintings and other objects. The messages conveyed by gold play on its qualities as the purest and most precious metal, unchangeable over time.[3] For objects featuring pearls and gold, the materials often became part of the message.

The sitter in Lorenzo Costa's *Woman with a Pearl Necklace* has not yet been identified, although the pearls on her cap, along with her pearl necklace, jeweled pendant, and clothing indicate that the portrait was related to her betrothal or marriage (fig. 15). The closest stylistic comparisons for the painting are with Costa's 1488 altarpiece for the Bentivoglio Chapel in San Giacomo Maggiore in Bologna, suggesting this woman was part of the Bolognese elite, perhaps even a member of the leading Bentivoglio family or their circle.[4] Although similarities with the women depicted in Costa's altarpiece provide the attribution and approximate time frame for the painting, the sitter's anonymity might be seen as an invitation to view her as a typical Renaissance woman. Yet she has a distinct personality and is presented with directness and empathy. She does not meet the viewer's glance but just avoids it. She wears a cap probably made of fine linen with small pearls attached in an elegant pattern. The cap contains much of her golden hair, but a lock escapes and a little bit of sheer drapery falls down the back of her neck, suggesting the flow of air around her. She wears a double strand of pearls, which conveys, as do the pearls on her cap, both her wealth and the virtues of purity and chastity. From this necklace hangs a gold pendant set with a large red stone, a small dark stone, and three pearls. This jewel marks her as a member of a wealthy family. It may be part of the dowry she brought from her own family or a jewel given to her by her betrothed or her husband as part of his counter-dowry, signifying her entry into her new family.

Presented in three-quarter view turned slightly to her right, the sitter may have been paired with her husband, shown in a portrait turning to his left.[5] Other clues suggest that this is a portrait of a recently married woman: the cap contains her hair, which a betrothed woman might wear in a looser style, and she wears dark-blue-green sleeves, while an unmarried or betrothed woman might have worn sleeves in brighter colors or patterns. Her bodice suggests a rich brocade, though abrasion to the surface of the painting seems to have effaced the deep yellow color of the silk and the shimmer characteristic of brocade woven with golden threads; it is as if only the underdrawing for the pattern remains. She also wears a sheer overgarment, its delicate dark edging probably joining at her waist. Even without knowing her identity or that of her family and husband, she represents a new union of families, with financial and political implications. She displays the virtues of purity, chastity, and beauty, as well as the wealth of her new household. She brings all the qualities required of the elite Renaissance bride, mostly conveyed through what she wears.

Objects connected with marriage and those displaying the virtues associated with married life act

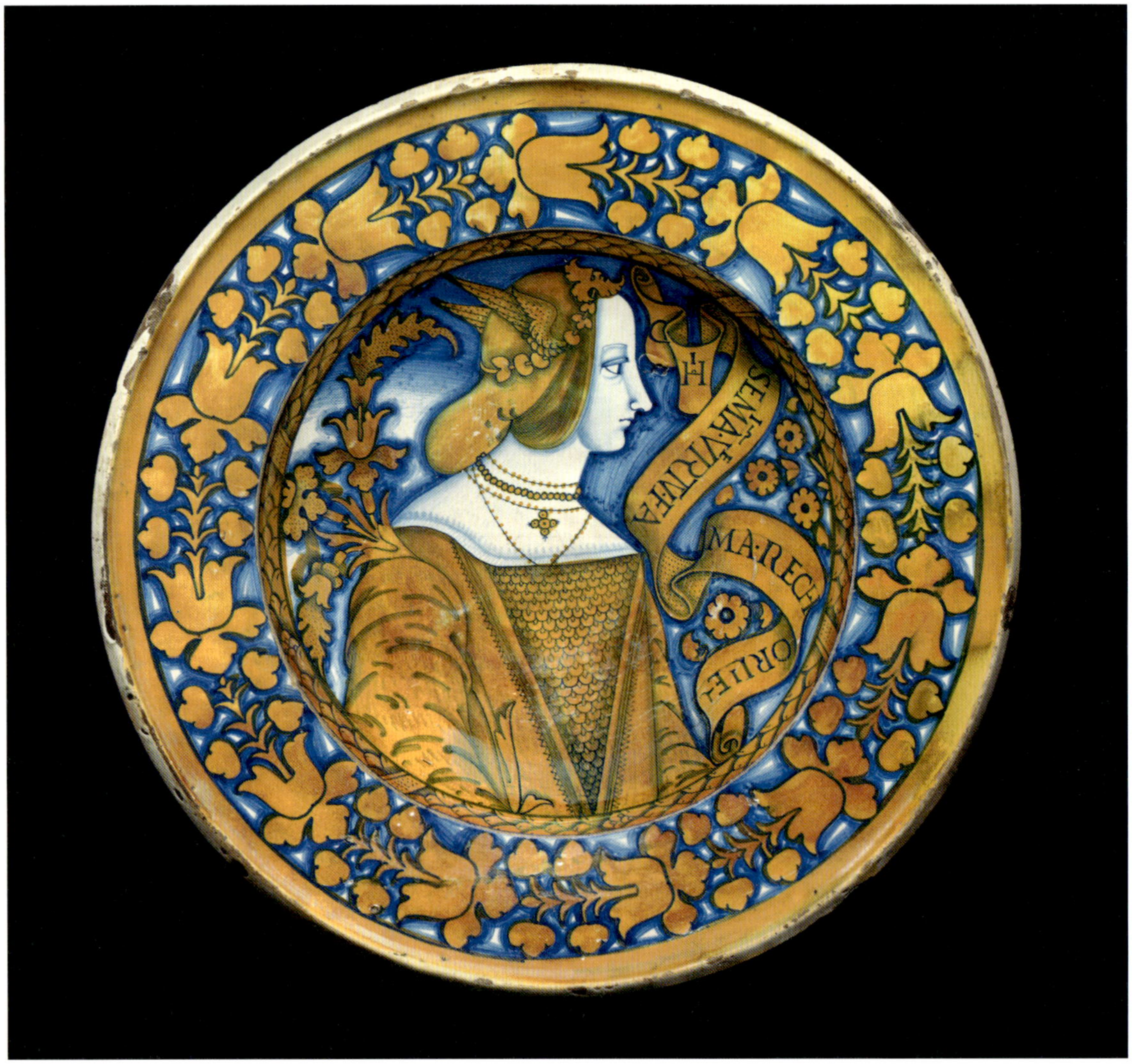

16 Plate with woman's profile, early 16th century, diam. 40.5 cm (16 in.)

as visual documentation of marriage's meanings for women and men in Renaissance Italy. A maiolica *piatto da pompa*, or display plate, for example, declares that virtue is required of women (fig. 16). The plate shows the profile of a woman dressed in brilliant gold, decked in jewels, and wearing an elaborate headdress. She may represent an unidentified historical figure or an idealized "*bella donna*," or beautiful woman, but she surely stands as a model of virtue for the Renaissance woman. A scroll, a common feature in such plates, unfurls alongside her, with the aphorism "Who sows virtue gathers fame."[6] The brilliant tones of the plate's luster glaze mimic the appearance of gold, a standard of excellence, purity, and value, and reinforce the message of the text. The blue and cream enhance the gold. The floral decoration underscores the notion of sowing and reaping, presenting female virtue as the basis for a fecund marriage and leading to the fame of the family. Such decorative plates might well have been commissioned or gifted at the time of a wedding, to stress the importance of virtue, the promise of fertility, and the ways that female virtue is at the root of a strong family life.[7]

The difficult luster-glazing technique characteristic of such display plates was achieved only by a

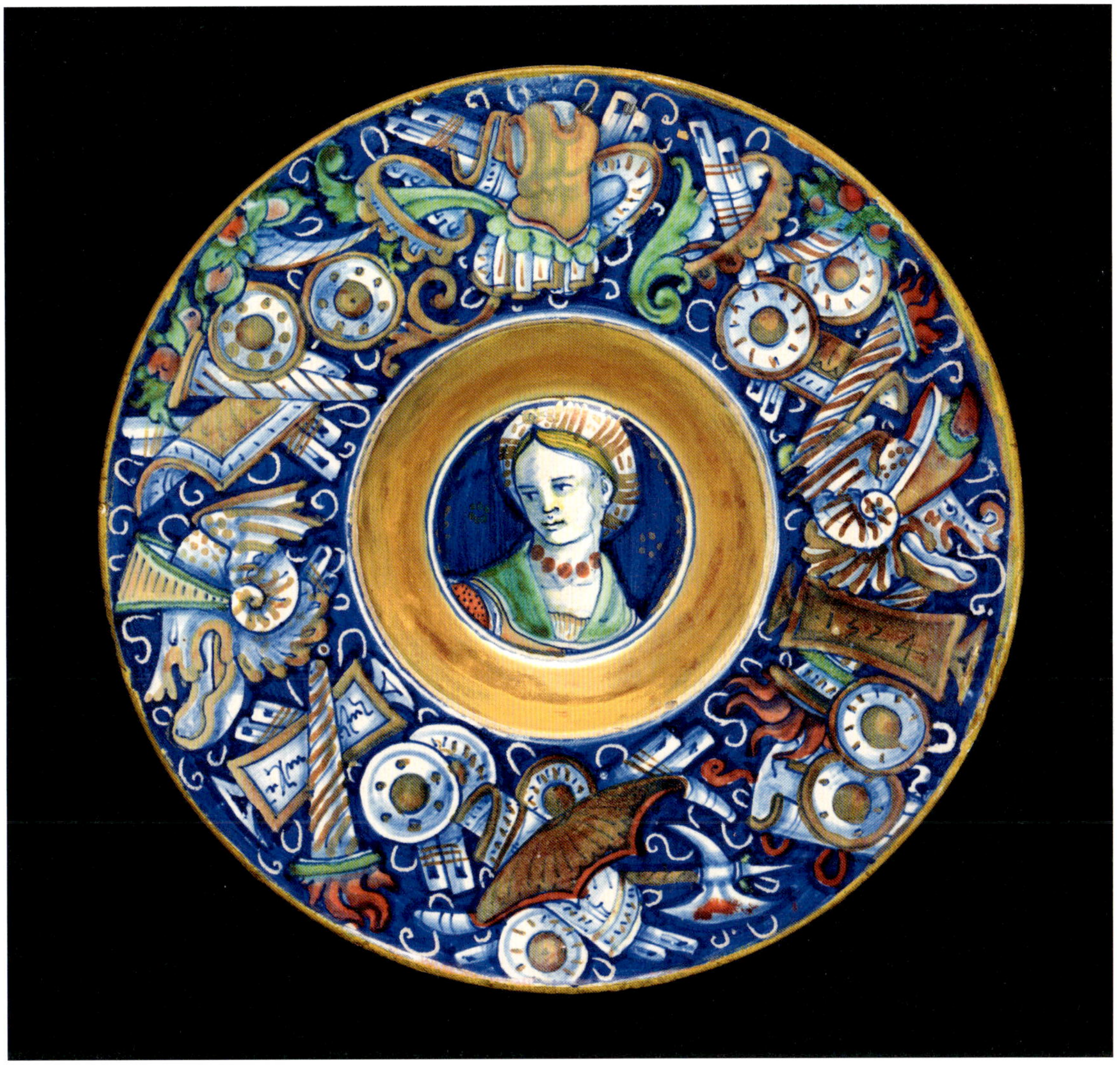

17 Probably by Maestro Giorgio Andreoli, Plate with female head and border with trophies, 1524, diam. 20.4 cm (8 in.)

handful of workshops in Italy at this time. A specialty of Islamic glazed earthenware production often made for export to the Italian market, the technique involved the application of a third layer of glaze, requiring a third firing of the object at a lower temperature in a smoky kiln. One of the most famous producers of this rare technique in Italy was Giorgio Andreoli, who was based in Gubbio. At the center of a small luster-glazed dish made by his workshop is the image of a woman wearing the bright clothing and cap of the typical Renaissance bride (fig. 17).[8] She wears a strand of beads made of coral, which was considered a protective material especially in childbirth and in the raising of healthy children. The characteristic red of coral embodies its almost magical qualities as a rare wonder of nature with links to the power and strength of blood coursing through the body.[9] Though Italian potters of the time were not generally able to produce red glazes, the luster-glazing technique allowed for the bright red of coral as well as fictive gold. This portrait is encircled by a particularly brilliant frame of simulated shining gold. Its rim is decorated with trophies, as if the manly virtues of strength and courage represented by arms, armor, and flaming torches surround and protect the woman at the

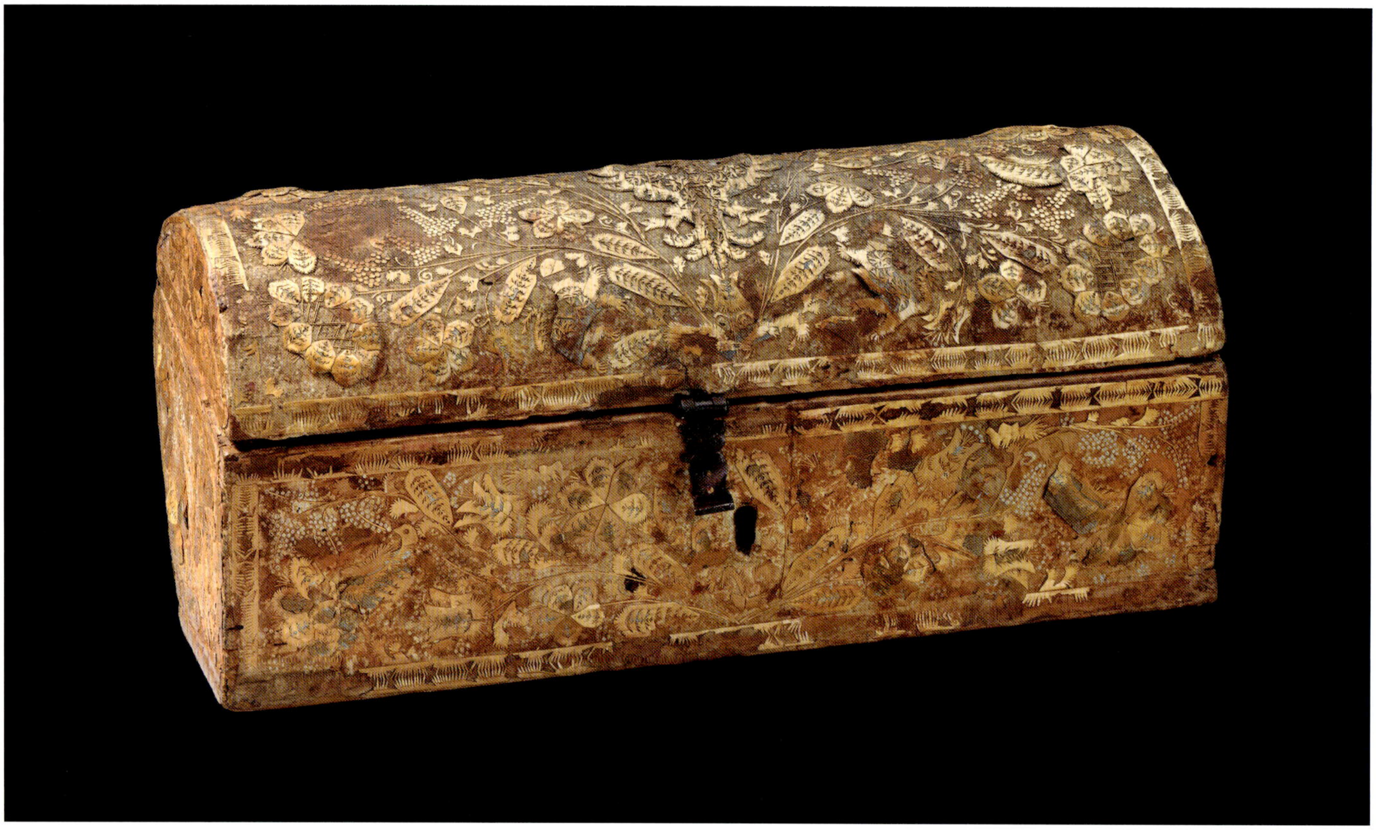

18 Casket, 16th century, length 43.2 cm (17 in.)

heart of this plate. But the arms have been abandoned and the battle is done. This celebration of the bride puts her, and her marriage, at the heart of harmonious civil life. The virtuous woman, surrounded by precious gold, with discarded arms now serving only as ornament, allows peace to reign.

The luster glazing on these plates produces images of golden splendor, created through artistic virtuosity rather than actual use of the precious material. Luster glazing emulating gold also guaranteed permanence of the message: like real gold, this luster did not diminish over time. Luster-glazed plates, however, were more likely to survive, while golden vessels might be melted down, sold, or pawned for the inherent value of the material. Even a humble wooden box decorated with cut straw could be symbolically elevated through a simulation of gold (fig. 18). Likely the work of a woman, this box's golden glow was achieved by enhancing the natural color of the straw through a process that included dampening the straw to treat and soften it, burnishing it to enhance its natural color, then cutting and setting the shapes on the box to catch the light.[10] Such boxes would have contained prized personal objects like jewels, small devotional objects like rosaries, and pieces of lace. The box's exterior golden effect also indicated the value of the objects inside.[11]

Marriage meant that people and goods moved across families, combining the wealth and status of both families into a new alliance. Cassoni would have served to transfer the goods of a newly married woman to the

OPPOSITE
19 Table cover, 17th century

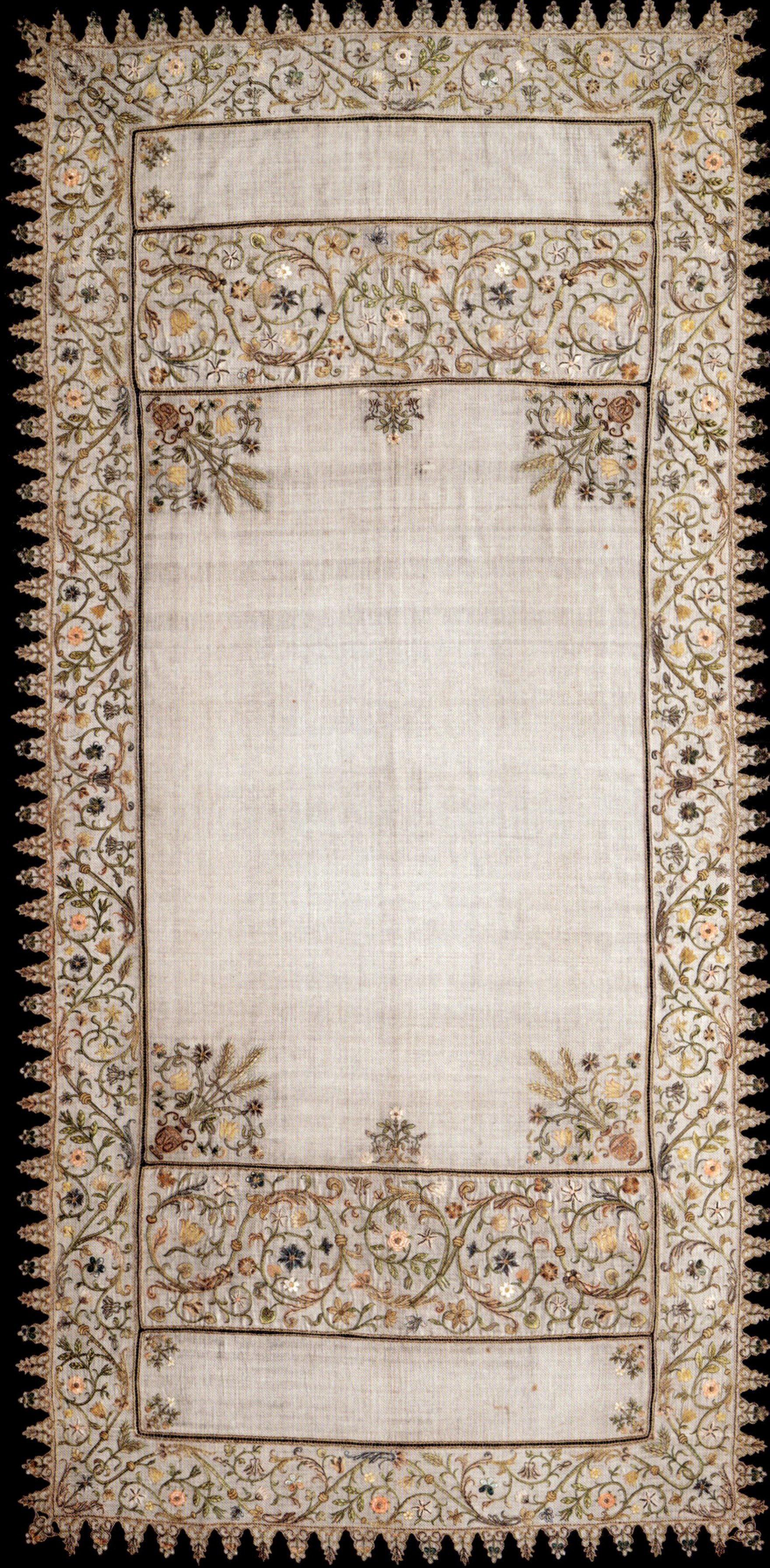

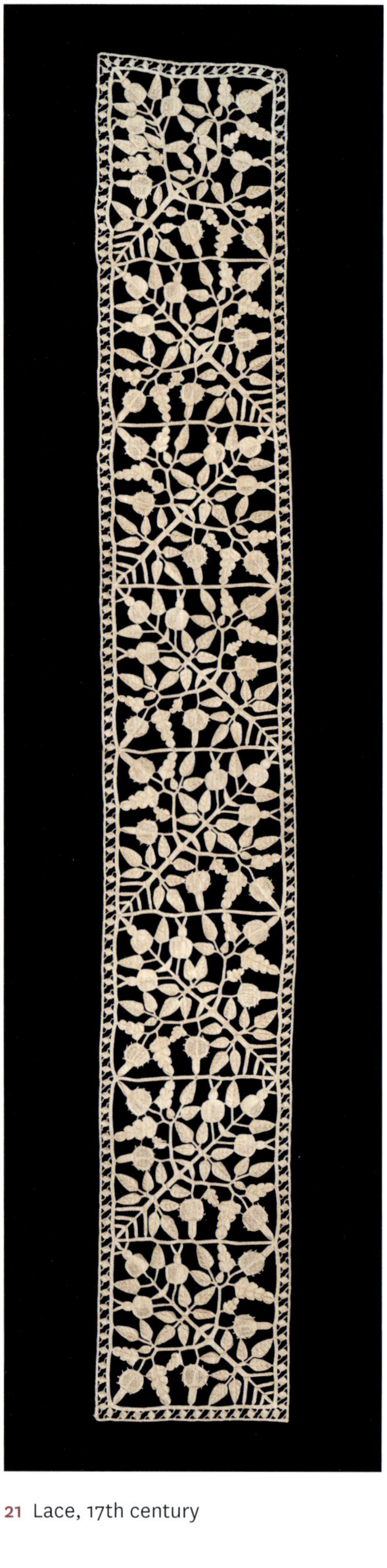

21 Lace, 17th century

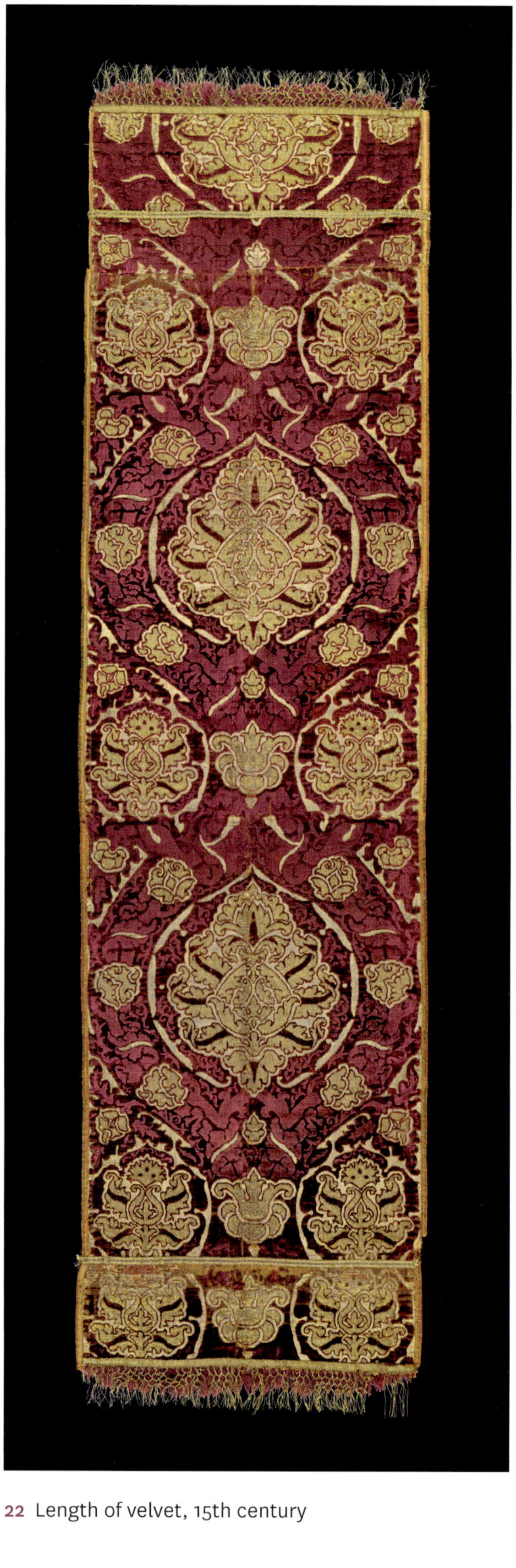

22 Length of velvet, 15th century

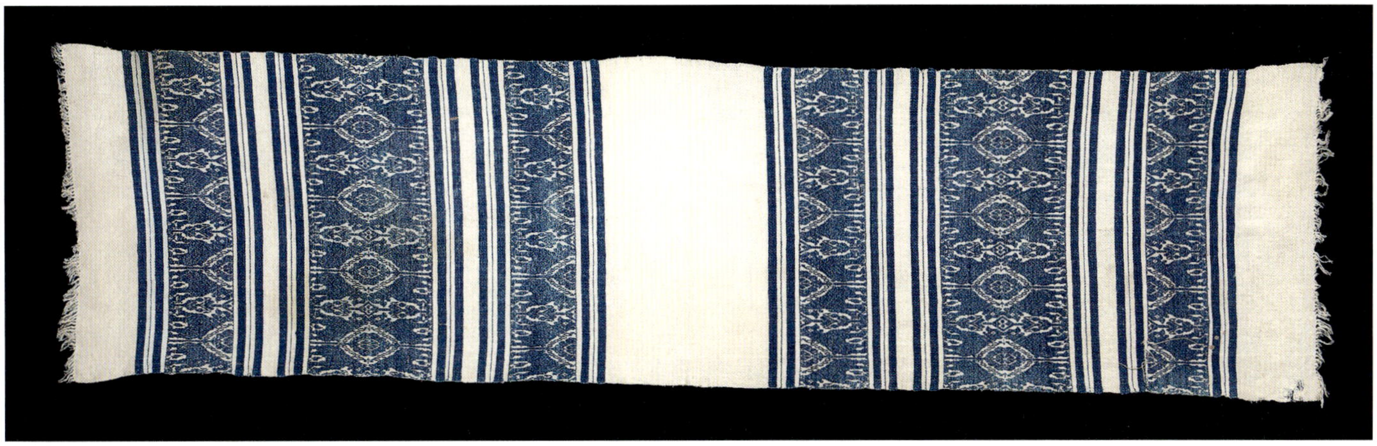

20 Towel, 16th–18th century

home of her husband. Painted with stories, covered with intarsia, or carved with decorative motifs, these chests contained clothing and household furnishings for the bride and her new family. The textiles that often filled these chests might include undergarments, sheets, and table linens—some edged in lace—and clothing and lengths of cloth in rich velvet or silk brocade; these were some of the most expensive items produced in Renaissance Italy. The tactile and intimate world of the Renaissance home comes across in surviving textiles. An embroidered tablecloth uses gold threads and brilliantly dyed thread to create floral patterns and images of flowers in vases of precious metal (fig. 19). Edged in small points also filled with embroidered florals, the entire border of the textile has extremely delicate pulled loops of gold thread. A more commonplace towel is decorated with a motif woven with blue thread (fig. 20). These cloths are often called Perugia towels, and while some were produced in that Umbrian town, they were made in many centers in Italy. Towels such as this were common for a wide variety of uses in the Renaissance home and appear in painted images as table covers, wrapped around babies after a bath, and hanging near fireplaces and in kitchen settings where they might have served a variety of domestic functions. A length of delicate lace, with floral decoration, could have been used to decorate the edges of clothing or other textiles (fig. 21). Lengths of velvet and silk embellished with precious gold would have been among the most valuable pieces in a Renaissance trousseau. A large panel like this sumptuous length of purple cut velvet with looped gold thread might have been used as a hanging to decorate a room for a festive occasion, or even displayed from a window when civic events took place (fig. 22). The fact that it survives in such excellent condition suggests that it was carefully taken care of and treasured.[12]

A maiolica inkwell displays several references to legal marriage and the joining of two families (fig. 23).[13] Two sets of profile portraits appear on the inkwell: a man and a woman shown individually on the sides and a couple facing each other across a roundel on the top. The roundel features clasped hands, signaling the marriage pact, and an inscription that reads "I give you my hand, give me the ring."[14] In Italian a wedding ring is called the *fede*, which also means "faith," and so the inscription is a play on words calling for fidelity in the union. It is possible, given the inkwell's decoration, that its functions may have included writing and recording marriage agreements, perhaps in a professional setting like the office of a notary. Alternatively, in a domestic setting, this inkwell could have reminded the owners of their vows and been used both when writing letters and when creating the sorts of documents that speak to the lifetime of a marriage: inventories of goods amassed by the couple and wills or agreements intended for the dispersal of those goods.

The imagery of clasped hands and paired profiles seen on the inkwell also often appears on jewelry.

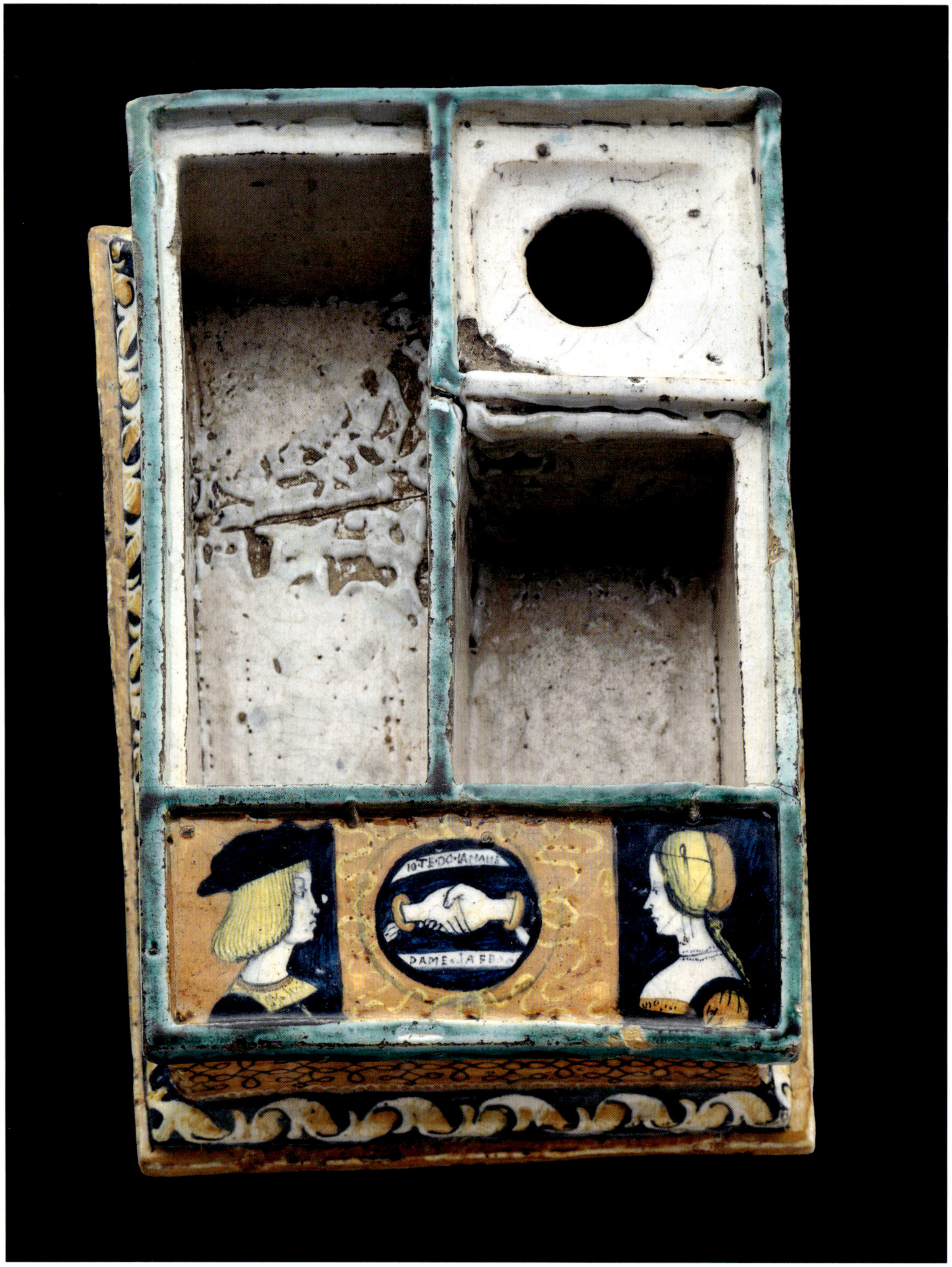

23 Inkwell, about 1500, length 27.9 cm (11 in.)

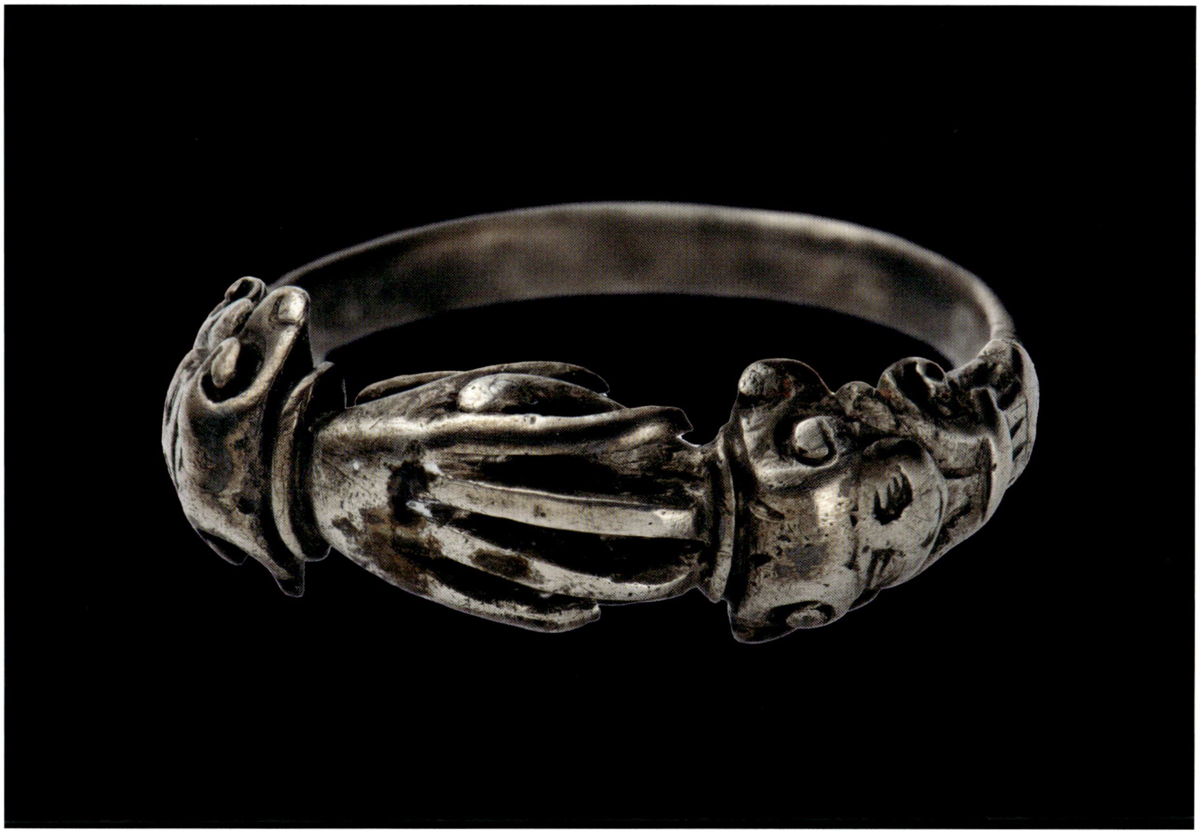

24 Betrothal ring, 15th–16th century

This betrothal ring combines the clasped hands and the ring of the legal ceremony of marriage into a message of faithfulness (fig. 24). Rings surviving from antiquity show clasped hands, suggesting ancient models for such Renaissance rings.[15] Profile portraits of a couple are seen on one side of a circular silver pendant with a gilded silver surround (fig. 25). The other side shows an image of the lamb of God, making it likely that it once held an *agnus dei*, a small disk of wax that was made from the remains of candlesticks used for Easter services in Rome (fig. 26). Blessed by the pope, these little disks were distributed to the faithful, who could take them home and keep them as signs of devotion.[16] They also took on talismanic qualities and were often kept near beds and cribs to guard the family from fire and flood, to protect women in childbirth, and generally to ward off evil. Because they were so fragile and often broke into pieces, containers were made for them, which might be worn like jewelry. This example may well have been worn by a man or a woman as a sign of piety and as an amulet when not safeguarding the family in the home. The couple on the container puts the extraliturgical devotional object into the world of Renaissance marriage and family; perhaps it was a gift to the bride to be worn or kept to encourage a fertile marriage and help ensure safe childbirth.

A portrait medal of Gracia Nasi the Younger offers a unique look at the importance of marriage in the Renaissance as well as revealing layers of meaning about family identity and self-fashioning (fig. 27). Once thought to represent her more famous aunt, Gracia Nasi the Elder (also known as Beatrice de Luna), this medal instead commemorates the marriage of the younger Gracia to her cousin Samuel Nasi. Gracia the Younger lived an extraordinary life in her own right.[17] She was a member of a powerful, wealthy, and illustrious Jewish

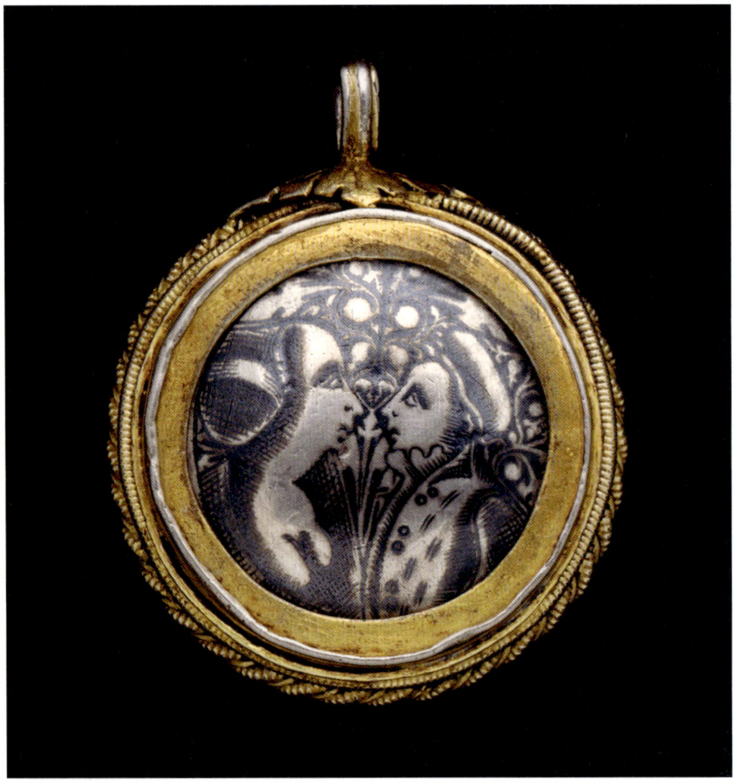

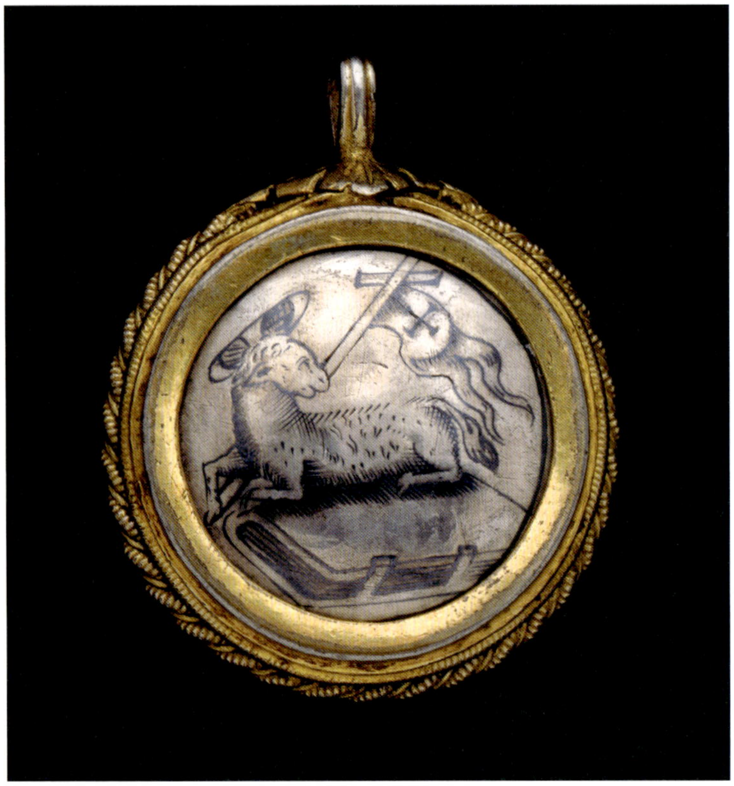

25 & 26 Marriage pendant, about 1455–65, 4.1 x 1.2 cm (1⅝ x ½ in.)

family that had to navigate the complex and sometimes dangerous circumstances of Jewish life in Renaissance Europe.[18] Gracia was born in Antwerp in 1540 to a family of New Christians—Jews who were forced to convert to Catholicism, though they often maintained their Jewish faith in secret—and was baptized with the name Beatrice de Luna, after her aunt. The family originated in Spain, moved to Portugal, where Gracia the Elder was born, and moved again several times to avoid anti-Jewish actions and violence. The family left Antwerp in 1544, having obtained safe conduct to settle in Venice, where they were able to live as New Christians. There they were also able to oversee their family businesses, which centered around trade and finance and engaged with key figures ranging from Ottoman sultans to popes, as well as powers across Europe, including England, France, and a number of Italian city-states.

As an eligible young woman from a wealthy family, Beatrice the Younger would have been a desirable match for the son of an elite Venetian family. As part of the Venetian safe conduct agreement, half the assets of the family were held by the Venetian mint to secure Beatrice's dowry, ensuring this money would enter the broader Venetian economy through her marriage. However, in a ploy likely arranged by her family to remove her from the Venetian marriage market and to keep the family's wealth intact, Beatrice was abducted in 1553 at the hands of two of her cousins and forced to marry one of them. The marriage that supposedly took place during her kidnapping was not recognized, and though both bride and groom were embroiled in legal issues around this event, it soon faded from memory. In 1555, accused of practicing their Jewish faith in secret, Beatrice and her mother, Brianda, appeared before the Venetian Council of Ten. They each declared to this governing body that they wanted to live openly as Jews, resulting in their expulsion from Venice. Given the power of the family and their relative good standing, they were able to negotiate the release of Beatrice's dowry. Beatrice and her mother moved to Ferrara, where other members of the family had lived at least from 1549 to 1552, as the city allowed Jews to live and practice their faith more openly than in Venice. In 1558 or 1559, Beatrice was betrothed and married to her cousin Bernardo, now known as Samuel Nasi (one of her kidnappers, but not the one she had supposedly married), and this medal was struck to commemorate the union.

The choice to have a medal made places this Jewish family in the world of elite Italian society, speaking the language of fame and self-fashioning that a Renaissance medal embodies, with its evocation of ancient prototypes.[19] That they chose to commemorate this marriage and to present an image of the young bride as the representative of her family is also telling, as portrait medals of women were relatively rare at this time. Her dress and jewels show her as a typical Renaissance bride, demonstrating the wealth and status of her family; given that her husband was also her cousin, she displays the consolidated wealth of her extended family. She is identified on the medal by her Jewish name, Gracia Nasi. With this medal, the family proclaims their Jewish identity and does so in Hebrew. No longer Beatrice de Luna, the name Gracia Nasi is written in Hebrew characters, unique on known surviving Renaissance medals and a bold statement.[20] It is not certain when or why the family began using their Hebrew name, but Gracia Nasi the Elder was using it by the time she left Ferrara for Constantinople in 1552. A Latin inscription identifies Gracia as eighteen years old when the medal was made, dating it to 1558. The use of both Latin and Hebrew advertises the family's knowledge of ancient languages and their right to claim the languages as their own.

It is striking that the family chose to commission a medal at all. Although the medal is a powerful statement of Jewish identity, it was made when life for Jews in Italy was becoming ever more difficult and dangerous. In 1555, the newly elected pope Paul IV began to persecute Jews in Italy. A number of Jews living in Ancona were murdered for their refusal to convert to Catholicism by order of the pope, and from Constantinople, Gracia the Elder sought to organize a boycott of the port. In 1559, shortly after their marriage, Gracia the Younger and her husband left Ferrara for Constantinople. Both her husband and her aunt died

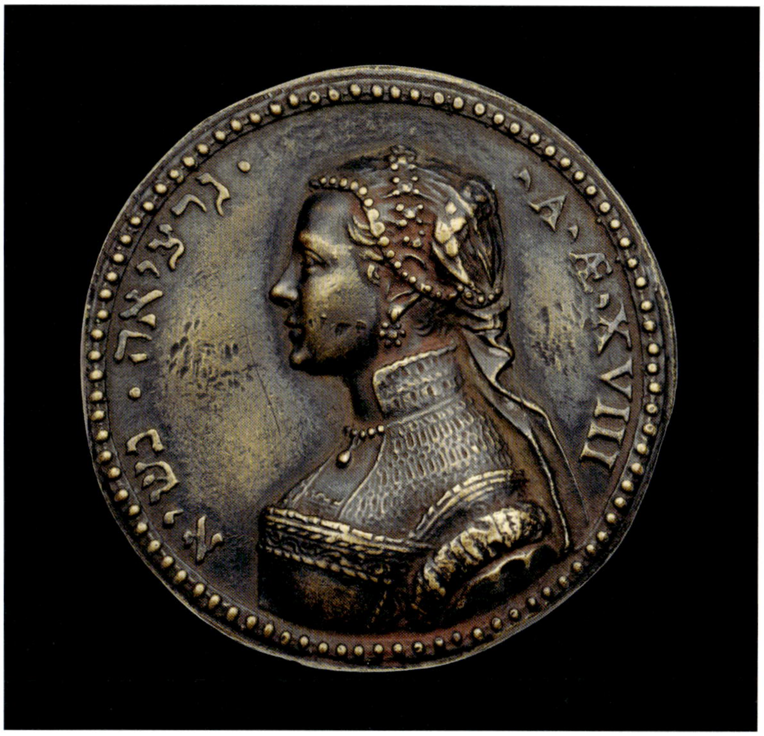

27 Pastorino di Giovan Michele de' Pastorini, *Gracia Nasi the Younger*, 1558, diam. 6.5 cm (2½ in.)

in Constantinople in 1569, and the family's standing diminished under Sultan Murad III, a serious reversal of fortunes.[21] By 1574, Gracia had returned to Ferrara, where she died in 1592. There is surely more to be learned about what brought Gracia Nasi the Younger back to Ferrara, but perhaps her return to the city where her marriage took place and her mother died was an indication of her lasting attachment to the city. After all, it was where she achieved her own greatest fame and agency, in service of her family's interests and recorded for history in the portrait medal commemorating her marriage.

Although associated with a specific moment in time, the objects surrounding a marriage would be kept in the home for years, if not decades, and then passed on through family members. Portraits, jewelry, decorative plates, and more would keep the ideals and hopes for a marriage alive. Messages intended for a young bride would become virtues for a married woman, informing her as she raised her own children.

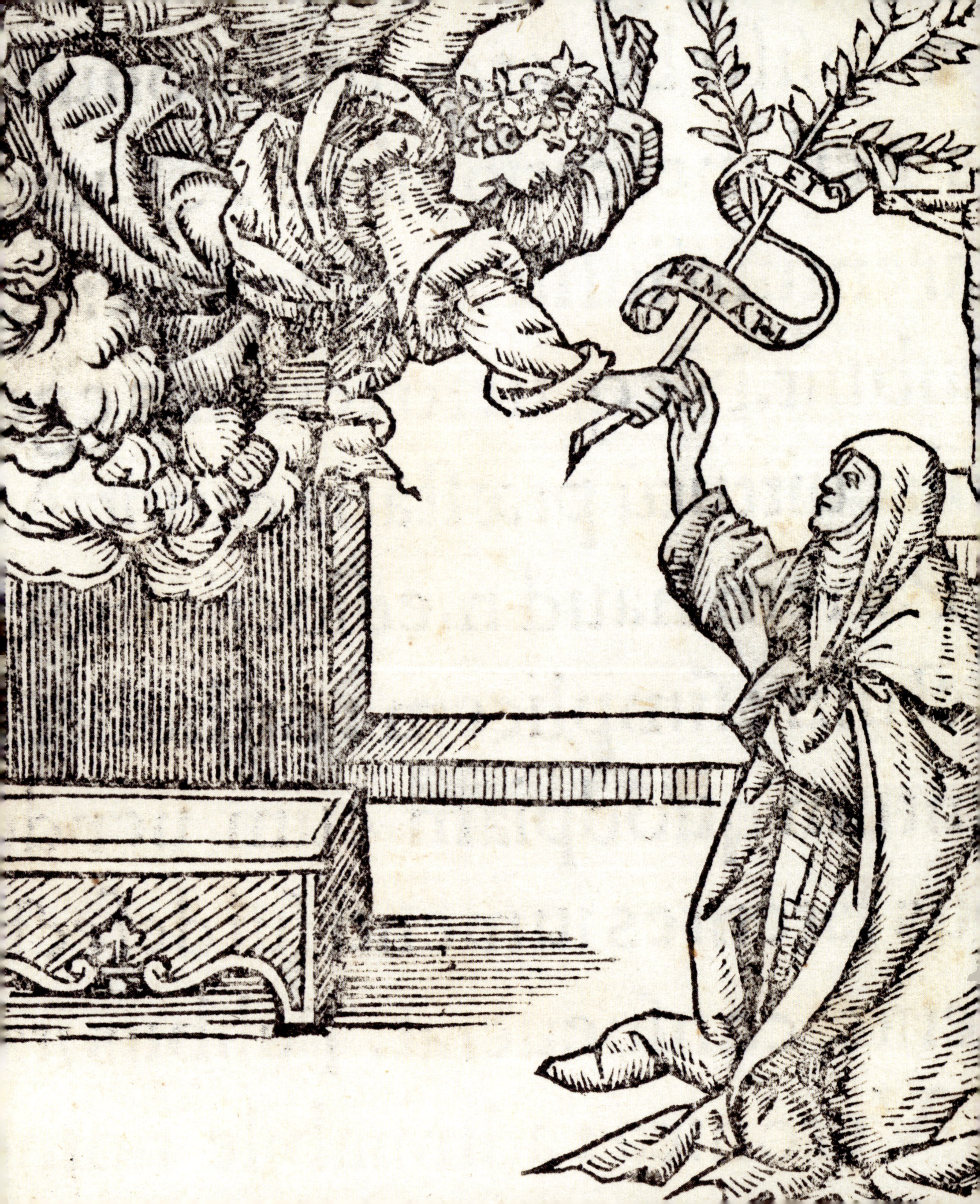
ET

Prayer and Practice

Religion pervaded life in Renaissance Italy for men and women alike. For Renaissance viewers, religious works of art spoke of ritual practices, devotional meanings, and spiritual messages.[1] For today's viewers, these works of art can illuminate spirituality and religious experience in ways that broaden our knowledge of women's lives, making it clear that women's creativity was inextricably bound with their devotional lives.[2] Although women were excluded from the priesthood and usually from the formal study of theology, they had great impact on faith, prayer, and practice. They attended Mass and listened to sermons, usually separated from the men.[3] In churches, in the home, or in convents, women prayed and meditated, read and wrote sacred poetry and devotional texts, and often served as the spiritual guides for their families. Private devotion in the home was usually the center of women's religious experience. They taught children about their faith, performed private rituals of prayer, and sometimes participated in more formal group activities through sodalities and lay organizations.[4] Women and girls also entered convents—sometimes following religious vocations, other times against their will,

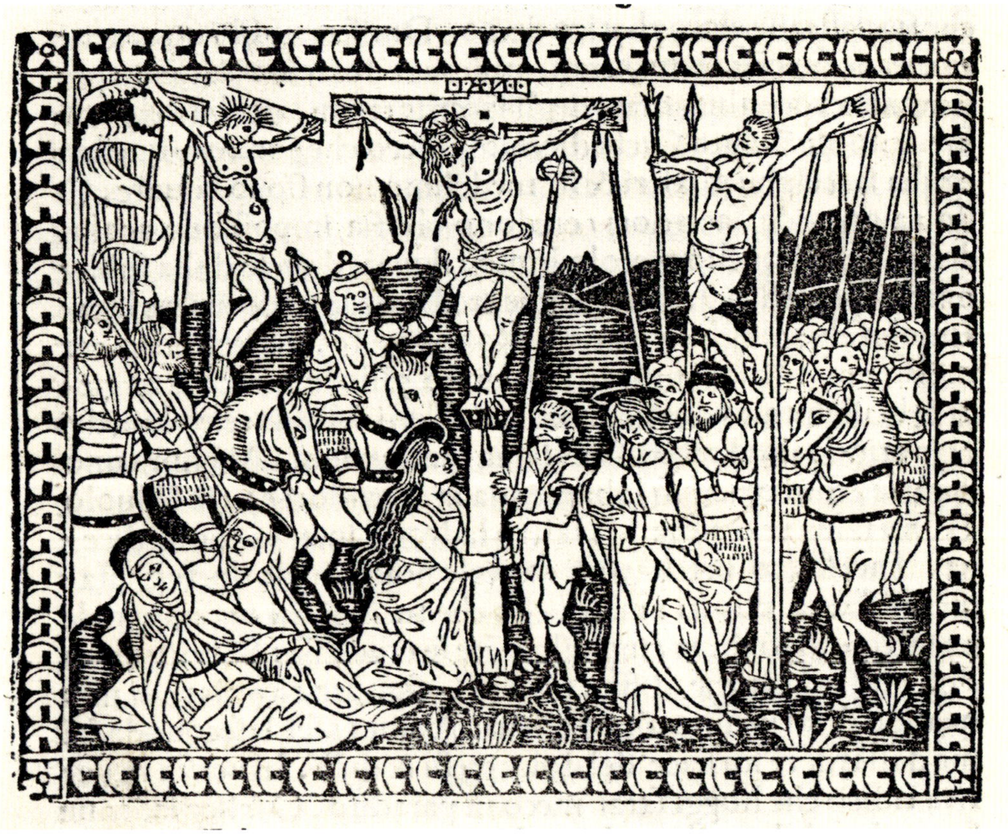

28 Woodcut from *Meditationi sopra la Passione*, Florence, about 1495

and sometimes for practical reasons. These communities often created outlets for women's devotional expression and creativity, not always possible outside such settings.[5]

Meditations on the Life of Christ, one of the most famous devotional treatises of the late Middle Ages, which remained popular throughout the Renaissance, was initially intended to be used by nuns.[6] Versions written in the vernacular were accessible to women who might be able to read Italian and could be read aloud. By presenting extended and detailed meditations on the life of Jesus, the treatise encouraged devotees to imagine themselves participating in the events recounted. By visualizing one's presence in these scenes and responding emotionally to them, a devotee would vividly experience them as if at firsthand. A fifteenth-century Florentine edition focused on the Passion, or the suffering and death of Christ, and called *Meditationi sopra la Passione*, includes a woodcut showing the Crucifixion: Mary is collapsed on the ground, supported by another holy woman, while Mary Magdalen kneels and embraces the cross (fig. 28). All three women respond to Jesus's suffering with intense grief and compassion, encouraging readers and viewers to do the same. Many works of devotional art in the Renaissance followed this same approach of inspiring an empathetic and emotional response in both male and female viewers.

A small panel depicting the Crucifixion, attributed to Bernardo Daddi and painted in Florence in the fourteenth century, was likely made for private use in the home or convent (fig. 29).[7] Mary faints with grief at left and is held by three women. Mary Magdalen embraces the base of the cross. To her right, a woman in purple kneels with hands joined in decorous prayer. This unidentified figure wears a halo, suggesting that she is a saint or blessed woman, but her contemporary

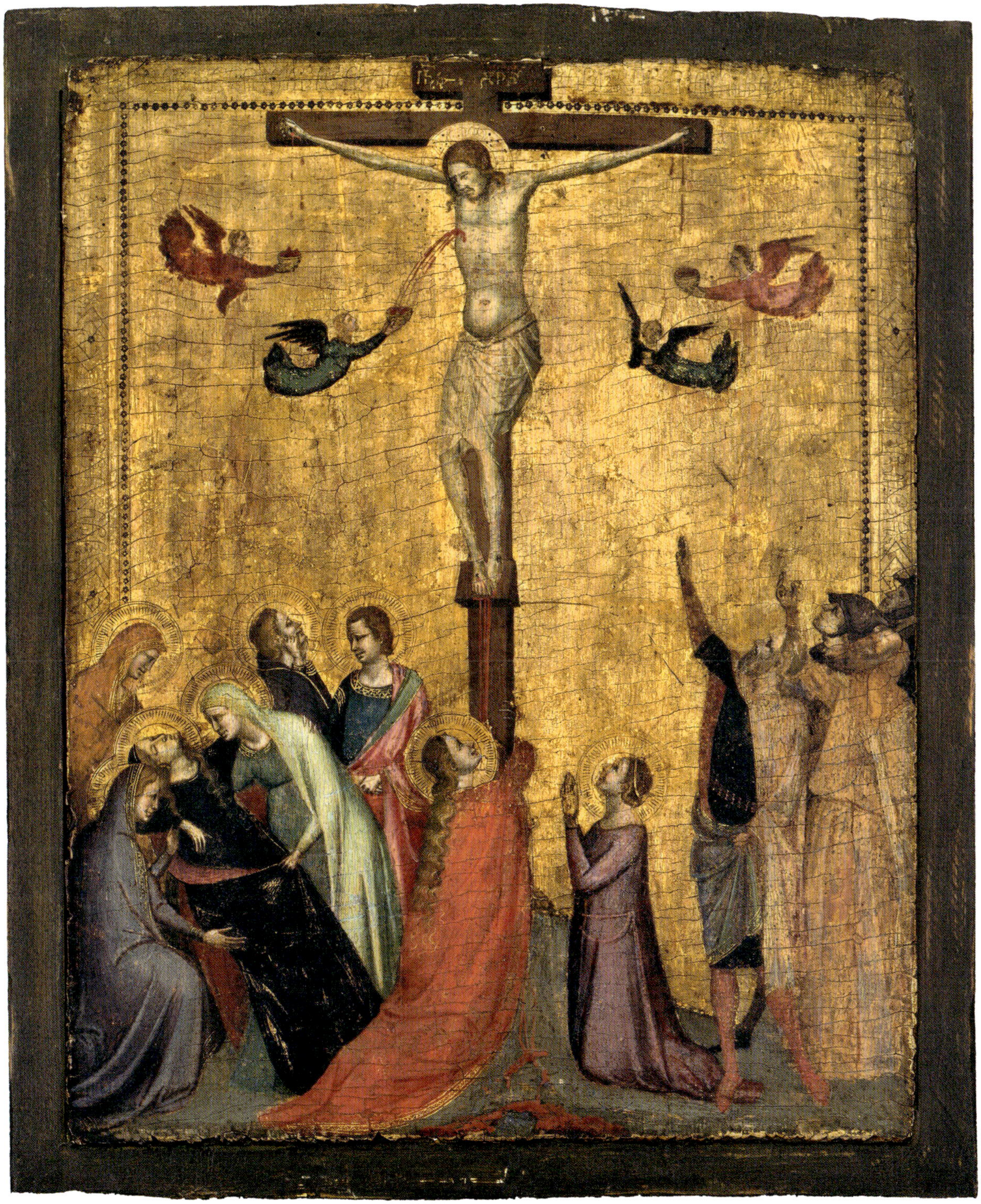

29 Bernardo Daddi, *The Crucifixion*, before 1328, 40.3 x 32.1 cm (15⅞ x 12⅝ in.)

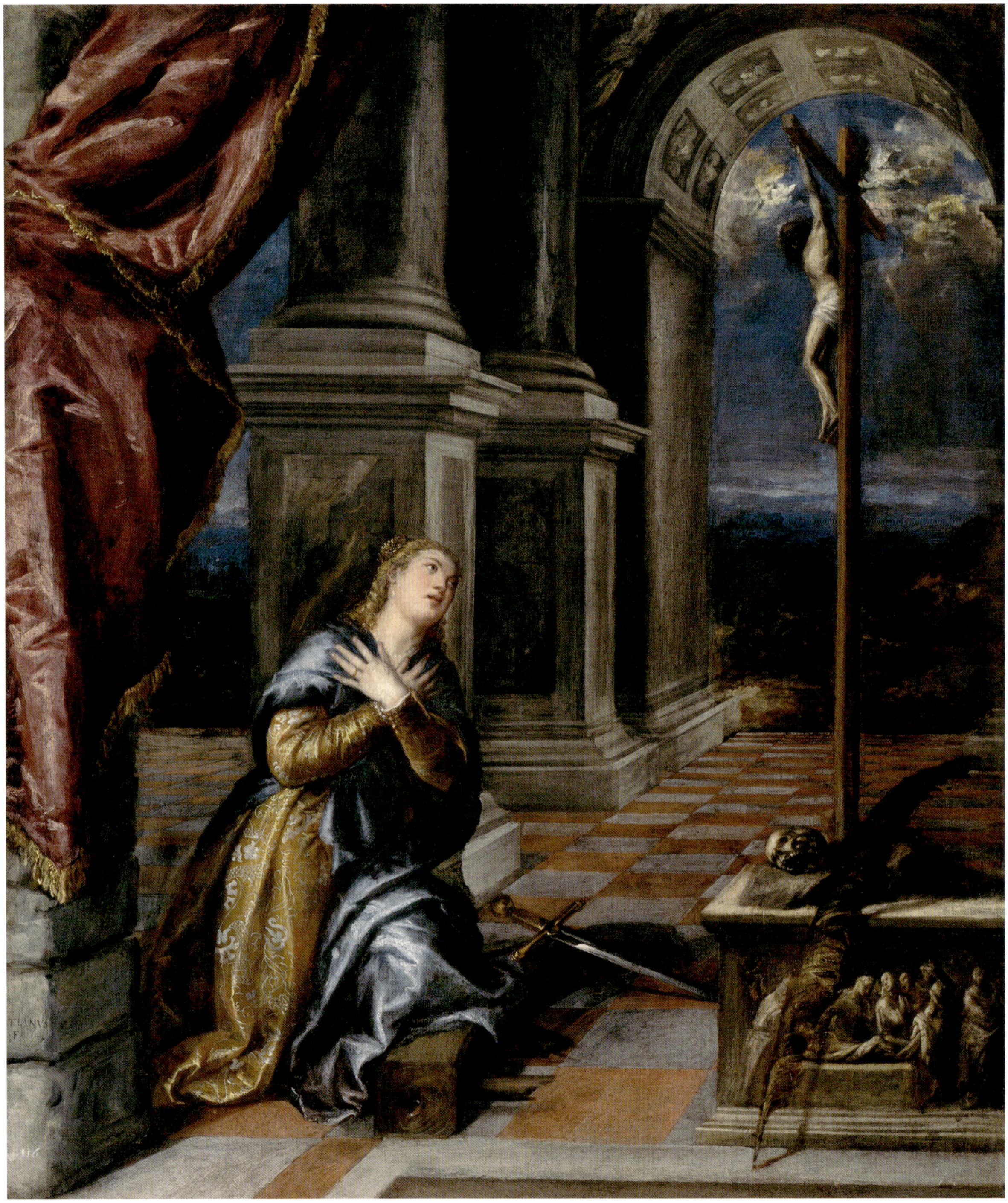

30 Titian, *Saint Catherine of Alexandria*, about 1567, 119.1 x 100 cm (46⅞ x 39⅜ in.)

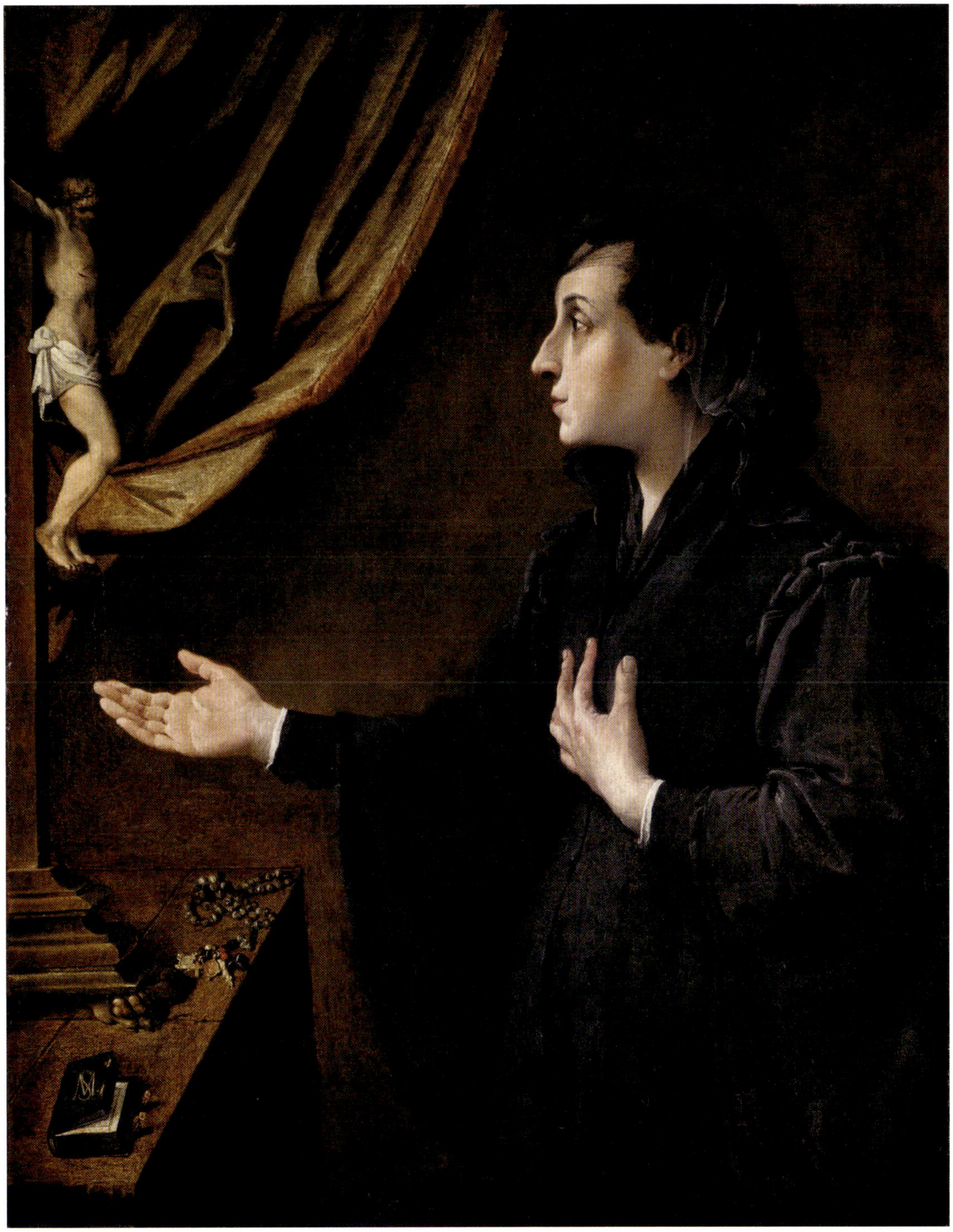

31 Ludovico Carracci, *Portrait of a Widow*, about 1585, 99.7 x 77.5 cm (39¼ x 30½ in.)

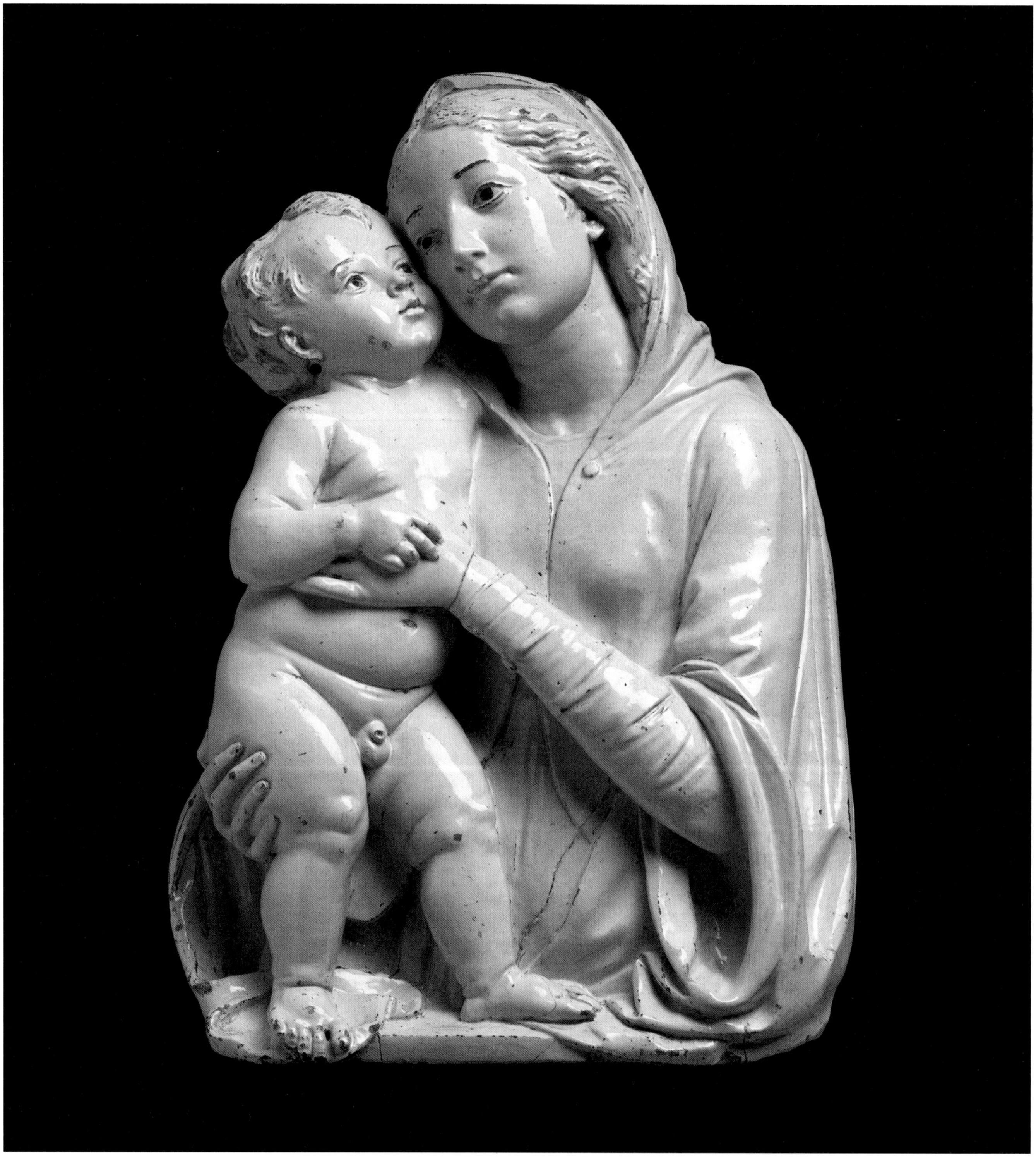

32 Andrea della Robbia, *Virgin and Child*, about 1500, H. 52.1 cm (20½ in.)

costume and lack of identifying attributes also make her a model for the woman who might use this painting for devotional purposes, encouraging the viewer to approach the scene through quiet contemplation. Seeing this painting, a female devotee would be encouraged to emulate the kneeling figure and imagine herself participating directly in the scene, internalizing the emotions expressed by the other women present there. In the Renaissance, women were considered more likely to feel and express deep emotion, and so they also served as role models for men to explore their feelings of grief and devotion to the body of Jesus.

Titian's *Saint Catherine of Alexandria* presents a powerful role model for prayer and meditation before a crucifix, a sculpted representation of Jesus crucified on the cross (fig. 30).[8] Catherine, dressed in the rich garments of an elite Venetian woman, kneels with her arms crossed in front of her chest and her head lifted in adoration. On the ground nearby are the broken wheel recalling her torture and the sword referring to her beheading, which identify her for the viewer. A large palm signifying her martyrdom rests on the base of the cross, drawing attention to the scene of Christ's entombment carved there and encouraging viewers to extend their meditation to this later scene about Christ's death. Catherine venerates the image of Jesus, which is presented here in a naturalistic way, as if it were both a sculpture of Christ on the cross and his actual body during the Crucifixion. This suggests the approach called for by the *Meditationi*: Meditation on an object can lead to imaginative participation in the event. The scene takes place in what appears to be a vaulted loggia with an arch at the back that frames the crucifix and opens onto a stormy sky and landscape. The scale of the figures seems small within such a vast space, transforming the scene into a visual metaphor for the transporting power of prayer. The curtain at the lower left is pulled aside as if to reveal this scene to the viewer, emphasizing the notion of spiritual revelation through prayer and meditation.[9] Possibly made for Cardinal Alessandrino (Michele Bonelli), this painting demonstrates that a female saint could provide a model for meditative, empathetic prayer for men as well as for women.

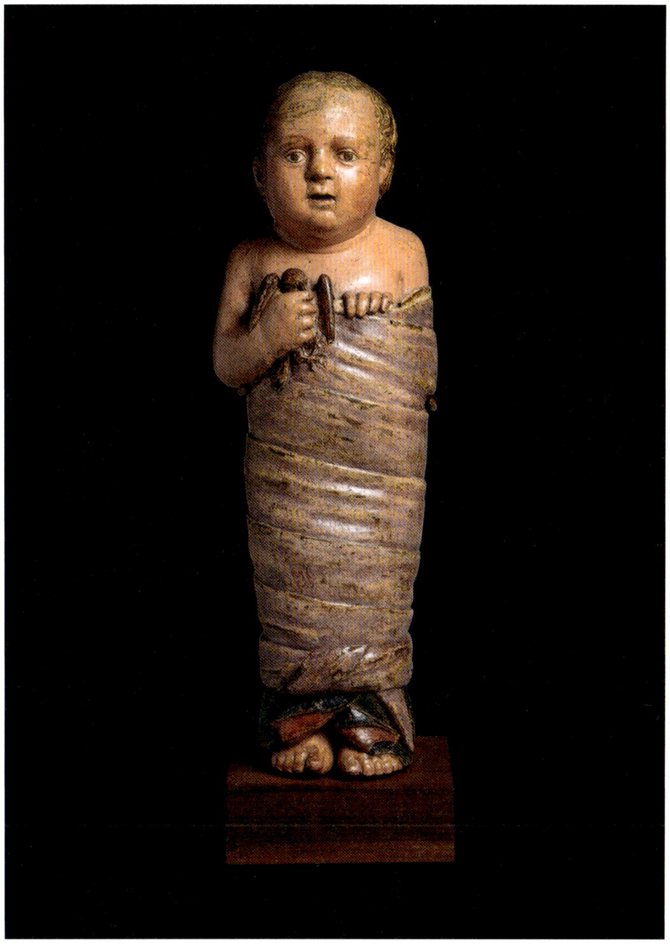

33 Mariano D'Angelo Romanelli, *The Christ Child Wrapped in Swaddling Clothes*, about 1375–1400, H. 46 cm (18½ in.)

Because women were seen as emotional and visionary in their devotional practice, their example encouraged men to experience similar responses.

Ludovico Carracci's *Portrait of a Widow* also shows a woman praying before a crucifix but in a more intimate setting, likely in her home (fig. 31). Not yet identified, the woman stands before an altar-like table with a crucifix, a prayer book personalized with the interwoven letters *M* and *S*, a rosary, and devotional tokens and medals arrayed before her, all objects that supported prayer.[10] As in the *Saint Catherine of Alexandria*, a curtain is pulled aside behind the figure, adding a sense of quiet and revelation. She wears the black clothing, headdress, and veil that mark her as a widow. Her

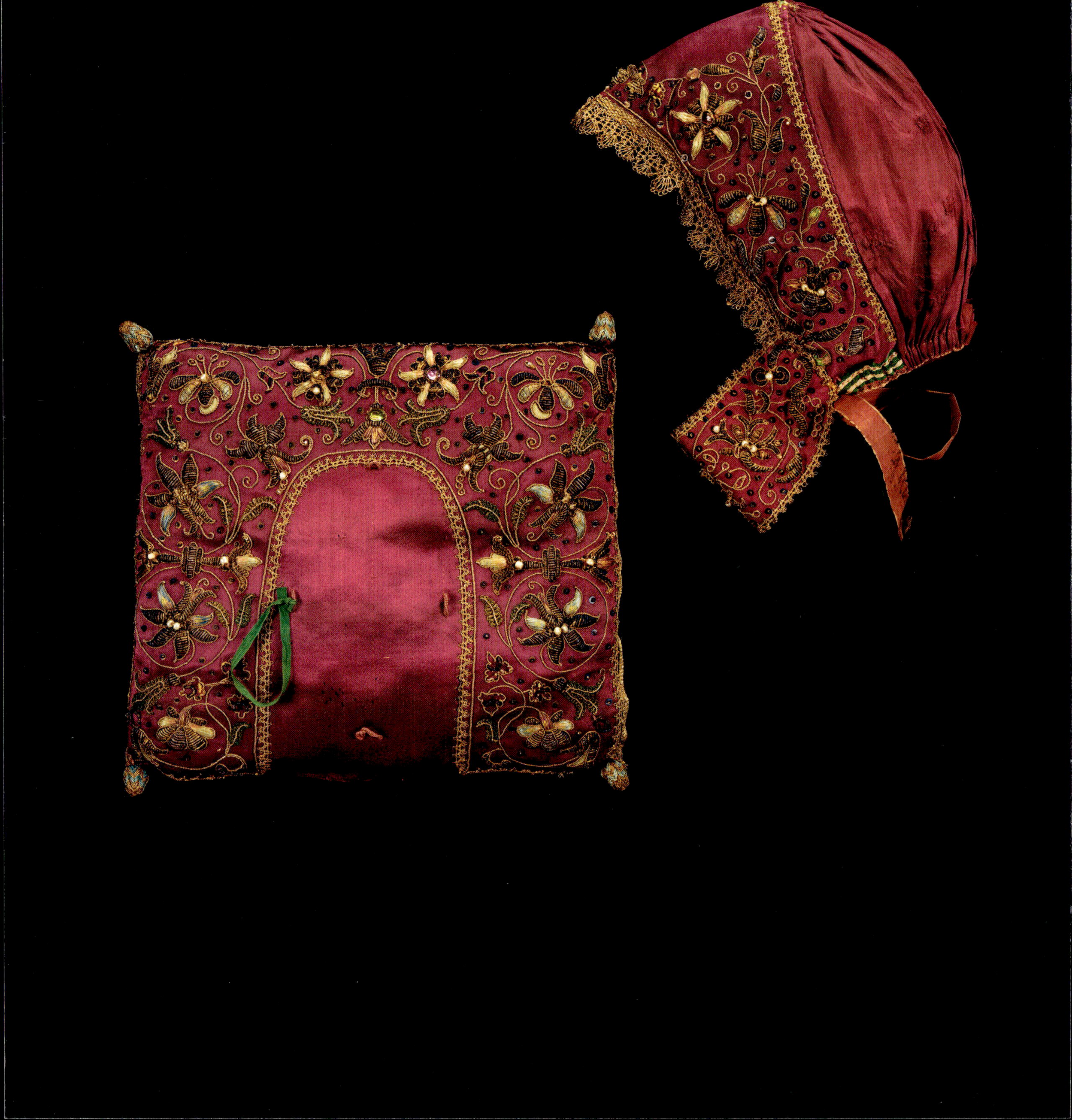

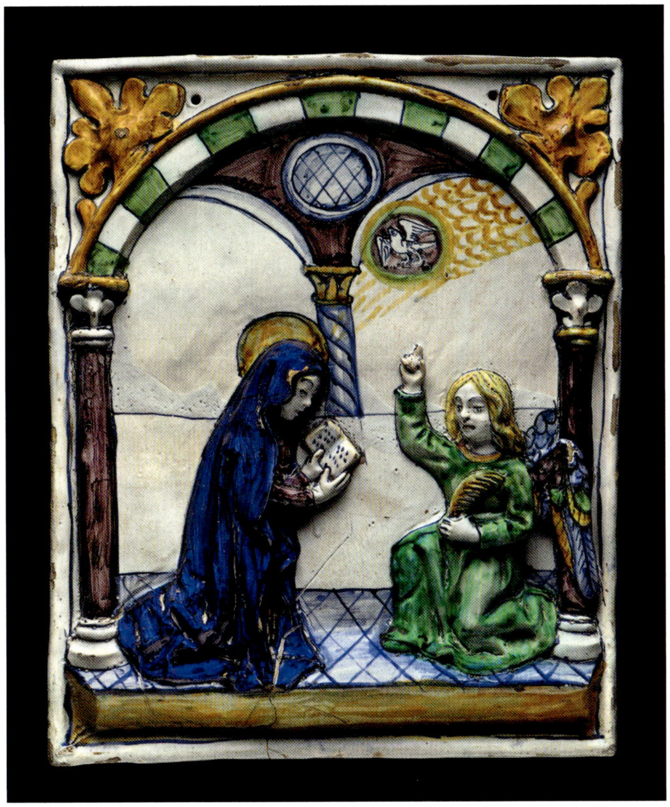

35 *The Annunciation*, late 15th century, 50.8 x 39.4 cm (20 x 15½ in.)

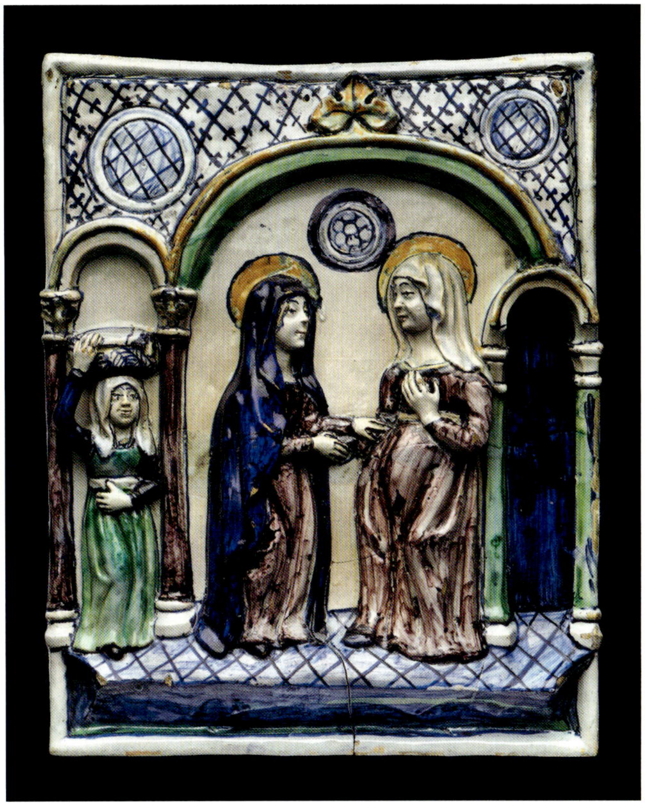

36 *The Visitation*, late 15th century, 50.8 x 39.4 cm (20 x 15½ in.)

gestures, one hand to her heart, the other palm open in acceptance, express her own devotion and invite the viewer to emulate her in prayer. She likely became the principal model of piety for her family upon the death of her husband. Widows in Renaissance Italy often took on greater responsibilities not just for the spiritual health of their families, but also for their financial well-being and social standing.[11] They sometimes took over family businesses and often had full control over the running of their households, achieving greater independence and agency. Carracci's widow, with the accoutrements of prayer that would have been familiar to those looking at the portrait, displays both strength and devotion.

Throughout their lives, women were responsible for the spiritual welfare of a household and for educating children about prayer and practice. Dominican friar, and spiritual adviser to several noble Italian women, Giovanni Dominici encouraged families, especially mothers, to create sites of holy play for children, where they might place flowers or jewels or light candles before sacred images.[12] Andrea della Robbia's *Virgin and Child* is a tender image of maternal love and an example of the most common type of devotional image made for the home (fig. 32). Small round impressions in the clay, visible near the necks of the figures, were likely made to allow the owners to apply jewelry to the sculpture, such as talismanic strands of coral beads. Coral was seen as a quasi-magical material that served as a protective agent especially for children, keeping them from illness and death and encouraging them to thrive and grow into healthy vital adults.[13] The tactile experience of placing such jewelry on the sculpture would honor

OPPOSITE
34 Cap and cushion, late 16th–early 17th century, cushion: 21 x 19 cm (8¼ x 7½ in.)

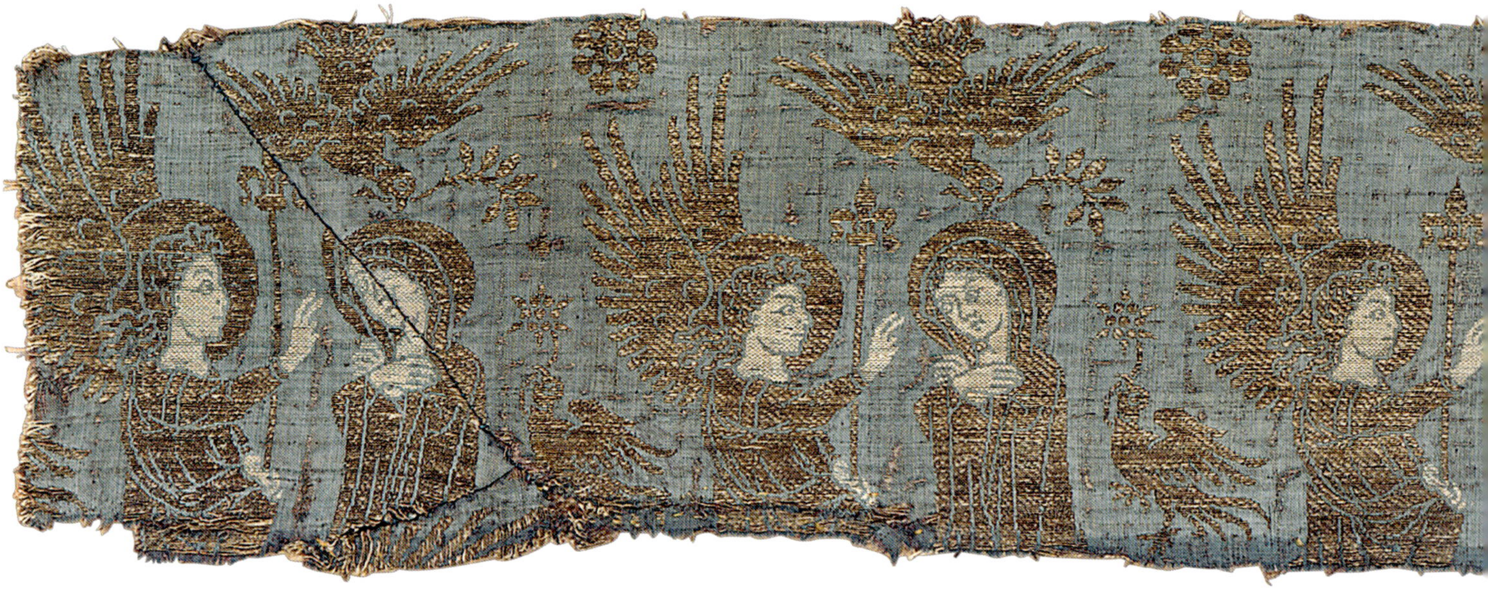

37 Fragment of a textile with the Annunciation, 14th–15th century

the holy figures as well as create a sense of closeness to them.

Young girls might be given small wood sculptures of the infant Jesus, and they often took such objects into convents or to their new homes as part of their marriage goods (fig. 33).[14] Though these doll-like sculptures are sometimes nude, this particular infant is tightly wrapped in swaddling clothes and holds a little bird. The figure is able to stand on its own, as a focus for prayer, but could also be laid down in a crib-like setting. Beautiful textiles were often created to use with these dolls such as this small pillow and cap made in red silk with delicate embroidery (fig. 34). Dressing these little figures and affectionately tending to them would encourage a sense of close interaction with Jesus, a devotional approach that is a characteristic aspect of women's religious practice. Although the use of such sculptures is not exclusive to girls and women, it is most closely associated with them, both in the home and in convents.

Considering how people prayed might help explain the form and function of certain works of art. A pair of maiolica reliefs may be seen as a visual evocation of the prayer Ave Maria, one of the most common prayers in the Catholic faith, with one panel depicting the Annunciation and the other the Visitation, episodes from the gospel of Luke (figs. 35, 36). The first line of the prayer references the Annunciation and quotes the words of the angel to Mary when she learns that, though a virgin, she is pregnant with Jesus. The second line comes from the Visitation, when Elizabeth recognizes that Mary is pregnant as her own child, John the Baptist, leaps in her womb in an acknowledgment of Jesus. Elizabeth's pregnancy was also considered miraculous, since she was old and had never been able to conceive a child. This scene of miraculous pregnancies deeply resonated with women who were or hoped to become pregnant.[15] In the relief depicting Mary and Elizabeth, both women smile, as does a servant who shares in the joy of the two blessed women. The attending woman is much like a viewer of this piece: privileged to witness this momentous encounter. One can imagine these two panels supporting the praying of the Ave Maria. They might have decorated a church, convent, or home, since this prayer was said ubiquitously, by men and women alike.

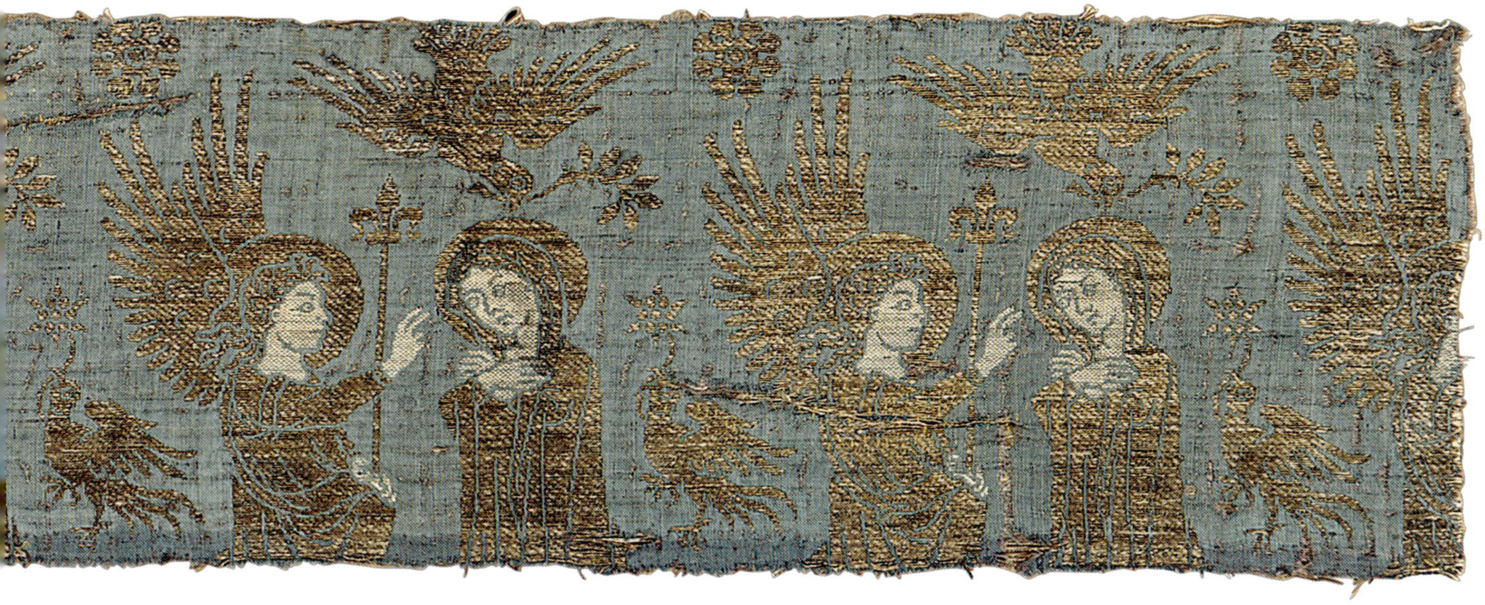

The practice of repeating the Ave Maria was a common mode of prayer and developed into the Rosary, where sets of seven or ten repetitions of this prayer were interspersed with the other most common prayer, Our Father.[16] A woven silk textile with a scene of the Annunciation repeated over and over speaks to this mode of prayer (fig. 37). Such textiles might be used in a home or convent, perhaps draped over the table that held objects like a crucifix for personal prayer. In religious settings, this textile might have served as an altar cover. The likely function of another woven textile, also with the scene of the Annunciation repeated vertically, was as part of a priest's vestment (fig. 38). Fragments with devotional imagery were often cut from larger garments as a way of preserving parts of clothing that was otherwise worn out or no longer used.

Textiles were a tactile and mobile form of devotional art and were often made and used by women.[17] Religious imagery might make its way into the home or convent through embroidered pictures, usually derived from drawings or paintings. One particular example shows the Pietà, or the scene of grief and lamentation after Christ's death, a frequent subject of devotional imagery in the sixteenth century (fig. 39). Here, Mary sits at the foot of the cross and holds the body of her dead son on her lap. This extremely fine embroidery retains its brilliant colors, suggesting it was well taken care of. The frame of the image is embroidered with decorative motifs and objects that recall moments in Jesus's suffering and death known collectively as the Instruments of the Passion, including the cloth with which a female disciple (Veronica) wiped his face at the top, and Christ's cloak at the bottom. A luxurious devotional image, its small scale suggests personal use, likely in the home, of a male or female owner.

Convents played a particularly important role in women's spiritual lives during the Renaissance.[18] Women went to convents mostly as young girls but also at other points in their lives, for example as widows. Convents provided safe havens for reformed prostitutes, who could repent and transform their lives, as well as accepted women who were ill and needed particular care. Religious communities could take the place of families in the lives of many girls and women, and so care, affection, joys, and sorrows would be shared by the women in a convent. Convents also played an important role in the

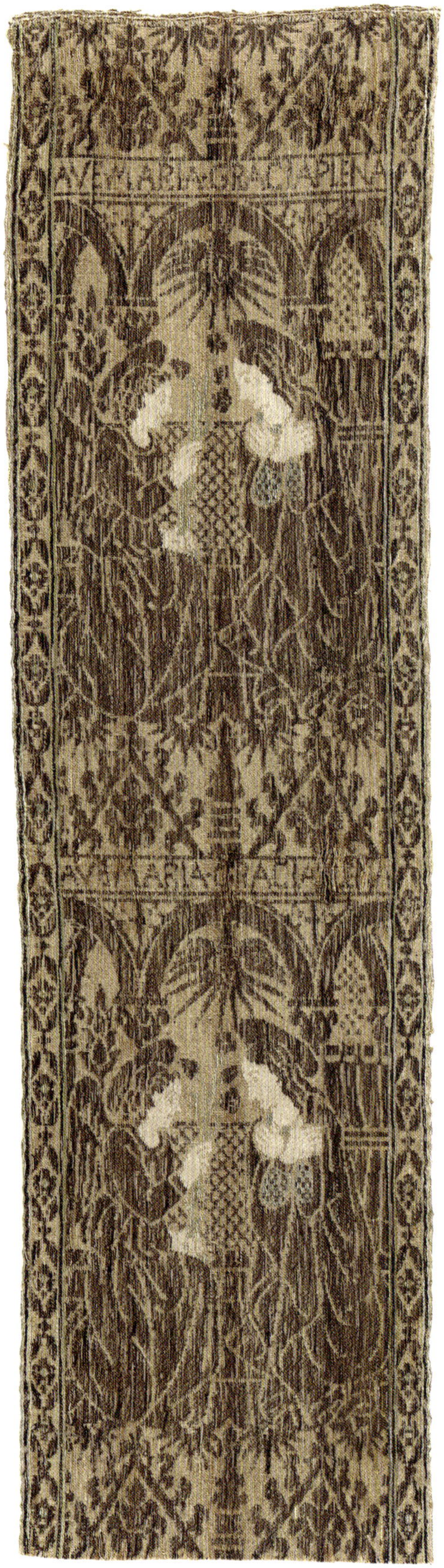

spiritual world of their larger communities, providing prayer and other services to people outside their walls.

Published in 1518, *Inexplicabilis mysteriis gesta beatae Veronicae virginis* (The Miracles and Deeds of the Blessed Virgin Veronica) presents the life Saint Veronica of Binasco (1445–1497), a nun in the convent of Santa Marta in Milan, and provides a window into the life of a convent.[19] Veronica was born to a poor farming family, and from an early age felt a deep religious devotion. Unable to read or write, Veronica was refused entry to a convent until Mary appeared to her in a vision, reassuring Veronica that she would learn these skills. Once at Santa Marta, she remained silent for many years, living a life of humble service to the community. She also received other visions in which she was taught to read and write by Mary, Jesus, and angels. Later in life, she experienced ecstasies and wept copious tears, which were gathered and saved as relics by her sisters. As word of her holiness and mysticism spread, she became known outside the convent and made many trips, including a journey to meet Pope Alexander VI.

The Latin text of this volume was written by Isidor Isolani, but was based on a life of Veronica written in the vernacular by one of her fellow Santa Marta nuns, Benedetta da Vimercate.[20] Benedetta, a teacher and a writer, recounted in her manuscript her own experiences of Veronica's life and holy deeds, as well as the recollections of other women in the convent. Its main purpose was to record for the community the extraordinary life, visions, and prophecies of Veronica. Benedetta's original manuscript is now in the Biblioteca Ambrosiana in Milan. Isolani's life, on the other hand, was an official hagiography, commissioned by the prioress of Santa Marta in 1517, twenty years after Veronica's death, and dedicated to King Francis I of France. The publication served Prioress Arcangela Panigarola's political and religious goals for her convent and sought to honor the saintly woman that the prioress saw as a spiritual role model for her community and herself. Isolani's book is illustrated with ten woodcuts of Veronica's visions,

38 Fragment of a textile with the Annunciation, 15th century–16th century

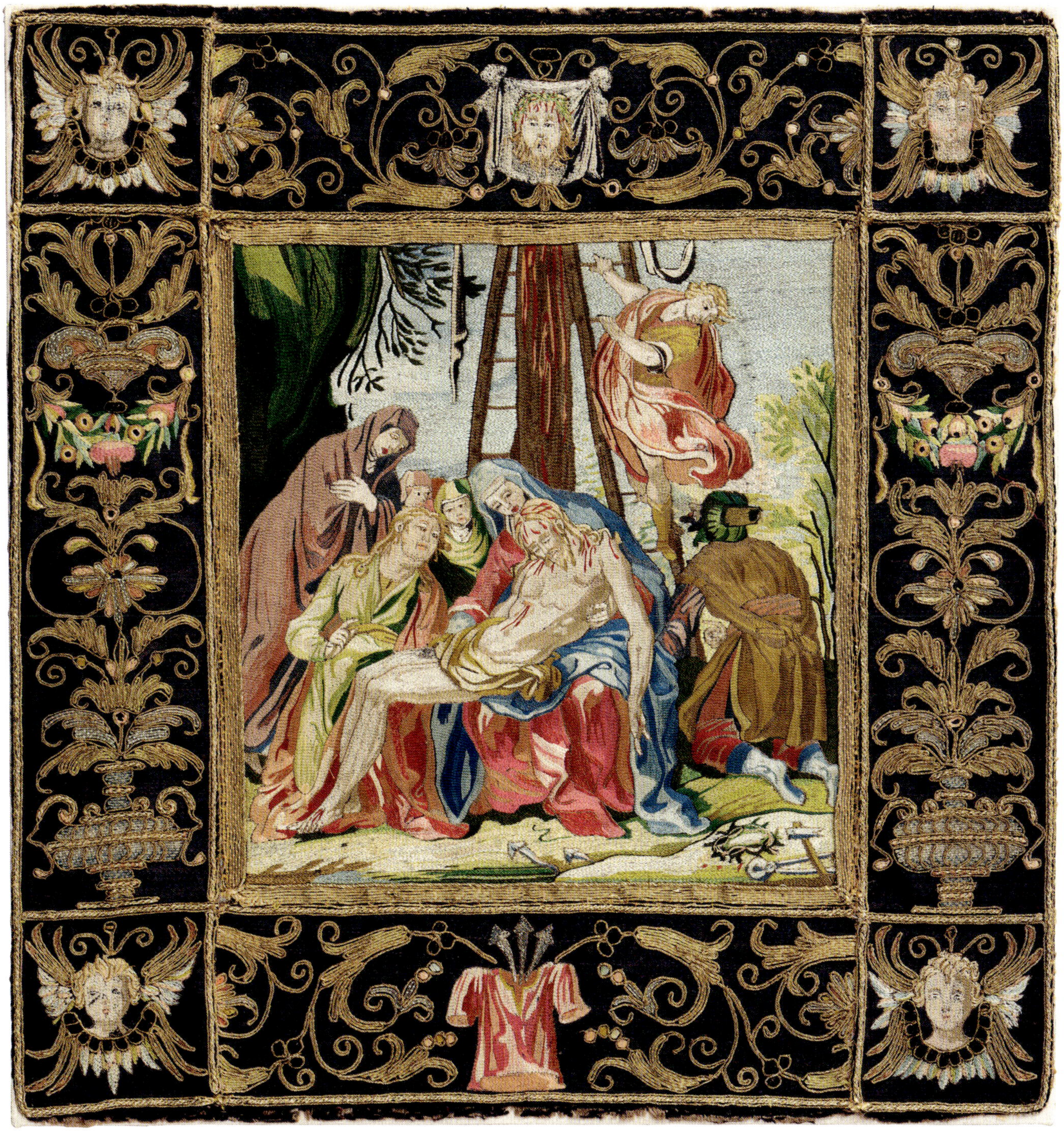

39 Embroidery with the Pietà, 16th century

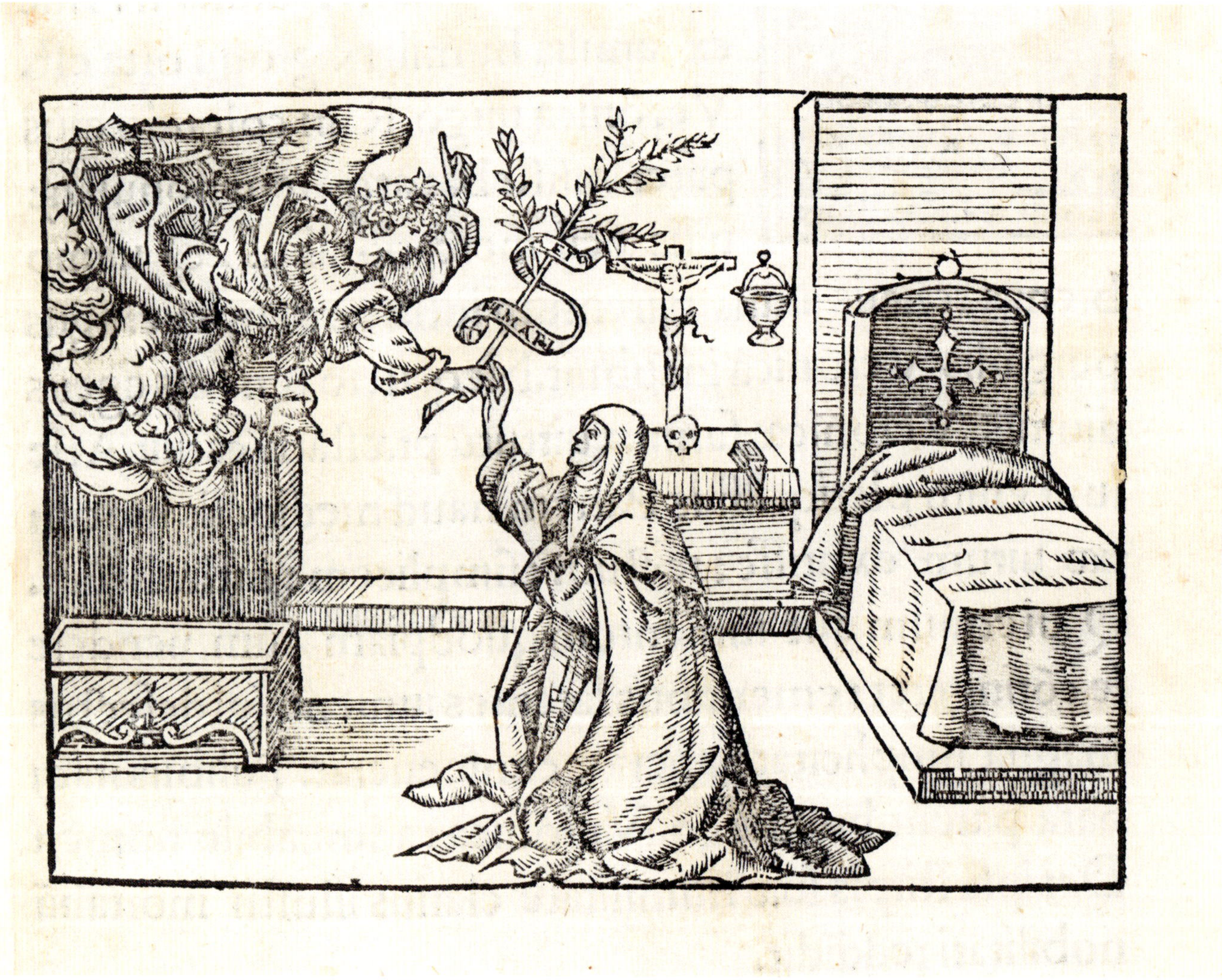

40

40 through 51 Woodcuts from Isodor Isolani, *Inexplicabilis mysteriis beatae gesta Veronicae virginis*, Milan, 1518

ensuring that even those who could not read Latin would understand the story.

The woodcuts introduce chapters in the book and show a series of episodes from Veronica's life, illustrating her visions and devotions; except for one, all are set in convent spaces. The first woodcut shows Veronica in her room at Santa Marta, kneeling in full robes (fig. 40). The room is furnished with a bed decorated with a cross on the headboard. Next to the bed is a small altar covered in a cloth with a crucifix, a small skull, and what seems to be a small box perhaps containing a book. Above the altar hangs a small basin, maybe filled with water for washing or holy water. An angel flies in from the upper left and gives to Veronica an olive branch with a scroll, reading AET. MARI, signifying that the branch is sent by Mary in heaven and is meant for Veronica to use for writing. The scene recalls the familiar imagery of the Annunciation, a sign of the grace that Veronica experienced through her visions.

The woodcuts that follow build upon Veronica's miraculous access to lessons in reading and writing and to Holy Communion. In the next image, Veronica is shown kneeling at the center, receiving bread from an angel, who again flies in from the upper left. A table covered with a cloth at left and the large piers to the right suggest a gathering space, possibly the dining hall, making the point that Veronica's sustenance is spiritual (fig. 41). Standing in a room with a large window opening to a landscape, Veronica, in the next scene, receives sacred reading lessons directly from Jesus (fig. 42). He holds a book and reads aloud to her while she focuses on the book in her own hands. She does not kneel before Jesus but stands on the same level, and by learning to read, gains direct access to his words. Next, Veronica kneels before an altar draped with a fringed cloth that is obscured by her vision of the infant Jesus surrounded by clouds (fig. 43). She kneels with her left hand humbly upon her heart and her right hand raised with open palm to accept the grace of this vision, which allows her to see Jesus standing on the altar where the Eucharist would be celebrated. This image recalls the little Jesus dolls that were given to girls and that could serve as devotional aids to encourage meditations on his

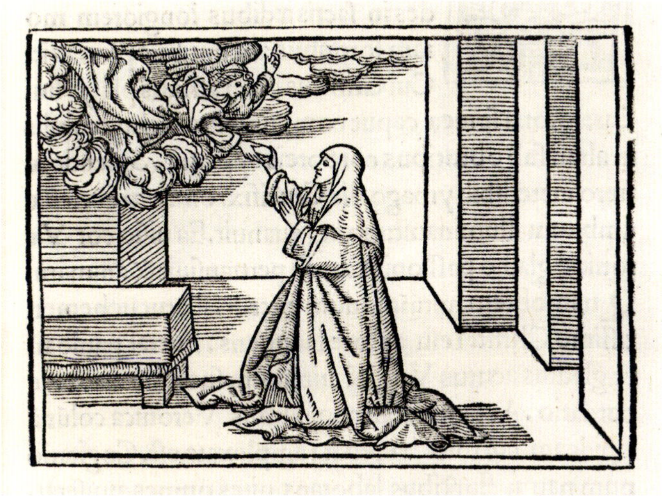

41

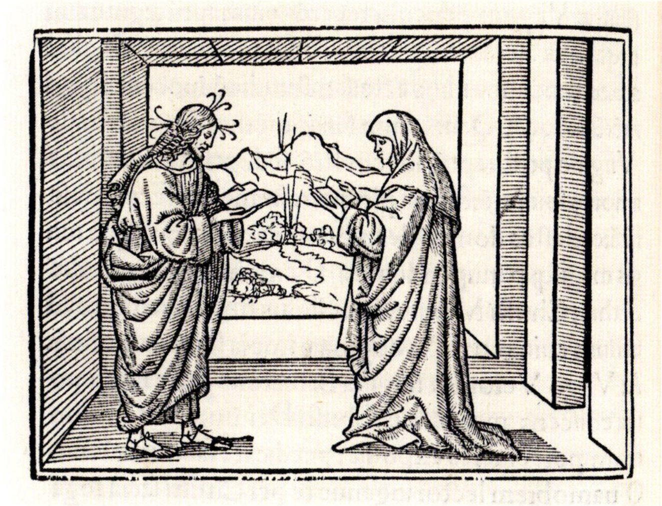

42

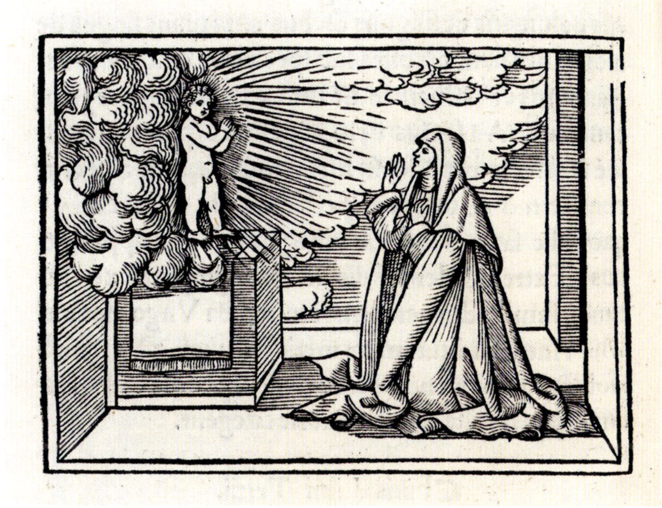

43

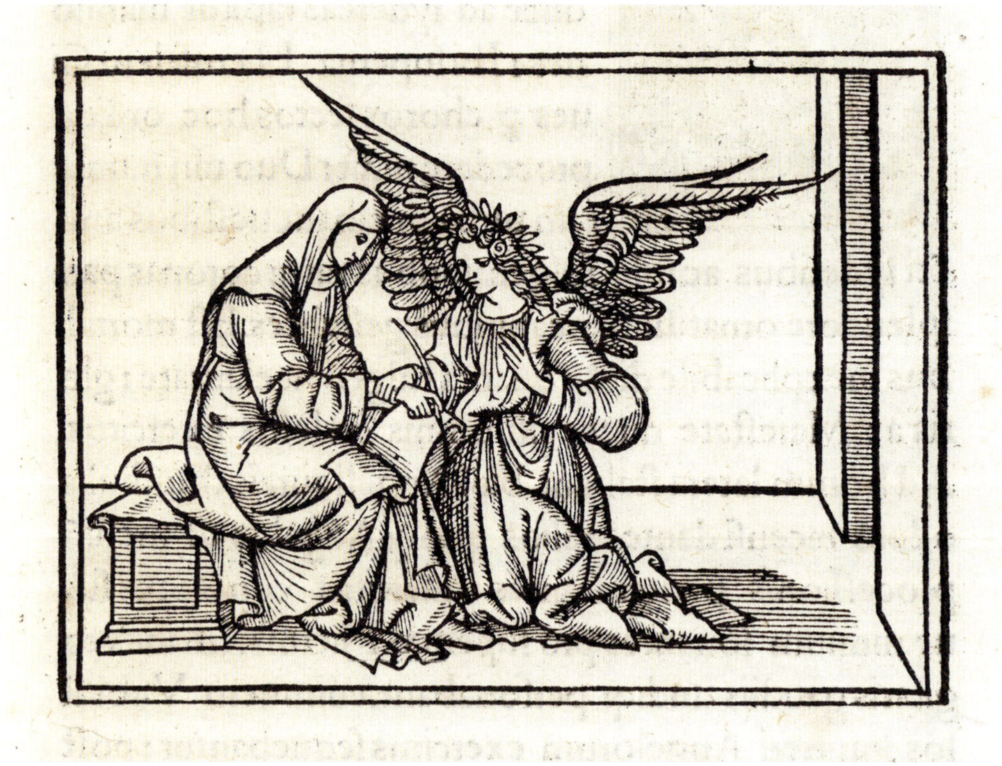

44

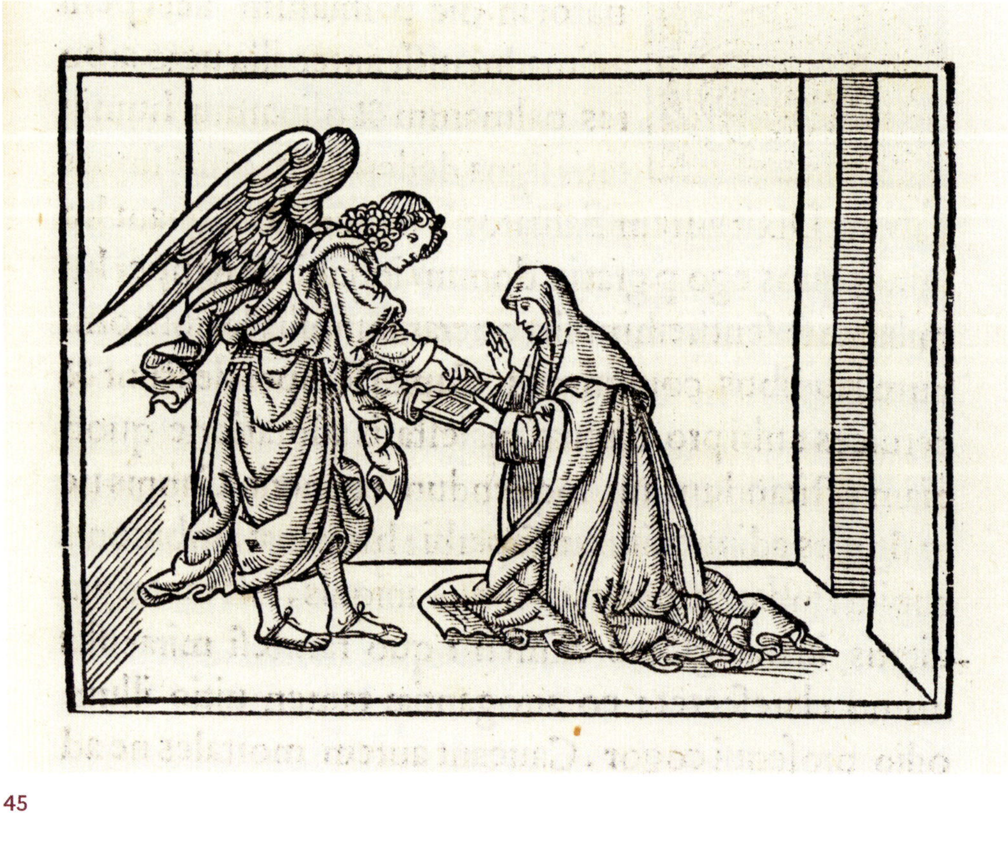

45

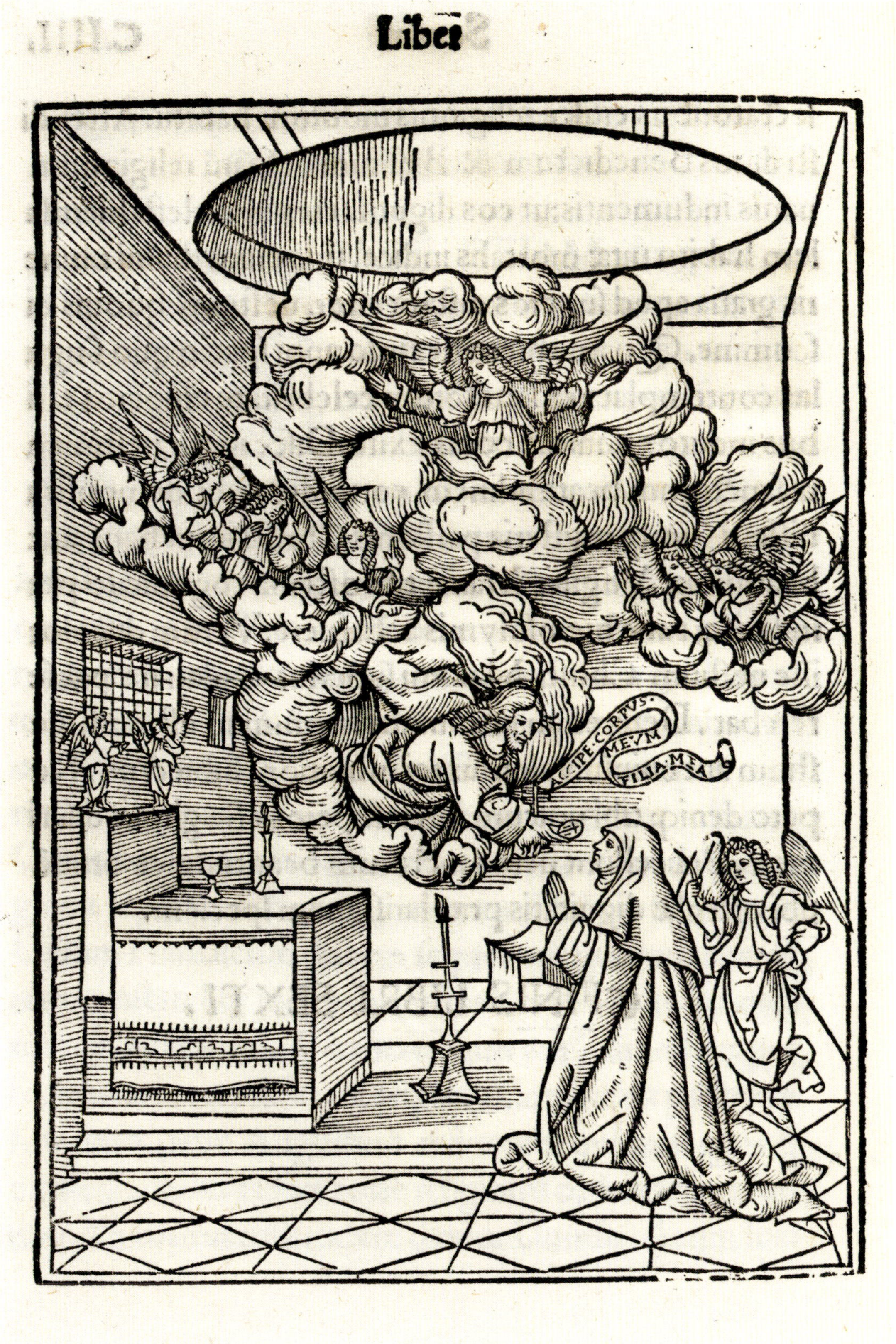

46

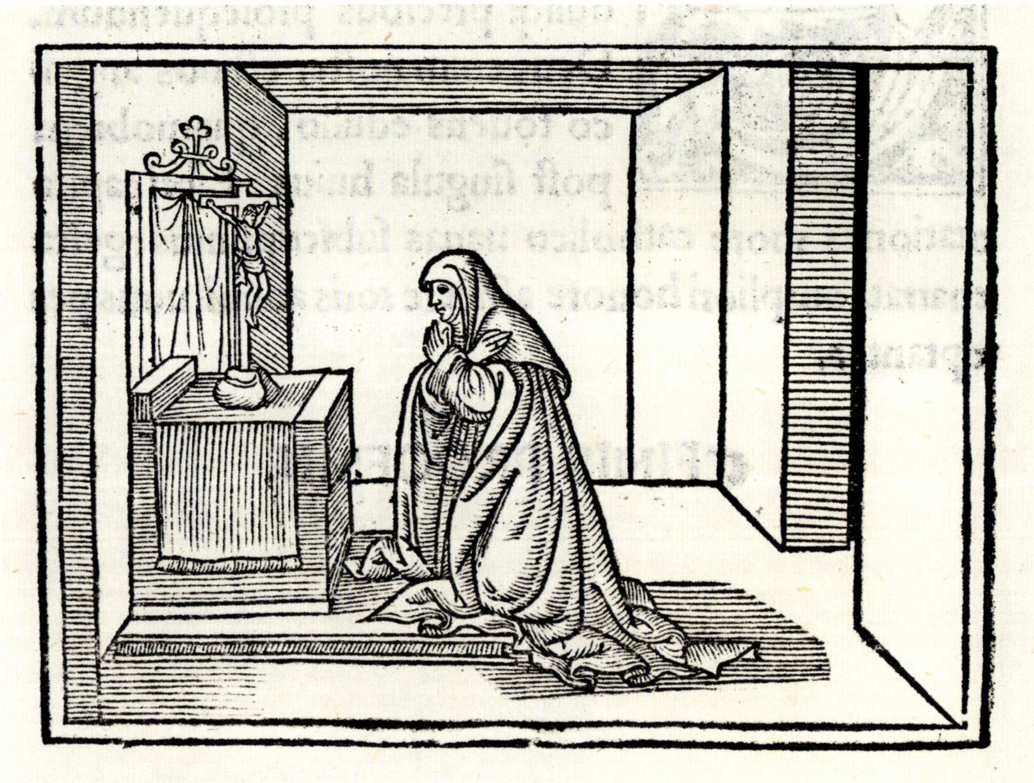

47

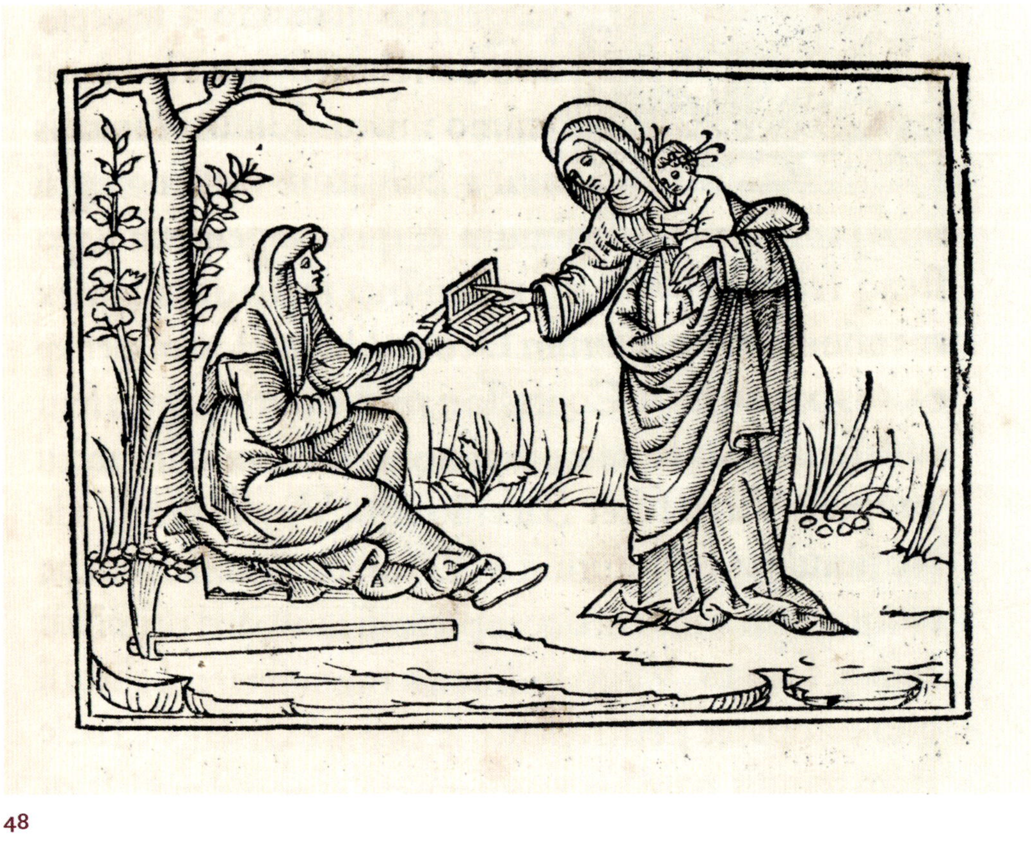

48

body. Two woodcuts follow that illustrate her writing and reading lessons. In the first, Veronica sits on a small bench, bent over a scroll unfurled on her lap, as an angel kneels at her side and guides her hand as she puts pen to paper, learning to write (fig. 44). In the second, Veronica kneels and holds her book out to an angel. The angel points out a passage, and Veronica gestures her acceptance of the message, evidence of her ability to read (fig. 45).

The only full-page image appears in the book twice, including as the last illustration: a spectacular vision of Jesus appearing before Veronica in what must be the convent church (fig. 46). The altar is decorated with a candle, a chalice, and sculpted angels. A large standing candleholder with a lit candle is set in front of the altar. Jesus flies down from the heavens through an oculus or vaulted ceiling. He moves through the clouds, accompanied by angels who point, express wonder, join hands in prayer, and seem almost to smile. Jesus holds a scroll that reads in Latin, "Take my body, my daughter," and extends the host, marked with a cross, to Veronica. This vision of Veronica receiving Communion directly from Jesus raises issues about women's access to the Eucharist, which could be restricted, especially in convent settings. Here, miraculously, Veronica is able to receive Communion directly from Jesus himself, without the intercession of a priest.

Two woodcuts are placed between this repeated scene. One shows Veronica at prayer in a smaller chapel space, kneeling before an altar with a crucifix; it is a simple scene of the kind of everyday devotion that all women might emulate (fig. 47). The penultimate woodcut in the book recounts Veronica's first vision, before she entered the convent, and asserts her humble beginnings and her vocation (fig. 48). Taking a break from working in the fields, she leans against a tree. She is dressed in ordinary clothes, her head shielded from the sun by a wide-brimmed hat, her hoe by her side, and a book in her hand. She extends the book to Mary—who has appeared to her holding the baby Jesus in her arms—indicating she has unsuccessfully tried to teach herself to read. Mary assures Veronica that the only letters she needs to know, and inscribe on her heart, are purity, detachment from earthly concerns, and devotion to the sufferings of Christ.

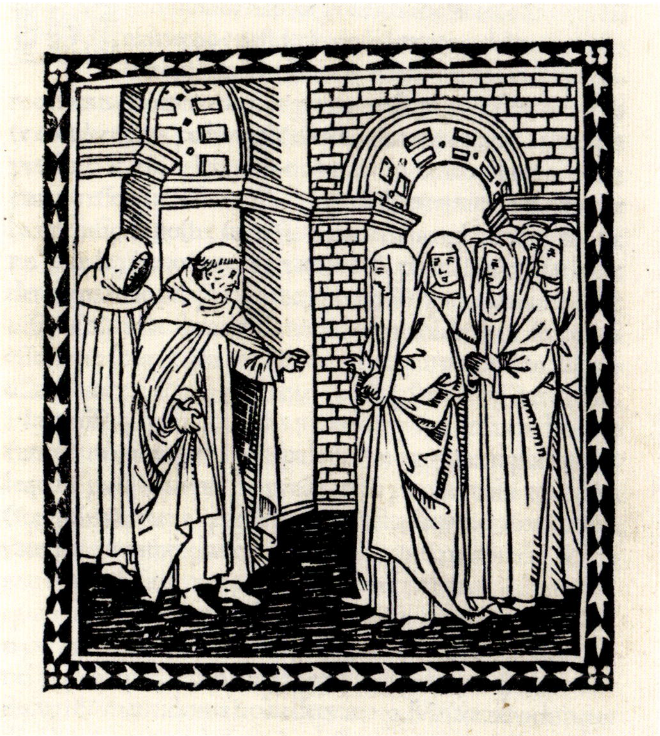

49 Woodcut from Girolamo Savonarola, *Predicha e revelationi*, Florence, 1495

Veronica's direct interaction—through prayer and visions, but also by being able to read and write—with Jesus, Mary, and the angels is key to her religious life. She is also depicted receiving the body of Christ through the Eucharist without the mediation of priests. For a convent audience, Veronica's story would emphasize the desire and need for direct access to scripture and to the Eucharist through Communion, central aspects of the faith that could be restricted for Renaissance women in general as well as for those in religious communities.

The stress in these woodcuts on reading and writing also highlights the important role convents played as one of the centers of education for girls who were placed in such communities for this purpose. Nuns were often able to at least read if not write, and not only did this serve the devotional practices and administration of the convent itself, but it also allowed nuns to share these skills with women outside the community.[21] Veronica's example shows how convent life could transform the experience of a poor, illiterate girl of great faith, but even more important, how she could fulfill her own vocation and transform the lives of other women as a model of diligence and devotion. With a book like this, Veronica's impact would reach beyond convent walls into the world of Renaissance life, as an example for both men and women.

In addition to being places of devotion, prayer, education, and service, convents could be centers of creativity, artistry, learning, and even business. Nuns were teachers, scribes, and manuscript illuminators. Several convents had printing presses where they produced books, broadsheets, and devotional prints for sale outside the convent. In some cases, nuns also acted as patrons for works of art commissioned not just for the private quarters of their communities, but also for public-facing spaces such as churches and facades of convents.[22] Enclosure rules were different for different orders, and sometimes there was considerable interaction with the outside world. An early-fifteenth-century manuscript presents *La santa regola di San Benedetto* (The Rule of Saint Benedict), recording the regulations and guidelines for nuns living in a Benedictine convent. One chapter offers guidance on how to welcome nuns who arrive as guests during pilgrimages, indicating that sisters did leave their convents on occasion. Veronica of Binasco, for example, made a number of trips during her life, including a stop in Florence, where she likely met

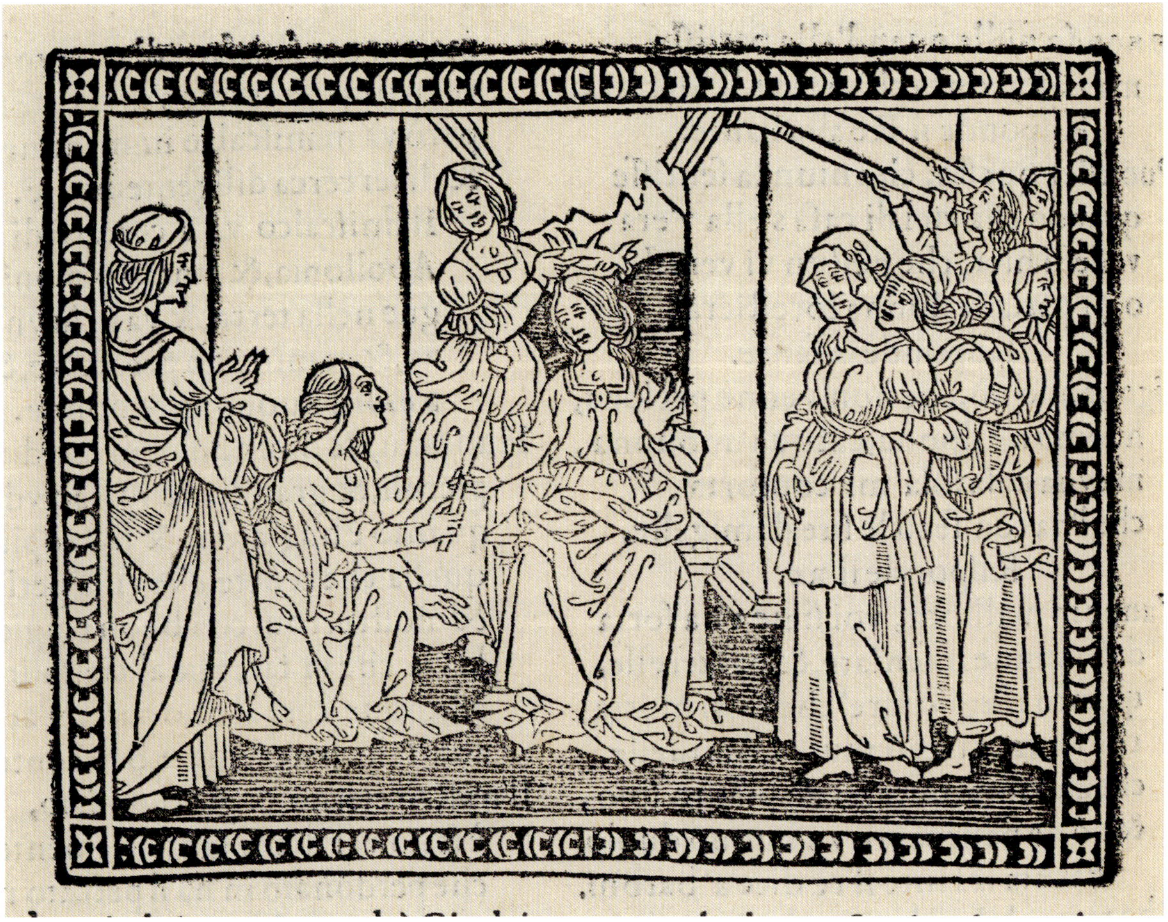

50 Woodcut from *La rappresentatione di S. Apollonia vergine, & martire*, Florence, 16th century

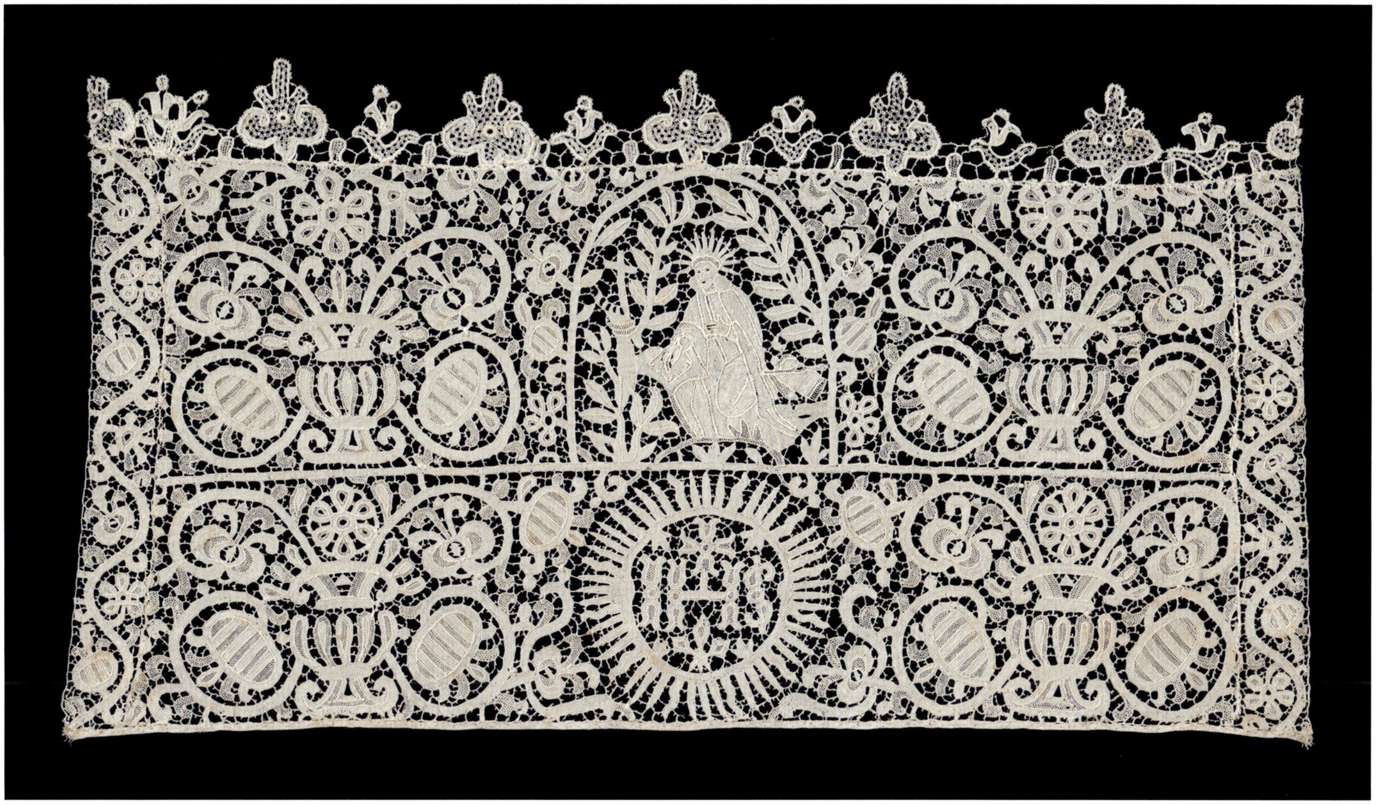

51 Lace, 17th century

the Dominican preacher and reformer Girolamo Savonarola. A fifteenth-century edition of his *Predicha e revelationi* (Sermons and Revelations) depicts nuns emerging from their cloister to meet him and a companion friar (fig. 49). The meeting is shown in an open space, possibly a courtyard in a convent or a public square, metaphorically suggesting that the work of Savonarola even reached women in enclosures.[23] Savonarola encouraged women's creative spirituality, and his impact on convent life was extensive in his own lifetime and beyond his death. This impact offers further proof that Renaissance women were engaged with the significant religious and political currents of their time.[24]

Nuns are recorded as singers, musicians, and composers, and sacred music was played and sung by women in convent churches that also served the lay public. The choir would sing in spaces shielded from public view, making it seem as if the music was produced by disembodied spirits. Convents with such choirs drew many visitors.[25] Convent theater would engage the community and enliven instruction about the lives of saints and stories from scripture.[26] *La rappresentatione di S. Apollonia vergine, & martire* (The Play of Saint Apollonia Virgin and Martyr) is illustrated with woodcuts recounting Saint Apollonia's life, torture, and martyrdom. Though it is uncertain if this sacred play was ever performed in convent settings, this woodcut evokes a stage, with a company of women surrounding the heroine seated on a throne, set in a shallow space (fig. 50).

The production of lace and embroidery was an important part of convent life, as both an educational

OVERLEAF
52 Torah binder, 17th century

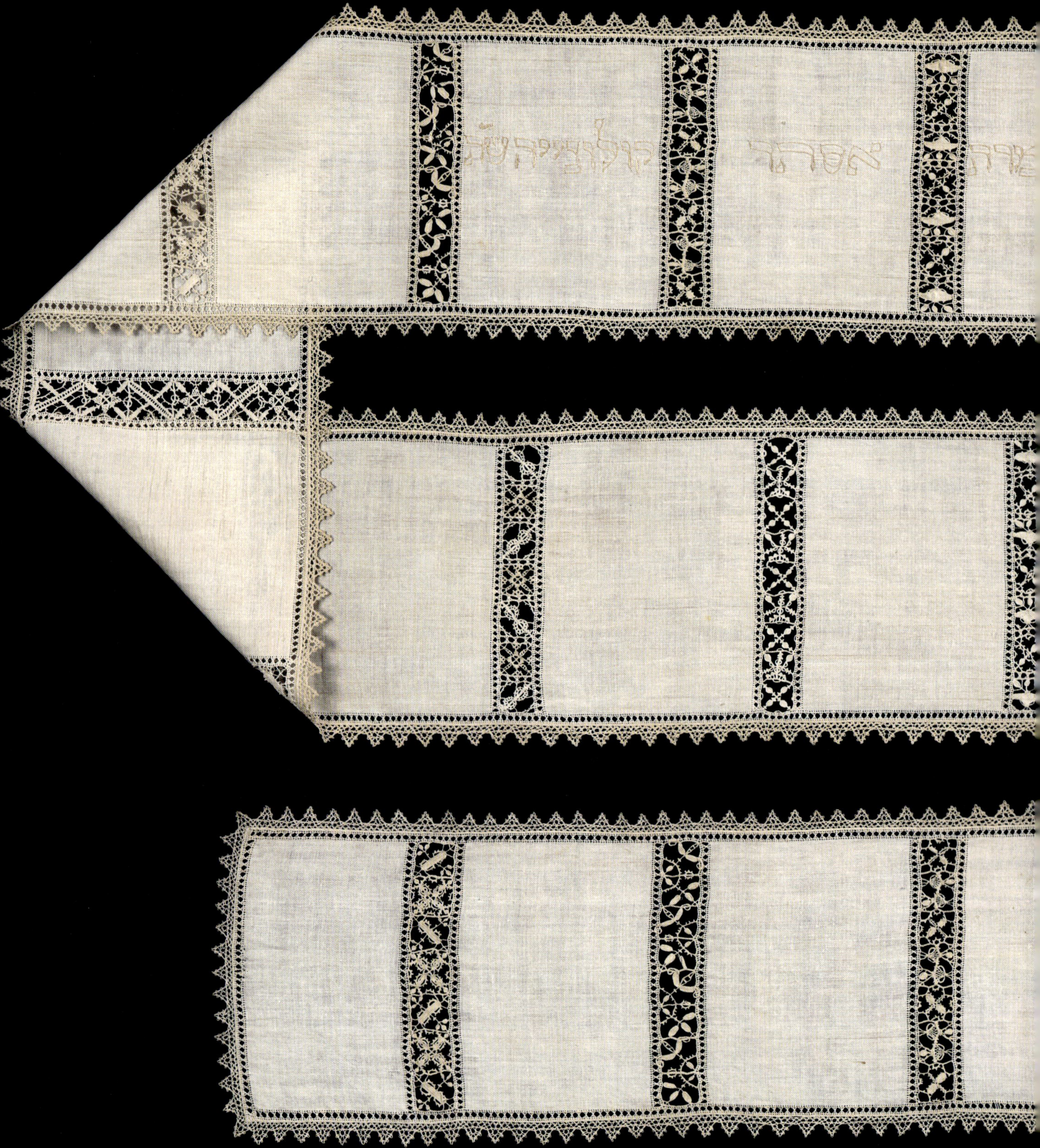
אסתר

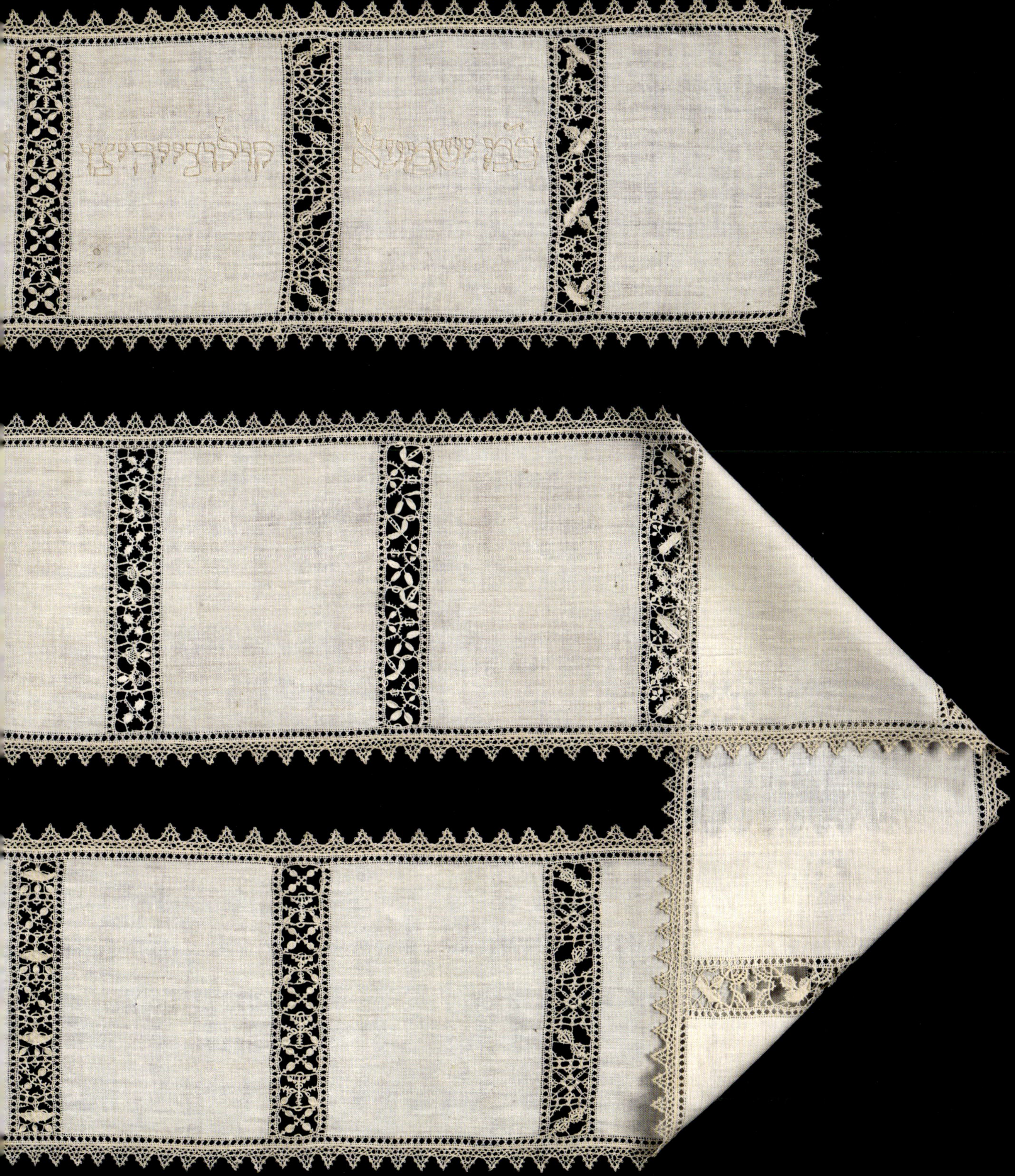

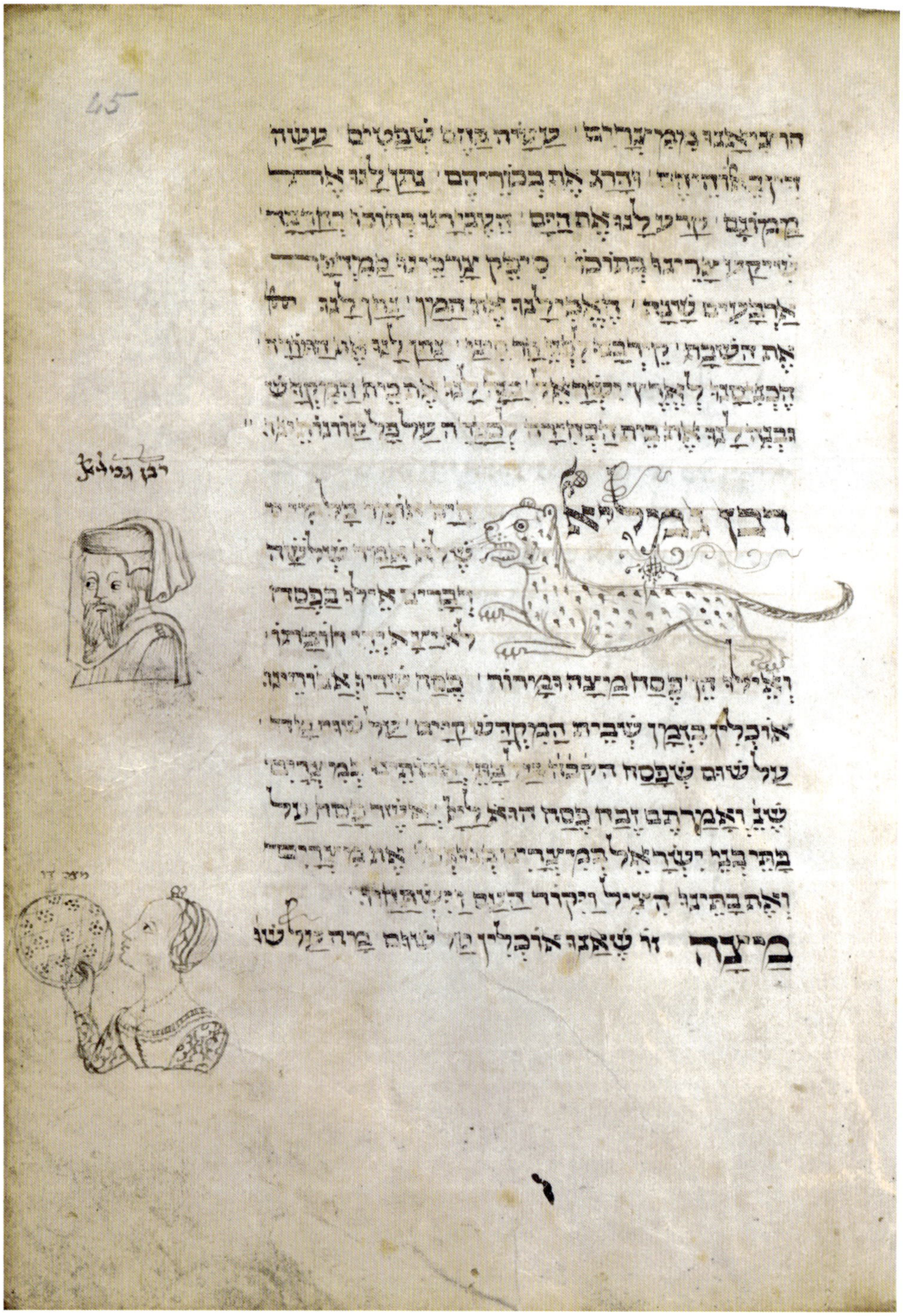

53

53 through 55 Joel ben Simeon, Prayer book (*Siddur*), Florence, 1469 activity and a source of income. Finished textiles were used for devotional purposes, but their creation could also have an impact through repetitive actions that could be meditative and encourage focus and discipline (fig. 51).[27] Such work might also increase familiarity with sacred narratives. One source recounts the story of a nun's vision of Saint Peter in terms of her own experience: "Whose face I recognized easily not only from having seen him depicted in churches, but also from having embroidered it at times."[28]

Though Catholicism was overwhelmingly the dominant religion in Renaissance Italy, there were numerous communities of Jews throughout the Italian peninsula, including in cities such as Rome, Florence, and Venice, and in court municipalities such as Mantua and Ferrara.[29] These communities were subject to episodes of anti-Jewish violence and shifting attitudes toward Jews. While some cities and towns supported the presence of Jews—though not always consistently—others expelled them, enacted compulsory conversion campaigns, or forced them to live in segregated areas. The first ghetto was established in Venice in 1516, and others soon followed in Rome and Florence. These uncertainties and dangers mean that every work of art that survives to reveal the Jewish experience in Renaissance Italy is especially precious.

Jewish rituals were performed both at home and at the synagogue. For Jewish women, practices that took place in the home were a central aspect of their religious lives, just as they were for Catholic women. In synagogues, as in churches, women were generally separated from men. Women were not allowed to read from or handle the Torah scrolls, but were able to honor the Torah by creating textiles made to be used in the synagogue.[30] This linen Torah binder features squares of white linen, joined together and embellished with strips of lace (fig. 52). The Hebrew inscription embroidered across several squares includes the name of a husband, Ishmael Colonia, and his wife Esther, along with the anagrams of the phrases "May the Rock and Redeemer guard him" and "Rejoicing in the Torah."[31] These textiles embody female creativity, skill, and devotion; when women made ornaments for the Torah, they were acknowledged for their handiwork, blessed, and praised.[32] The Italian liturgy includes this blessing: "He who blessed our matriarchs, Sarah, Rebecca, Rachel, and Leah, may he bless every daughter of Israel who makes a mantle or cover in honor of the Torah." This is characteristic of Italian Renaissance practice, as is the fact that a few surviving prayer books written for women alter part of the morning prayers to express specific thanks for being "made a woman and not a man," a small but almost astonishing recognition that women were valuable in their essence and by their very nature as women.[33]

Women's participation in Jewish ritual practice in the home is brought vividly to life in a prayer book from Florence made in the 1460s by Joel ben Simeon, one of the most significant Jewish artists and scribes active in fifteenth-century Italy.[34] Made for a father and his daughter, Maraviglia, the book includes a number of illustrations of people praying and performing religious rituals. In one illustration, a young woman holds a matzah, the unleavened bread called for by Jewish practice (fig. 53). In another, she lifts a cup during the Havdalah ceremony, which marks the end of Shabbat (fig. 54). Her clothing suggests this is a well-off family, able to afford the precious cup that was surely the work of a skilled goldsmith. In another drawing, the young woman, along with a young man, lifts a basket of food for Passover, creating a happy sense of shared ritual (fig. 55). On other pages, she points to important sections in the text and is shown bowing her head in prayer. It is unknown if this prayer book was commissioned for a specific occasion, but perhaps it was linked to the young woman's betrothal as an effort by her father to stress her beauty and wealth but also her pious behavior. She is shown decked out in the rich clothes and jewels of a young eligible woman. Whatever its origins, the prayer book makes clear that women were central to devotional practice in the home. Her interaction with sections of the text also demonstrates that she was able to read, and the book itself calls attention to the fact that in Renaissance Italy, some Jewish woman were literate, including in Hebrew.

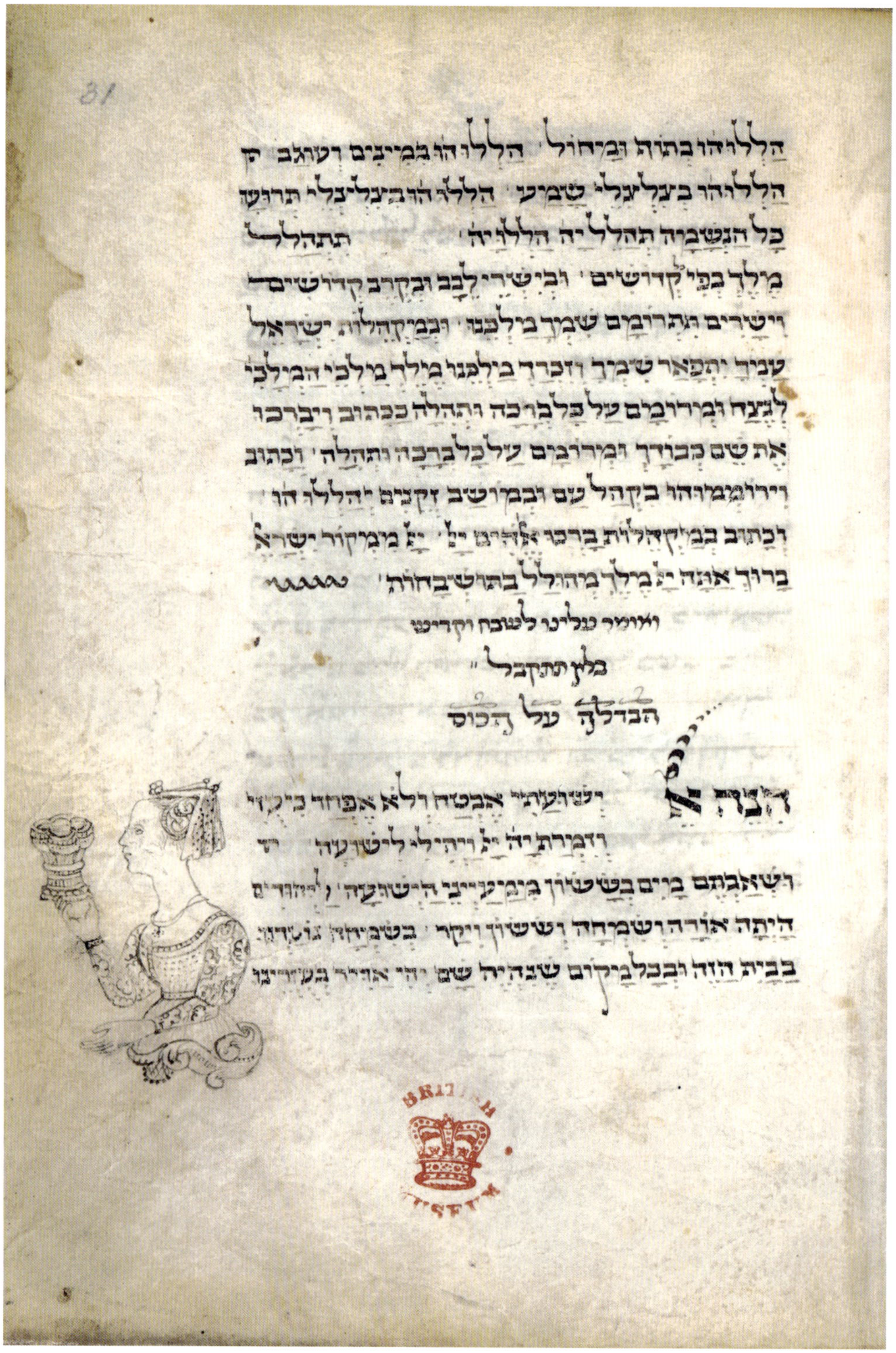

31

הללויהו בתוף ומחול · הללוהו במינים ועוגב · יה
הללויהו בצלצלי שמע · הללוהו בצלצלי תרועה
כל הנשמה תהלל יה הללויה · תתהלל
מלך בפי קדושים · ובישרי לבב ובקרב קדושים
וישרים תתרומם שמך בלבנו · ובמקהלות ישראל
עמך יתפאר שמך וזכרך בלבנו מלך מלכי המלכי
לנצח ומרומם על כל ברכה ותהלה ככתוב ויברכו
את שם כבודך ומרומם על כל ברכה ותהלה · וכתוב
וירוממוהו בקהל עם ובמושב זקנים יהללוהו ·
וכתוב במקהלות ברכו אלהים יי׳ · יי׳ ממקור ישרא׳
ברוך אתה יי׳ מלך מהולל בתשבחות ·

ואומר עלינו לשבח וקדיש
בלא תתקבל

הבדלה על הכוס

הנה אל ישועתי אבטח ולא אפחד כי עזי
וזמרת יה יי׳ ויהי לי לישועה · יד
ושאבתם מים בששון ממעיני הישועה · ליהודים
היתה אורה ושמחה וששון ויקר · [illegible]
בבית הזה ובכל מקום שנהיה שם · יהי אדיר בעזרינו

54

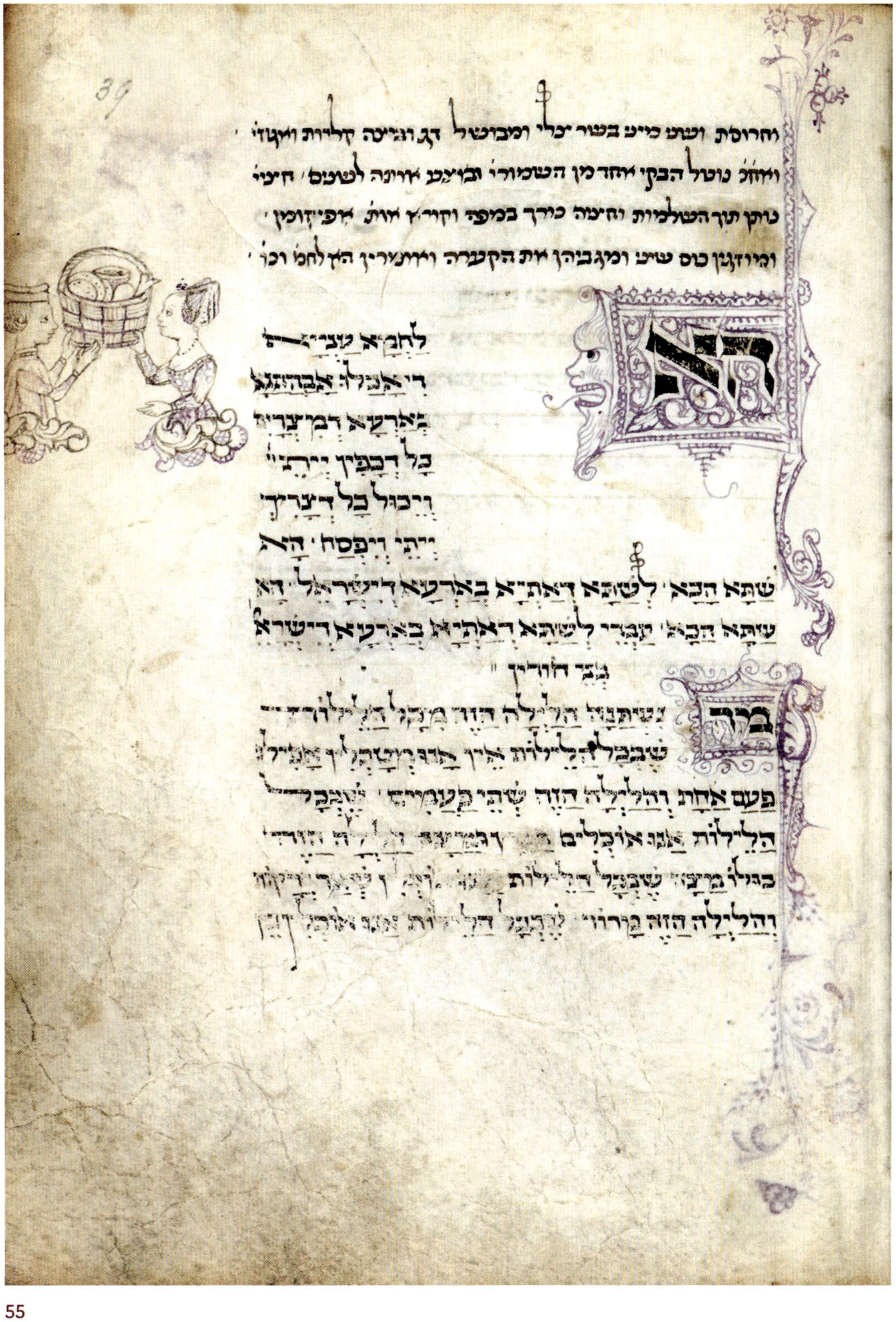

55

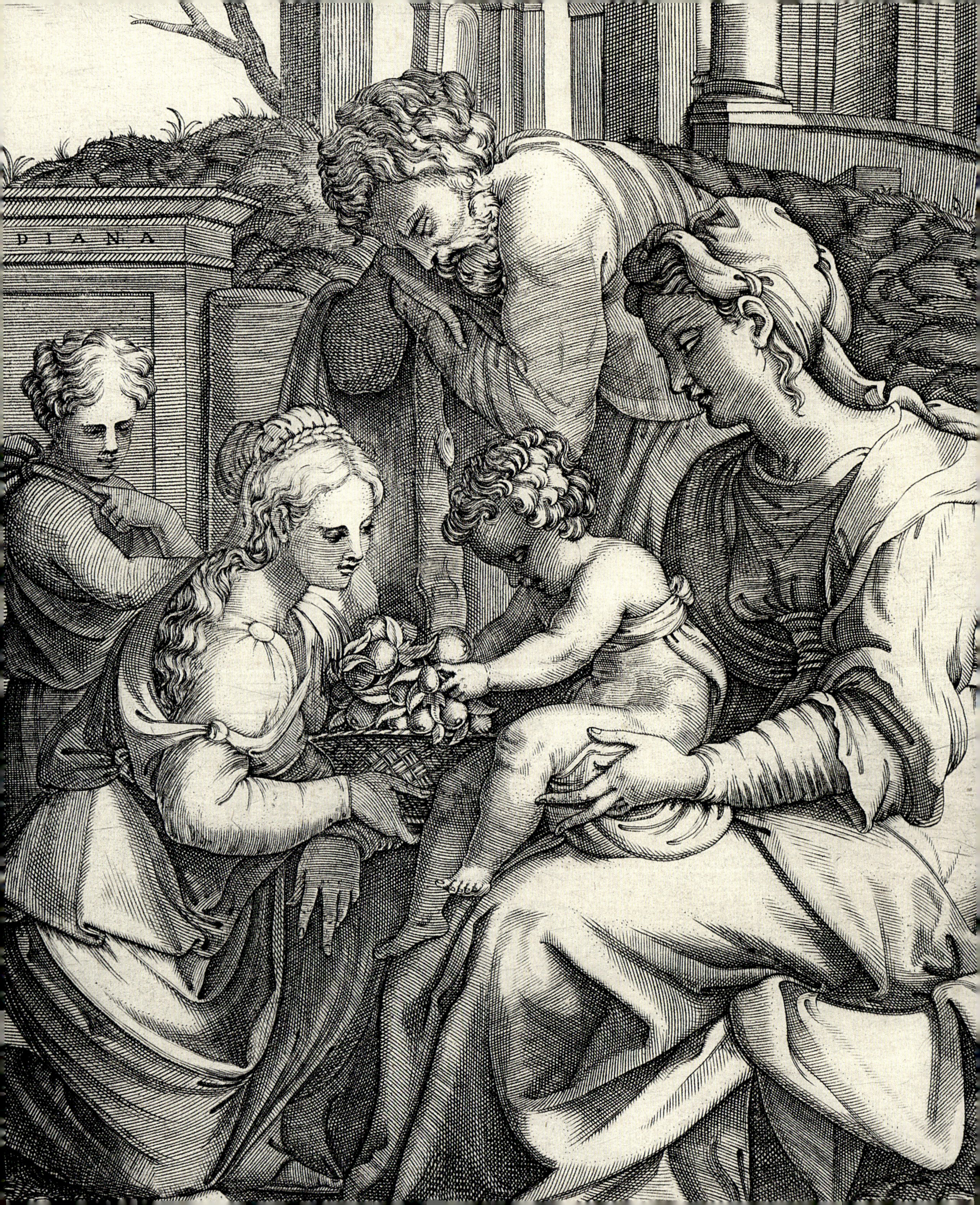
DIANA

Artists Known and Unknown

Women who pursued creative professions in Renaissance Italy included artists, writers, poets, musicians, and singers. Female artists were often categorized as exceptional, with their creativity and success leading them to be seen as "wonders of nature."[1] Women themselves often played into this notion of exceptionality as a strategy to shape their fame. Working in fields dominated by men, women had to overcome many obstacles, beginning with access to training, materials, and workshops.[2] Success for a woman required certain circumstances, and often depended on her family's profession and willingness to support her artistic pursuits. Most commonly, if she was part of a family with a workshop, she might be called upon to help with the family business and would thus learn the trade, be it painting, sculpting, engraving, modeling clay, or carving wood. Lavinia Fontana, Barbara Longhi, Artemisia Gentileschi, Isabella Catanea Parasole, and Diana Mantuana all learned their crafts in this way. A painter might marry into the family of another painter, perhaps continuing to practice her art alongside her husband. Others relied on the support of their family to be able to learn and develop the skills needed to succeed. Sofonisba Anguissola is the paradigmatic example of an artist supported and promoted by a father who was not an artist himself. Women who were placed by their families in convents might learn and practice their trade there, be it painting or lace making.[3] Widows often took over their husband's businesses, including workshops. By the early seventeenth century, women's names were included in the ranks of the Florentine Accademia del Disegno and the Roman Accademia di San Luca, artistic sodalities that provided members with opportunities for learning and networking.[4] In Bologna, the home of Lavinia Fontana, record numbers of women artists are named in documentary sources.[5]

Literacy and artistic success often went hand in hand for women: Support for the education of women was fundamental for female creativity to thrive in all fields.[6] Works by female poets and writers were published in increasing numbers in Renaissance Italy; Vittoria Colonna's book of poems, published in 1538, was the first single-authored printed book of poetry by a woman in Italy. Though famous as a gifted poet, Colonna did not seek to publish her poems, and this first edition was produced without her permission. The publisher in Parma had gathered together her poems, which circulated among her friends and in literary circles. A number of editions followed, with her consent, including one published in Venice in 1542 (fig. 56). As the frontispiece with its elaborately decorated framework states, it includes twenty-four spiritual sonnets, poems, and a treatise on the triumph of the cross.[7] The book is about six and a half by four and a half inches, presenting her writing on an intimate scale and making the volume easy to hold or carry about. Colonna became a role model for women writers in her day. She maintained a close friendship with Michelangelo Buonarotti, and their artistic exchanges included poems by both and drawings by Michelangelo.

Sofonisba Anguissola's long career was exceptional in a number of ways, not simply because she was a woman.[8] She painted more self-portraits than any other artist, male or female, in Renaissance Italy. She and her father, Amilcare, devised strategies to bolster her fame that included presenting herself in self-portraits.[9] It is vital to clarify that the perception of her as exceptional because she was a woman was part of this construction of her artistic identity, as it was for many creative women. Sofonisba made self-portraits early in her career to advertise who she was and what she was capable of. Such images could be given to people who were in a position to make her famous, or they could be a sort of calling card to help find her a secure place to work. Collectors like the writer Annibale Caro specifically sought out Sofonisba's self-portraits. In 1558, Caro wrote to Sofonisba's father, saying he wanted a self-portrait to be able to display two wonders at once: the work itself and the artist.[10] Sofonisba's exceptional talent but also her exceptional gender enhanced the value of the work for Caro.

Not an artist himself, Amilcare had to find teachers for his talented daughter. Sofonisba and her sister Elena were sent to the workshops of painters to learn to paint, a bold decision on their father's part. Sofonisba in turn taught her younger sisters to draw and paint. One of those sisters, Lucia, showed promise equal to that of Sofonisba, but died young. Around 1556–57, Amilcare struck up a correspondence with Michelangelo, considered the greatest living artist, and sent him one of Sofonisba's drawings, depicting a laughing girl teaching an older woman to read. Michelangelo praised her efforts and countered with the challenge that she draw a companion piece of a weeping boy. She responded with a drawing of her little brother Asdrubale bitten by a crayfish, crying in pain. Sofonisba was among a small group of artists whose talents and careers were encouraged by Michelangelo through the exchange of ideas and drawings.[11] In 1566, Giorgio Vasari visited the Anguissola home in Cremona as he worked on his second edition of *Le vite de' più eccellenti pittori, scultori, e architettori* (The Lives of the Most Excellent Painters, Sculptors, and Architects). By this point, Sofonisba's fame was already well established, and the book's publication in 1568 would help spread word of her reputation even further.[12]

A self-portrait, painted when Sofonisba was around twenty-six years old, reveals much about this early period of establishing her fame (fig. 57). At just over three inches tall, this miniature advertises

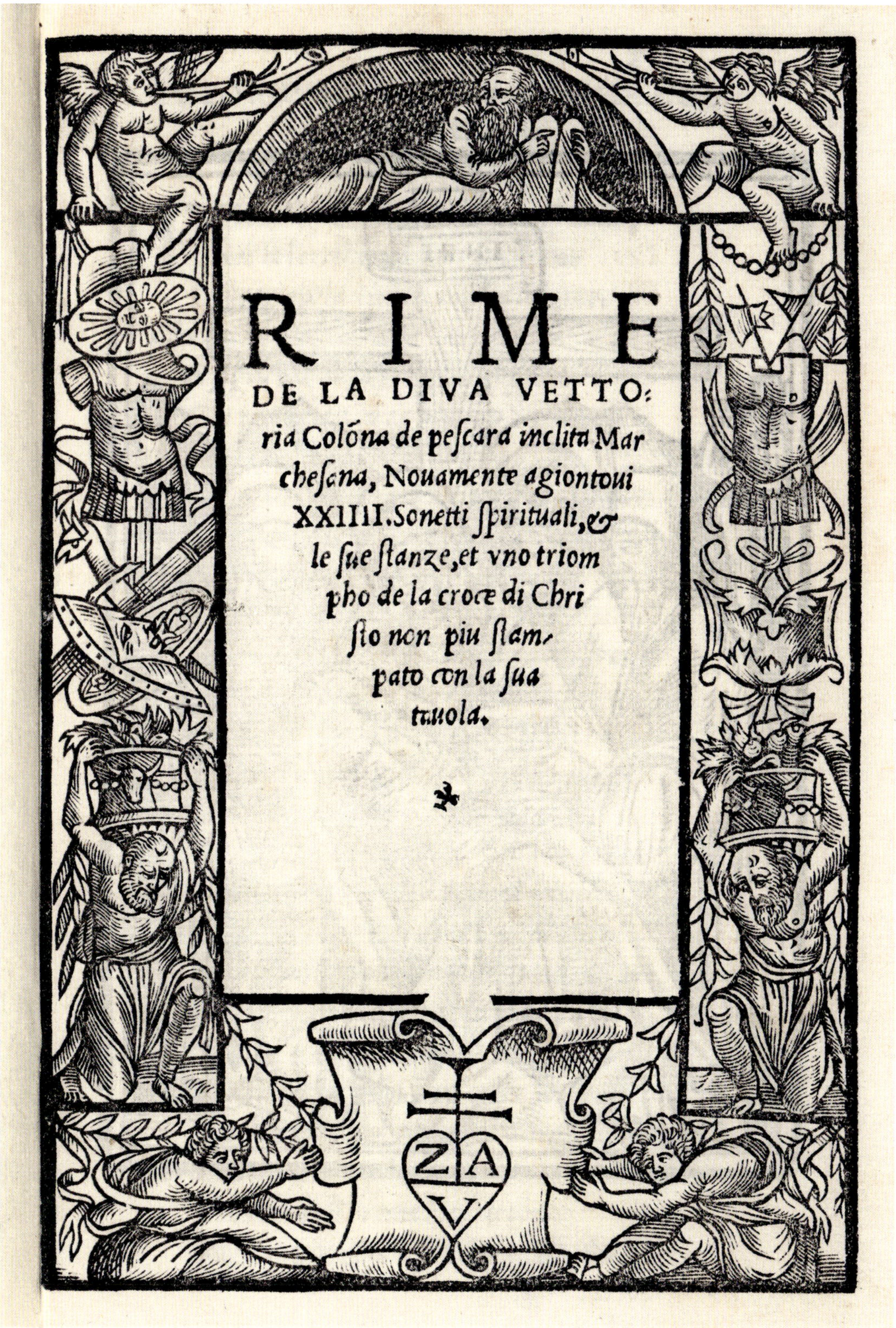
RIME
DE LA DIVA VETTO:
ria Colõna de peſcara inclita Mar
cheſana, Nouamente agiontovi
XXIIII.Sonetti ſpirituali,&
le ſue ſtanze,et vno triom
pho de la croce di Chri
ſto non piu ſtam-
pato con la ſua
tauola.

Z A V

56 Frontispiece from Vittoria Colonna, *Rime*, Venice, 1542

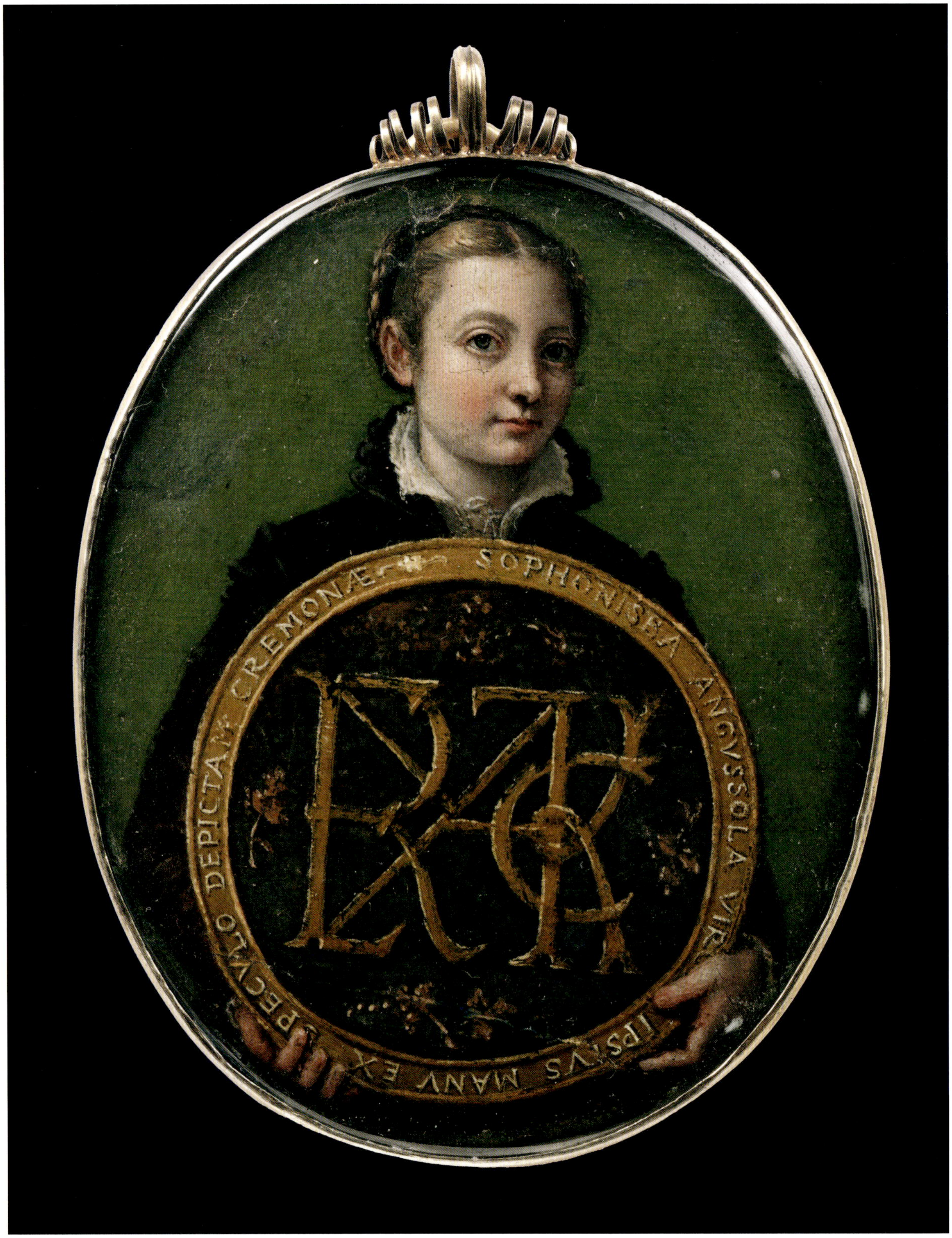

57 Sofonisba Anguissola, *Self-Portrait*, about 1556, 8.3 x 6.4 cm (3¼ x 2½ in.)

Sofonisba's skill at painting on a small scale, a valued specialty. Because she painted so many self-portraits, the artist is recognizable by her golden hair, large eyes, fair skin, and slightly smiling mouth. She is dressed simply, wearing a black jacket over a lace-trimmed white shirt, the same clothes she wears in most of her self-portraits, including one where she shows herself at work painting *Virgin and Child*.[13] Her figure is set against a plain green background, and she holds a large roundel in front of her body, almost like a shield. This roundel has not yet been associated with any known objects. It may be the reverse of a mirror or another image, or the side shown may be the primary one, serving to display the cipher at the center, surrounded by small floral decorative motifs and Sofonisba's signature. The signature reads "SOPHONISBA ANGVSSOLA VIR[GO] IPSIVS MANV EX [S]PECVLO DEPICTAM CREMONAE" or "Sofonisba Anguissola the maiden painted this with her own hand from a mirror in Cremona." The cipher of interwoven letters at the center is a popular form of Renaissance puzzle.[14] The letters of her father's name, Amilcare, can be discerned, but so can other letters and possible meanings. For example, the names of the ancient female painters Iaia and Marcia can be found here. According to literary sources, both of these women painted self-portraits using mirrors. Certainly, the inclusion of her father's name is a tribute to his efforts on her behalf.

The hands of the artist play an important role here, as they support the roundel but also remind the viewer that they are the hands that made this work and will make others. Sofonisba cleverly includes a visual pun. Her left thumb masks the letters "GO" in the word "VIRGO" so that it instead reads "VIR," or the Latin for man and the root of the words *virtuosity* and *virtuoso*.[15] Sofonisba plays on the notion of *virtù*, commonly understood in the period as manly virtue as well as talent, and claims the title virtuosa for herself. The signature also proclaims her literacy, including the competence and confidence to include a play on words in Latin while conveying a powerful message about her own abilities. Her sure, steady gaze attests to her ability to see herself, and those around her, with skilled eyes.

Sofonisba and Amilcare's efforts ultimately paid off, with Sofonisba earning a position at the Spanish court, as a lady-in-waiting to Philip II's consort Isabel de Valois. One of her duties was to teach Isabel to draw and paint. She was also expected to produce works of art for the court, especially portraits, sharing her gifts to earn her place. The fact that she was a woman and an artist would have made her an especially appealing member of the court, given her rare talents and exceptional abilities. Sofonisba achieved great fame and success over her long life, working in several cities, including Madrid, Genoa, and Palermo, and continuing to paint into her old age. She would also continue to teach late into her life. In July 1624, the young painter Anthony Van Dyck sought her out in Palermo and drew sketches of her. He recounted in his diary that Sofonisba had given him advice about how best to light the face of an elderly person, among other things. He was struck by her agile mind and steady hands, as well as her unhappiness that her poor eyesight prevented her from painting. She was in her nineties.[16]

Lavinia Fontana was born into a family of artists and subsequently became the head of her family's workshop, a common enough occurrence for male artists but extremely rare for a woman.[17] Her father, the painter Prospero Fontana, ran an important workshop in Bologna, where Lavinia and her brother worked as assistants before she inherited and began running the shop. She produced large-scale altarpieces and history paintings as well as works on a smaller scale. Her *Virgin Adoring the Sleeping Christ Child*, with its small size and unusual coved shape, was probably made for a domestic setting, likely set into a piece of furniture in a bedroom (fig. 58).[18] In a dark room, with a nocturnal landscape beyond, the baby Jesus is fast asleep, one arm behind his head, and Mary moves to cover him with a transparent veil. The child's pose, with his right arm draping down off the bed, evokes not just a deep sleep but also death and asks the viewer to meditate on his future. This painting is a pared down version of a devotional subject frequently depicted by Lavinia, the Madonna of Silence. Usually done on a larger scale but for a domestic setting, Lavinia's representations of the scene include the young

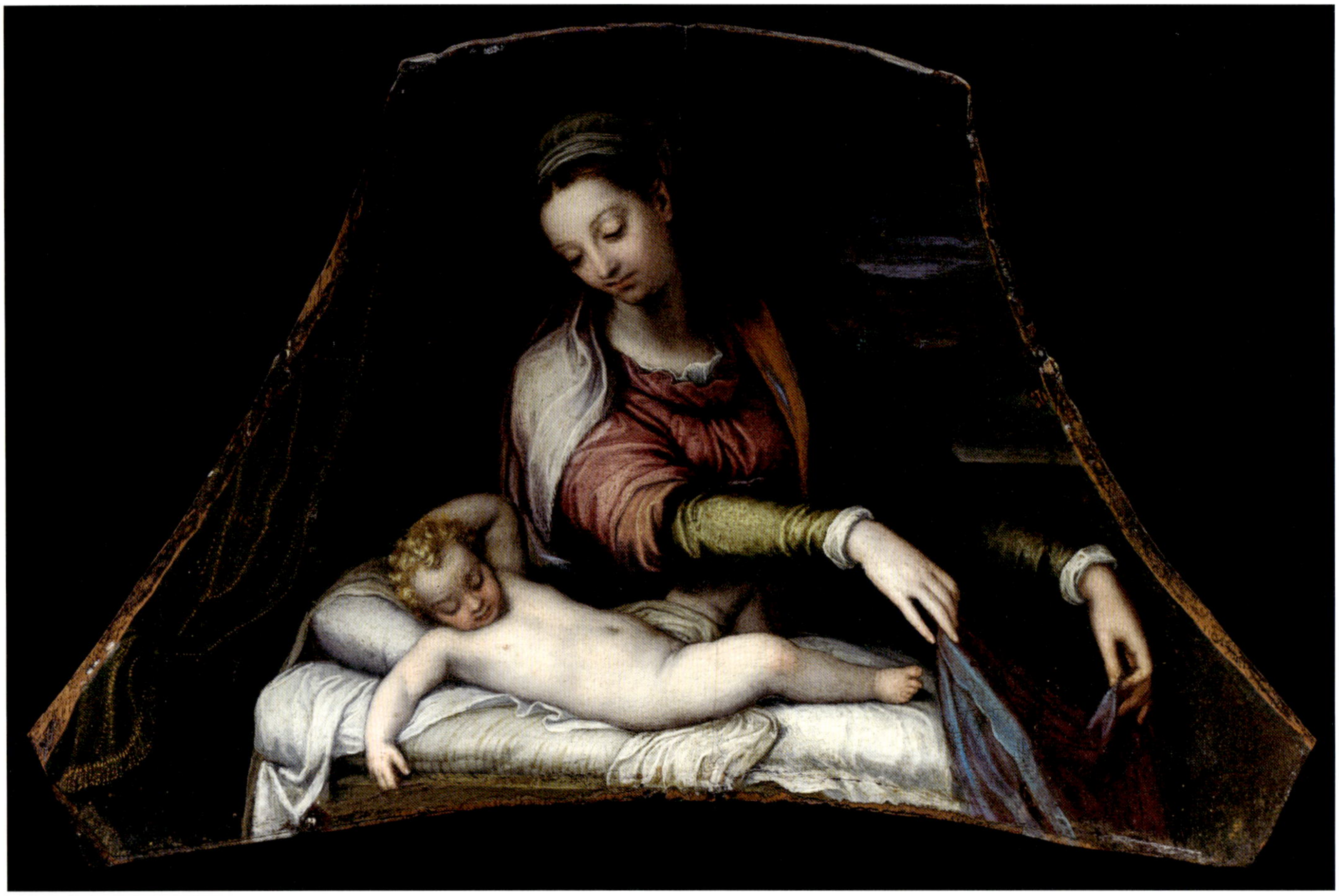

58 Lavinia Fontana, *Virgin Adoring the Sleeping Christ Child*, about 1605–10, 15.2 x 25.4 cm (6 x 10 in.)

Saint John the Baptist signaling for silence as he, Saint Joseph, and Mary watch the child Jesus sleep. Here, perhaps the viewer takes on the role of Saint John and calls for silence. The *Virgin Adoring the Sleeping Christ Child* might have decorated a crib, where a baby could sleep protected by Mary and Jesus. Or the work might have been part of a bed, where a mother-to-be might look forward to a beautiful, healthy, quiet baby. Lavinia herself had eleven children and surely understood the longing for quiet time for prayer and contemplation and was familiar with a quietly sleeping baby needing protection.

Barbara Longhi, like Lavinia Fontana, was part of a family of artists.[19] The daughter and sister of painters, she became known for devotional images such as the *Virgin and Child* (fig. 59). This small-scale devotional painting shows Mary nursing the baby Jesus, an often-depicted subject.[20] The baby suckles and looks at the viewer, as a few small drops of milk escape his lips. Mary's milk was evidence of the physical bond between mother and child, so much so that liquids believed to be drops of Mary's milk were held as relics in churches and shrines. For the Renaissance viewer, these drops would encourage contemplation of Jesus's humanity and remind the faithful of the spiritual sustenance he provides. The painting's small scale and the infant's direct gaze make it a representative example of devotional prayer guided by images. The viewer was encouraged to feel a sense of intimate contact with Jesus, while the drops of milk signified the spiritual nourishment that a devotee sought from such images. Religious reformers in the later sixteenth century

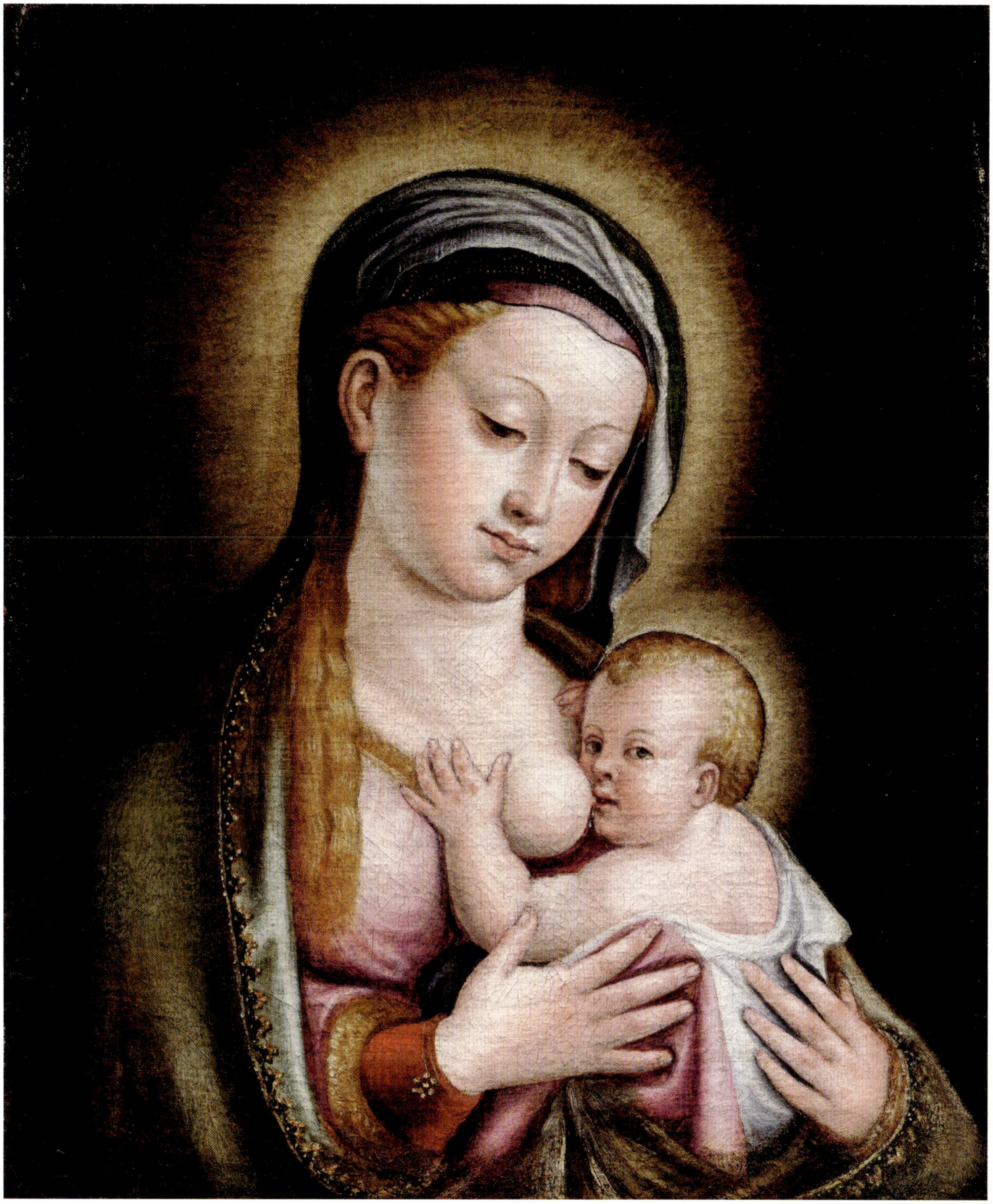

59 Barbara Longhi, *Virgin and Child*, 36.2 x 29.5 cm (14¼ x 11⅝)

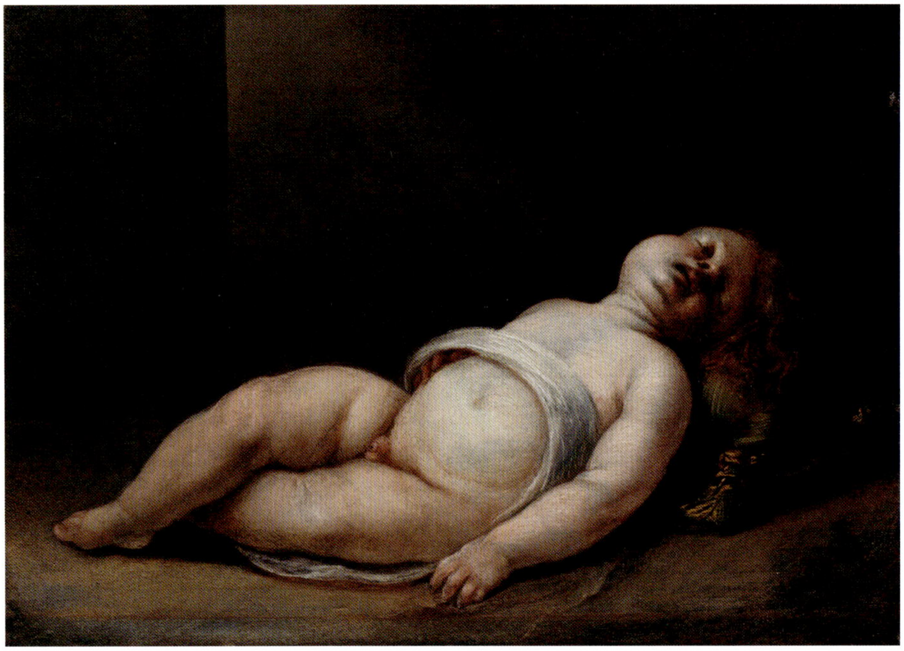

60 Artemisia Gentileschi, *The Sleeping Christ Child*, 1630–32, 12.4 x 17.5 cm (4⅞ x 6⅞ in.)

scrutinized representations of the nursing Madonna, as they feared such images might stir lustful feelings in men who viewed them.[21] As a result, they became less common, but Barbara Longhi returned to the theme many times. Perhaps she painted these images specifically for women, or for nuns in convent settings, where the subject remained popular.[22]

Artemisia Gentileschi's *Sleeping Christ Child* depicts an infant in a deep sleep, with relaxed muscles and head thrown back (fig. 60).[23] The copper support enhances the luminous quality of the scene. Gentileschi, like Fontana and Longhi, was the daughter of an artist and learned her trade in her father's workshop. This painting may represent the sleeping baby Jesus, with the drapery encircling his body referring to the winding cloth of the dead Christ. However, an inscription scratched into the back of the copper plate seems to read "EROTE" (small boy or Eros), and a contemporary print of the painting that includes a skull suggest that the identification as the infant Jesus is not completely certain. Painted on a small scale, this may have been a devotional object, encouraging the viewer to contemplate the soft flesh of Jesus. The painting's quietude, infused with a golden light, creates a sense of intimacy and invites close observation.

All four of these paintings are relatively small, an accident of collecting, availability, and a reflection of the art market over time, but also a result of historical factors. These painters all worked on larger-scale paintings, and Fontana and Gentileschi produced monumental altarpieces and canvases as well.[24] For women, painting on a small scale was one response to the challenge of having limited access to the workshops and studio assistants necessary for larger commissions. Working in a domestic setting on a smaller scale was also easier for women, given the restrictions on their lives. Thus, the subject matter of portraits, still lifes, and devotional images, all of which work well on a smaller scale, tend to dominate works by women in this period. They were, therefore, often praised for their precise, refined painting styles—suited to smaller works—rather than their creativity and bravura. But Fontana and Gentileschi were not alone in painting large-scale works. The Florentine nun Plautilla Nelli, for example, also painted monumental works, including a *Last Supper* for her convent's refectory.[25]

Diana Mantuana, commonly known today as Diana Scultori, learned her craft in her family's workshop in Mantua and made her career as a printmaker.[26] Her father was an engraver and sculptor who worked for the Gonzaga court, and he taught Diana and her brother Adamo the skills needed to engrave copperplates. It was through her father that Diana would have obtained drawings made after the work of other artists, especially that of Giulio Romano, the most important artist working in Mantua in the early sixteenth century. Diana's *Latona Giving Birth to Apollo and Diana on the Island of Delos*, for example, is based on a work by Giulio and shows the Roman goddess Latona after giving birth to Zeus's children Apollo and Diana (fig. 61). Likely made in Mantua, the print is signed with just Diana's first name at the lower left. The inclusion of her signature speaks to Diana's sense of her accomplishments. By using just her given name, perhaps Diana aspired to join the ranks of Michelangelo and Donatello, known immediately as a great printer and a woman, without needing to call out her family ties. Diana's career was given an early boost by Vasari, who visited the family shop in Mantua in 1566. There he met "two sons who engrave copper plates divinely, and what is more marvelous, a daughter named Diana also engraves so well that it is a wonderful thing: and when I saw her, a very well-bred and charming young lady, and her works, which are most beautiful, I was stunned."[27]

In 1575, Diana and her husband, the architect Francesco da Volterra, moved to Rome, where he was more likely to gain important commissions. In Rome, she produced architectural prints after her husband's drawings, using her own fame to help to attract architectural commissions for him. Diana herself attained rare status in Rome; she was able to obtain a papal privilege for her work, highly unusually for a printmaker. This meant that she had full rights to her copperplates and the prints taken from them, and therefore only she

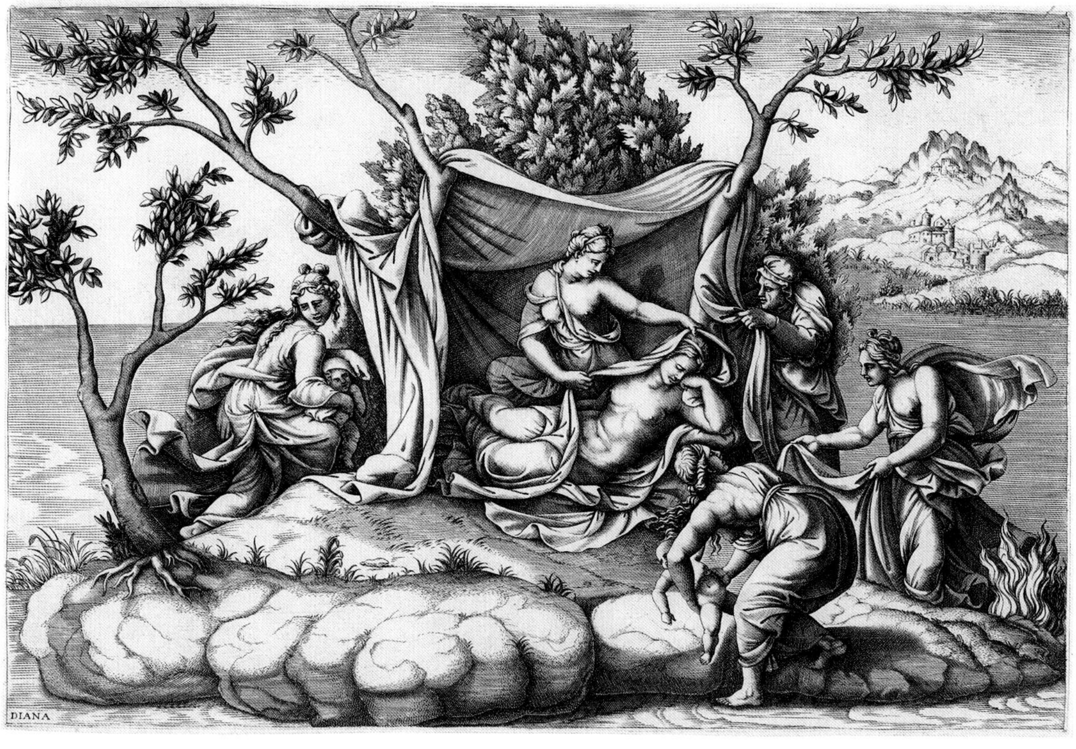

61 Diana Mantuana, *Latona Giving Birth to Apollo and Diana on the Island of Delos*, 1561–65

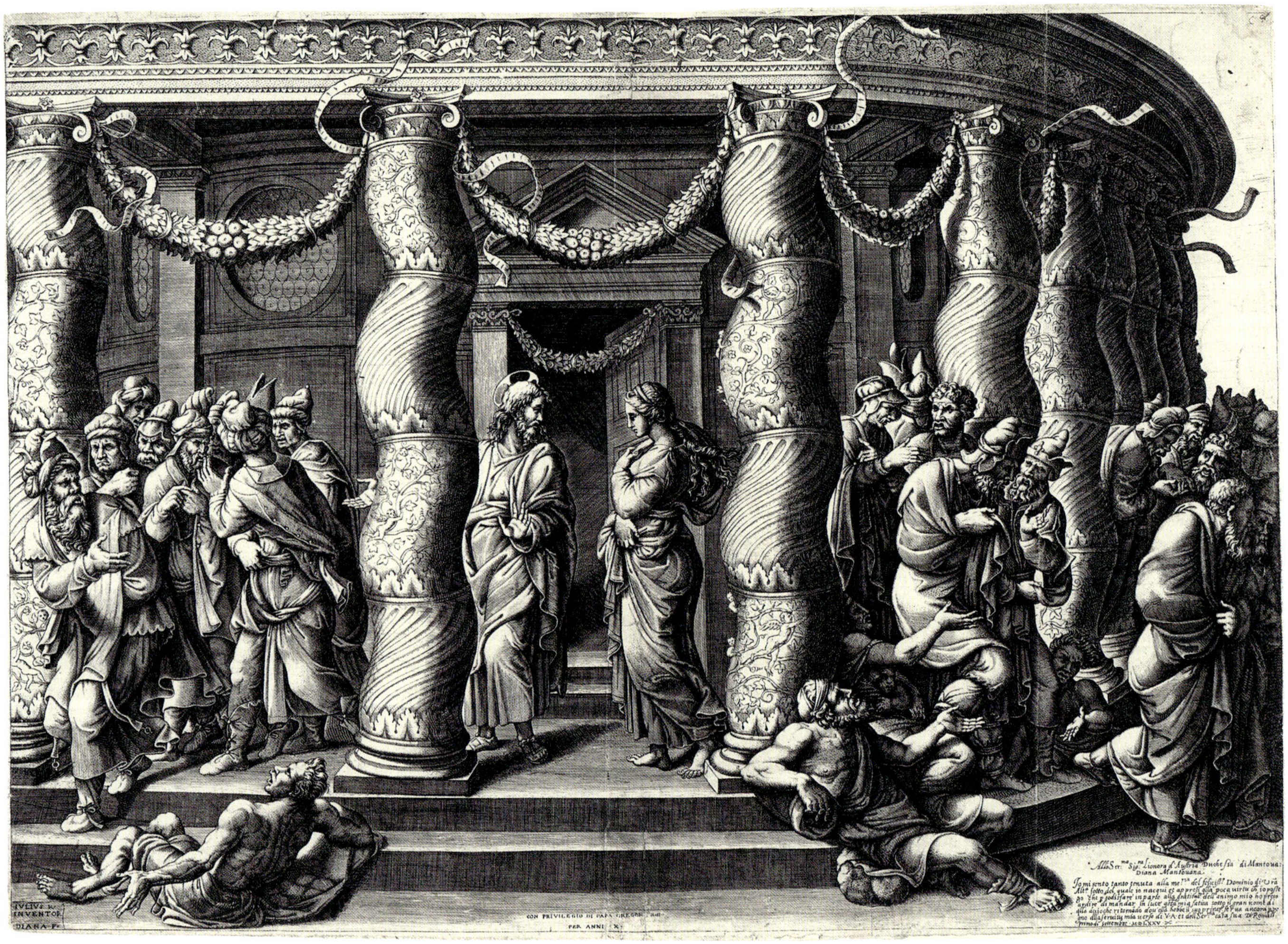

62 Diana Mantuana, *Christ and the Woman Taken in Adultery*, 1575

could market, sell, and be paid for her prints; anyone who infringed on these rights would be severely fined.[28] Dated September 1, 1575, *Christ and the Woman Taken in Adultery* includes notice of the papal privilege at the bottom, which translates to: "With the Privilege of Pope Gregory XIII for 10 years" (fig. 62). Based on a work by Giulio Romano, as noted in the Latin signature that translates as "Giulio Inventor, Diana made it," the image shows Jesus refusing to condemn a woman brought to him by a group of scribes and Pharisees, and instead asks if any of them were free of sin. Jesus stands with the woman on the porch of the Temple while the crowd begins to move away. The image is directly related to a tapestry cartoon by Raphael, *Saint Peter Healing the Sick Man*, which used the famous twisting columns of Saint Peter's Basilica to set the scene, as they do here.

Diana included a dedication here that translates as "To her Serene Highness Lady Eleonora of Austria, Duchess of Mantua/ Diana Mantuana/ I feel myself so tied to the memory of Your Ladyship's most fortunate dominion, under which I was born and learned what little *virtù* I possess, that to satisfy in part the gratitude in my soul I have been so bold as to bring this work of mine to light under her great name, in order that, returning to where it had its beginning, it serves her prince again, as a token of my service to Your Highness and your most serene house."[29] Diana used dedications on her prints to flatter and honor important potential patrons, such as Eleonora of Austria, the Duchess of Mantua, or to display her own connections, identity, and stature. The inscription here illustrates a keen understanding of court politics. With one image, Diana emphasized her associations with Rome and Mantua, illustrated her connection to artistic forebears, and celebrated her ambitious achievements.

A print based on the work of Francesco Salviati also includes just her first name, in the top left (fig. 63). Elsewhere, she signed her name as Diana Mantuana, further connecting herself with the Mantuan court and a line of famous artists. For example, *The Virgin and Child*, again after Salviati, is signed in Latin with "Francesco Salviati Inventor, Diana of Mantua was engraving this in Rome" (fig. 64). A print done after a drawing of a famous ancient sculpture is signed inconspicuously near the base of the statue with "Diana Incidebat," or "Diana was engraving this" (fig. 65). Diana's use of signatures, dedications, and inscriptions would shape a contemporary's view of her work, priming the viewer to appreciate her skill. No other printmaker had been given the kind of papal privilege she attained. She, like Raphael, Michelangelo, and Giulio Romano before her, became an artist associated with the most prestigious patron in Renaissance Rome, the papacy.

Along with her husband, Diana became part of the artists' association the Compagnia di San Giuseppe,

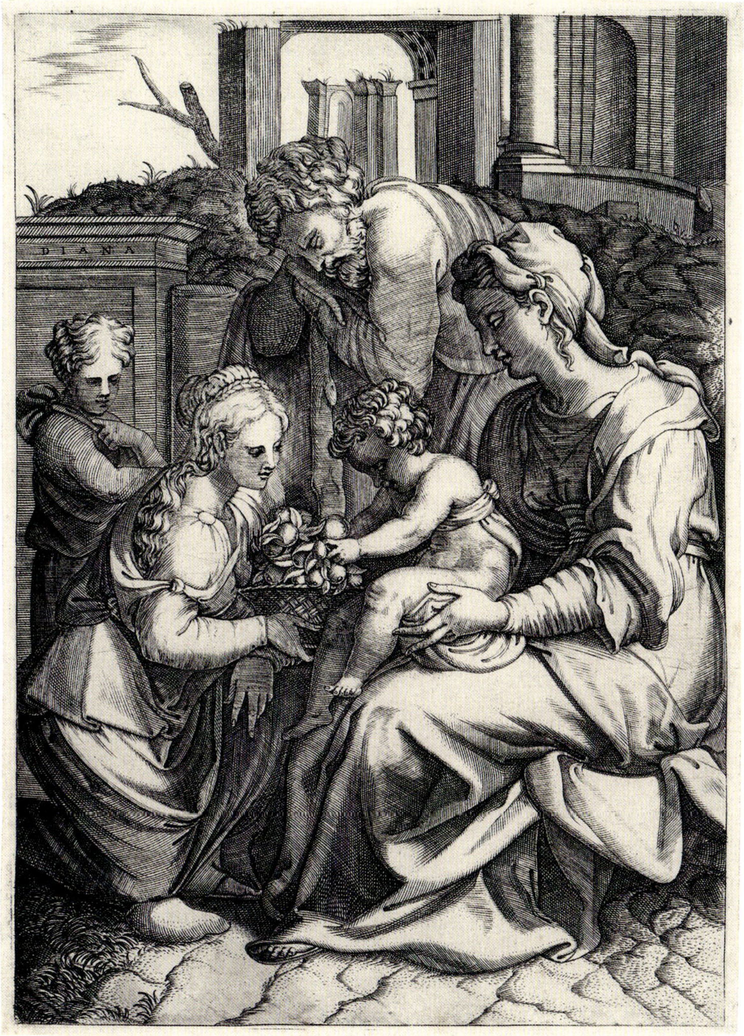

63 Diana Mantuana, *The Holy Family*, 1575–76

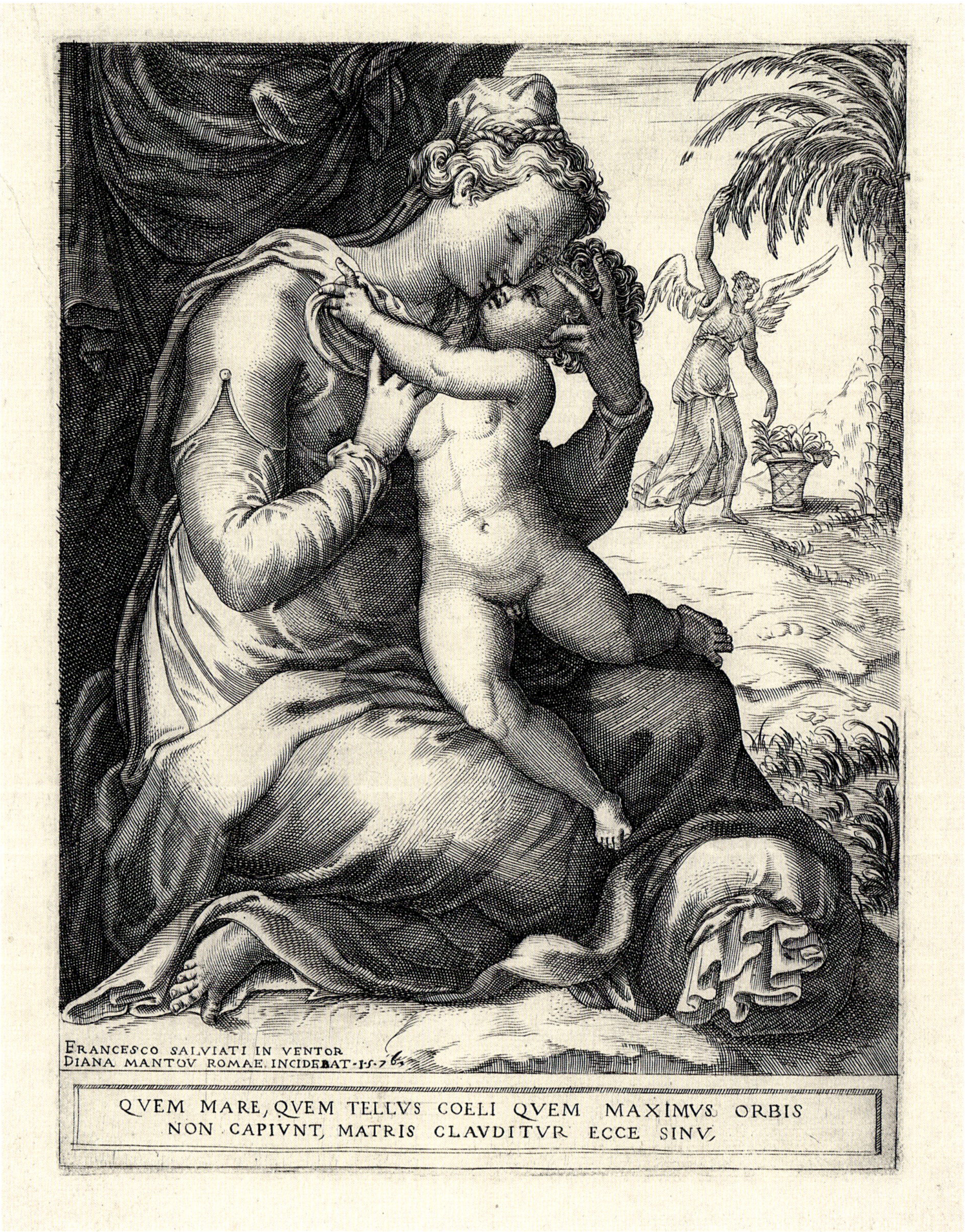

64 Diana Mantuana, *The Virgin and Child*, 1576

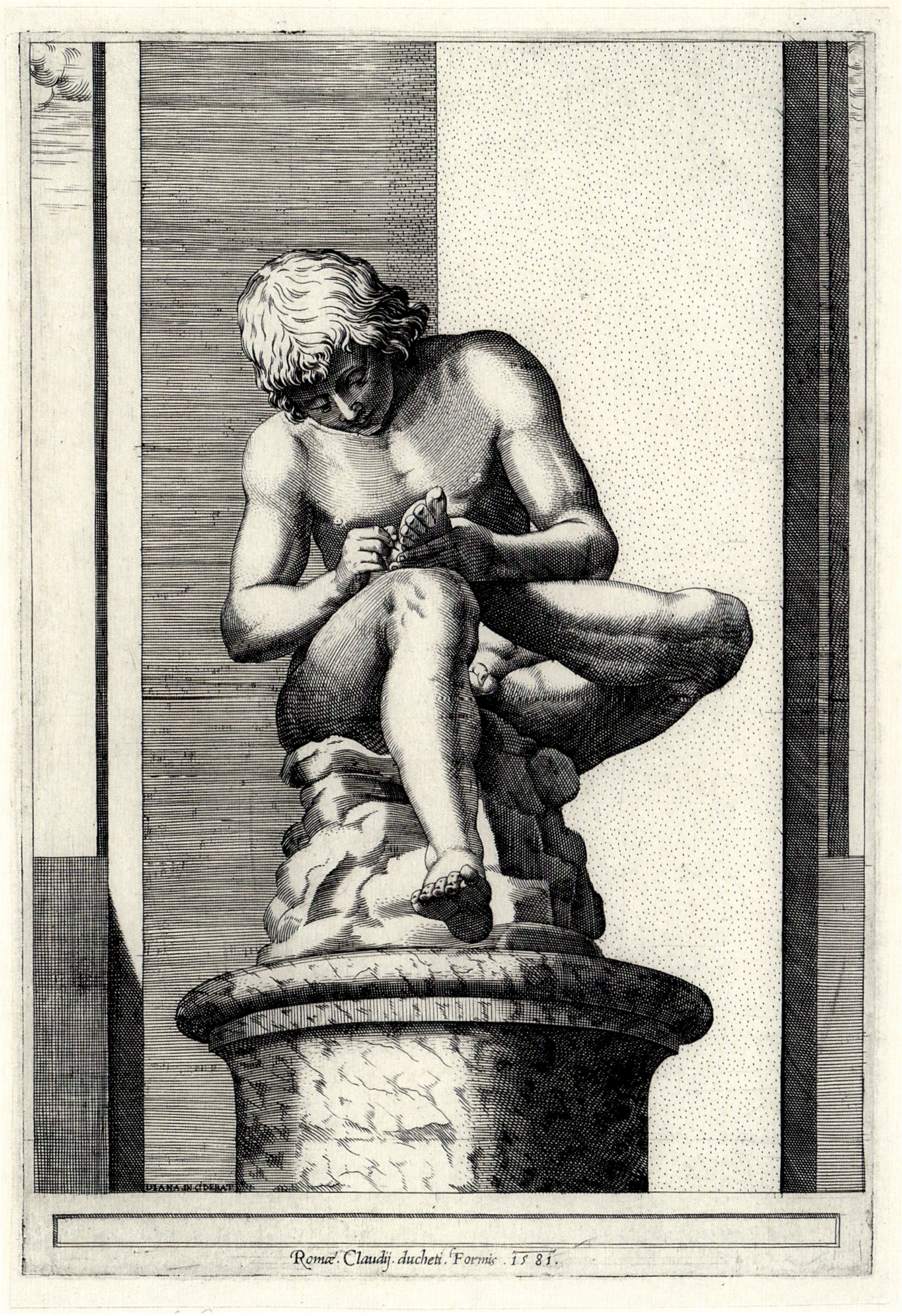

65 Diana Mantuana, *The Thorn-Puller*, 1581

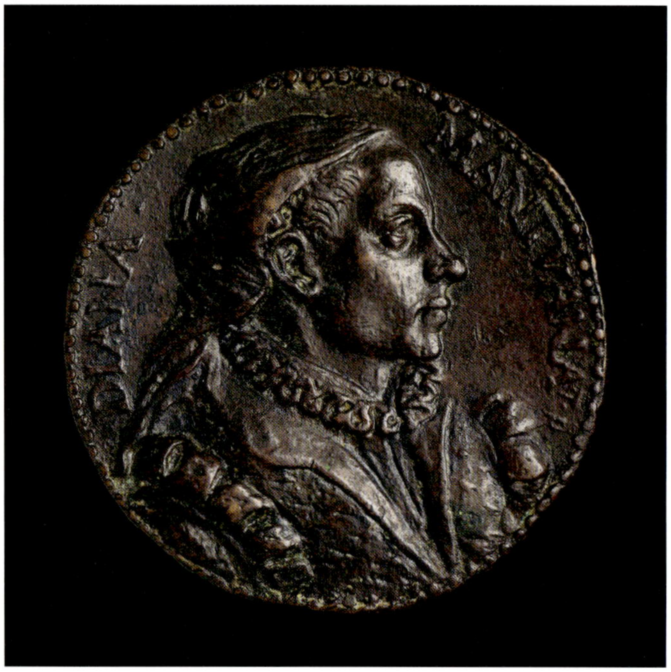

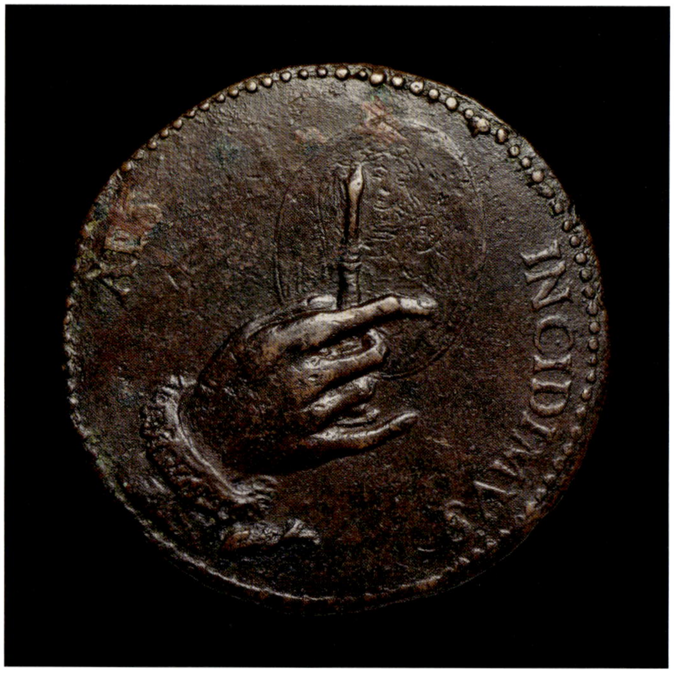

66 & 67 Medal of Diana Mantuana, 16th century, diam. 4 cm (1⅝ in.)

but as a woman, she was not allowed many of the professional benefits and was restricted to religious activities and fundraising for poor women's dowries. A medal representing Diana, one of a pair, with the other of her husband, suggests Diana did not let these restrictions influence her ambitions. A rare example of a Renaissance medal of a woman artist, one side shows a portrait of Diana in profile (fig. 66).[30] The reverse shows a woman's hand, with her long, slender fingers holding a burin and incising an image of the Madonna and Child, with an inscription that translates as "We engrave copper (or bronze)" (fig. 67). This imagery evokes Saint Luke, whose legend recounted that he painted Mary and Jesus. This medal elevates the art of engraving but more specifically the work of a woman engraver's hand, and, of course, Diana herself.

Women played key roles in the textile industry in Renaissance Italy, one of the most lucrative areas of manufacturing in the period. Women made lace, embroidered, and wove silks and velvets (fig. 68). Because most guilds that regulated textile production generally excluded women, women's names do not often appear in records, and only rarely are any textiles signed, but it should always be considered a possibility that a textile may have been made by a woman. Similarly, works made in humble, natural materials like cut straw, a skill known to have been practiced by women, especially nuns, in the Renaissance, were very likely made by women whose names will never be discovered (see fig. 18).[31] Documents also attest to the work of nuns in convents, major contributors to the production, especially of textiles for devotional use. In the context of convents, women would sometimes intentionally not sign their works or leave records of their individual accomplishments, since often this work also served a devotional purpose, and vows of humility would prohibit seeking recognition for a creative achievement.[32] Female textile makers needing to earn a living, or at least their keep, were recorded in business documents such as payment logs. The Venetian lace industry, for example, relied on the underpaid, grueling work of poor women.[33] A woodcut from Cesare Vecellio's compendium of global costumes includes a "woman of Ischia" with spindles in her hand (fig. 69). The accompanying text praises her industry, as she worked to support her household.[34]

Isabella Catanea Parasole upended the era's accepted notions about women's creativity in the field of lace pattern books. These books typically contained designs invented or compiled by men and served as models for women's work.[35] Through their intricate and visually engaging designs, they also encouraged fantasy and contemplation, providing pleasure and instruction to their generally female audience. Male authors often dedicated the works to powerful women, seeking associations and patronage that might support their careers. These dedications also lauded the male author's creativity, curiosity, and industriousness in producing the book. Parasole achieved professional success by publishing a number of books featuring her own lace-making patterns illustrated with her own woodcuts.[36] She rejected the idea of needlework as a mere pastime and presented herself as an artist with agency, as is evident in the dedications of her books to noble and royal women, including, for example, Princess Elisabeth of Austria, wife of Philip IV of Spain. Her lace designs are inventive fantasies, and the graphic power of the black-and-white woodcuts makes a strong visual statement (fig. 70). Her designs also reflect actual lace production, as seen in this intricate strip of lace (fig. 71). As with Diana Mantuana, Parasole learned her craft in her family's workshop, which produced carved wooden objects including dolls and small boxes. Used to hold small personal items such as jewels, pieces of lace, and devotional objects, these boxes were often lined with paper printed with decorative motifs, also produced in the family shop. Like many artists before her, Parasole played on the exceptional aspect of being a woman in a trade that was usually reserved for men. She followed the tradition of using florid titles for such books, linking the practice of lace making with female virtue. Her 1625 book was called *Gemma pretiosa delle virtuose donne* (The Precious Gem of Virtuous Women). Given the obvious virtuosity demonstrated by the book's author, the title takes on an ironic tone.

Women working with textiles also played an important role in the Jewish communities of Renaissance Italy, and these works include some of the few examples where a woman put her name on her handiwork. Torah binders are used to keep the scrolls from unrolling while stored in the ark in the synagogue. Because the Torah is the most holy object in the Jewish

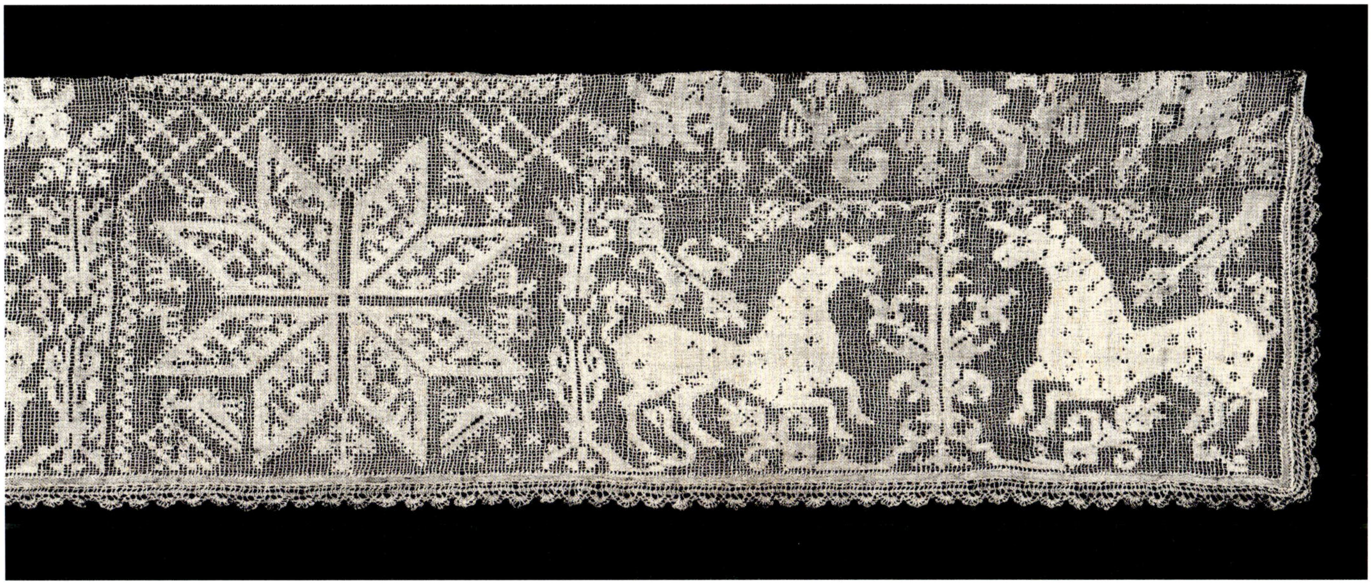

68 Detail of lace, 16th century

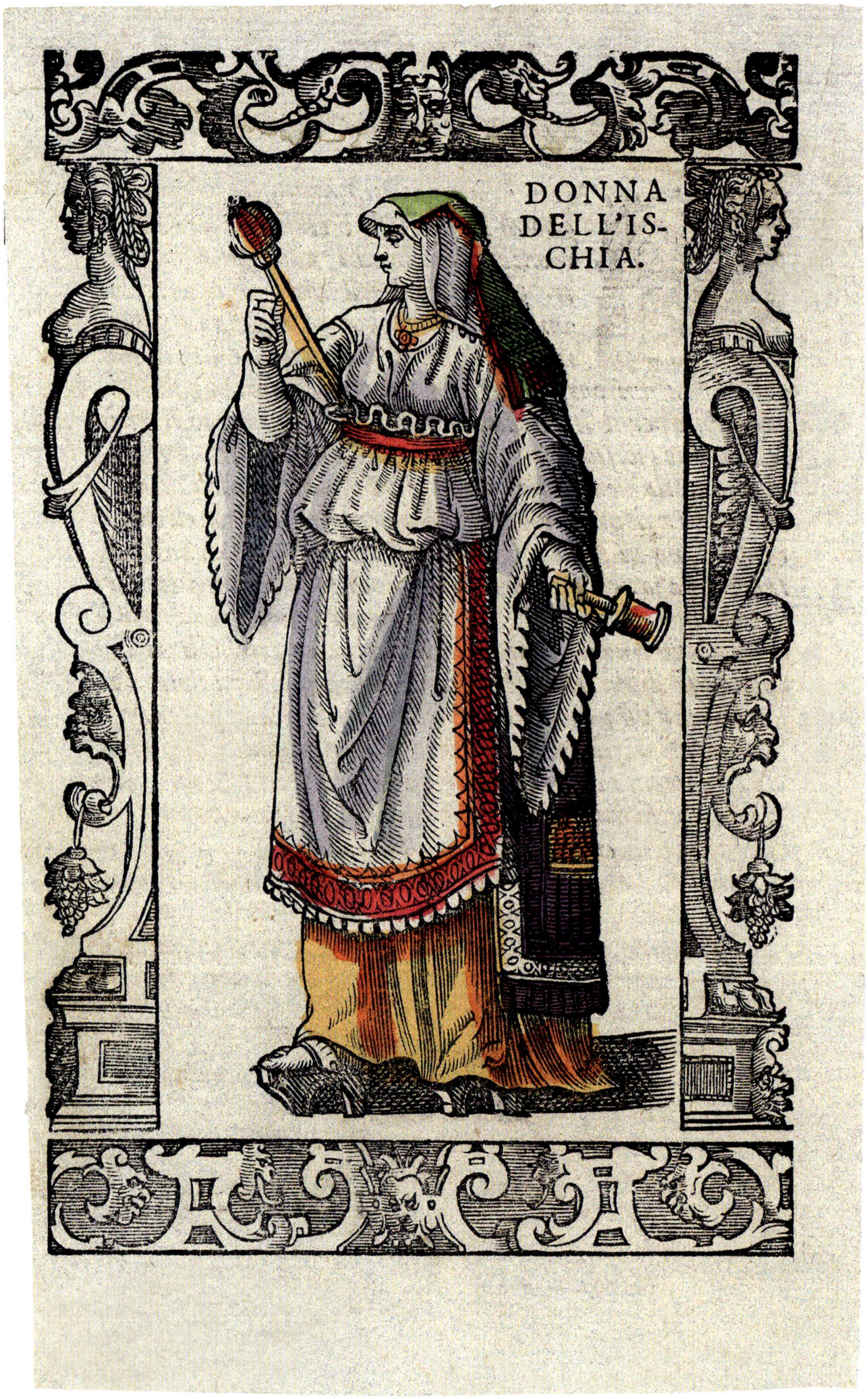

69 *Donna dell'Ischia* from Cesare Vecellio, *De gli Habiti Antichi et Moderni di Diversi Parti del Mondo*, Venice, 1590

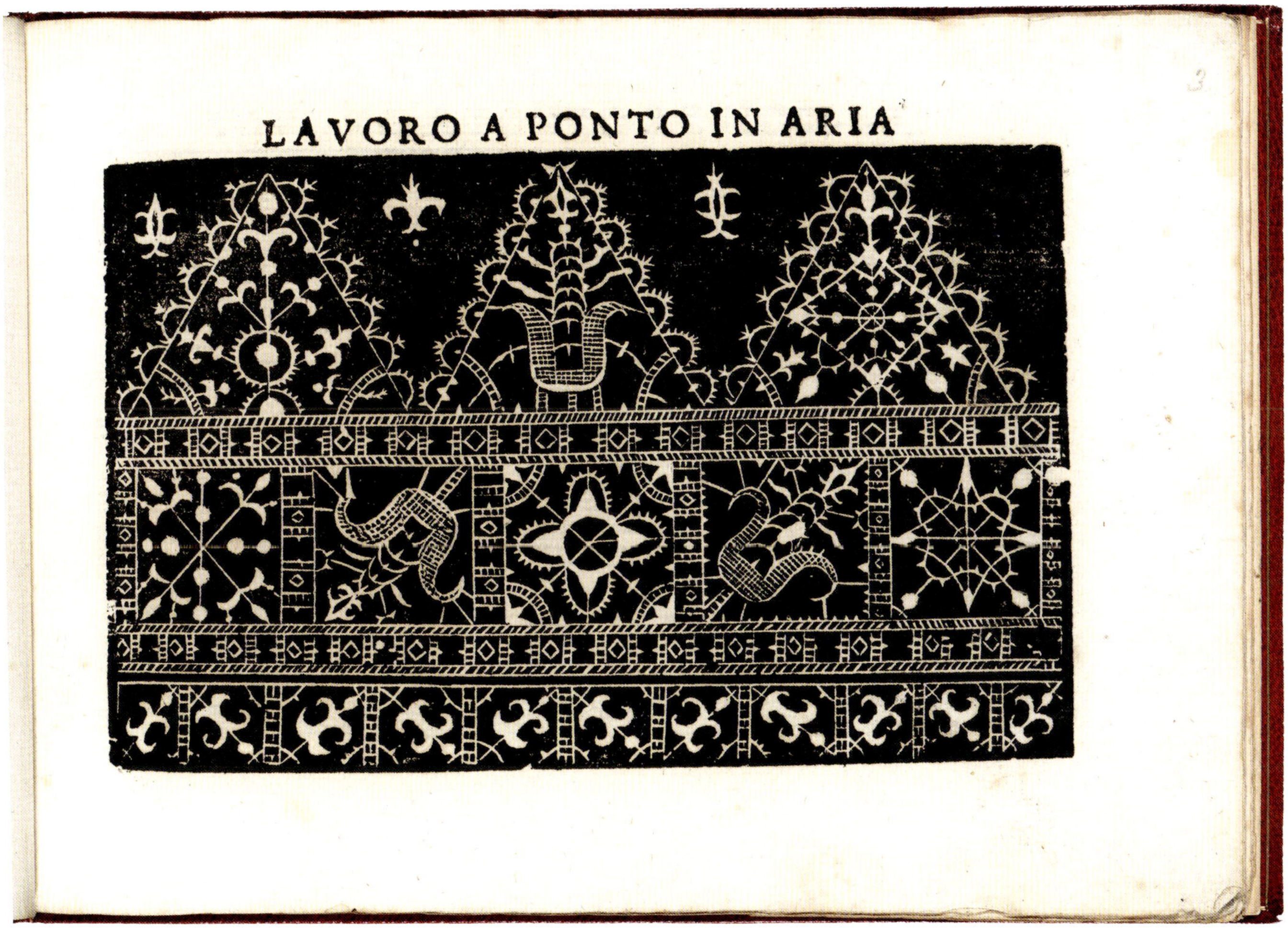

70 Isabella Catanea Parasole, woodcut from *Gemma pretiosa delle virtuose donne*, Rome, 1625

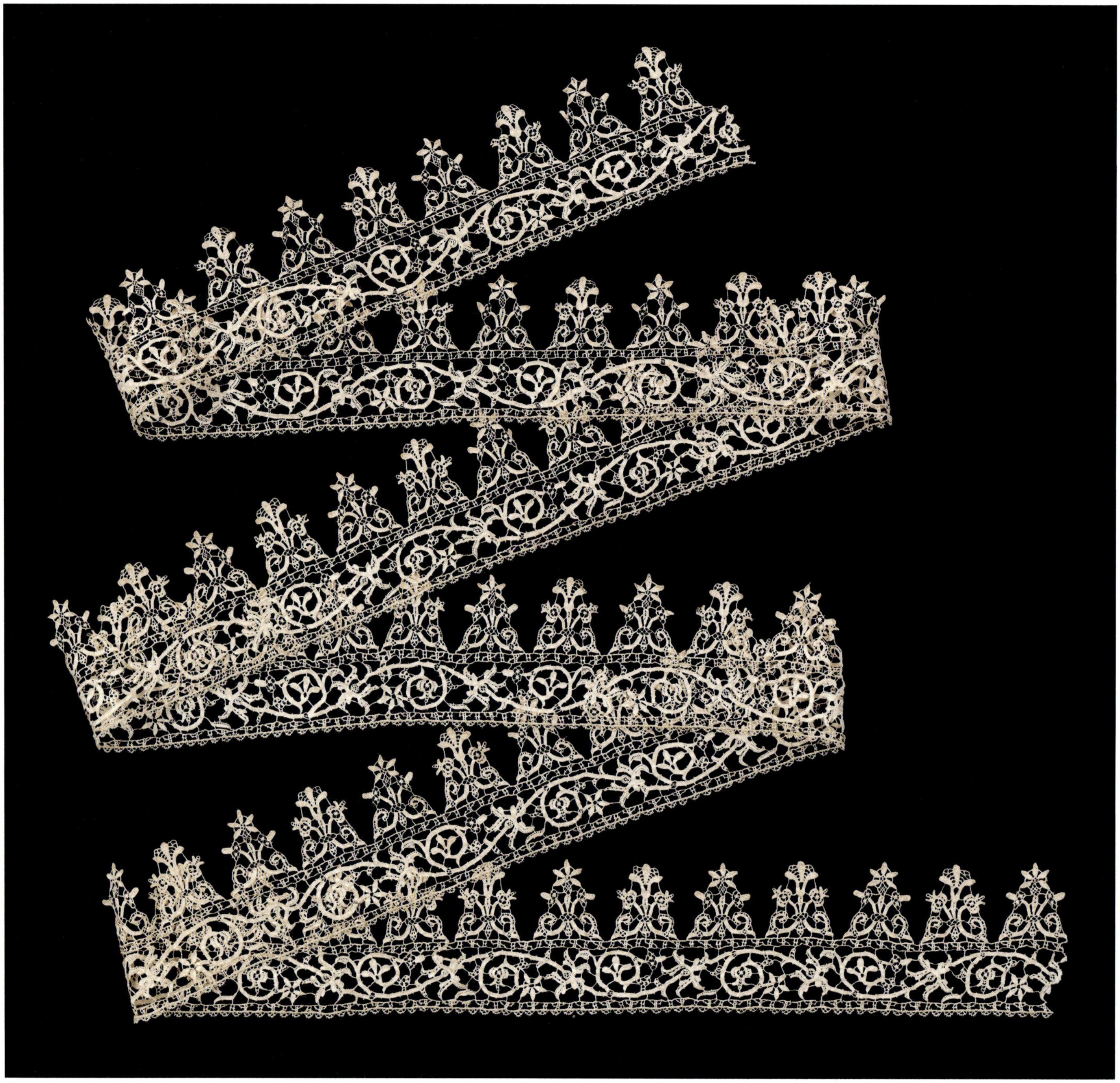

71 Lace, 17th century

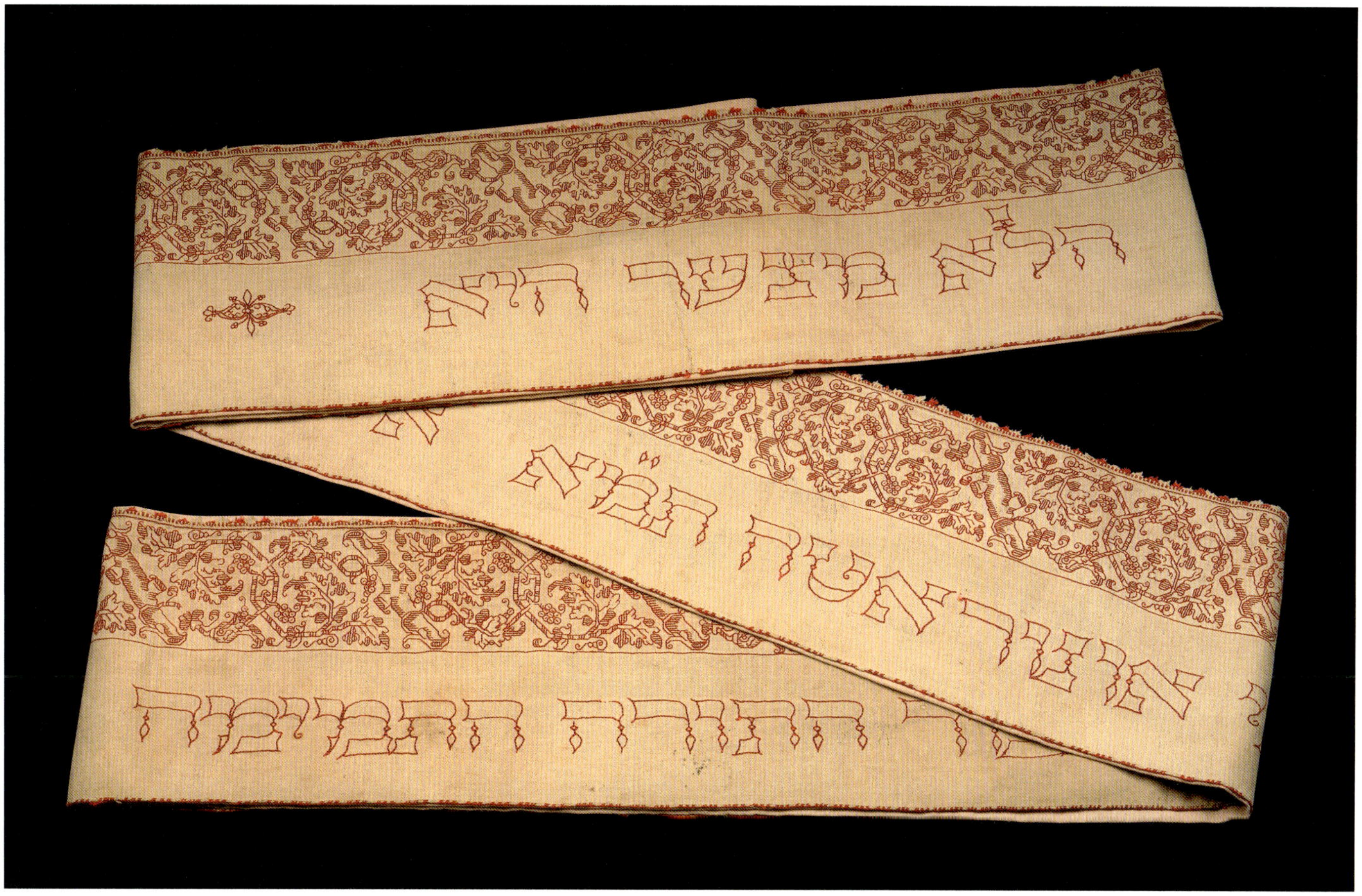

72 Honorata Foa, Torah binder, 1582–83

faith, women gained special blessings for making any textile in its honor. Torah binders were made by sewing together pieces of fabric, often embellished with embroidery or lace, and featured stitched dedications expressing the personal act of piety and devotion in making such an object for donation to a synagogue. These long pieces of fabric also can be symbolically compared to the swaddling of a beloved child.

On one of the earliest known Italian Torah binders, made in 1582–83, Honorata Foa dedicated her work in an embroidered inscription: "In honor of the pure Torah, my hand raised an offering, I Honorata . . . wife of . . . Samuel Foa . . . , 'it is such a little one', the year 5343" (fig. 72).[37] Her reference to her small hand recalls the importance of the creative hands in Anguissola's self-portrait and on the reverse of Diana Mantuana's medal. Dedicating a work in honor of the Torah is typical of Italian practice, as opposed to the custom of inscribing a blessing for individual boys in northern European practice. The inscription reveals a sense of appreciation for women's contributions to the faith, to family, and to community unique to Renaissance Italy. This appreciation of the value and worth of women's work is also expressed in a chapter of the biblical Book of Proverbs, summarized in Christine de Pizan's *The Book of the City of Ladies*. Christine presents the biblical chapter as an example of the value of women's work and how it could, and should, be valued by all.[38]

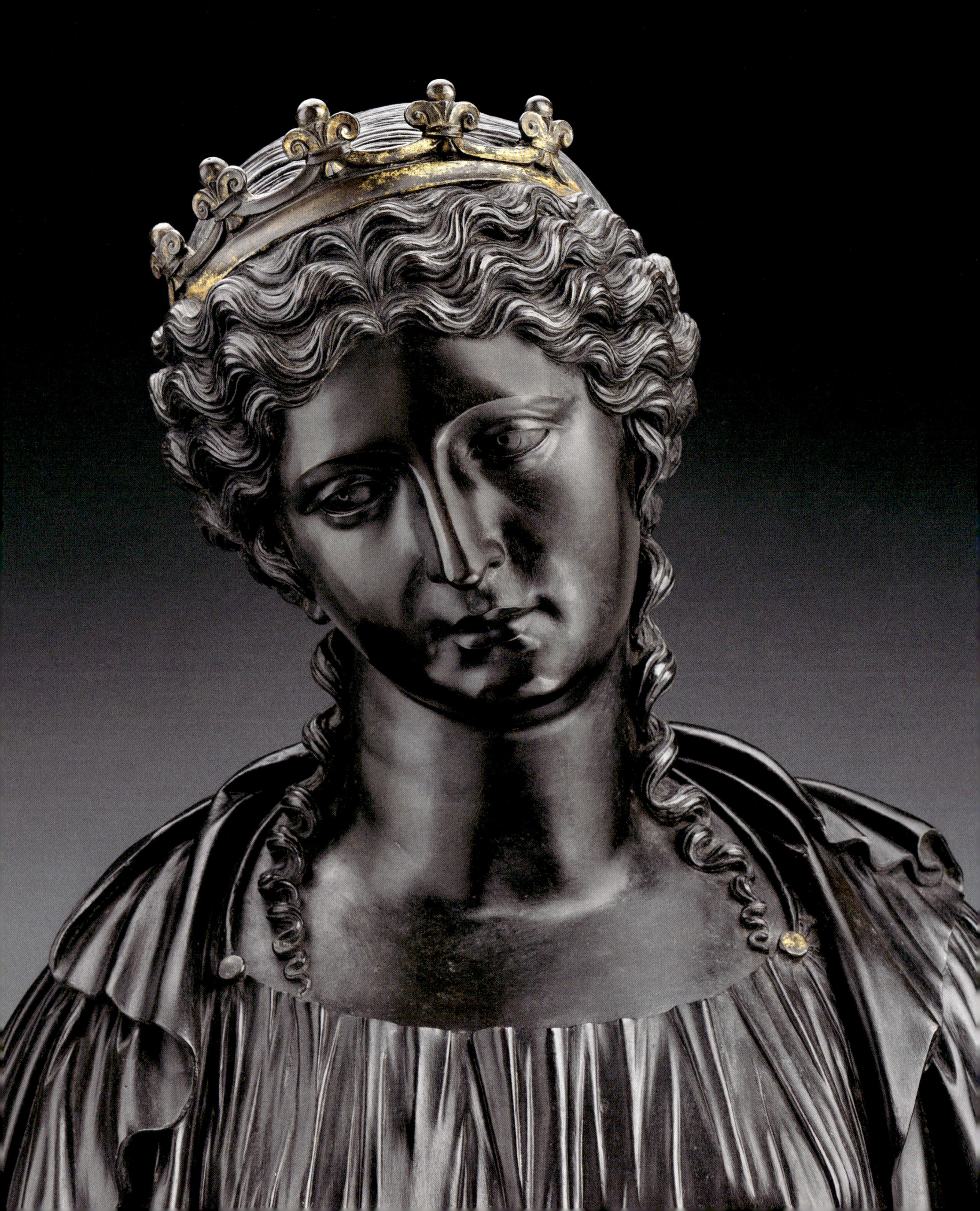

Illustrious Women

Pier Jacopo Alari Bonacolsi's bronze bust of Cleopatra, made in Mantua probably in 1519–21, is a Renaissance rethinking of one of the most famous women in history.[1] Cleopatra was the last Ptolemaic queen of Egypt, who committed suicide by the bite of a poisonous asp when her kingdom was conquered by Rome. Her story fascinated writers in Italy, although their interpretations varied. In the fourteenth century, writers presented her in a negative, moralizing context. Dante, for example, placed her with the lustful in the second circle of hell in *The Divine Comedy*. In *De mulieribus claris* (On famous women) Boccaccio states: "Cleopatra . . . became an object of gossip for the whole world . . . She gained glory for almost nothing else than her beauty, while on the other hand she became known throughout the world for her greed, cruelty, and lustfulness."[2] By the early sixteenth century, a more sympathetic view of Cleopatra expressed by some ancient writers was gaining popularity.[3] Plutarch, in his *Life of Antony*, details Cleopatra's efforts to save her kingdom from Roman conquest, including an affair with Julius Caesar and an alliance with and marriage to Marc Antony. When Egypt was ultimately defeated, Marc Antony killed himself, and the grief-stricken Cleopatra also chose suicide rather than being transported to Rome to be displayed as a spoil of war in Augustus Caesar's triumphal procession. Bonacolsi, also known as Antico, shows Cleopatra not in the act of committing suicide or dying from the poisonous bite, but rather contemplating her fateful choice. The idea of presenting a powerful woman deep in thought, which encourages viewers to consider her story from a contemplative, empathetic perspective, adds a new facet to the Renaissance presentation of the figure of Cleopatra.

Antico's *Cleopatra* is elegantly and chastely dressed; her hair is adorned with jewels, she wears a gilded crown with pearls, and holes in her earlobes suggest that she once wore real earrings (fig. 73). Her evocative expression imparts a quiet sense of melancholy, as if she is caught up in her thoughts. Her tilted head and downcast gaze imply meditation. Because this image goes against common ideas about Cleopatra and presents an alternative way of thinking about her, the snake that slithers along the channel of the molding on the socle becomes essential in identifying her. The socle, unique among Antico's bronze busts, is a segment that does not support the sculpture but acts more like a tablet for an inscription. The partial socle and snake were cast as part of the bust, suggesting that Antico did not want to risk the separation of this small detail from the figure.[4] Furthering the idea that this bust represents Cleopatra are the pearls, often included in Renaissance images of her, that decorate her crown. In a famous episode, she dissolved one of her most valuable pearl earrings in vinegar and gave it to Marc Antony to drink, winning a bet that she could provide the most expensive meal.

Antico worked for the Gonzaga family at the court of Mantua. It is very likely, though not confirmed in documentary sources, that *Cleopatra* was commissioned by Isabella d'Este, Marchioness of Mantua and one of the most powerful patrons and collectors in early-sixteenth-century Italy.[5] In 1519 Isabella was preparing to move into new apartments, leaving her old rooms to her son who had come of age and was ruling

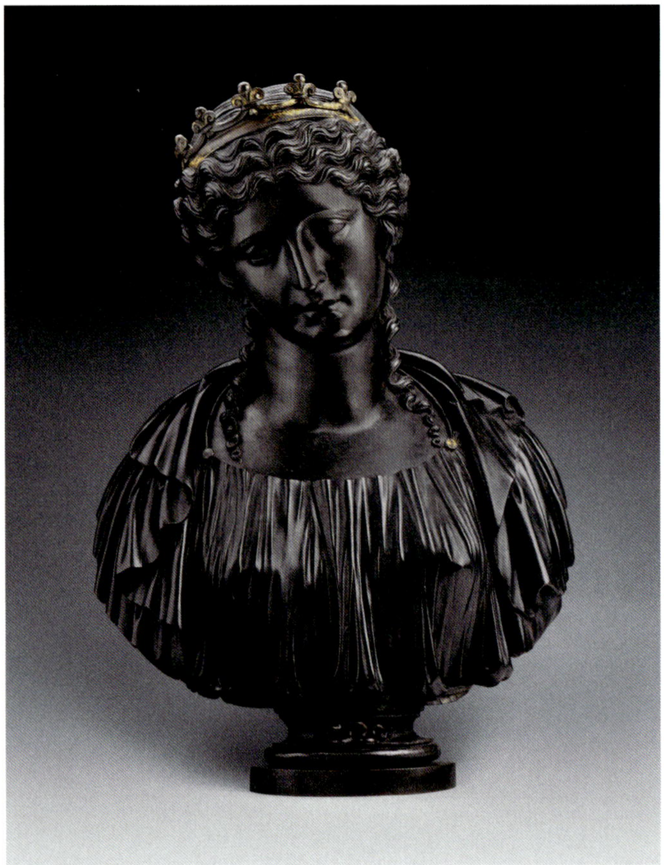

73 Pier Jacopo Alari Bonacolsi, *Cleopatra*, about 1519–22, H. 64.5 cm (25⅜ in.)

independently after a period when the widowed Isabella acted as regent. In a letter to Antico, she commissioned a number of bronze busts to decorate her new rooms, and the *Cleopatra* may have been part of this group. It is likely that Isabella played a fundamental role in how this sculpture took shape.

Documentary sources and other works of art confirm that Isabella was deeply interested in Cleopatra. A letter she received from her agent in Rome in February 1512 mentions an ancient statue of a reclining woman thought to be the Egyptian queen (fig. 74).[6] This letter is one of the earliest written sources for the marble statue, which was displayed by Pope Julius II in the recently built Belvedere court at the Vatican along with his other prized antiquities. Although recognized as representing Ariadne by the early nineteenth century, the statue was identified as Cleopatra in the early

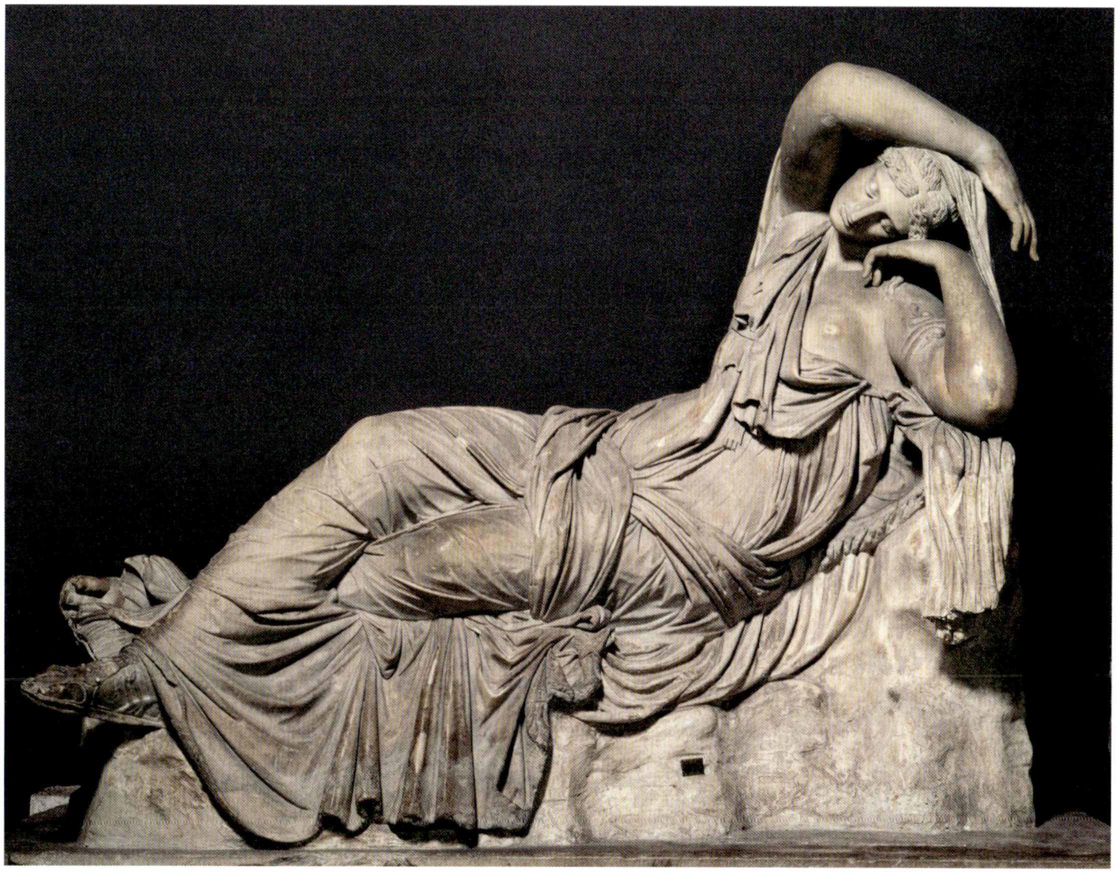

74 *Sleeping Ariadne*, early 2nd century A.D., length 195 cm (76¾ in.)

sixteenth century based on the figure's armlet in the form of a snake.[7] The small detail of a snake was enough to lead to this identification, as it seems to for Antico's bust as well. The deep, death-like sleep of the figure, along with her bared breast, also coincided with Renaissance ideas about Cleopatra as a tragic heroine. Inspired by the ancient statue, Baldassare Castiglione wrote a poem, likely known to Isabella d'Este, in the voice of the sculpture and its sitter, presenting Cleopatra as a complex character and a noble queen: "Whoever you are who sees these arms bitten by harsh snakes and eyes grown dim in eternal night carved in this marble, do not believe that I lay down in death unwilling. For a long time my conquerors forbade me to break off my life, doubtless so I, a captive queen, might be borne in a thronging triumphal procession… But virtue and noble desire for an honorable death overcame shameful life and the tyrant's snares, for freedom was achieved by death, and I felt no chains. I went down to the waters of the Underworld a free shade."[8]

Isabella commissioned a small bronze version of the Vatican sculpture for her *grotta*, where it was placed below a bust of Marc Antony, thus reuniting the lovers. It was also near one of her greatest sculptural treasures, Michelangelo's now lost *Sleeping Cupid*. She paired Michelangelo's figure with a *Sleeping Cupid* believed to be by the ancient Greek sculptor Praxiteles.[9] Given Isabella's interest in creating relationships among the sculptures in her collection, Antico's *Cleopatra* may have been conceived in dialogue with its ancient predecessor, the Vatican *Cleopatra*, in a similar artistic conversation across time and distance.

Renaissance viewers like Isabella may even have been aware that the Vatican marble was believed to be

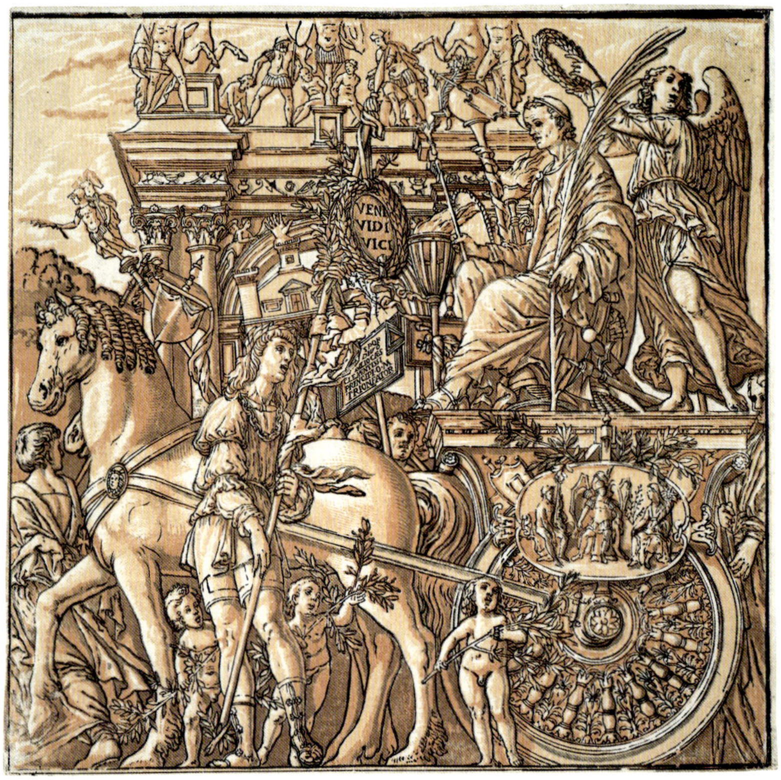

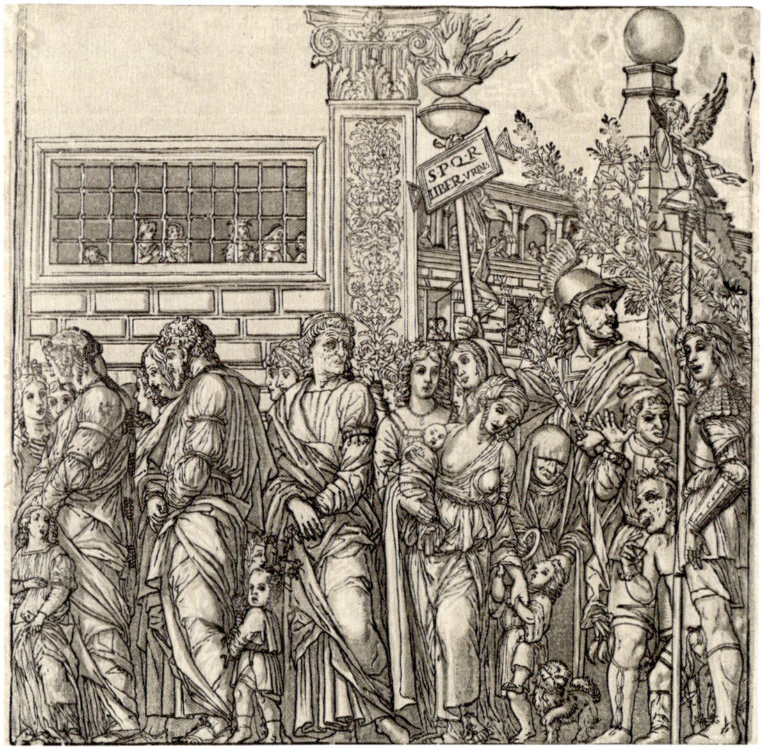

75 Andrea Andreani after Andrea Mantegna, *Julius Caesar on His Chariot*, 1599
76 Andrea Andreani after Andrea Mantegna, *Captives*, 1599

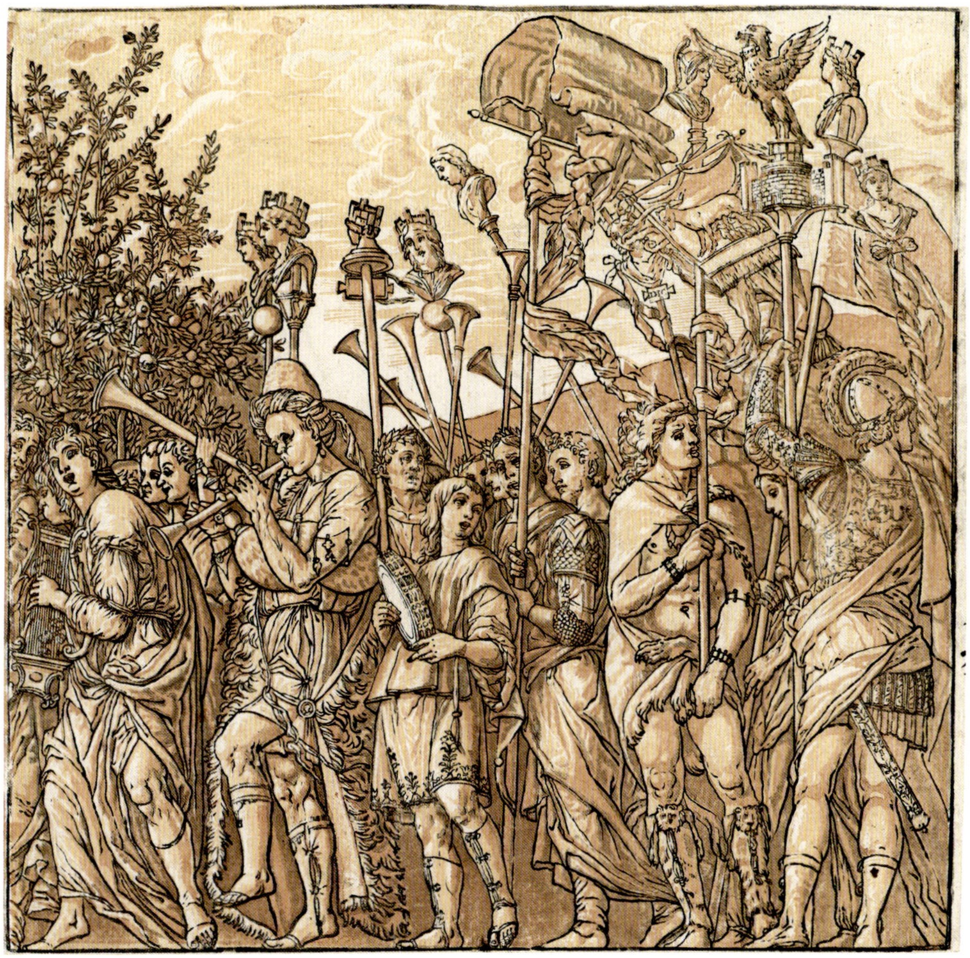

77 Andrea Andreani after Andrea Mantegna, *Musicians and Standard-Bearers*, 1599

the actual effigy that the victorious general Augustus, unable to bring the living Cleopatra to Rome, included in his triumphal procession, the marble standing in for the queen. The topos of living marble—hard stone that almost seems alive through the sculptor's carving—was often used in discussing the Vatican marble and could be interpreted as weakening Cleopatra's triumph over Augustus. She could be considered present in the "living stone" of the marble sculpture despite her suicide.[10] One of the most famous commissions of Isabella's husband, Francesco II Gonzaga, was Andrea Mantegna's *Triumphs of Caesar*, a series of paintings presenting an imaginative reconstruction of the kind of triumphal celebrations that Cleopatra sought to avoid.[11] These paintings have stood for centuries as a powerful evocation of the Roman triumph as general type. Prints after the original cycle also circulated widely, spreading its fame. These compelling images would have been present in both Isabella's and Antico's minds as the bust of Cleopatra was being created. Three prints from the series show different sections of the procession: Caesar on his chariot, captives paraded through the streets, and the musicians and standard-bearers marching, all demonstrating the power of the victor and the pathos of the prisoners (figs. 75, 76, 77). In the scene of the standard-bearers, busts quite similar to Antico's are set onto poles held high about the crowds and may have inspired Antico when creating his bust of Cleopatra.

Antico's *Cleopatra* is a deeply imaginative work that presented new sensibilities and ideas about what

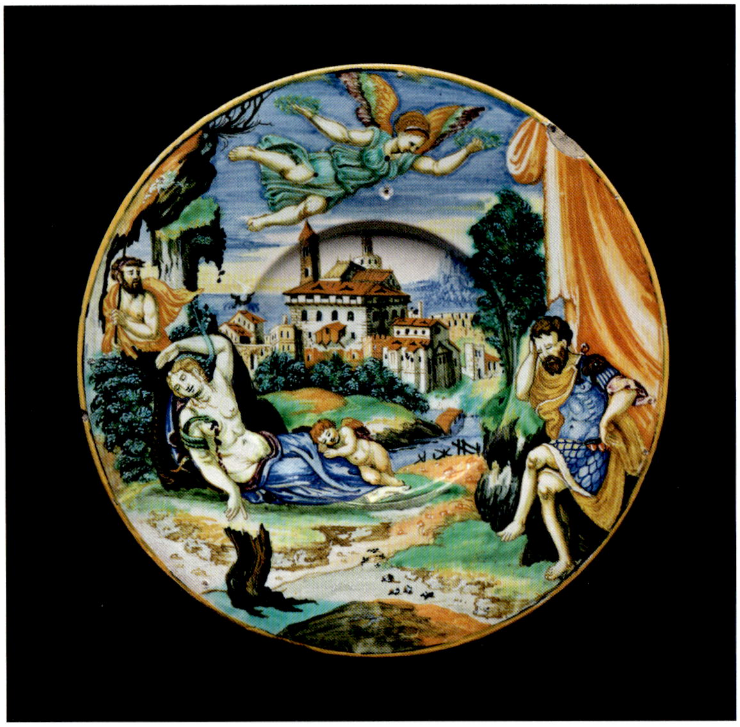

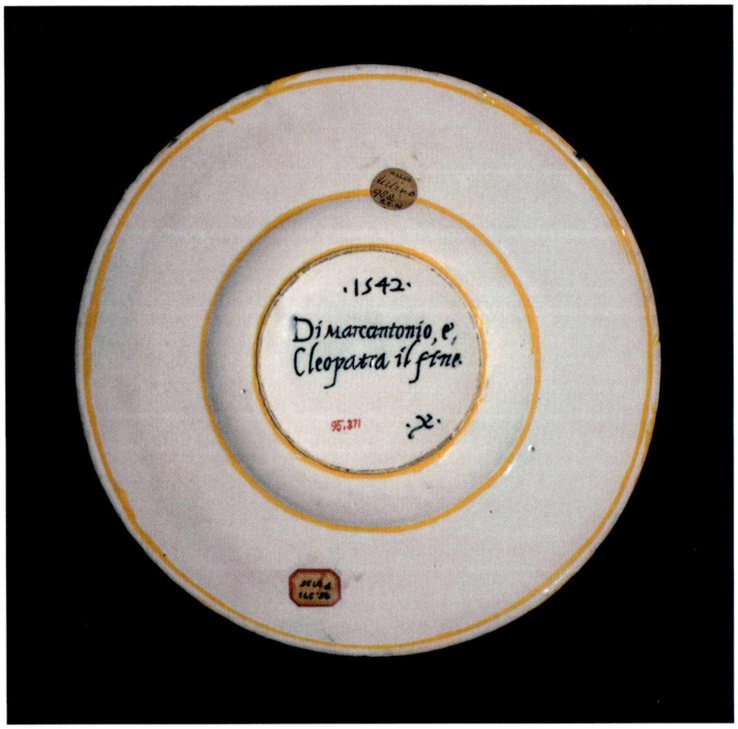

78 & 79 Francesco Xanto Avelli da Rovigo, Plate with Cleopatra and Marc Antony, 1542, diam. 26.4 cm (10⅜ in.)

women could accomplish, through exploration of the story of an ancient queen, images of Roman triumphs, and the evocation of the Roman portrait bust form. Antico's smallest details are thought provoking: a socle that seems to support but does not, a snake that kills but confers victory, and a tragic death countered by the complex workings of the animated soul. This Cleopatra demonstrates her power through her ability to think and to choose.

While bronze was one of the most expensive and honored materials of Renaissance art, important messages were also conveyed in humbler materials. Plates made from maiolica, tin-glazed earthtenware, provided delightful visual and intellectual stimuli at court gatherings, whether in use or on display, depicting scenes from ancient history, the Bible, or poetry. A maiolica plate attributed to Francesco Xanto Avelli, working in Urbino, presents Cleopatra in what at first seems to be a more typical Renaissance depiction based on the Vatican *Cleopatra* (fig. 78). On the left is Cleopatra, reclining with her breasts bared and arm draped over her head. Her pose here links the painted figure directly to the Vatican *Cleopatra*. At right is Marc Antony, dressed in armor and seated with his legs crossed and his eyes closed, perhaps contemplating his own suicide. At the top of the plate, the winged figure of Fame holds crowns above the heads of the lovers. Cupid sleeps curled up on Cleopatra's legs. To the left of Cleopatra is a man wearing a yellow cape and moving away from the scene. Although he has not been convincingly identified, he may be the servant who delivered to Cleopatra the basket of fruit that concealed the poisonous asp. In the distance is a cityscape that might represent Urbino. On the back of the plate, written in blue glaze, is text that translates to "Of Marc Antony and Cleopatra. The End" (fig. 79). The plate's decoration does not include a coat of arms, device, or inscription that could connect it with a broader service, series of stories, or a specific patron, but it comes from a highly sophisticated court setting.

The plate's imagery and inscription stress the couple's tragic love story. Cleopatra's breast, bitten by the snake, bleeds copiously, leaving no doubt as to her fate. The sleeping Cupid signifies the end of their

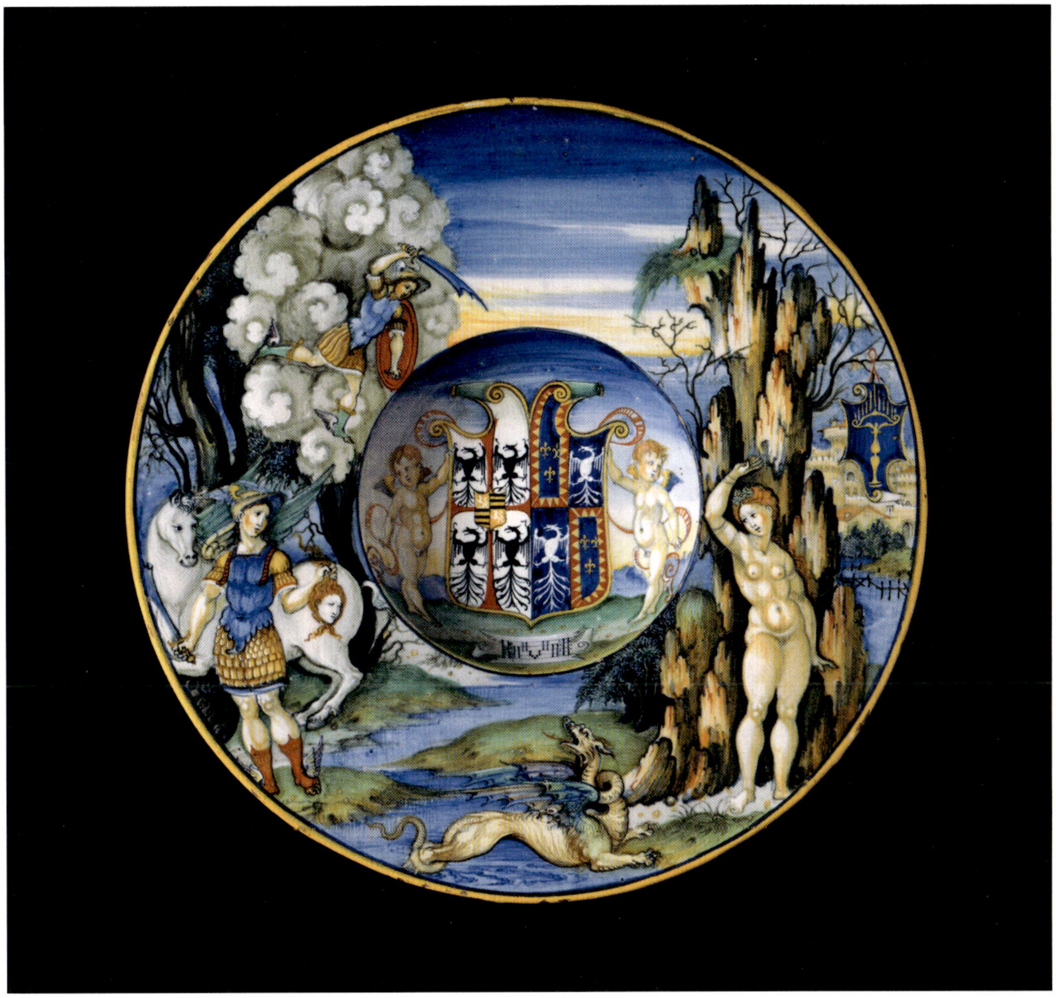

80 Nicola da Urbino, Plate with Perseus and Andromeda, about 1524, diam. 26.8 cm (10½ in.)

love in death, though it hints at reawakening. This is one of a number of details that point to a more positive, empathetic view of Cleopatra, one that aligns with Antico's presentation. Her partial nudity, as in the Vatican marble, demonstrates her place among ancient heroines such as Lucretia, a Roman noblewoman who also committed suicide to maintain her honor and that of her family. On this plate, both lovers are shown, the inscription on the back links them, and the crowns held by Fame relate to Renaissance wedding celebrations.[12] Although Cleopatra's relationships with men often defined her fame in negative ways, in this representation, the pathos of the lovers' shared choice of suicide, their devotion to each other as husband and wife, and the power of a love that will transcend death tell a different story.

The brilliance of the Urbino court is also demonstrated by a plate that is part of a large service commissioned by Eleonora Gonzaga, wife of Francesco Maria I della Rovere and Duchess of Urbino (fig. 80).[13] Sent by Eleonora as a gift to her mother, Isabella d'Este, the plate speaks to a particular mother-daughter relationship as well as the networks of powerful women across the Italian courts and the importance of maiolica in Renaissance life. This service was intended for use at Isabella's country retreat and this plate takes its subject from Ovid's *Metamorphoses*, a favored source for narrative painting in the period. Three stories from the life

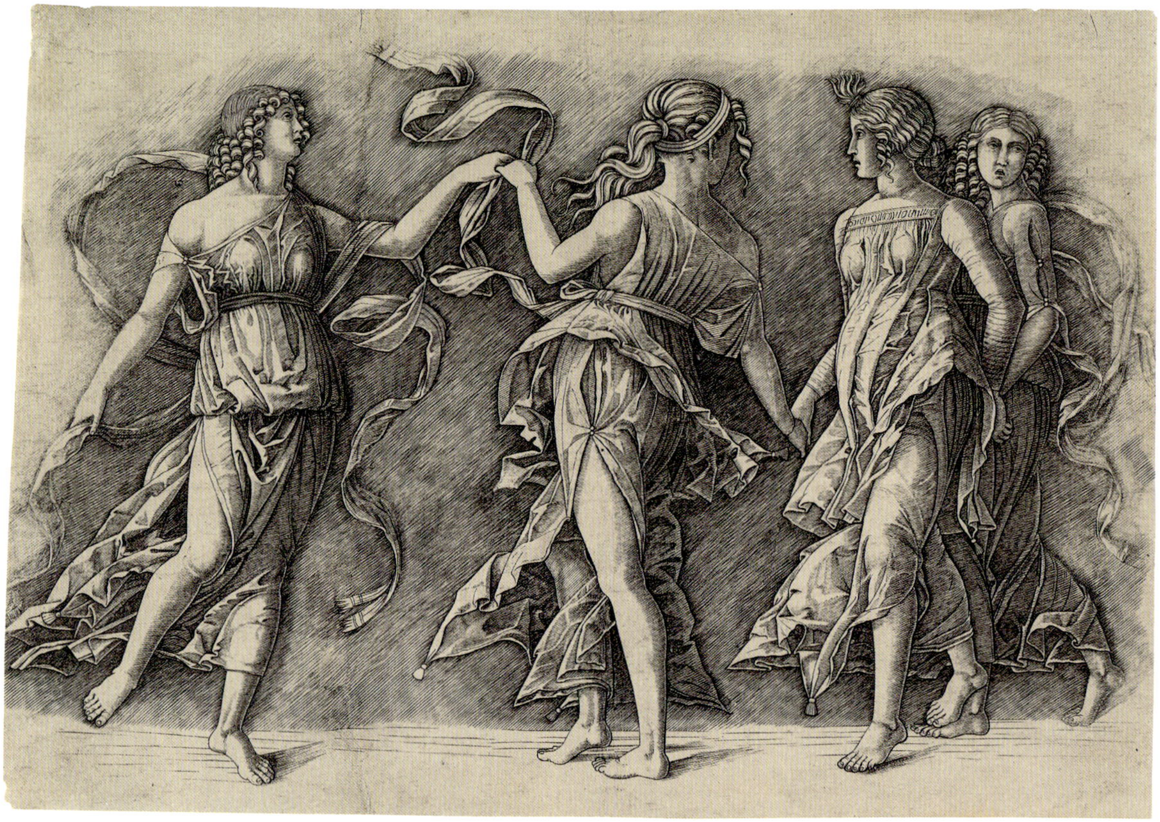

81 After Andrea Mantegna, *The Four Muses*, about 1497–1505

of Perseus are shown including his flying in to slay the sea monster, rescuing Andromeda, and displaying the head of the slain Medusa. Urbino in the early sixteenth century was a center for refined maiolica production, and Eleonora commissioned the service from one of the most famous and skilled maiolica painters of the day, who elevated the humble material through his exceptional artistry. The commission allowed Eleonora to share the finest art the Urbino court had to offer with her family while also displaying her own position as duchess of one of the most illustrious courts in Italy: patron in her own right and not just as her mother's daughter.

The power of dynastic roles and strategic political marriages is made clear in the inclusion of Isabella's coat of arms at the center, the impaled arms of Este and Gonzaga. Isabella's personal ideals are visualized in two of her devices included on this plate: the blazing candelabrum on the right illustrating brilliance and the musical staff with rests and pauses signaling silence.[14] Set just below the coat of arms, the musical banner perhaps conveys a sense of her desire to withdraw from dynastic responsibilities to read, think, and play or listen to music.

Isabella pursued these interests in her *studiolo*, or private study, where she surrounded herself with artworks large and small. One of the large paintings that decorated the walls there was Andrea Mantegna's *Mars and Vensus* (or *Parnassus)*, which includes the dancing muses also depicted in *The Four Muses* (fig. 81). It is telling that this group was excerpted.[15] Sometimes described as the "Tenth Muse," Isabella was a patron of dancers and musicians and an amateur musician and dancer herself. She was taught to dance as a young child in Ferrara by a Jewish dancing master. The freedom and grace of the Muses' movements as well as their loose

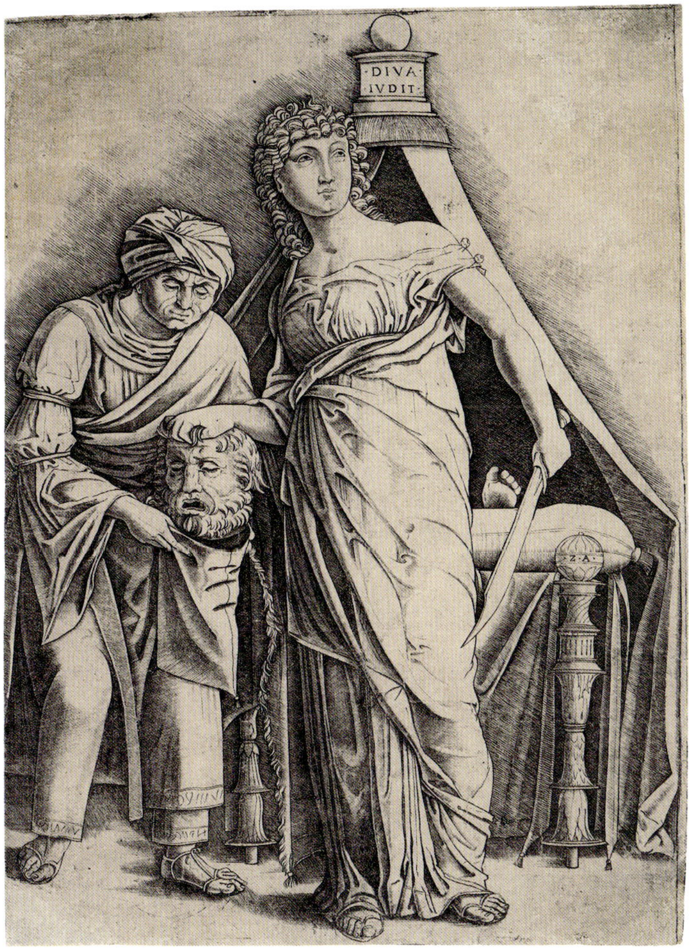

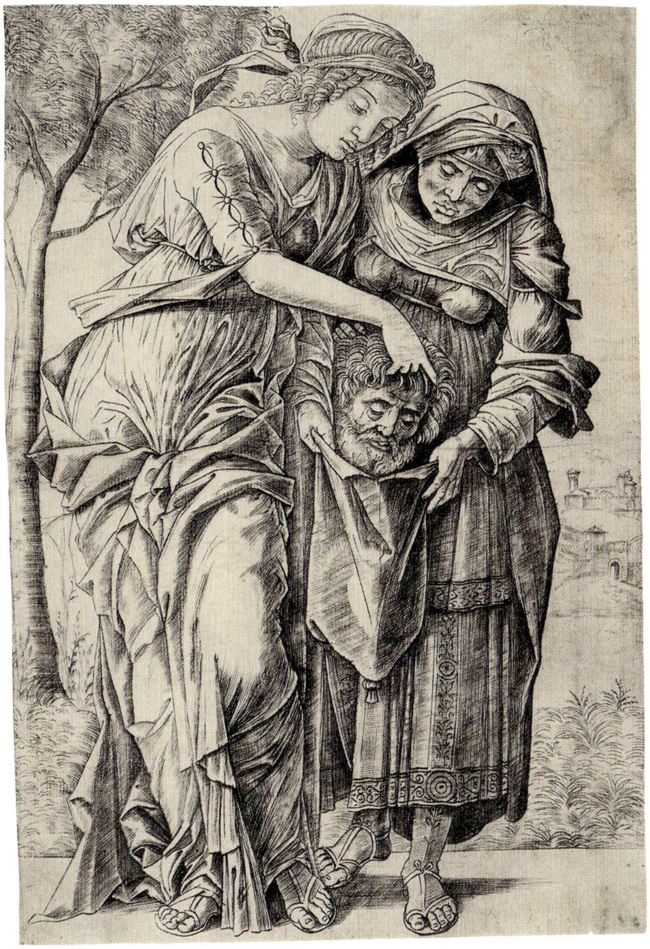

82 Attributed to Giovanni Antonio da Brescia after Andrea Mantegna, *Judith with the Head of Holofernes*, about 1490–1507

83 Girolamo Mocetto after Andrea Mantegna, *Judith with the Head of Holofernes*, about 1500–1510

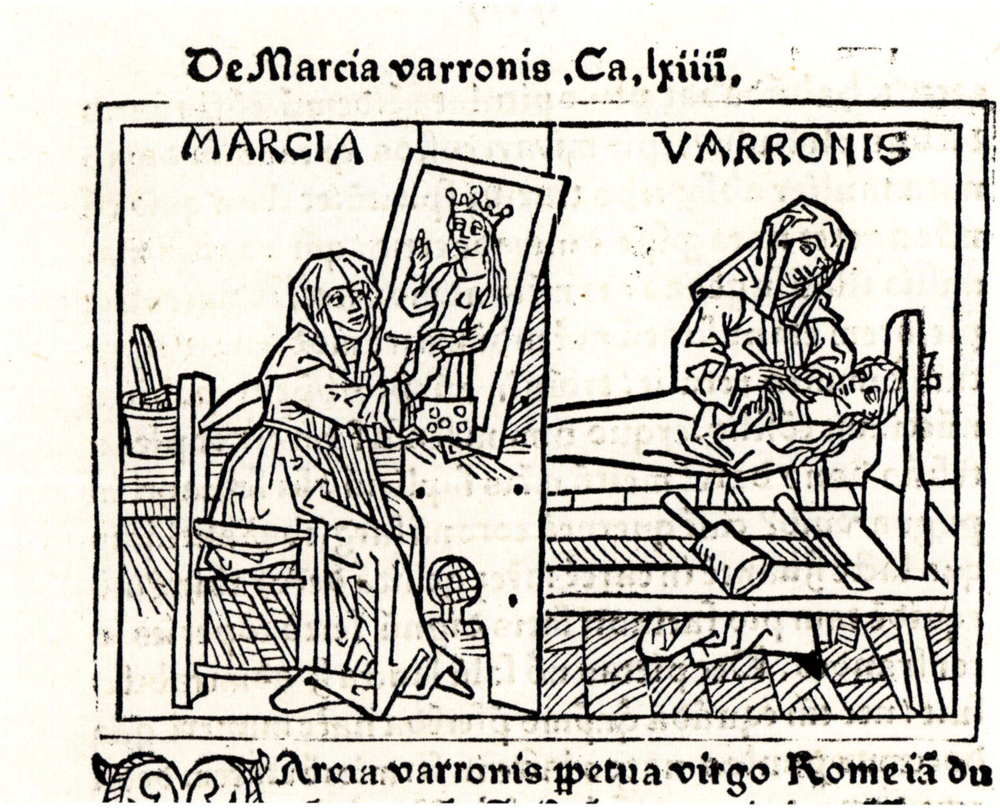

84 Woodcut from Giovanni Boccaccio, *De Claris Mulieribus*, Ulm (Germany), 1473

garments and hair create an image of lightness and physical freedom that Isabella and other women at court must have relished.

Two prints, also based on paintings by Mantegna, depict Judith and her servant Abra with the head of Holofernes (figs. 82, 83).[16] Both show the moments after Judith has killed Holofernes, as she prepares to bring his head back to her people with the help of Abra. This image of two brave women explores female heroism and stresses how the women worked together to commit this dangerous act, focusing on shared effort rather than Judith's independent actions. In the second print, Abra seems to be depicted as a Black African, based on her facial features.[17] This is not the first instance of an African person being depicted at the Gonzaga court. Mantegna's ceiling frescoes in the ducal palace's Camera picta (better known as the Camera degli Sposi, or Room of the Bride and Groom) include a Black woman among the court ladies playfully looking down at the family members gathered below through a fictive oculus. Isabella specifically sought out African people for her court, although as rarities more than as individuals, and little is known about them. Ample documentation speaks to Isabella's life and how she crafted her own image, but the stories of so many others remain undiscovered. Works of art like this print are a testament to their presence.

A thriving literary and visual culture developed around the idea of the illustrious woman in Renaissance Italy, particularly in court circles.[18] Boccaccio's *On Famous Women*, first published in 1361–62 and detailing the lives of mythological and historical women, was a touch point for subsequent writers. An early edition printed in Germany in 1473 includes woodcut illustrations such as an image of the ancient Roman artist Marcia shown working as a painter and as a sculptor (fig. 84). Boccaccio did help to spread the fame of creative women, despite his often moralizing and sometimes misogynistic views, like his portrayal of Cleopatra. Christine de Pizan's early and powerful efforts in her *The Book of the City of Ladies* expanded the canon of illustrious women, and presented pointedly positive interpretations and role models for women. A writer who supported her family with her work, she argued forcefully and broadly for the worth of women; it was women who learned to turn weaknesses into strengths and were able to negotiate ways of exerting their power, intellect, and creativity despite the limitations they experienced. She included saints and contemporary women alike and praised and contextualized the work of women in the home. It seems possible that copies of her treatise, published in France, made their way to northern Italy in the fifteenth century. Bolognese writer Giovanni Sabadino degli Arienti, for example, presented certain arguments that echo ideas that Christine put forward. His work can be interpreted as shifting the discourse toward more favorable views of women's lives and possibilities, especially for the elite women of the courts. In *Gynevera de le clare donne* (Ginevra On Famous Women) of 1492, he discussed not ancient but modern Italian women who, for example, acted as rulers in their husbands' absences, as Isabella and Eleonora would both eventually do. He also extolled women's virtues in the context of running households, work that underpinned civic life and stability. Arienti sent a copy of his book to Isabella, likely hoping to gain support from her, and she thanked him, writing, "We will carefully read it and we will endeavor to follow the footsteps of those illustrious women."[19]

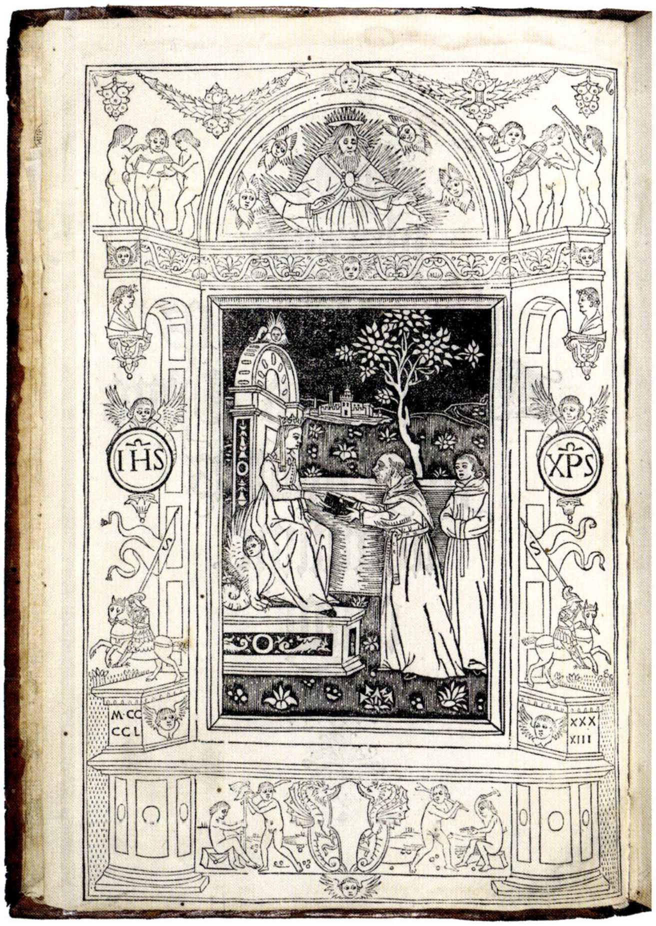

85 Frontispiece from Jacopo Filippo Foresti, *De plurimus claris sceletisque mulieribus*, Ferrara, 1497

Jacopo Foresti's *De plurimus claris sceletisque mulieribus* (Concerning Famous Women), published in 1497 in Ferrara, was dedicated to Beatrice d'Aragona, Queen of Hungary.[20] The frontispiece to the volume includes an image of Foresti, an Augustinian friar, presenting the book to Beatrice (fig. 85). Framed almost like an altarpiece, this scene is set in a garden, with Beatrice seated on a throne and her castle in the distance. A second illustration from the book shows a woman working in her study, surrounded by books (fig. 86). This illustration appears several times, accompanying biographies of learned women, among them Isotta Nogarola (1418–1466), one of the most famous scholars and writers of her day.[21] Born in Verona, she was well educated, wrote in Latin, and was connected to a network of humanists in Venice and the Veneto. She and other learned women in her family were role models for intelligent, scholarly women, a practice that was reinforced by their inclusion in works like Foresti's. Although Foresti valorizes contemporary women's intellectual and literary pursuits, he also maintains some negative views of women and uses the same moralizing tone as Boccaccio.

Isabella's own courtier Mario Equicola produced *De mulieribus* (On Women) in 1501. Equicola's book has been characterized by scholars as a turning point in Italian writing on women, as he purposely sought out

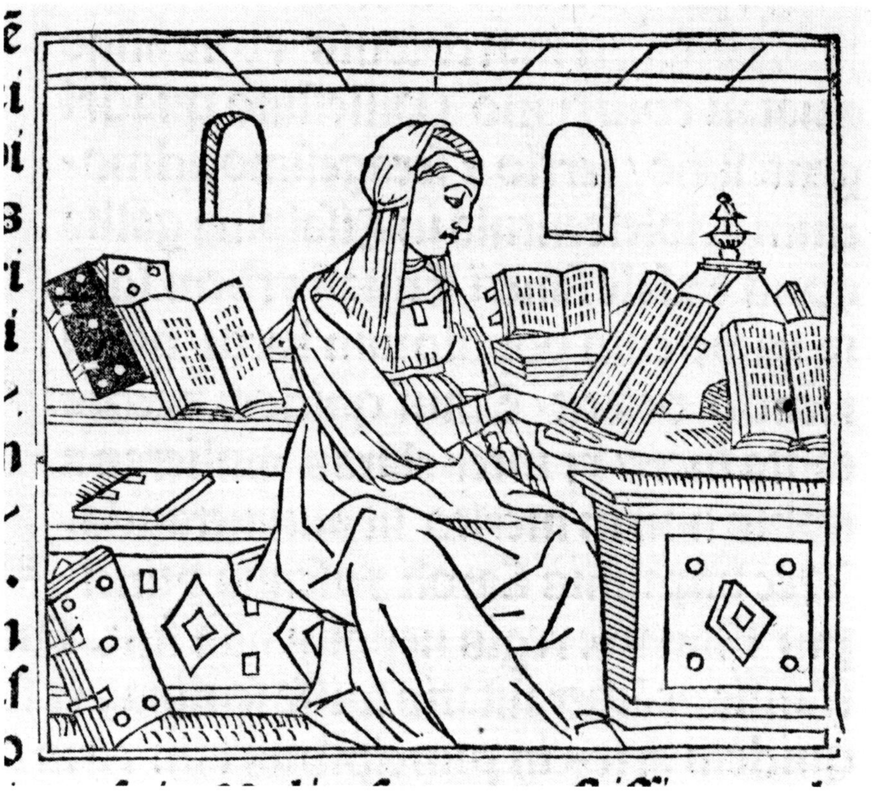

86 Woodcut from Foresti, *De plurimus claris sceletisque mulieribus*, 1497

positive role models and openly contended that women could do anything.[22] Equicola's contemporary illustrious women include Isabella herself and her friends Margarita and Cornelia Cantelmo, the latter of whom commissioned the book. In it, Isabella is presented in the most flattering way, as worthy of the ancients: "If the nature of the universe allowed, surely antiquity would wish to claim as its own the present lady Isabella d'Este, Mantua's first lady."[23] The Cantelmo sisters were women of intellect and patrons of the arts, and as part of Isabella's closest circle, they helped to add luster to her court.

Equicola presents Isabella as an example for women throughout history—past, present, and future—and indeed, Isabella's story is remembered today. However, it is hard to know the full stories of those women who did not have the power, wealth, and elite status of an Isabella d'Este or an Eleonora Gonzaga. The women in their circles, like the Cantelmo sisters, also achieved much, as writers, artists, singers, dancers, ladies in waiting, and servants, though their positions were always more precarious.

Taken together, it is striking how many literary and visual depictions of female exemplarity include violence by or against women. Such images typically revolve around women's bodies, often naked. Cleopatra and Lucretia both chose death before dishonor and committed suicide. One of the most famous prints of the Renaissance is by Marcantonio Raimondi, after the painter Raphael, and shows Lucretia, who was raped by Tarquin, who then threatened to besmirch her name if she revealed his violent act (fig. 87).[24] Though she did expose his crime, her innocence was proven, and her father, husband, and other male family members acted to avenge her, she still chose suicide. This print shows her with one breast bared about to stab herself, glorifying her extreme act of heroism. Lucretia's tragic suicide inspired her family to fight against the aggressive forces represented by Tarquin, eventually leading to the

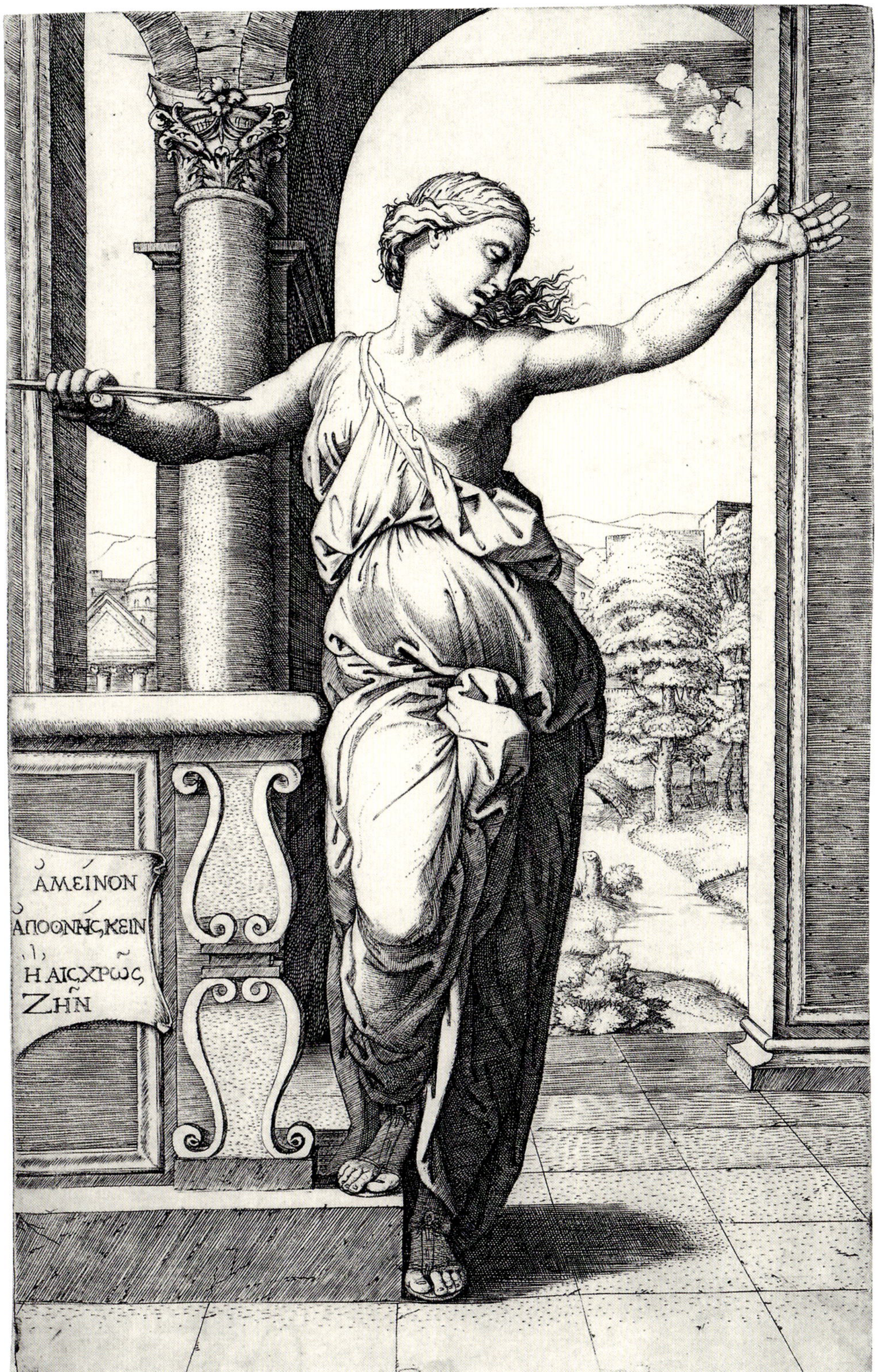

87 Marcantonio Raimondi after Raphael, *The Death of Lucretia*, about 1511–12

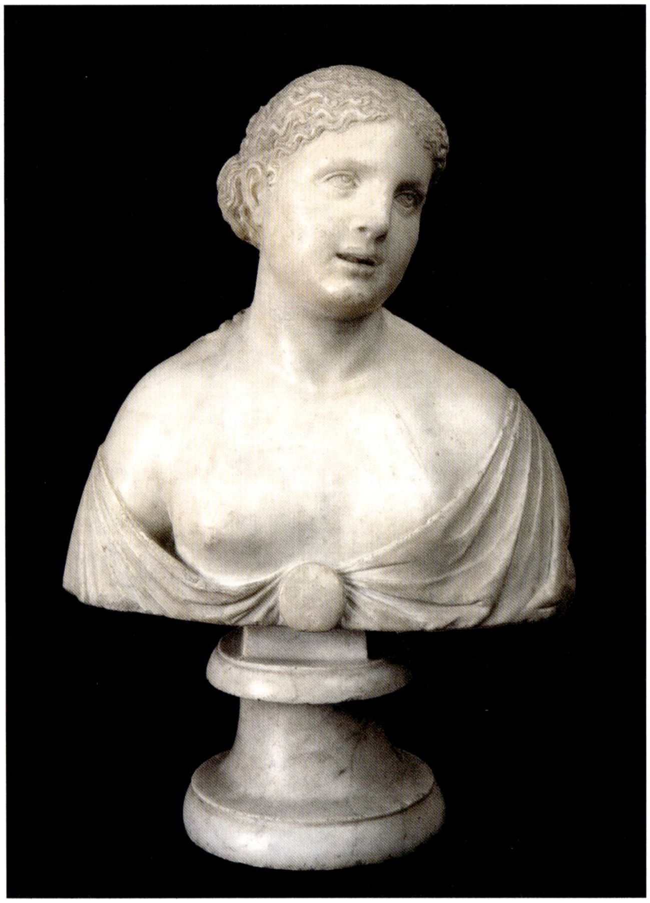

88 Antonio Minello de' Bardi, Bust of a classical heroine, early 16th century, H. 34.9 cm (13¾ in.)

establishment of the Roman Republic. A small marble bust presents an unknown woman, her hair carefully contained in a decorative headdress, her mouth open in anguish, and with her breasts mostly exposed (fig. 88). Though unidentified, she stands in for all such Renaissance heroines, and again calls out the radical nature of Antico's *Cleopatra*, powerful in thought yet chastely dressed.

The biblical figure Salome was used as a pawn by her mother to obtain revenge against Saint John the Baptist. Salome danced so beautifully for King Herod, that he promised her anything she desired, and, at her mother's behest, she requested John's head. Bernardino Luini painted the moment when Salome receives the Baptist's head on a platter (fig. 89). Unlike the triumphant and virtuous Judith holding the head of Holofernes in victory, Salome turns her head away, deep in thought at the result of her actions, perhaps realizing its meaning and her role in it.[25] Luini's *Salome*, like Antico's *Cleopatra*, presents the power of women's minds, showing her deep in thought and expressing quiet resistance in the face of violence and shame.

There are some contexts where extreme violence is used to illustrate fortitude and faith. The martyrdoms of saints, for example, involve horribly torturous deaths for men and women alike. In one print, based on a composition by Raphael, Saint Cecilia is shown suffering her execution in a cauldron of oil, with hands joined in prayer (fig. 90). The severed heads of her brothers are held up for her to see in the hope of swaying her devotion while their bodies lie scattered around. She would be considered as an exemplar of faith for all, but it must be noted that here, she stands naked at the center of a crowd of mostly male spectators.

The Sabine women were kidnapped and violated in the service of the foundation of the city of Rome. One of the most famous sculptures made in Renaissance Florence shows a nude woman being held up by one man while another man kneels nearby; she struggles to escape as fingers press deeply into her flesh. Carved in costly white marble by the court sculptor Giambologna for the Duke of Florence and set into the Loggia dei Lanzi in the central civic square, it was dubbed the "Rape of the Sabine Woman." The sculpture achieved further renown through the production and circulation of prints like a chiaroscuro woodcut (fig. 91).[26]

Despite the violence, women were frequently cast as peacemakers, and for Christine de Pizan, the Sabines were examples of this idea.[27] A large maiolica plate presents a corrective to the violent story by showing the reconciliation of the Romans and the Sabines, a peace created through the sacrifices of the Sabine women (fig. 92). The acts of violence are made to seem justified by the positive outcomes. Yet knowledge of the stories does not erase the painful aspects of seeing women tortured, raped, or presented nude for the male gaze.

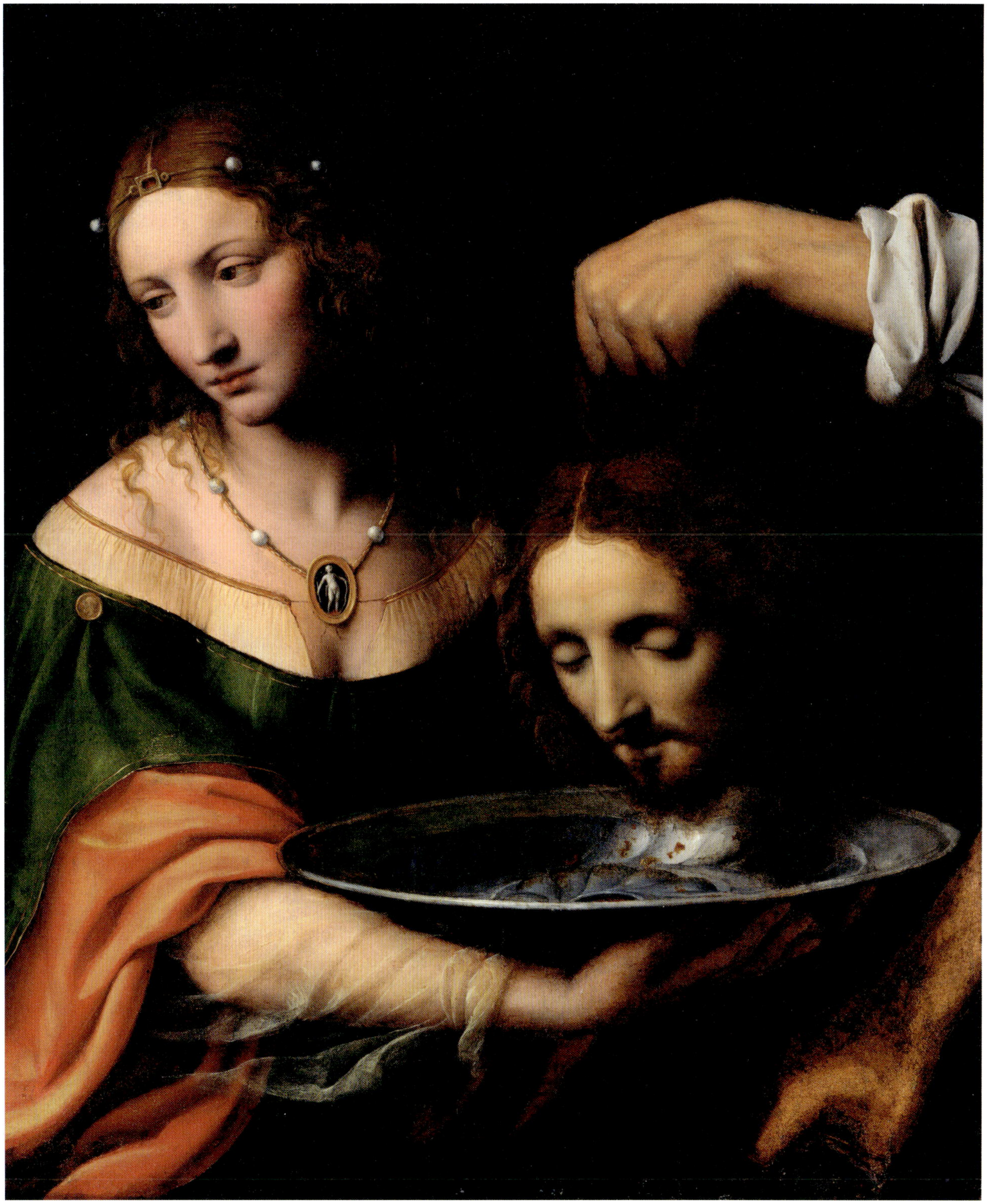

89 Bernardino Luini, *Salome with the Head of Saint John the Baptist*, 1515–25, 62.2 x 51.4 cm (24½ x 20¼ in.)

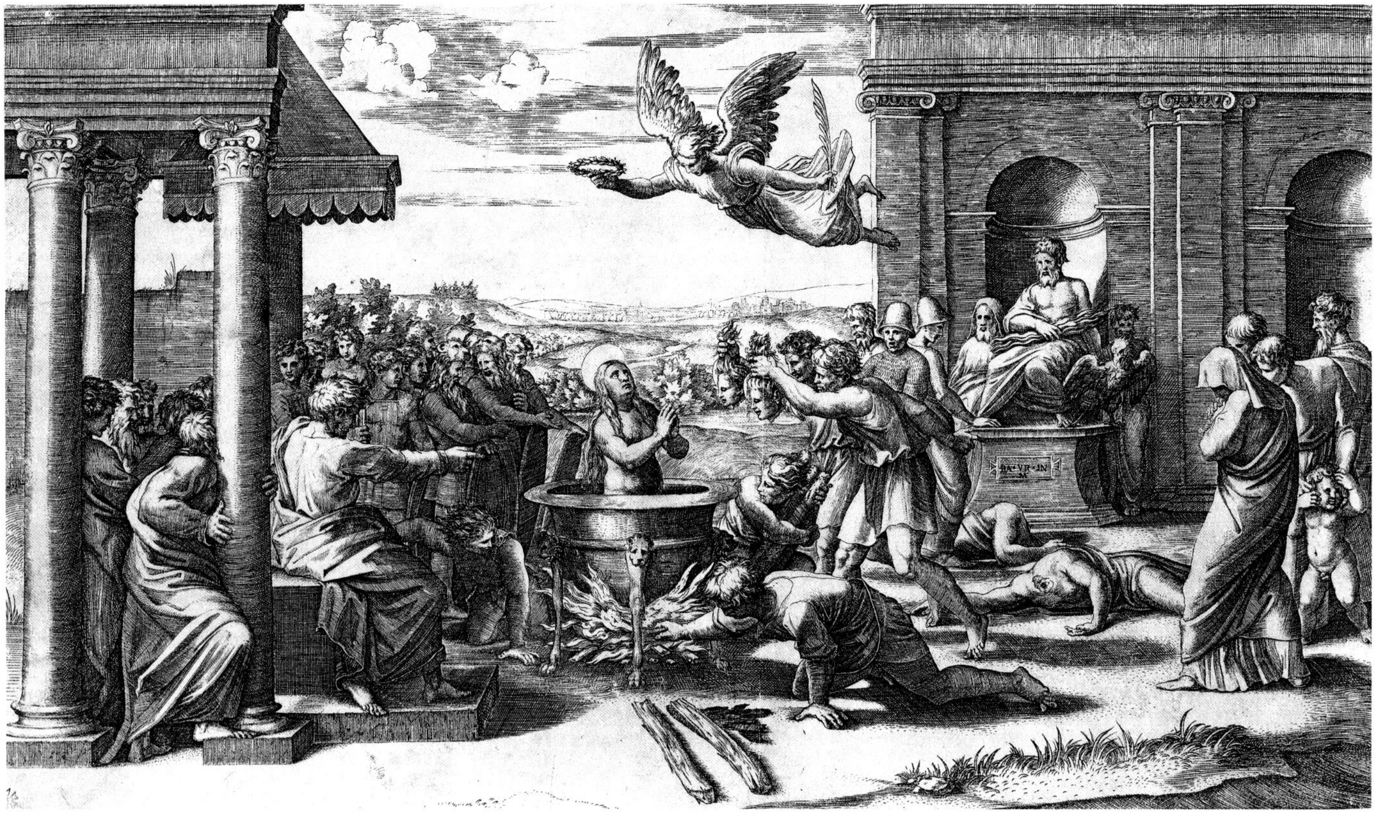

90 After Raphael, *The Martyrdom of Saint Cecilia*, early to mid-16th century

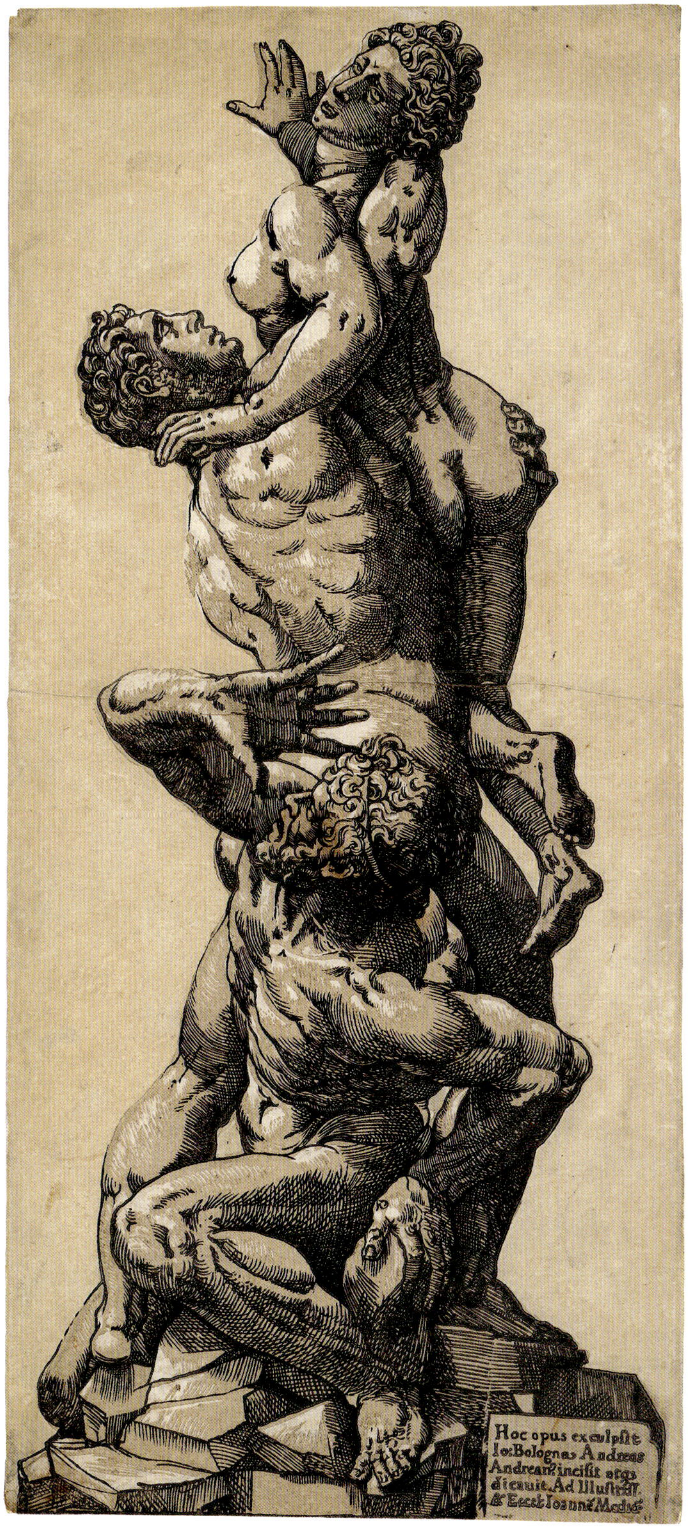

91 Andrea Andreani after Giambologna, *The Rape of a Sabine*, about 1584

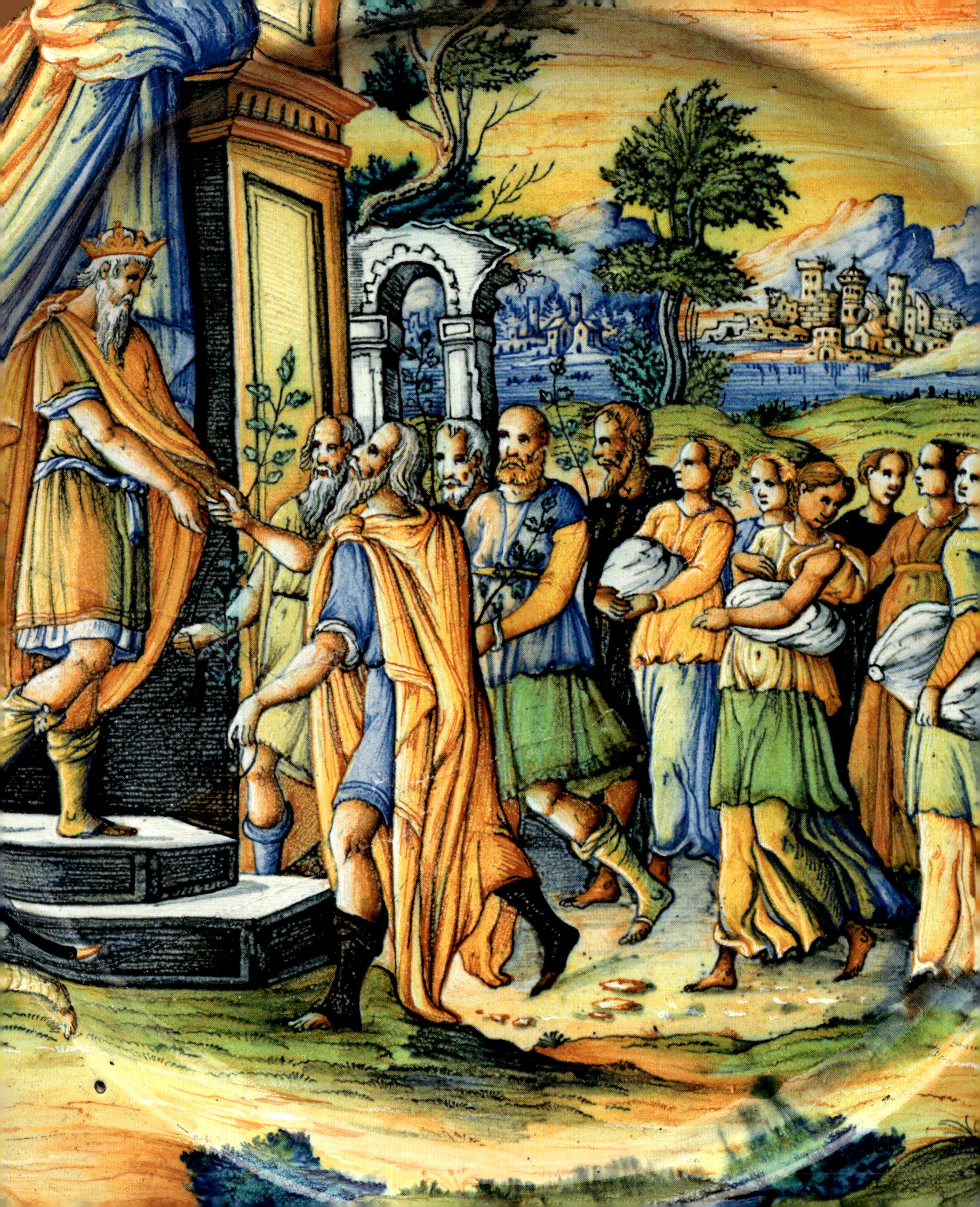

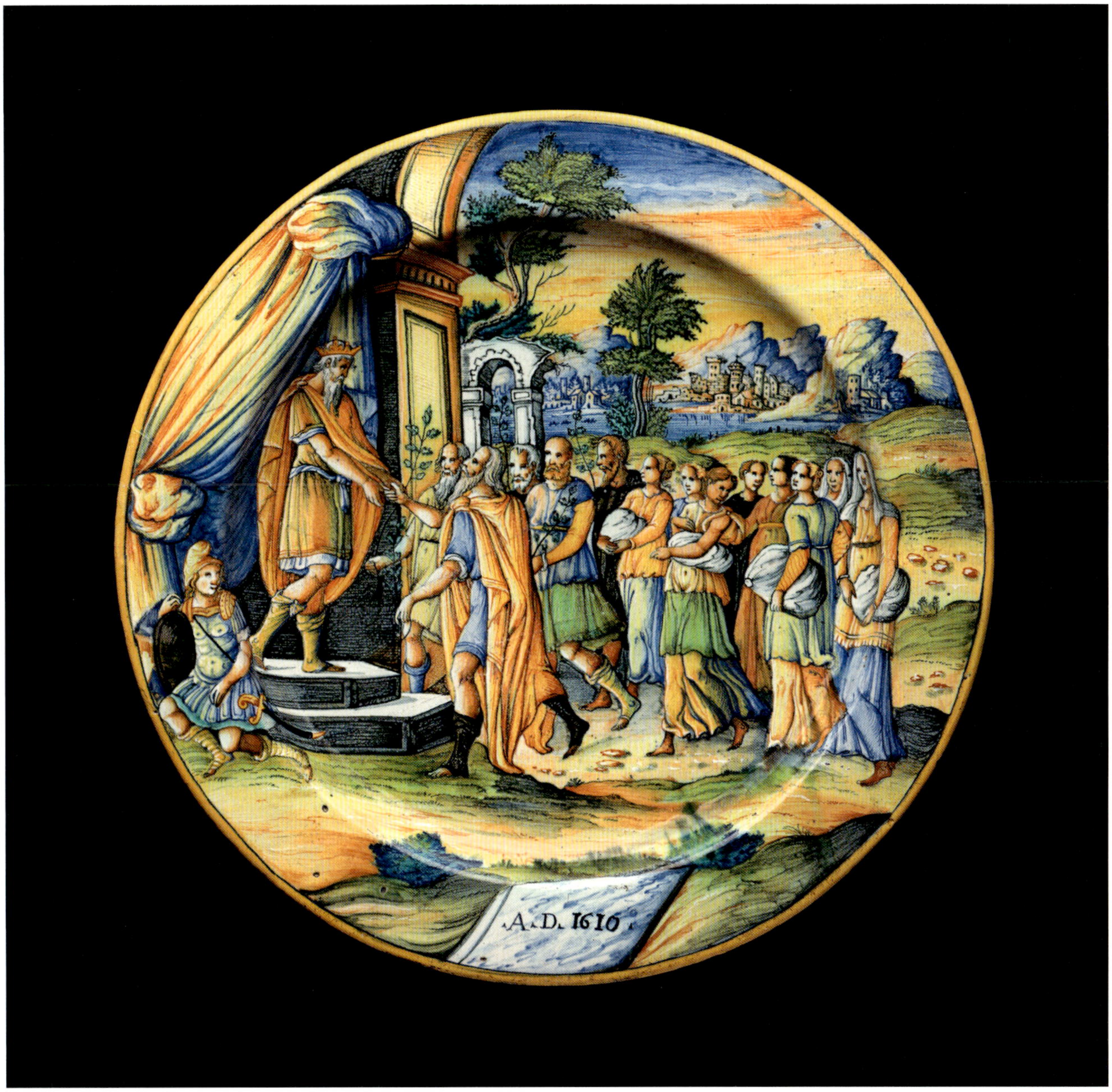

92 Alfonso Patanazzi, Plate with the reconciliation of the Romans and the Sabines, 1610, diam. 49.2 cm (19⅜ in.)

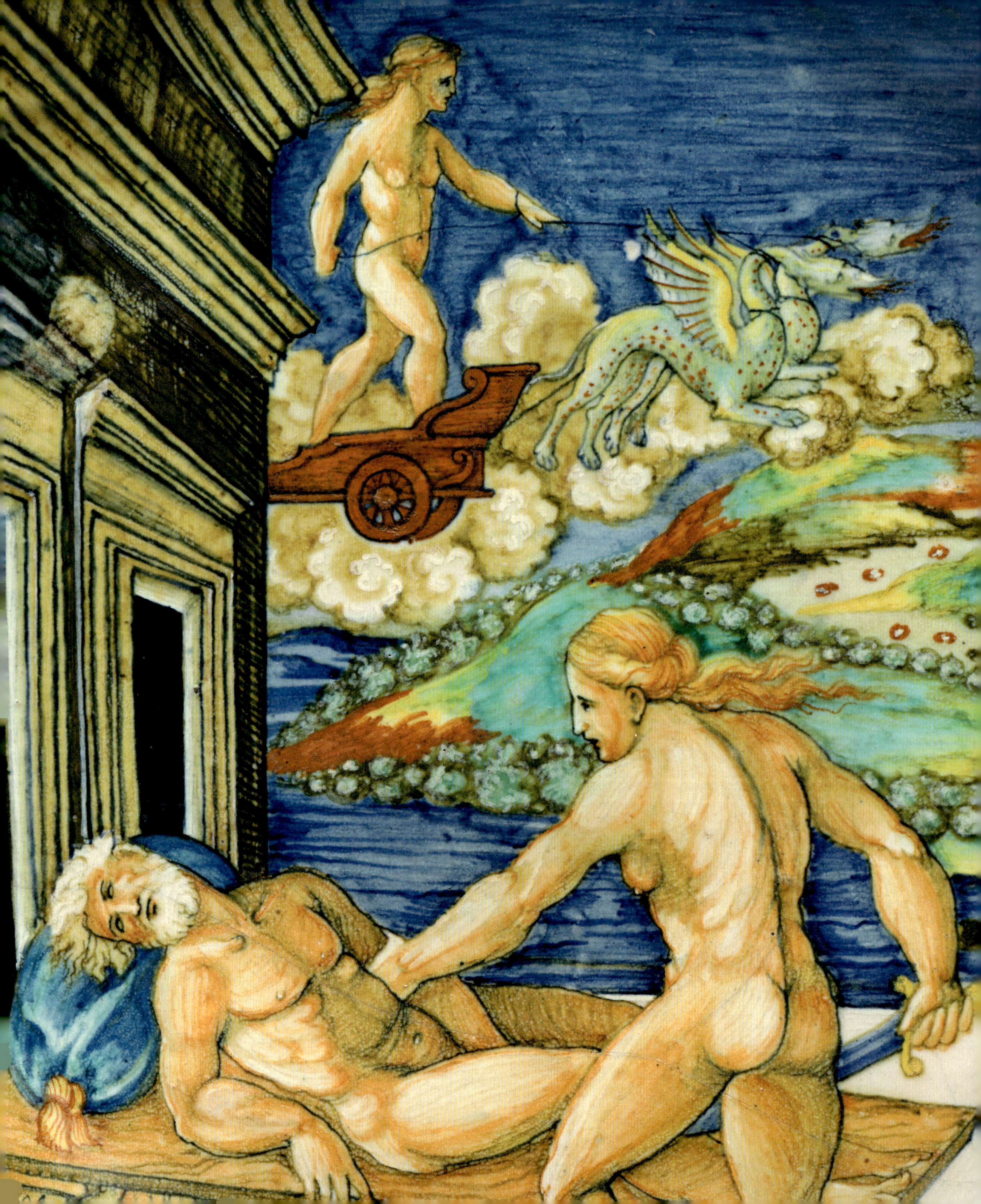

Science and Sorcery

Women in Renaissance Italy were healers in their own homes, in hospitals, and in convent settings.[1] At home, women often created remedies and treated their families for common ailments. Some kept books of secrets or recipe books for medicines and cosmetics, and a familiarity with herbs, plants, flowers, and their uses was common among Renaissance women. Isabella d'Este, for example, was known for the perfumes she created and sent to other women as gifts.[2] Women gathered and shared recipes, and could source ingredients either at apothecary shops or from their own gardens. Women were also midwives and wet-nurses, and they nursed children and patients in hospital settings. Renaissance documents reveal that nuns in convents created medicines to treat their own immediate communities but also sold these remedies through convent pharmacies, an important source of income and social interaction.[3] Nuns who were experienced as pharmacists in turn taught younger sisters these practices. The daughters and wives of apothecaries might learn the family trade and, as widows, for example, might go on to run these family businesses. Women operated mostly outside the guild structures that regulated the world of medicine and pharmacy, and so social networks and the sharing of knowledge and ideas, tested through practical application, were crucial.[4] A woman's training was typically developed through the practical application of accumulated wisdom and experiment.

Works of art provide clues to women's involvement in the world of Renaissance medicine. Maiolica drug jars, produced in a variety of shapes and decorated with colorful patterns or figural imagery, were ideal for storing medicinal ingredients. On pharmacy shelves, labels and ornaments indicated their contents to the apothecary, and their shiny, hard, and brightly colored glazed surfaces could be easily wiped down, conveying cleanliness and helping to engender trust in customers.[5] Similarly, at home, they could serve as storage pots for medicines or as vases for flowers and plants, enlivening interior spaces. The decoration on this tall maiolica drug jar known as an albarello includes knots—often featured in textile pattern books—and pearls—frequently worn by women for their associations with purity, virtue, and family wealth—both of which suggest it might have been owned or used by a woman (fig. 93). Labeled with the word for poppy, it probably contained a sleep aid. An albarello probably made in Sicily around 1600 is decorated with an image of the young John the Baptist, suggesting that it might have been made for a religious institution like a convent or owned by someone with a particular feeling of devotion to the young saint (fig. 94). Though neither of these can be definitively associated with use by women, they provide examples of jars that might have served women in the context of their homes or in convents.

Women's knowledge of the natural world and the medicinal properties of plants could also lead to suspicion. Renaissance representations of sorceresses can reveal perceptions about the power of women's knowledge while also hinting at the ambivalence that such knowledge might create. A maiolica plate depicts two scenes from Ovid's *Metamorphoses* featuring the sorceress Medea (fig. 95). In the foreground, Medea prepares to rejuvenate her father-in-law Aeson by exsanguinating him and replacing his blood with a potion that would

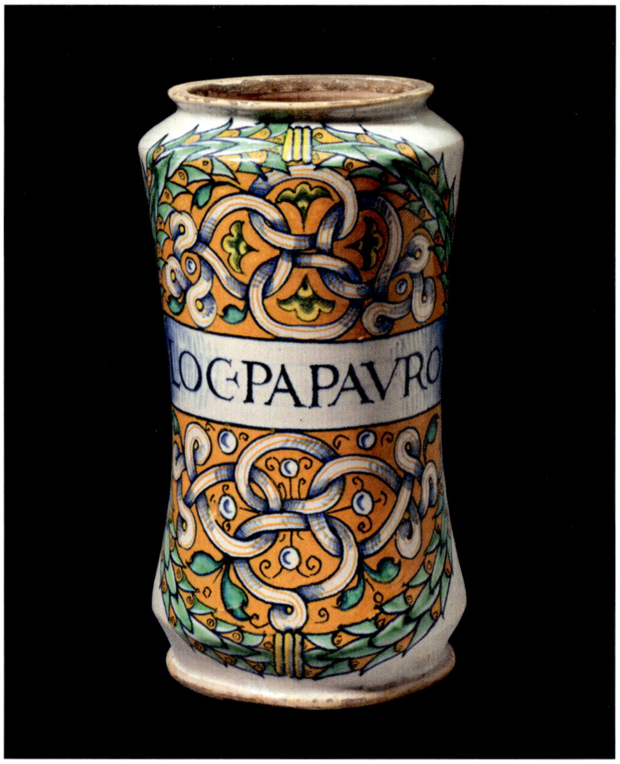

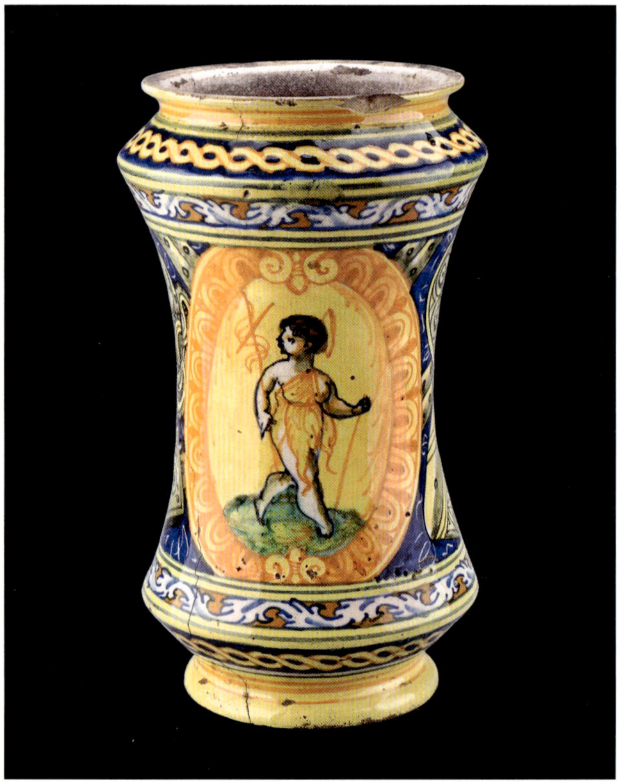

93 Albarello, early 16th century, H. 21.6 cm (8½ in.)
94 Albarello, about 1600, H. 24.5 cm (9⅝ in.)

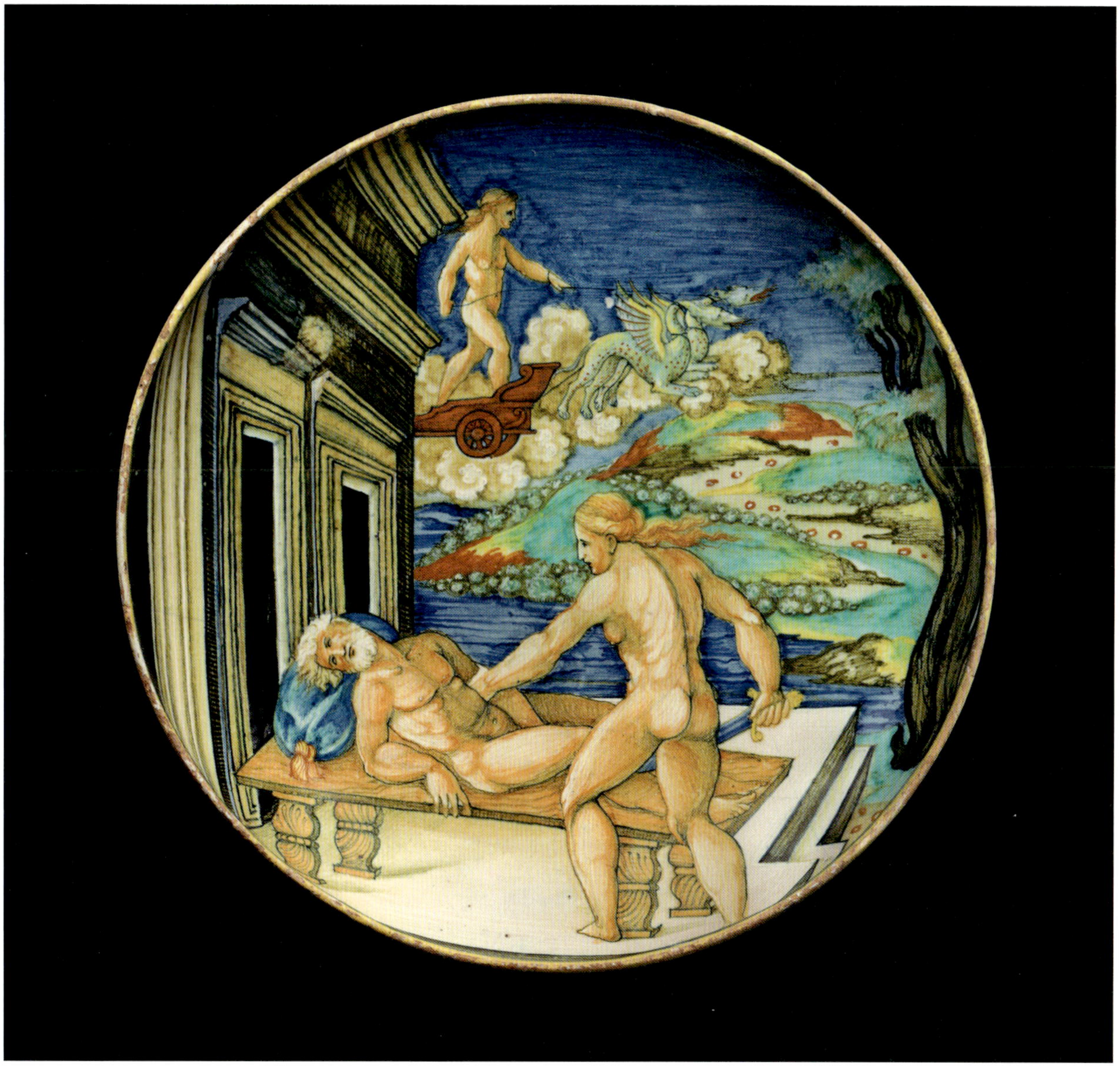

95 Plate depicting Medea and Aeson, about 1530, diam. 26 cm (10¼ in.)

grant him forty more years of life. With a sword in her right hand, she turns away from the viewer, showing her muscular back and preparing to take action. Her left hand grasps Aeson's left arm as he lies on a wooden bench. His head rests on a soft blue pillow with golden tassels and, with eyes open, he turns his head to expose his neck. He braces himself for the terrifying action to follow with his legs crossed and his right hand gripping the bench. Medea anchors herself in a wide stance and focuses her gaze on Aeson. Her long golden-red hair, though tied back, flies out behind her, suggesting quick, decisive movement. The action is set as if on a stage, with stairs on the right leading up to the platform. Above this scene, Medea appears again, standing in a flying chariot drawn by winged dragons. Here too, she is completely naked. She flies amid the clouds and over a landmass complete with hills, a seashore, and the suggestion of a pathway curving off into the distance. According to Ovid, Medea spent nine days and nights searching for the plants, roots, herbs, flowers, and other ingredients needed for her potion; the depiction of Medea, a powerful woman taking flight, at the top of the plate represents this journey and reveals her tenacity as well as her knowledge of the natural world.[6]

Medea was one of the most complex women in ancient Greek mythology.[7] She was the daughter of King Aeëtes of Colchis, the niece of the famous sorceress Circe, and the granddaughter of the sun god Helios. She is best known for the horrific acts she committed, especially the murder of her two sons, an act of vengeance after Jason's betrayal and rejection. Yet here she is shown as a powerful heroine, using her courage and knowledge to grant Jason his request that she restore youth to his elderly father. This plate celebrates Medea's knowledge of the human body and potion making. Her confidence in her actions is demonstrated by her nude figure and her focused attention. The trust Aeson shows in her abilities speaks to her standing in their family.

The heroic presentation of Medea's nude body displays a sort of unnaturalness that may have colored the Renaissance viewer's perception of her powerful actions. Her figure seems more like that of a man than of a woman. This is a typical way of characterizing female power: a strong woman must take on masculine characteristics, making her less of a woman and more of an exceptional virago, or warrior.[8] The physical power evident in her nude body might have unnerved a Renaissance viewer, male or female. It may also have delighted those same viewers. Medea's story was usually understood for its supreme tragedy, but these episodes could bring insight into the complexity of her character. In both scenes, her body is strong and muscular; she is presented in powerful stances, acting with great strength of body, mind, and spirit. Her flight in search of ingredients stresses her wisdom and knowledge, as well as her powerful control over the dragons. This scene stands in contrast to frequent imagery that represented Medea fleeing in that same chariot after she had exacted her vengeance on Jason by killing their children as well as his new bride. Here, the depictions of Medea stress what she did to help Jason and his father, using her powers and wisdom for their benefit. The viewer is asked to reexamine Medea's story before condemning her later actions.

This maiolica plate does not have an identifying coat of arms or an inscription on the back. Masterfully painted, it is attributed to an important though as yet unidentified artist, the Painter of the Apollo Basin, and probably dates to around 1530. Its subject matter suggests an elite setting where it might have served several purposes. Maiolica painting was one of the principal means for depicting stories from ancient history and mythology in a vivid and tactile way. Often based on prints that illustrated such books as the *Metamorphoses*, historiated maiolica plates brought these stories out of the study and into the more social realm of the Renaissance court or wealthy home. These types of plates were used at the table for special occasions or displayed when not in use, and no doubt they sparked conversation, perhaps even game playing.[9]

It is impossible to know what discussions might have developed around this particular plate. Who at the table knew their Ovid well enough to recognize this scene, rarely represented in art? Perhaps the women at the table called attention to the visceral power shown in Medea's body or traded jokes about their own potions

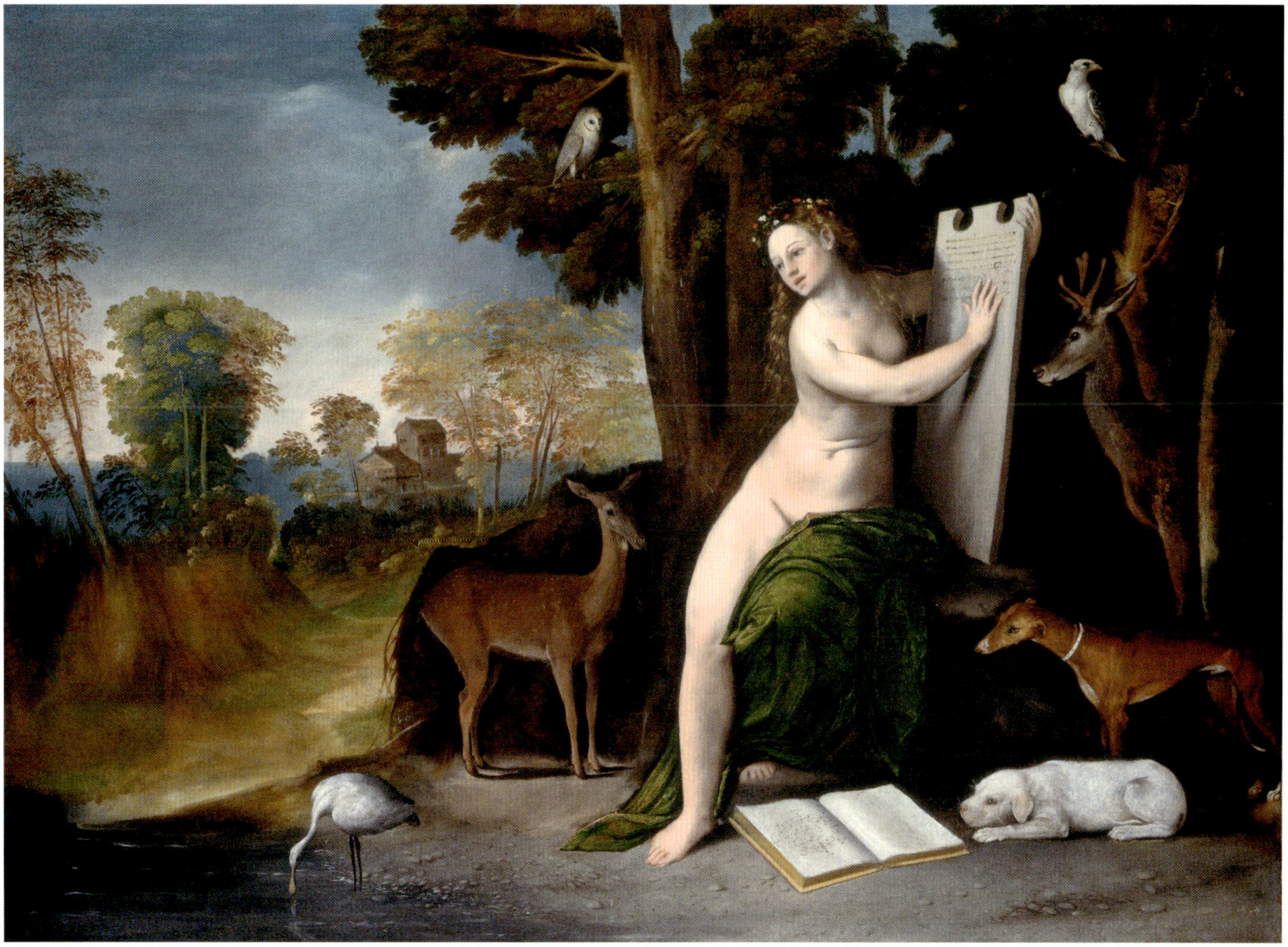

96 Dosso Dossi, *Circe and Her Lovers in a Landscape*, about 1525, 100.8 x 136.1 cm (39⅝ x 53⅝ in.)

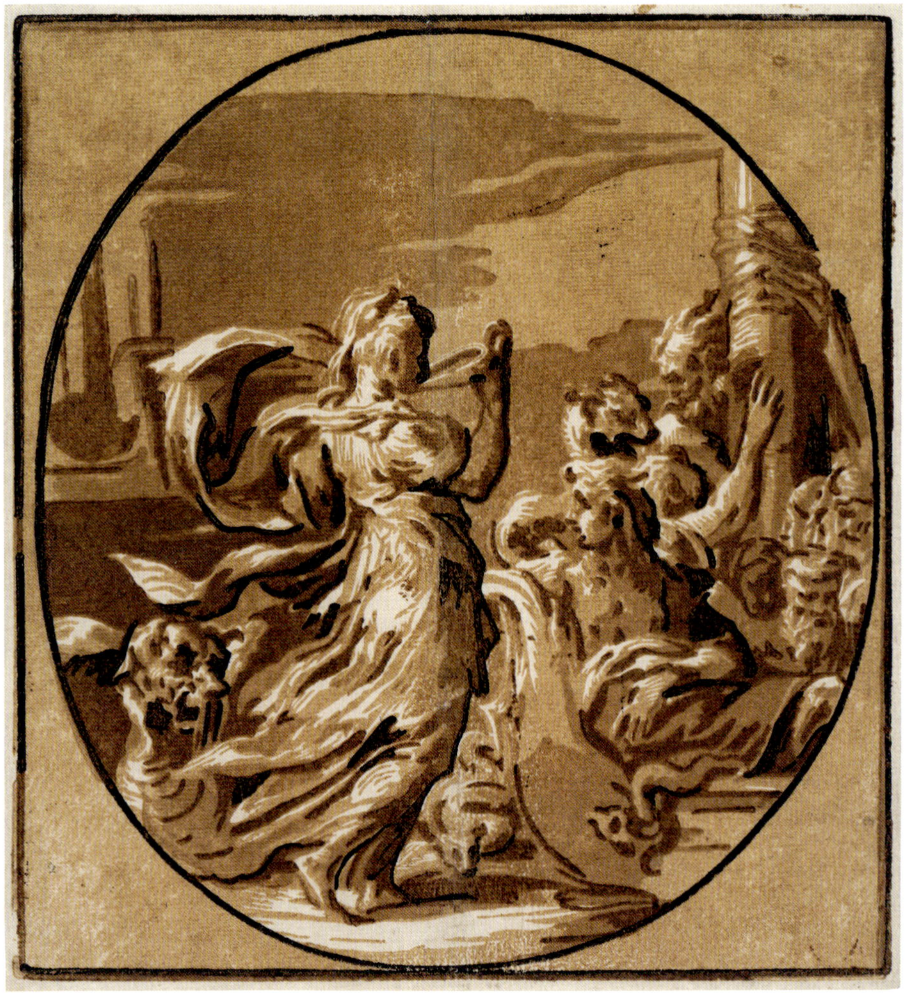

97 Antonio da Trento after Parmigianino, *Circella Drinking with the Companions of Ulysses*, mid-16th century

for youth and longer life. Italian noblewoman, regent, and alchemist Caterina Sforza, famous for her book of secrets and scientific knowledge, for example, had at least one such potion in her compendium. Perhaps the conversation turned toward Medea's violent acts of revenge, her masculine physique seen as an indication that she was an "unnatural" woman. Did the discussion reveal the suspicions and anxieties that a woman's power might prompt in a social environment where women's lives were carefully controlled? Would someone have called the conversation back to the fine quality of the painting or the literary source for the scenes? And might the women at the table, when they retired to their own studies, have taken out a copy of Ovid to learn a bit more about this sorceress Medea and consider her own role as healer or maker of cosmetics in a different, more powerful way?

Medea was the niece of the famous sorceress Circe, who was frequently represented in Renaissance art and literature.[10] Because Circe's island kingdom was thought to be set along the western coast of Italy, she was the sorceress most associated with the region. Circe's story originally comes from Homer's *Odyssey*. Daughter of Helios and the water nymph Perse, she lived alone on the island of Aeaea and was visited by Odysseus and his men. Circe initially enchanted the

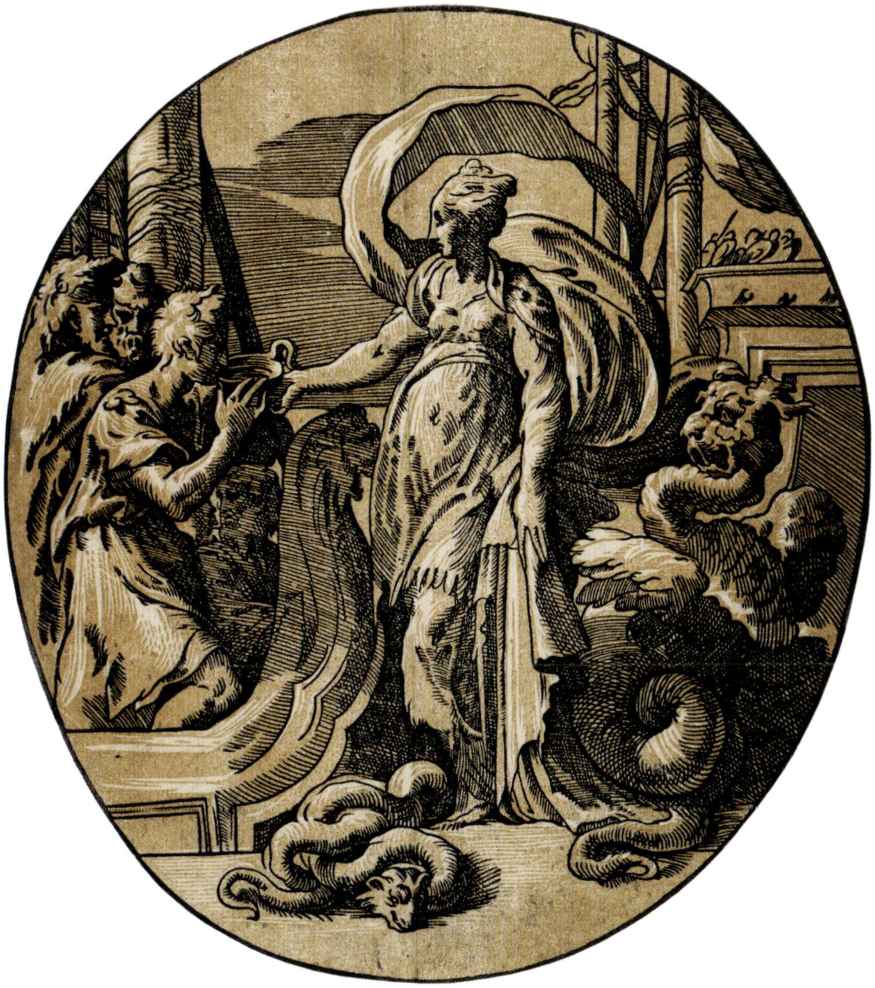

98 Antonio da Trento after Parmigianino, *Circella Giving Drink to the Companions of Ulysses*, mid-16th century

men, giving them a potion to turn them into swine, until a warning came from the god Mercury. Given the god's threat, she reversed her spell, and ultimately Odysseus and his crew enjoyed themselves on Circe's island for a year, with Circe giving birth to Odysseus's son. Around 1518, Ferrarese painter Dosso Dossi depicted Circe seated in a peaceful, bucolic setting, surrounded by her animal companions (fig. 96).[11] She holds a large tablet while an open book showing a pentagram rests at her feet; these are her spells and secrets, though they are illegible here. Renaissance viewers would see beyond the peaceful scene depicted and assume all of the animals were victims of Circe's spell, and would perhaps search their expressions for anthropomorphic qualities.

Circe's story held mysteries that engaged people in this period. Her magical ability to harness the transformative power of nature and to blur the boundary between human and animal touched on themes that fascinated scholars and philosophers during the Renaissance.[12] Writers in the sixteenth century explored the qualities shared by humans and animals, including Niccolò Machiavelli, who compared men to lions and foxes in his political treatise *Il Principe* (The Prince). Florentine writer Giovanni Battista Gelli considered the ambiguities that such imaginative transformations might result in. In his *La Circe*, Odysseus interviews the

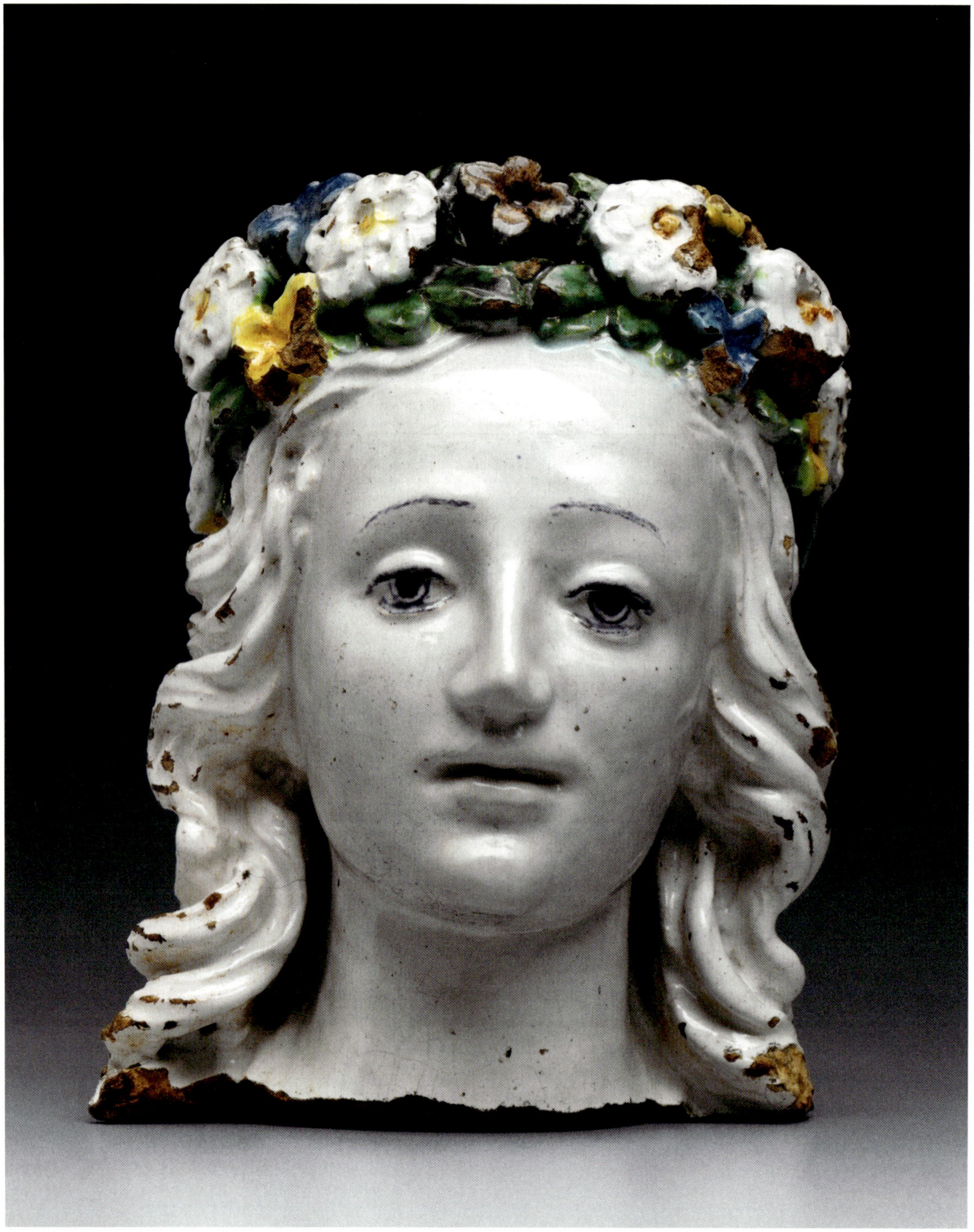

99 Giovanni della Robbia, *Flora*, about 1500, H. 17.5 cm (6⅞ in.)

animals Circe has transformed, and all but one tells him they would rather remain animals, since men were generally so unhappy.[13] Such ideas led to discussions about what these imagined transformations might tell people about their own nature.

Two woodcuts after Parmigianino have sometimes been thought by scholars to represent Circe as a beautiful woman offering a drink to Odysseus's men (figs. 97, 98).[14] In both prints she is shown with her flowing garments swirling around her. In one, she holds an elegantly shaped vase out to a man; in the other, she herself drinks in an effort to convince her companions that the contents are safe. Fooled by the sorceress, the men are turned into snakes and gryphons. Parmigianino's enchantress displays the lightness and grace that defined beauty in this period, but here beauty masks treachery.[15] It is likely that these two prints illustrate a fifteenth-century poem by Matteo Maria Boiardo, *Orlando Innamorato* (Orlando in love), which tells the story of the sorceress Circella, a character inspired by Circe. Boiardo describes frescoes that decorate a loggia, with scenes of Circella turning men into creatures including snakes and hybrid beasts as here and drinking of her own potion, episodes that do not occur in Circe's story. So, here Parmigianino works from these descriptions of paintings in a poem to create seductively beautiful images. In the poem, these episodes were supposed to warn Orlando and his men not to drink.

In the late sixteenth century, Moderata Fonte presented her own rethinking of a powerful sorceress's story from a woman's point of view.[16] In her epic romance *Floridoro*, she invents the character of Circetta, the daughter of Circe and Ulysses and a benevolent sorceress, with lessons to teach. Circetta is a chaste sorceress who turns unworthy men into trees rather than beasts. She leads readers to reconsider her mother's actions in a more favorable light: "And be silent, you who say unjustly / that she transformed his companions into beasts, / for she never, if not forced,/ caused displeasure to whoever turned to offend her."[17] By presenting Circe through her daughter's eyes, Fonte emphasized the good that women healers and sages could do and headed off criticism of women's arcane

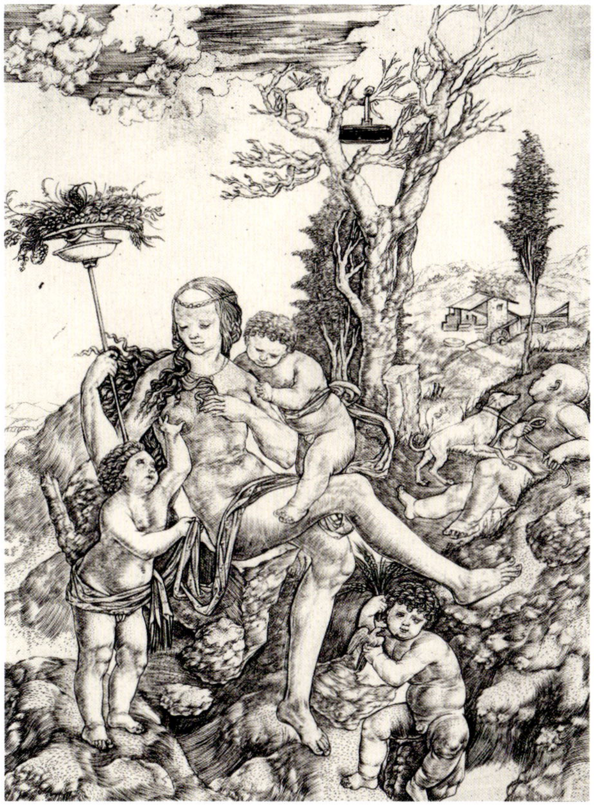

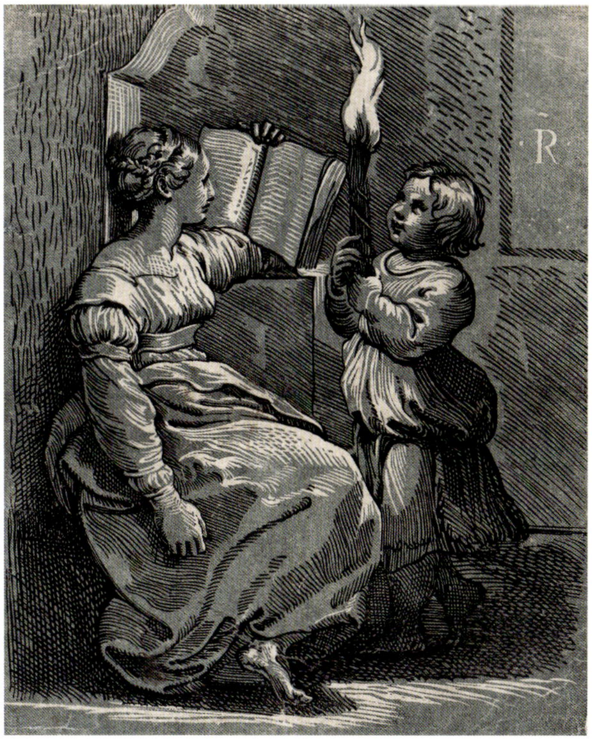

100 Il Robetta, *Allegory of Abundance*, about 1510–1520
101 Ugo da Carpi, *Sibyl Reading*, early 16th century

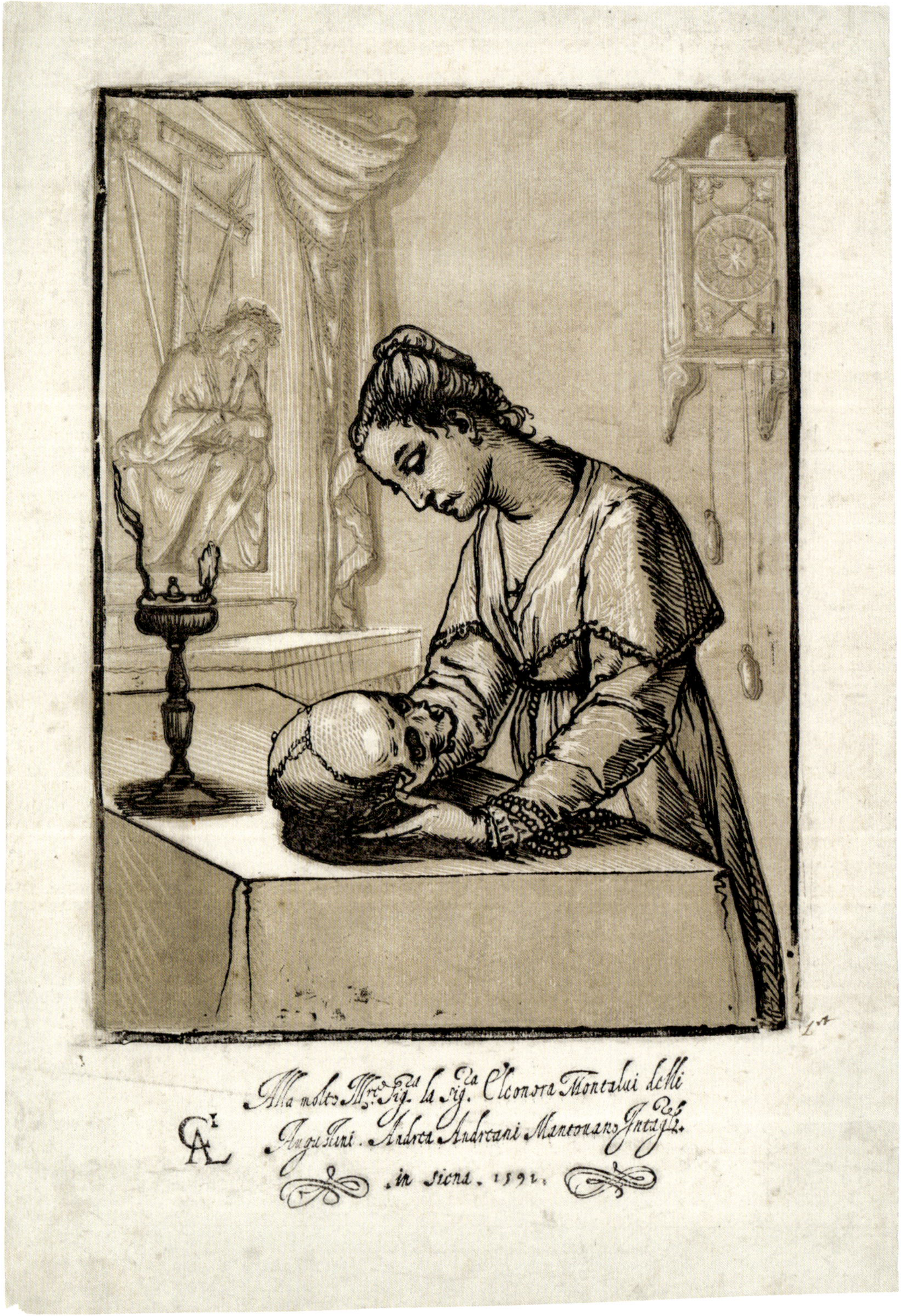

102 Andrea Andreani, *Woman Contemplating a Skull*, 1591

knowledge, all part of her general call for women's education and a recognition of women's superior intellectual abilities.

Women in Renaissance Italy who were thought to have magical powers were sought out for potions and spells, and provided care and healing remedies on a private basis.[18] These women often lived precarious lives, quietly practicing their skills for payment or support. They are often recorded in documents only when things go wrong and their remedies fail, resulting in charges of witchcraft brought against them. With such accusations, a woman's healing powers were interpreted as part of the frightening world of sacrilege and the occult, which had to be controlled through justice and severe punishment.

Women in this period were also more generally associated with nature itself.[19] Allegories of nature, spring, and abundance, and depictions of the goddesses Flora and Ceres, all find their way into Renaissance imagery. *Natura*, *Primavera*, and *Dovizia* are all feminine nouns in Italian and are visually represented as women. Giovanni della Robbia's sculpture of the head of a woman with a wreath of flowers in her hair is a fragment that was once part of a larger statuette and may be an image of Flora, the goddess of spring (fig. 99). In the home, such an image would have evoked a sense of verdant renewal with the benevolent female goddess overseeing the household's well-being.[20] Il Robetta's print of a nude woman seated in the countryside surrounded by children is an allegory of abundance (fig. 100). Unlike the rocky landscape around her, this woman projects an image of plenty. She is a vivid embodiment of the link between the nurturing female body and the regenerative aspects of nature. Through the gestation and birth of children, women's bodies held the power to effect transformation. The female body contained mysteries that were linked to the mysteries of nature.

Female education was still a contested topic in Renaissance Italy. While some advocated for the education of women and numerous areas of study were opening up to women, this was still generally the exception. From imaginary sorceresses to home healers, the divisions between magic and science were still being drawn. Women found themselves at the nexus between these two realms, and the education of women was at the heart of this issue. A woman shown reading deep into the night, for example, is labeled a Sibyl or seer, a role model for female intuition and wisdom (fig. 101).[21] Her book is illuminated not by candlelight but by a flaming torch held by a little boy, becoming almost an allegory of enlightenment. This image might also quietly assert the value of allowing women to develop their intellect. A print of a woman in her study, examining a skull, also could suggest the importance of female education (fig. 102). She works by the light of a lamp and is overseen by a devotional image of Christ on one wall and a clock on the other. Clock and skull point to the idea of a memento mori, which admonishes viewers to remember their mortality and the passage of time. Is this a vanitas image, reminding the young woman holding the skull that she too will age and die? Is it a representation meant to remind the viewer of a repentant saint like Mary Magdalen, often shown with a skull? Or could she be an artist studying anatomy? Or a writer contemplating mortality by the light of the oil lamp on her table? The print was dedicated to Eleonora Montalvi, wife of Ippolito Agostini, a leading citizen of Siena in the 1590s. It presents a complex subject that defies easy identification and reveals the complexities of women's intellectual and spiritual lives.

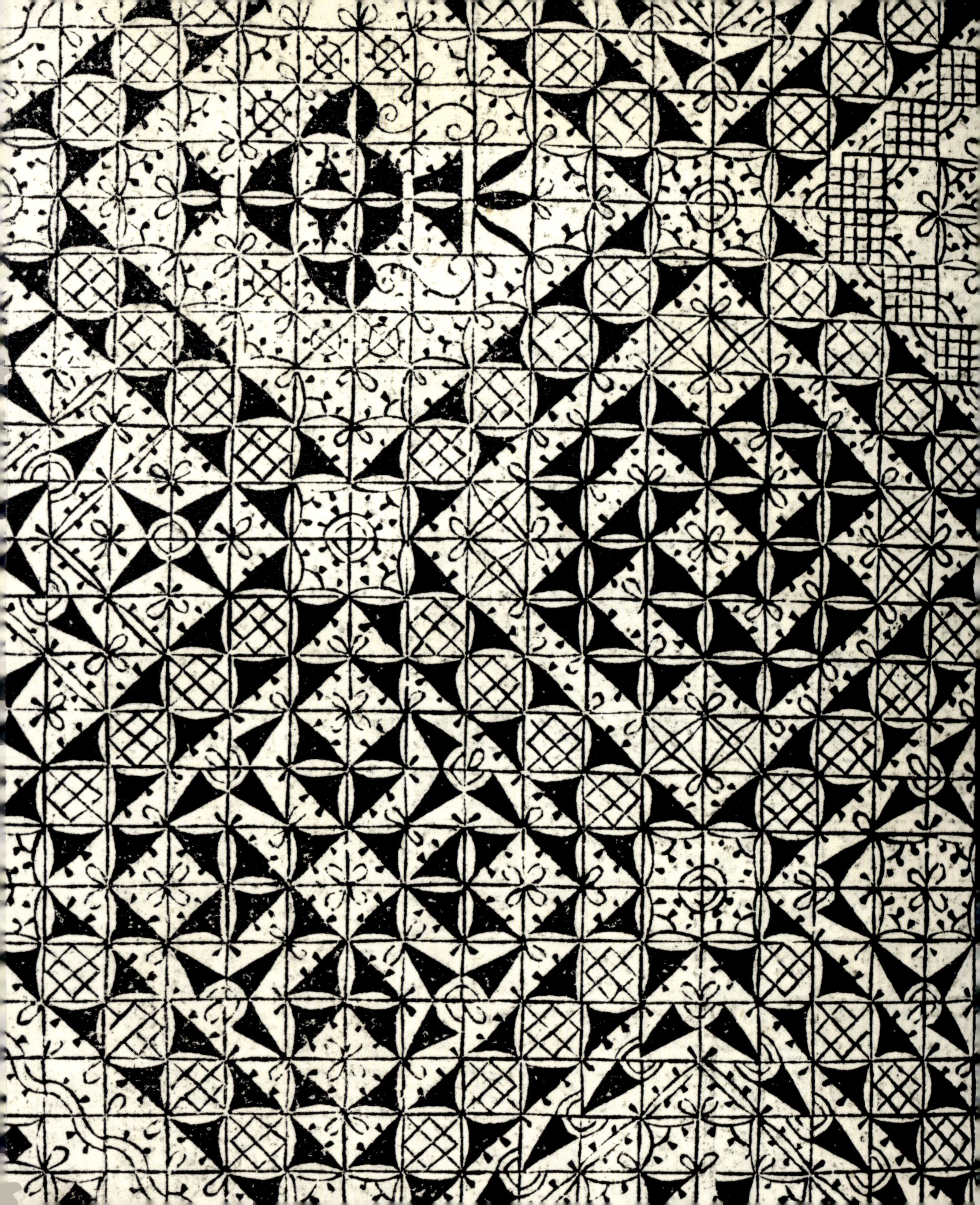

Hands and Minds

Women in Renaissance Italy were deeply engaged as makers and users of textiles, and their handwork demonstrated creativity, skill, and industriousness.[1] Women often learned to make lace and embroidery as part of their education, in order to furnish their homes and, in certain environments like convents, as a business that helped bring fame and income to their communities. Textile making was also associated with ideas about virtue and the control imposed upon women, encapsulated in notions that women should use their hands and not their minds, and employ the needles and pins of textile work rather than the pens and ink of intellectual endeavor.[2] In ancient poetry and myth, women who engaged in the needle arts were presented as models of virtue. For example, Penelope, the wife of Ulysses, was famous for her loyalty and devotion to her husband, expressed through her weaving. She held off suitors who assumed her husband was dead by weaving a shroud for her father-in-law, promising to consider their overtures only once it was finished. Every day, she worked at her loom, and every night she undid her work. In Renaissance Italy, where her story was known from works by Homer, Ovid,

Boccaccio, and Christine de Pizan, among others, Penelope became a paragon of the virtue of chastity. Various interpretations of the story at the time show that women's work raised complex questions. Penelope would be praised for her ingenuity in using her textile production as a shield against unwanted suitors and denigrated for performing useless work, since she toiled at her loom but ultimately produced nothing. Primarily, however, she was held up as an exemplary wife, chaste and loyal.[3]

Lace-pattern books, which became popular in Italy in the middle of the sixteenth century, espoused models of behavior for women, especially through the books' titles, while providing guidance for the creation of lace.[4] These books also illustrate how Renaissance women were able to stretch boundaries for their work and for themselves. For their Renaissance audience, usually female, pattern books provided ideas for lacework and circulated knowledge of popular motifs and types of lace. They served a practical function, which may explain why they do not survive in greater numbers. Individual woodcuts may have been pulled out for use or pricked to make copies. The woodcuts have a powerful graphic impact that their original owners surely appreciated and, for modern viewers, they provide insight into the meanings and appeal of ornament

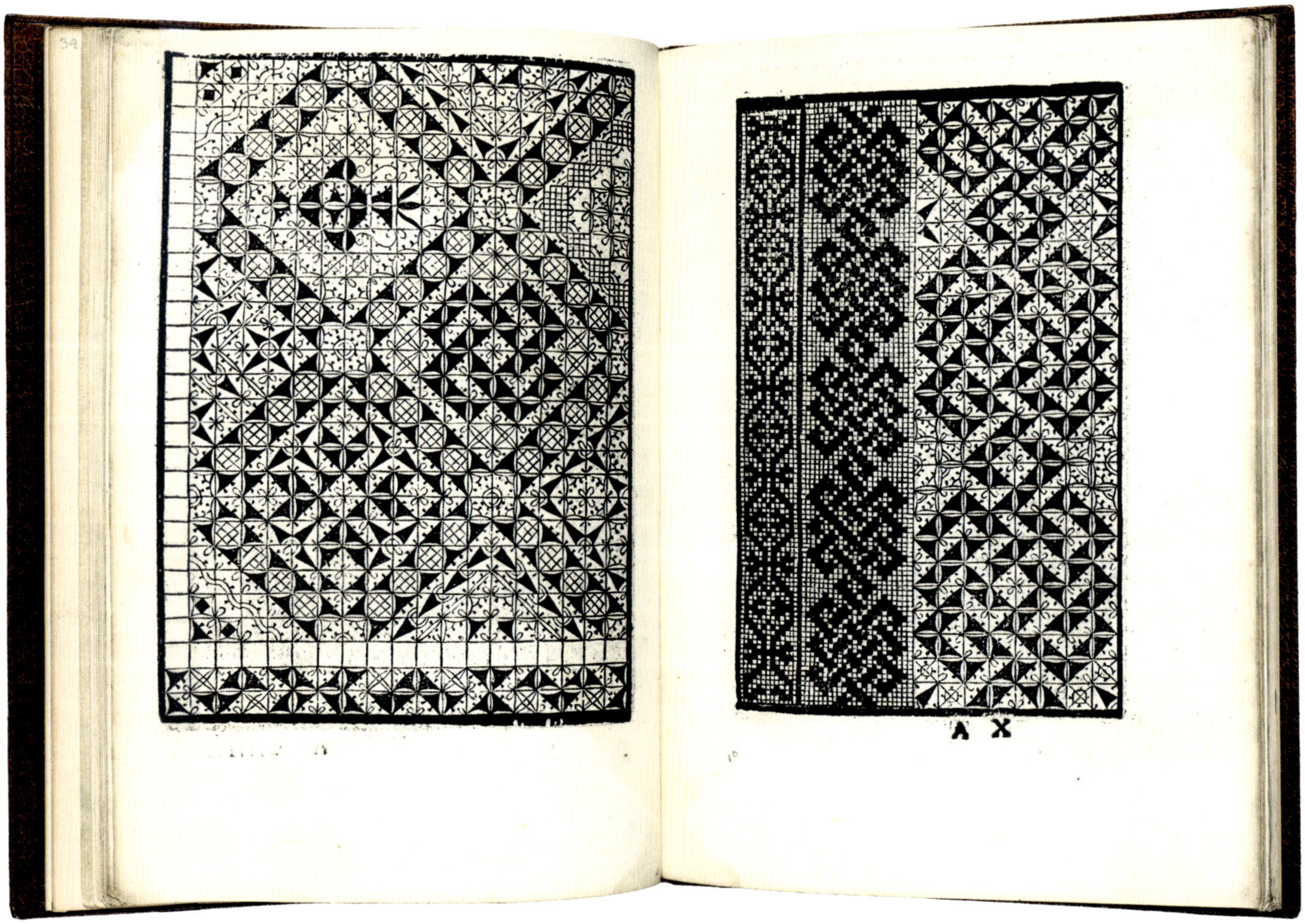

103 Domenico da Sera, *Ornamento de le belle e virtudiose donne*, Venice, 1543

in the Renaissance. The compiler of each volume, usually a man, created new patterns but also chose among known motifs that had international reach, so that the production of the books took on an aspect of broad intellectual pursuit that reflected well on both owner and author. The books generally included a frontispiece and a dedicatory page, sometimes including minimal text on the pages of the designs themselves, naming the types of lacework that were illustrated. The woodcuts would have encouraged those looking at them to identify and select favorites, respond with curiosity and delight, and perhaps inspire their own inventions as well. This period of contemplation and exploration of the user's preferences would proceed or replace the actual work. Sometimes the volumes included pictorial woodcuts offering aphorisms on how lace making could instill or describe virtue in women, possibly intended to inject humor or irony into the book.

One of the earlier Italian lace-pattern books, dating to the middle of the sixteenth century, is *Ornamento de le belle e virtudiose donne* (Ornament of Beautiful and Virtuous Women) of 1543. Compiled by Domenico da Sera and printed by Matteo Pagano in Venice, it has forty-five woodcuts (fig. 103). Its frontispiece features a decorative framework that includes male figures, satyr masks, winged putti holding lengths of drapery, and a kneeling woman holding up a cup set between palms and flowering plants at the top of the page (fig. 104). In an inset scene at the bottom, six women are shown engaged in the production of textiles. The setting is probably an elite home that opens to a wide landscape. At left, a seated woman holds her embroidery or lace on a pillow on her lap, and with her left hand she uses dividers to help measure from a pattern held by another woman. Working with an instrument also employed by architects and sculptors, this practitioner uses both her hands and her mind. At right, a woman is seated at a loom, with two women looking on, one carrying a basket of goods. By the time of this book's publication, the craft of weaving was becoming more regulated by guilds, meaning that much of the work was being done by professional male weavers.[5] However, this image indicates that weaving, like other textile crafts, was often

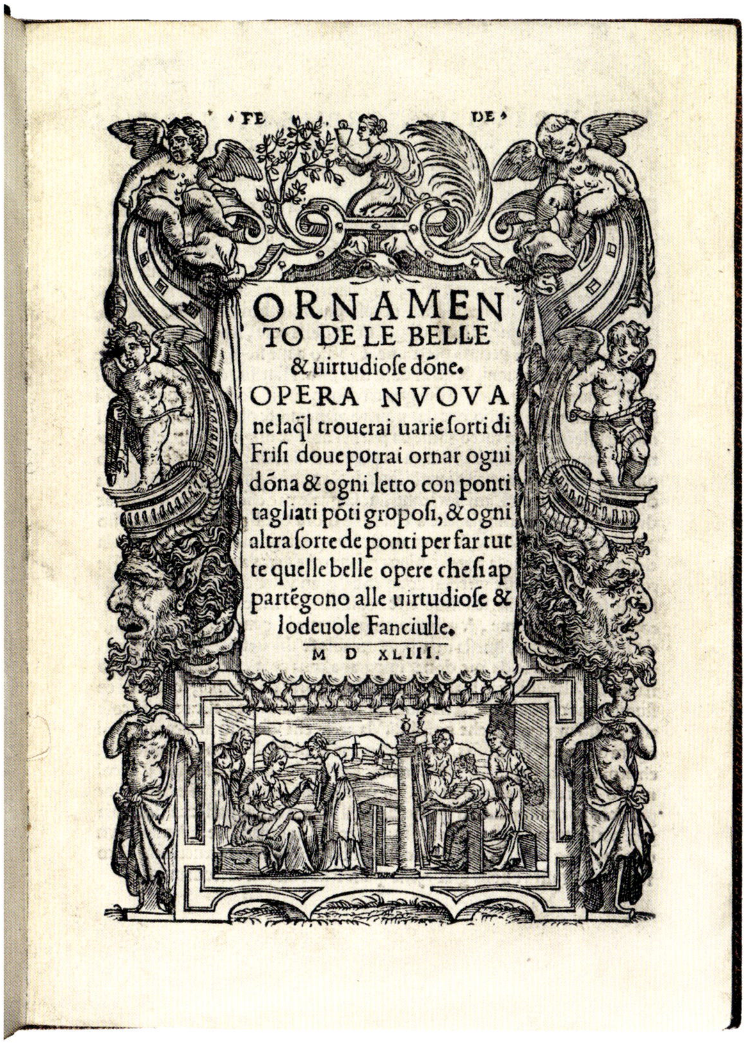
FE DE
ORNAMEN
TO DE LE BELLE
& uirtudiose dōne.
OPERA NVOVA
ne laq̄l trouerai uarie sorti di
Frisi doue potrai ornar ogni
dōna & ogni letto con ponti
tagliati pōti groposi, & ogni
altra sorte de ponti per far tut
te quelle belle opere che si ap
partēgono alle uirtudiose &
lodeuole Fanciulle.
M D XLIII.

104 Frontispiece for Da Sera, *Ornamento de le belle e virtudiose donne*, 1543

practiced in the home, where many women produced their textiles. The women who help or observe in this scene are more simply dressed: they may be servants or elders, passing on their own accumulated knowledge.[6] The two scenes show how women worked together, creating networks across age and class boundaries in the home. The text framed above reveals the goal of the book:

> A new work in which you will find various types of *frisi* [friezes] by which you can

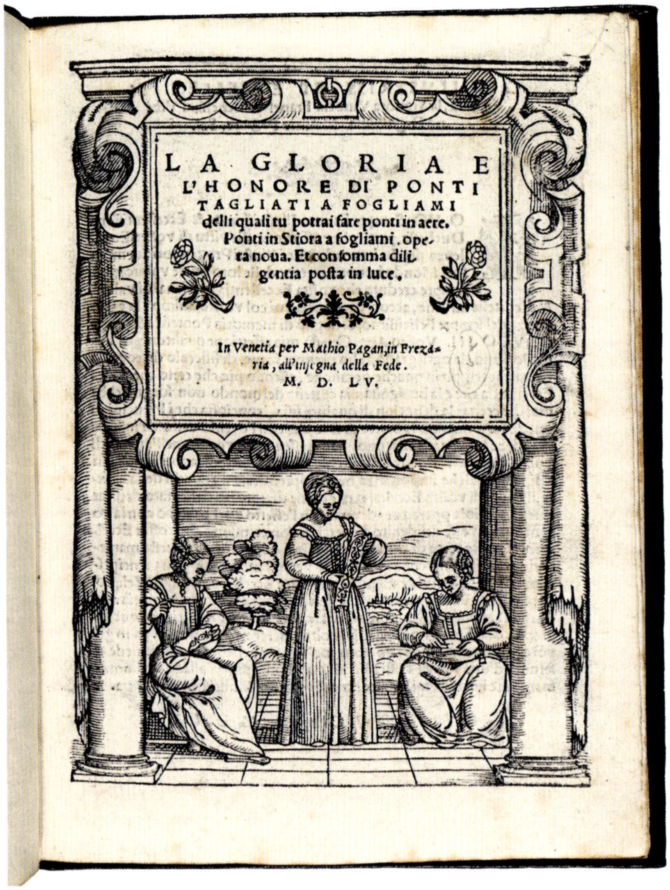
LA GLORIA E
L'HONORE DI PONTI
TAGLIATI A FOGLIAMI
delli quali tu potrai fare ponti in aere.
Ponti in Stiora a fogliami. opera noua. Et con somma diligentia posta in luce.
In Venetia per Mathio Pagan, in Frezaria, all'insegna della Fede.
M. D. LV.

105 Frontispiece for Matteo Pagano, *La gloria e l'honore di ponti tagliati a fogliami*, Venice, 1555

> ornament every woman and every bed with *ponti tagliati, ponti gropposi* [types of lace: cutwork and knot work] and every other type of *ponti* to make all those beautiful works that are appropriate for virtuous and praiseworthy girls.

Matteo Pagano compiled and printed *La gloria e l'honore di ponti tagliati a fogliami* (The Glory and Honor of Cutwork in Leaf Point Patterns) of 1555. Its frontispiece shows three women in a columned space set before a landscape (fig. 105). One woman stands at the center and displays a finished panel with a decorative motif, and the other two sit with pillows on their laps, copying not from a pattern book but from the completed example held by the standing woman. This scene demonstrates the way knowledge of this sort was shared and taught among groups of women, and how handiwork was learned by example and perfected through practice. It offers a view into a world of women working and learning together.[7] Rather than the moralizing tone of Da Sera's opening, Pagano's frontispiece focuses on his own accomplishment in putting the book together:

> The glory and the honor of *ponti tagliati a fogliami* from which you can make *ponti in aere punti in stiora a fogliami*. New work. And with the highest diligence brought to light. In Venice by Matteo Pagano, in Frezaria, with the mark of the Fede.

Pagano dedicates the book to the noblewoman Vittoria Farnese, Duchess of Urbino (1519–1602), setting it into a courtly context (fig. 106). Many of these books are dedicated to high-ranking, wealthy, and powerful women. The authors, like Pagano, would be seeking support and recognition for their own work. Such dedications also encouraged women of lesser status to link themselves, through this virtuous lacework, to higher ranks of society. Even in a moralizing context, women's power and agency are called out.

Cesare Vecellio's *Corona delle nobili et virtuose donne libro primo* (Crown of Noble and Virtuous Women Book One), published in Venice in 1591, includes two images accompanied by witty verses that play on notions of art making and women's virtue, both framed in fictive lace panels, as if the patterns contained in the book had been put to use. The first shows a sculpture of Venus standing on the back of a tortoise, pointing at her head and holding an apple, the prize recognizing her beauty at the Judgment of Paris (fig. 107). The caption above toys with the idea of her beauty, translating as: "It is fitting that the goodness and not the beauty of the woman should be revealed." Behind her is a portico, with two women on the left focusing industriously on their needlework, and on the right, a sculptor working with hammer and chisel on a marble statue.

This juxtaposition of women's work with the work of the male sculptor in marble introduces the notion of a *paragone*, a comparison like the debate on the relative virtues of painting and sculpture. The inscription speaks in the voice of the sculpture at the center: "I am Venus, made of fine marble by the wondrous hands of the learned Phidias. In me you see the gentle and humane acts of a woman, full of kindness. I rest atop a tortoise, which stays at home and is silent all the time." The interweaving of themes of industry, artistry, silence, and virtue would surely engender various responses from men and women alike.

The second image shows a fox seated under a tree, holding the bust of a woman with a fancy hairdo and pearls around her neck (fig. 108). Here, the caption reads: "That intellect is more worthy than beauty." Below, the little story translates to "The fox found a head so well formed by a fine sculptor, and which, you would have said, lacks only spirit, so worthy was the diligence and artifice. The fox took it in hand and said: oh head so perfect and gentle, but empty of intellect." Both of these illustrations seem geared to engage and flatter the book's audience by praising the goodness and intellect of real women over both industry and the beauty of a sculpted image. In both woodcuts the idea of a paragone offers an opportunity to consider the relative merits of women's work, in the soft material of textiles in relation to marble, the hard material of the sculptor,

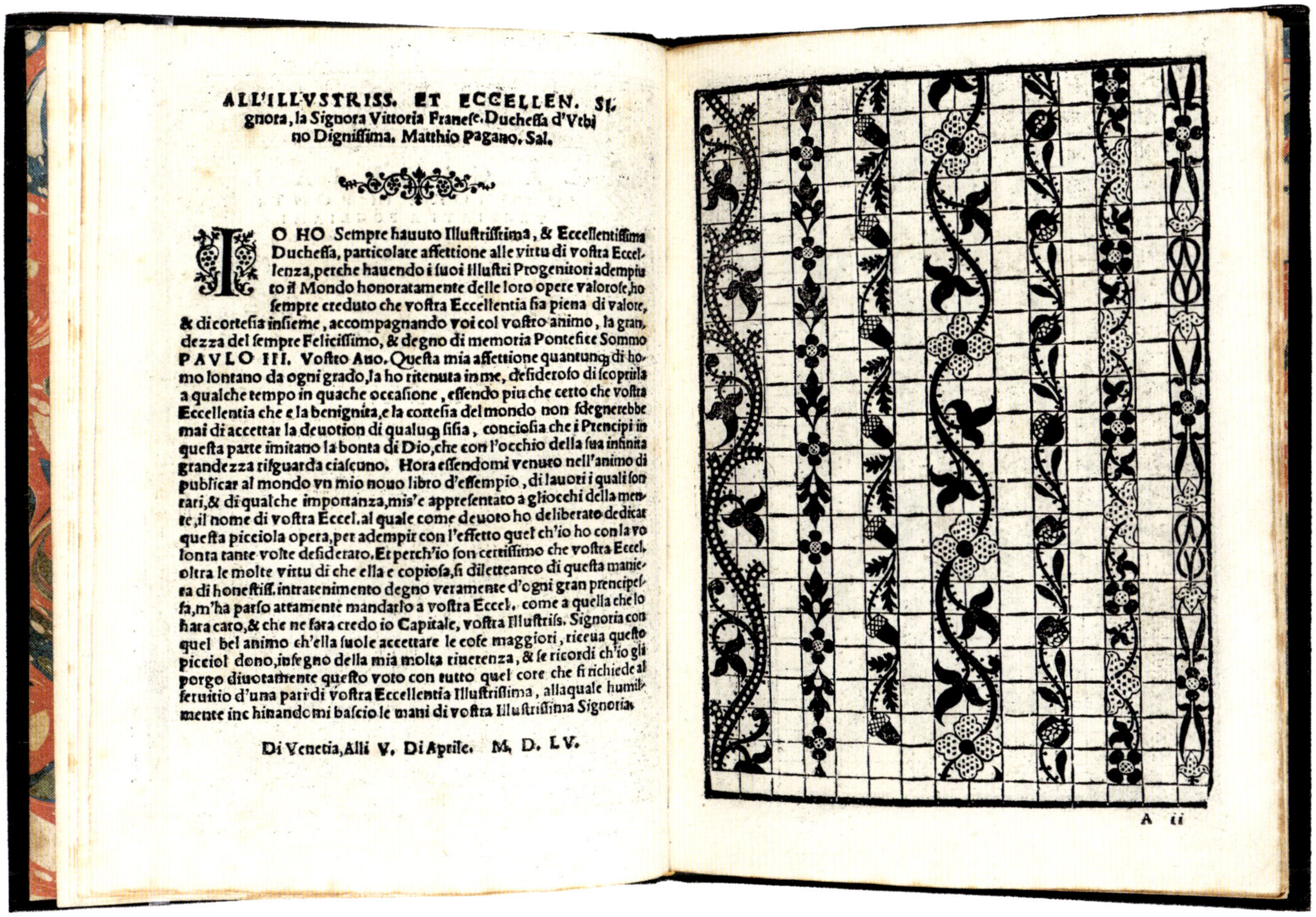

106 Pagano, *La gloria e l'honore di ponti tagliati a fogliami*, 1555

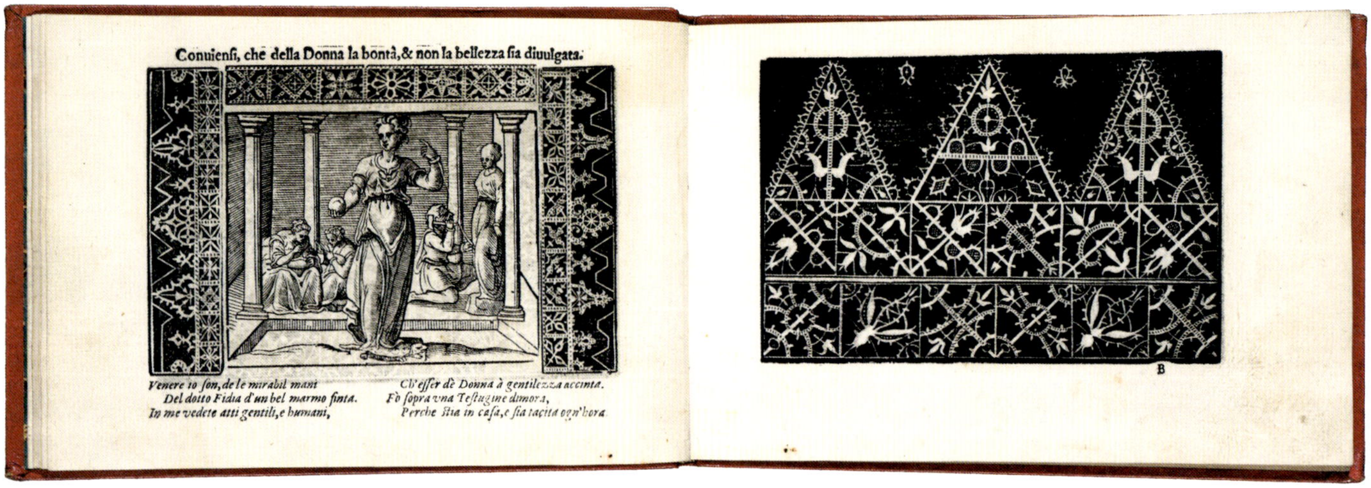

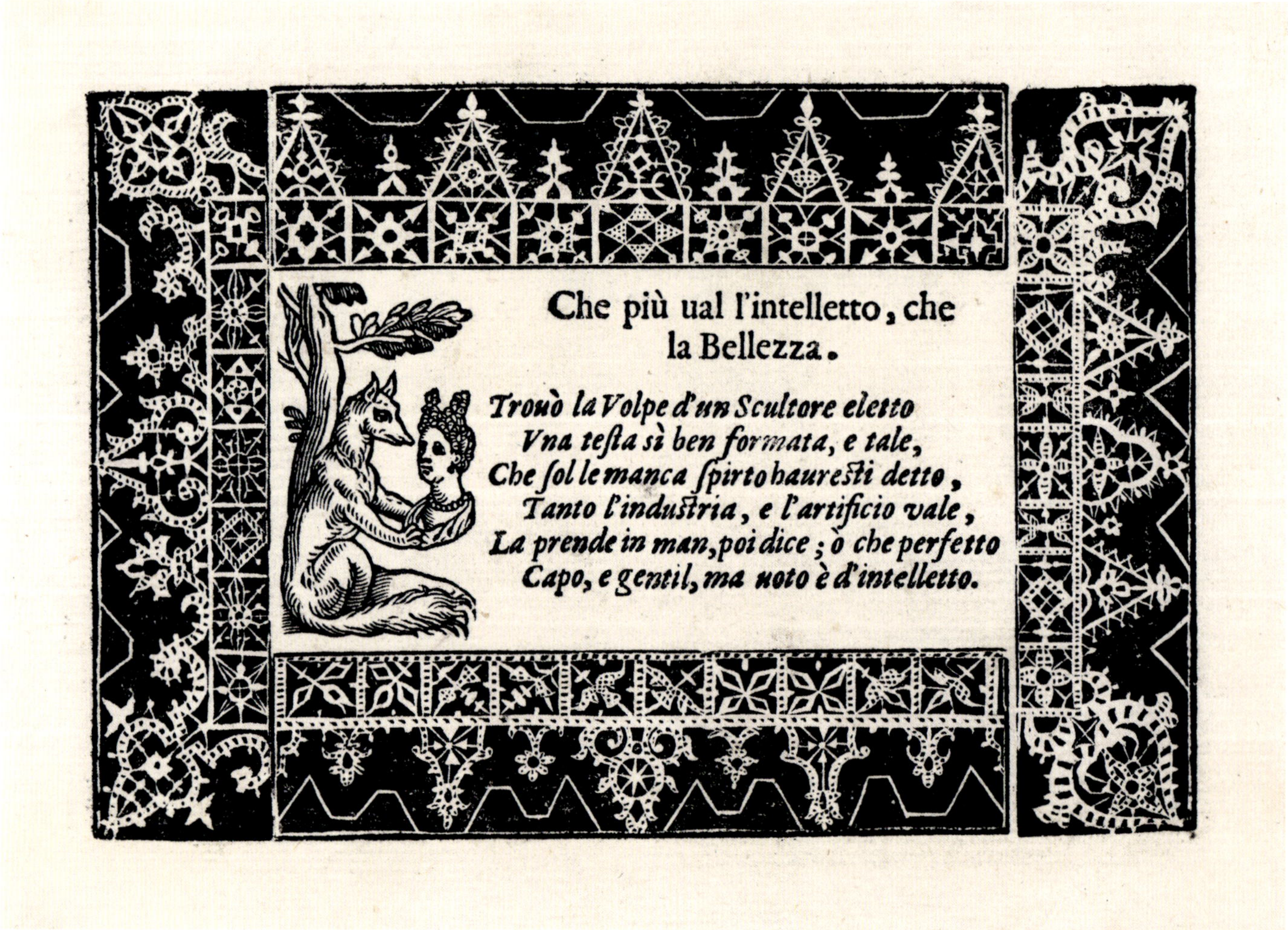

107 & 108 Woodcuts from Cesare Vecellio, *Corona delle nobili et virtuose donne libro primo*, Venice, 1591

and to compare contemporary women textile artists to the ancient sculptor Phidias.[8] Pagano, too, in one of his lace-pattern books, described women's needlework as "painting with a needle, just like Apelles," making a comparison between needle artists and the famous ancient painter.[9] Vecellio himself was a painter as well as a designer and compiler of lace patterns.[10] These witty pages display his sophistication and appreciation for the range of possible interpretations of ornament, as well as women's handiwork and artistry.

Isabella Catanea Parasole broke boundaries by producing a series of pattern books that enjoyed great success, enhanced by the fact that she was a woman. Like her male counterparts, Parasole dedicated her books to elite female patrons. Unlike her male counterparts, she could speak to her patrons as a woman, which would surely resonate with them. Her books display her creativity and agency in design and judgment and demonstrate her understanding of the techniques of lace production as well as her virtuosity in making woodcuts (see fig. 70).[11] Because of the association of lace making with feminine virtue, she produced these within an acceptable framework for women's work. The frontispieces of her books, including in this volume, call specific attention to the fact that these are Parasole's designs, emphasizing the notion of her exceptionality as a woman producing these patterns and indicating her fame as designer and creator. The title, *Gemma pretiosa delle virtuose donne* (Precious Gem of Virtuous Women) is followed by this description "Where are to be seen most beautiful works of *Pont'in aria Retticella di Maglia e Piombini*. Designed by Isabetta Catanea Parasole" (fig. 109).[12] This was the last book of six produced during Parasole's lifetime, most of which had appeared in numerous editions, another indication of her fame.[13] She also embodied women's potential, serving as a role model for female readers to embrace their own creativity and value their own judgment.

These pattern books illustrate how artistic knowledge was shared and passed down, and how women might break tradition to find creative roles for themselves, as Isabella Parasole did. Some lauded the discipline that activities such as lace making and

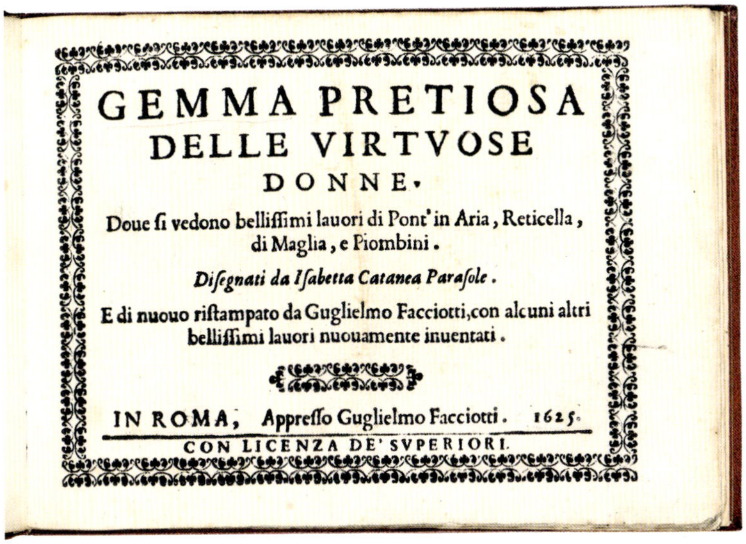
GEMMA PRETIOSA
DELLE VIRTVOSE
DONNE.
Doue ſi vedono belliſſimi lauori di Pont'in Aria, Reticella, di Maglia, e Piombini.
Diſegnati da Iſabetta Catanea Paraſole.
E di nuouo riſtampato da Guglielmo Facciotti, con alcuni altri belliſſimi lauori nuouamente inuentati.
IN ROMA, Appreſſo Guglielmo Facciotti. 1625.
CON LICENZA DE' SVPERIORI.

109 Frontispiece for Isabella Catanea Parasole, *Gemma pretiosa della virtuose donne*, Rome, 1625

embroidery could instill in practitioners and saw these practices as helpful in preparing women for intellectual endeavors. Pietro Bembo, one of the most famous intellects and writers of his day, encouraged his thirteen-year-old daughter, Elena, to develop her mind, to study Greek and Latin, and to read and write. He advised her not to waste time learning music, which might make her seem vain and frivolous; instead, he counseled her to read and do needlework.[14] Laura Cereta, scholar, humanist, and poet, recounts that her training in needlework in the convent where she was educated taught her discipline and how to focus her mind, both of which helped her as a writer.[15]

These books lead to a consideration of lacework made by women and its many uses. Lace became more common in Italian life during the course of the sixteenth century: on clothing, on textiles for domestic and religious use, and as part of ritual practice. In addition to decorating the collars and cuffs of elite men's and women's clothing, lace inspired the decoration of shoes and fans. These platform shoes known as *chopines*, worn by Venetian women both at home and when going out, are decorated with silk tape and rope as well as leather cut to resemble simple lace patterns (fig. 110). This fan

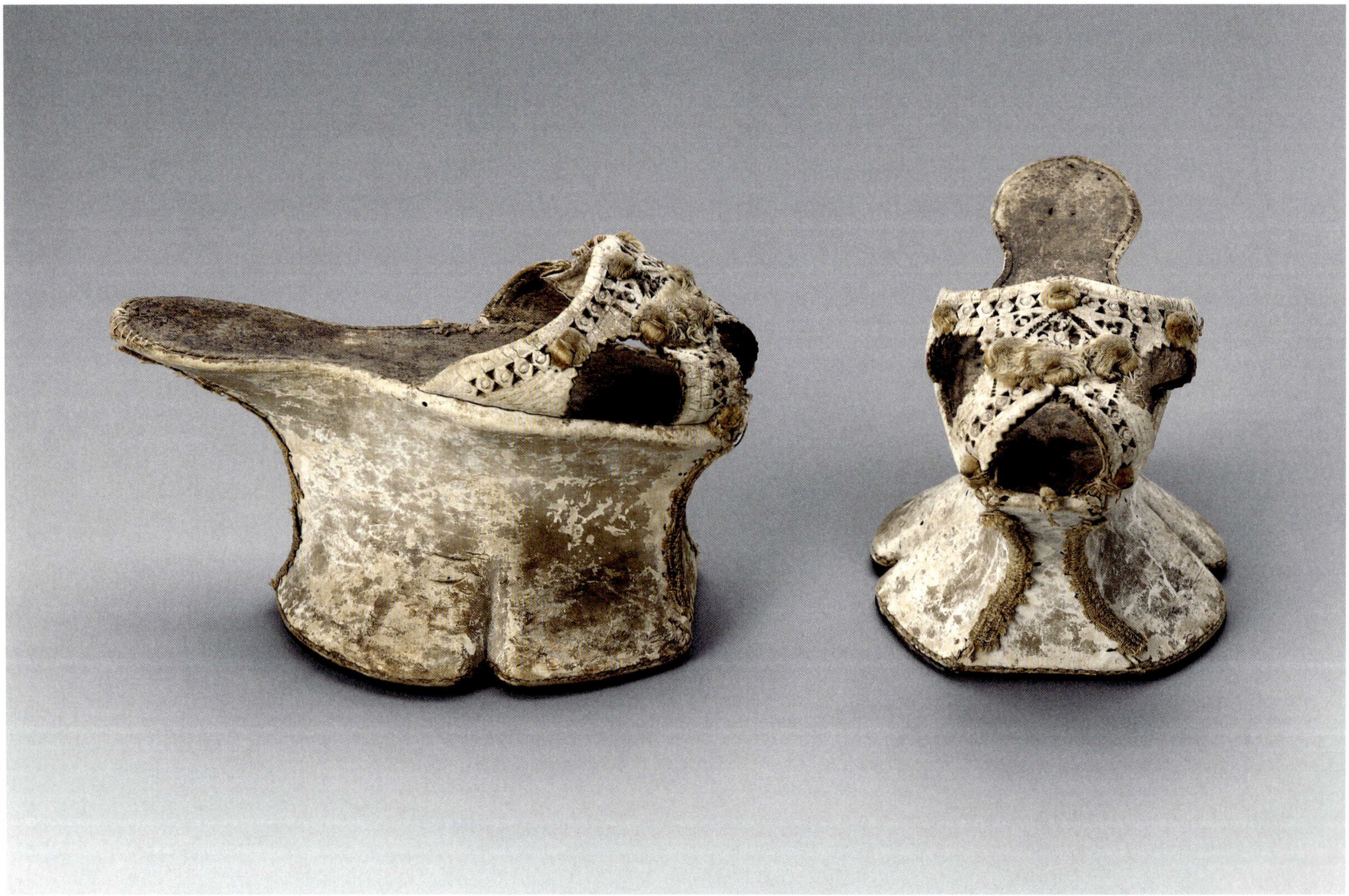

110 Chopines, 1610–20

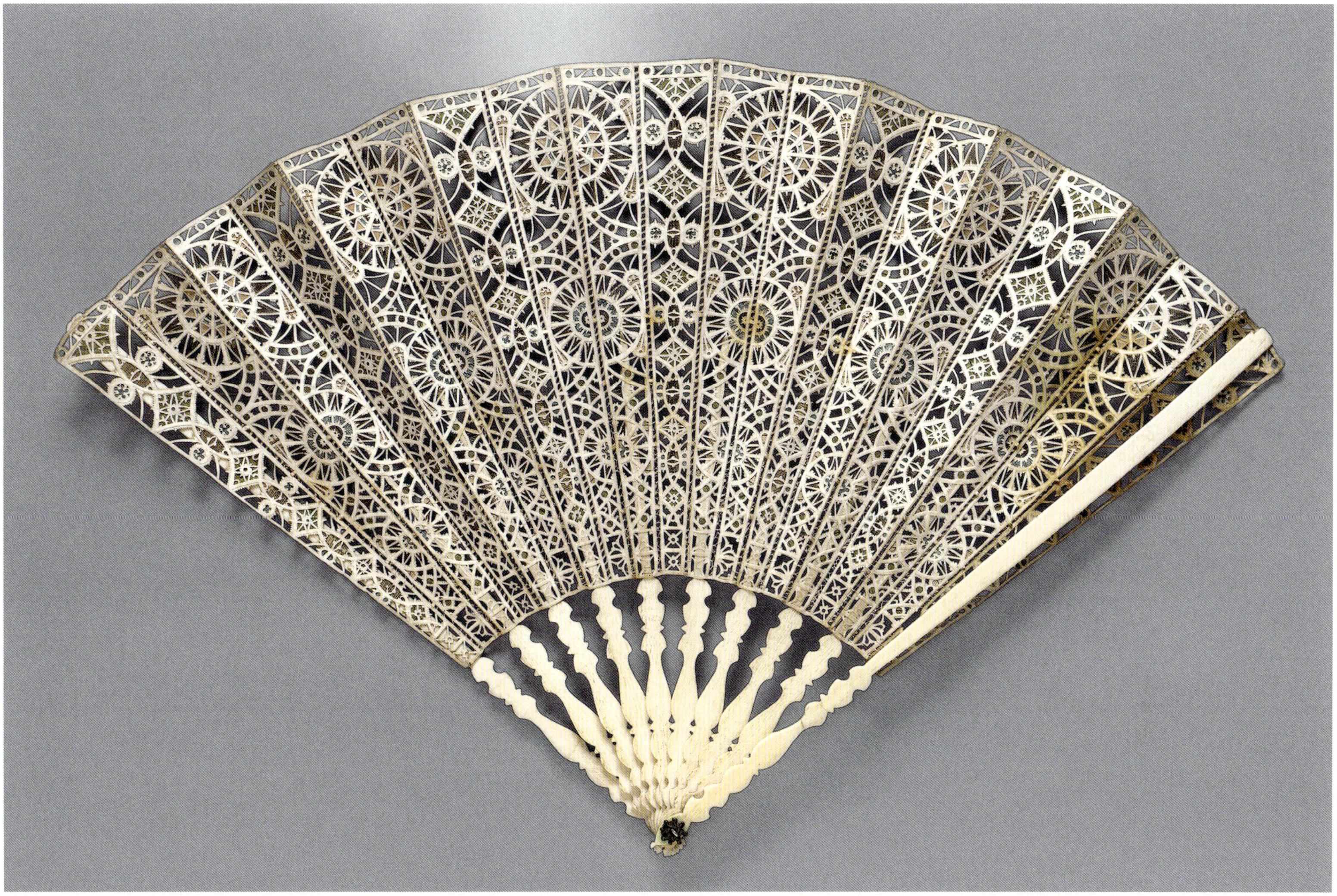

111 Découpé folding fan, about 1590–1600

112 Towel, 17th century

displays elaborate patterns of stars and circles very similar to those found in lace patterns, emphasized by the contrasting-colored silk insets against which the intricately cut skin is shown (fig. 111). Beautiful table covers ornamented with lace were used in private homes, and lace edges decorate the panels of a Torah binder, donated by a Jewish couple to their synagogue (fig. 112; see fig. 52). Women's work adorned many walks of life in Renaissance Italy.[16]

Books that record the customs and costumes of the Renaissance provide a glimpse of how women lived and dressed.[17] In Giacomo Franco's *Habiti d'houmeni et donne venetiane* (Clothing of Venetian Men and Women), published in Venice in 1610, a scene of young women riding in gondolas shows them "going to visit their relatives in convents," clearly recording certain aspects of women's lives (fig. 113). Elite Venetian women were very restricted in their movements in the city, so this sort of outing allowed them to see and be seen. In each gondola a well-dressed woman peers out, her long golden hair streaming down her back.

These types of costume books also provide insight into how women of different social statuses might be recognized by what they wore or might use their clothing to shape their images. For example, women of all classes in Venice wore high chopines (fig. 114).[18] For an elite woman, chopines would allow her to display great lengths of rich velvets and brocades. When she went out, she would always have someone to help support and accompany her (fig. 115). Courtesans, who in Venice held relatively high status, registered with the civic government and moved in elite circles, dressed

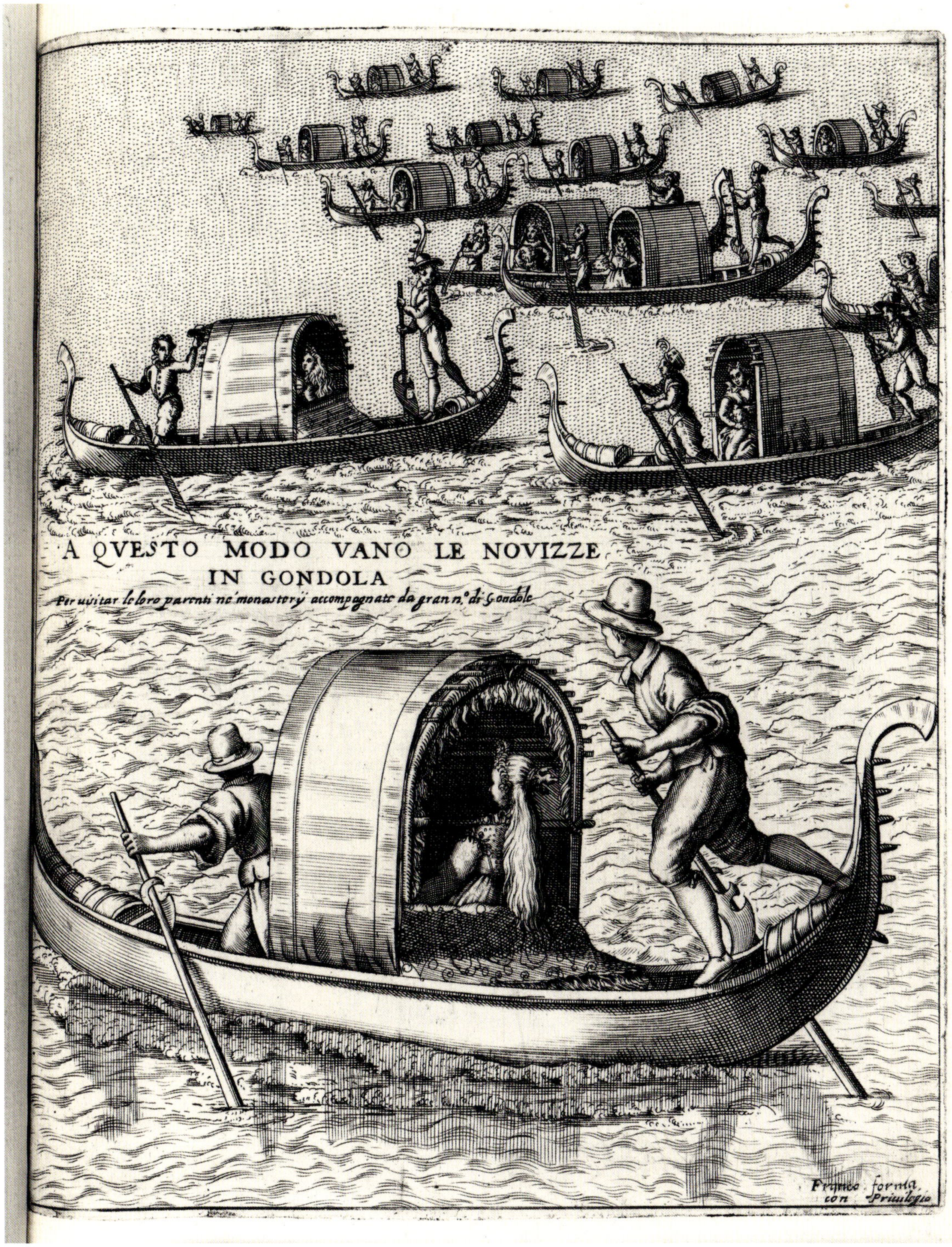

113 Woodcut from Giacomo Franco, *Habiti d'houmeni et donne venetiane*, Venice, 1610

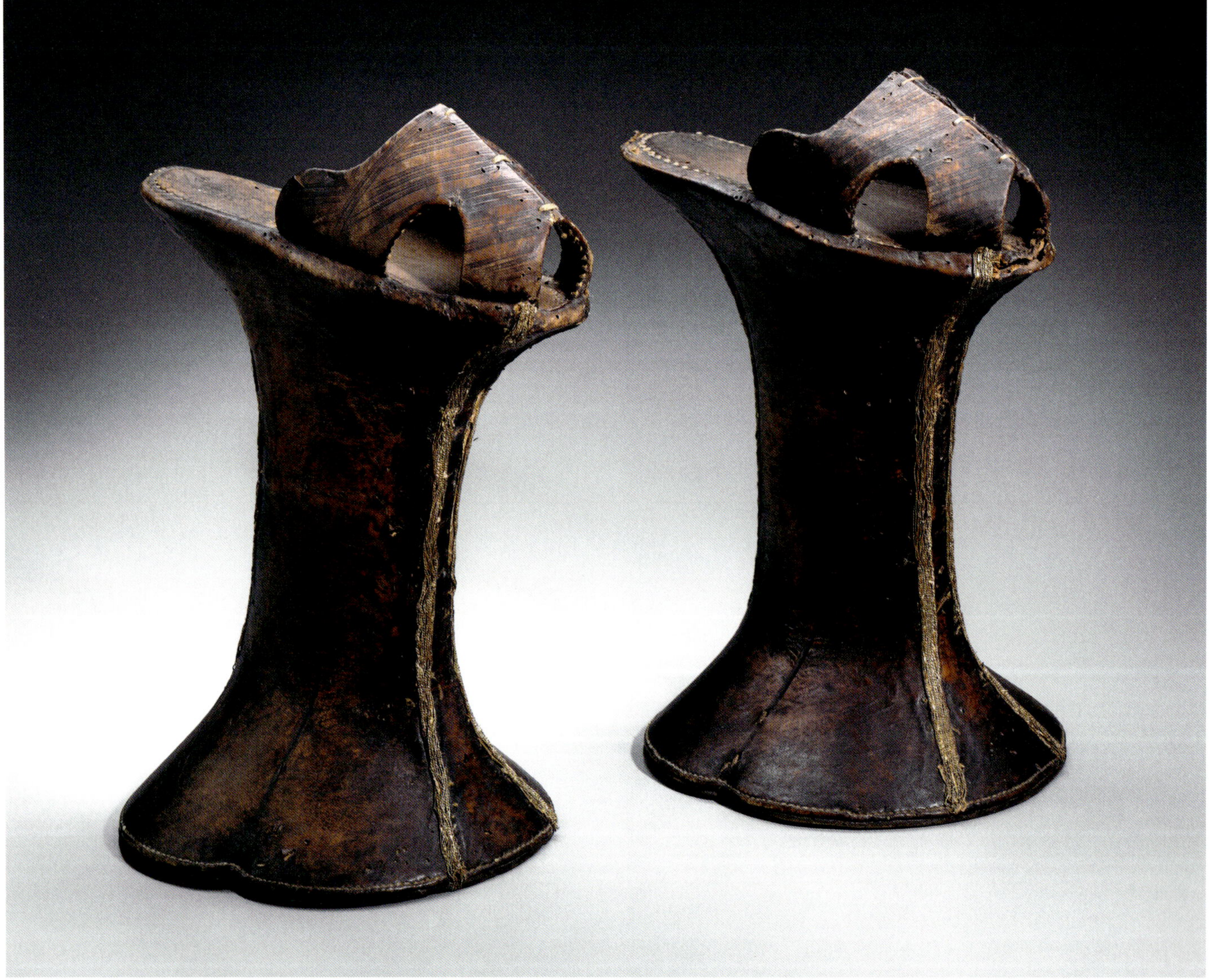

114 Chopines, about 1590–1610

almost exactly like their noble counterparts (fig. 116). Their lives and livelihoods depended, however, on the patronage of their male clients. Sex workers who had to navigate the streets would also wear chopines, but usually had to make their way on their own, an indication of their vulnerability and a metaphor for how precarious their lives could be. On the other hand, in a hand-colored sheet from Pietro Bertelli's 1589 costume book *Diversarum nationum habitus* (Costumes of Various Nations), the woman labeled as a "Venetian courtesan" pulls her long skirt aside to reveal both her high chopines and her masculine pantaloons, clearly dressing for the erotic charge of both emulating and undercutting the fashions of elite Venetian women (fig. 117).

Cesare Vecellio's most famous work is his 1590 book, *De gli habiti antichi et moderni di diversi parti del mondo* (The Ancient and Modern Clothes from All Over the World).[19] A compendium of costumes of men and women from ancient to modern times, it demonstrates the same spirit of collecting, describing, and compiling images that characterized lace-pattern books. His own pattern book was published a year after this title. For *Gli Habiti,* Vecellio put together well over four hundred woodcuts with descriptions that celebrated the diversity of styles, costumes, and people that he ardently sought out and reproduced. He lauds his own city of Venice, which was one of the most important crossroads for people from all over the world thanks to its role as a major trading center for the Mediterranean world. His images of women reveal layers of social and economic status as well as stages of life, from noblewomen to farmers, from children to elderly women, from young brides to widows. A woman from Ischia carries spindles and wears the shoes that made farmwork possible (see fig. 69). In his description of her clothing, Vecellio writes that in Ischia most women spin cloth, work the land, and are rarely idle. A simpler chopine, lower and made of softer leather, is a good example of more practical footgear for women (fig. 118). Vecellio describes how widows wear veils to express their grief, whereas courtesans use veils to hide their faces and create a sense of mystery and seduction (fig. 119).[20]

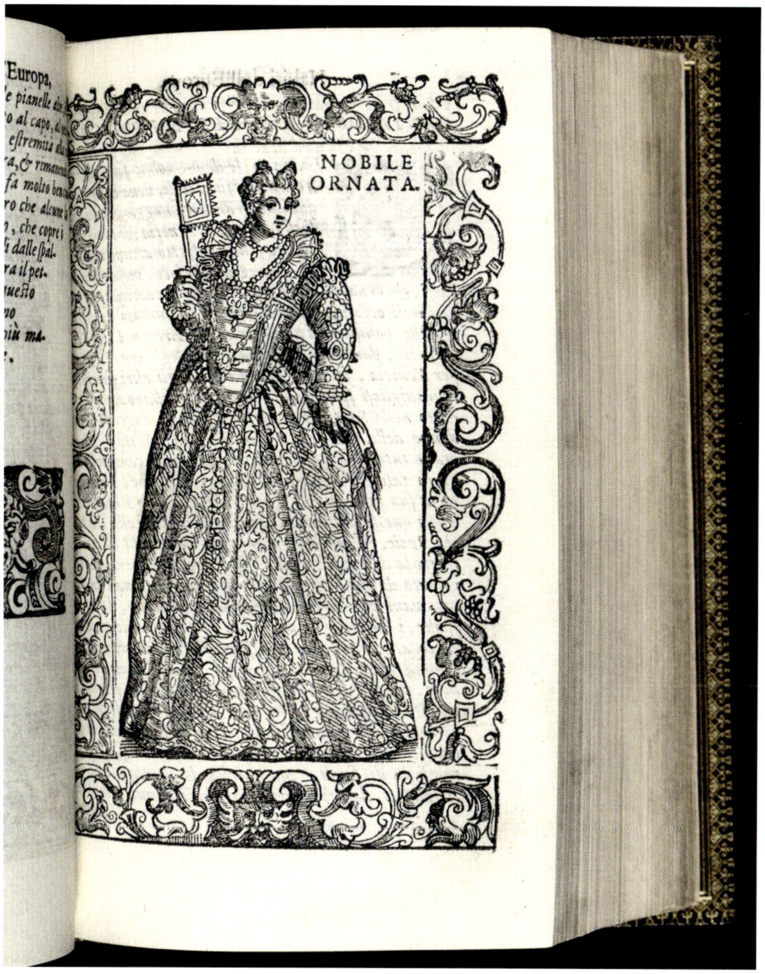

115 Woodcut from Cesare Vecellio, *De gli habiti antichi et moderni di diverse parti del mondo*, Venice, 1590

Among others, Vecellio included a noble matron from Naples who carries, "like all Neapolitan woman," a beautiful rosary; a middle-class woman from Silesia with her daughter; a Neapolitan baroness, carrying a fan; a woman from Naples in a style of clothing no longer worn; a splendid noble matron from Sicily dressed for public festivities; a noble Roman bride dressed for going out; a woman from Gaeta, which he describes as "full of splendid gardens, which supply all of Italy with apples, oranges, limes and lemons" (figs. 120–125). Vecellio's curiosity about the world provides a snapshot of a wide variety of women's lives, showing his determination to record and present them to his readers and viewers, and making clear that every woman has a story to tell.

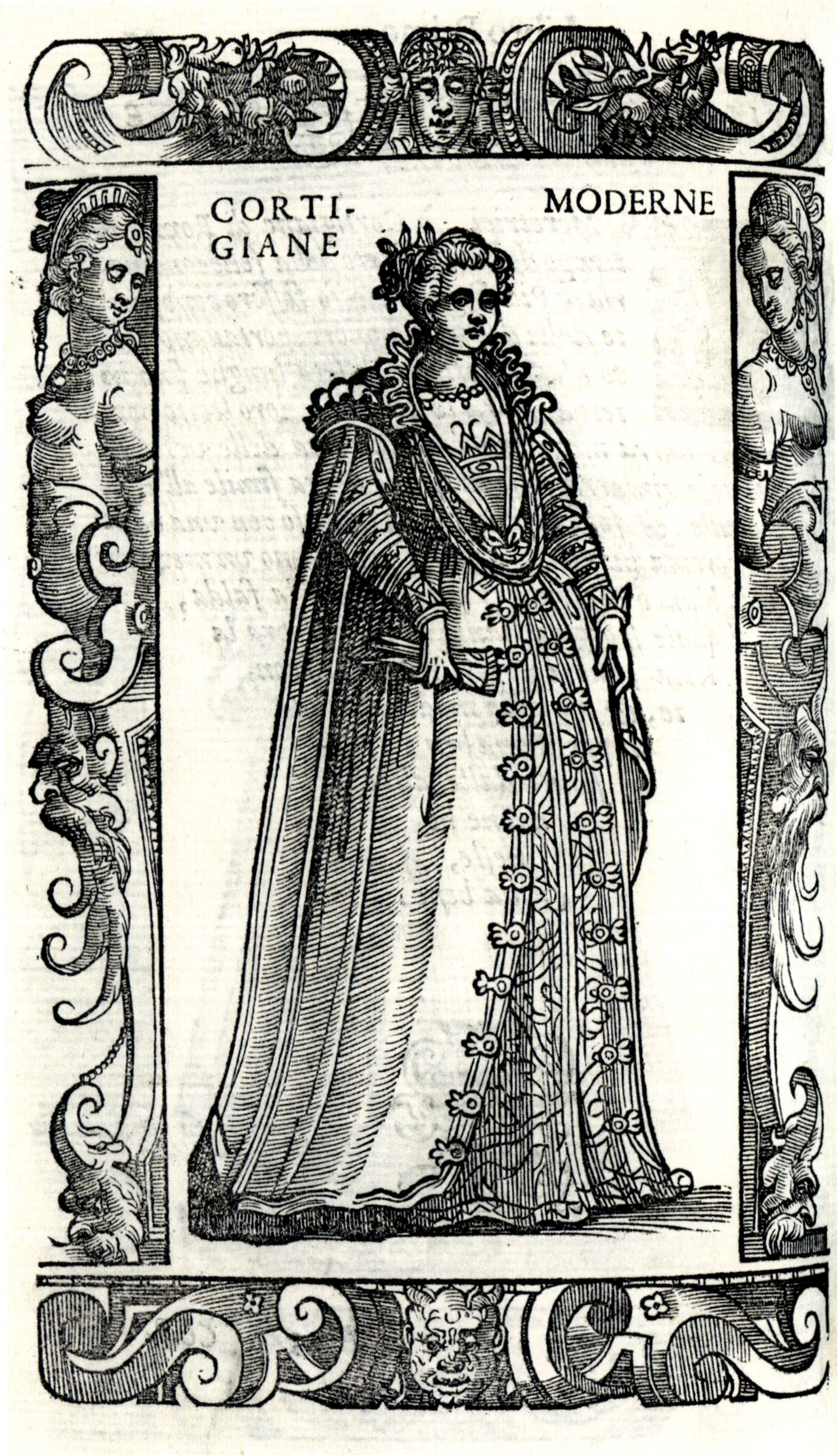

116 *Cortigiane moderne* from Vecellio, *De gli habiti antichi et moderni di diverse parti del mondo*, 1590

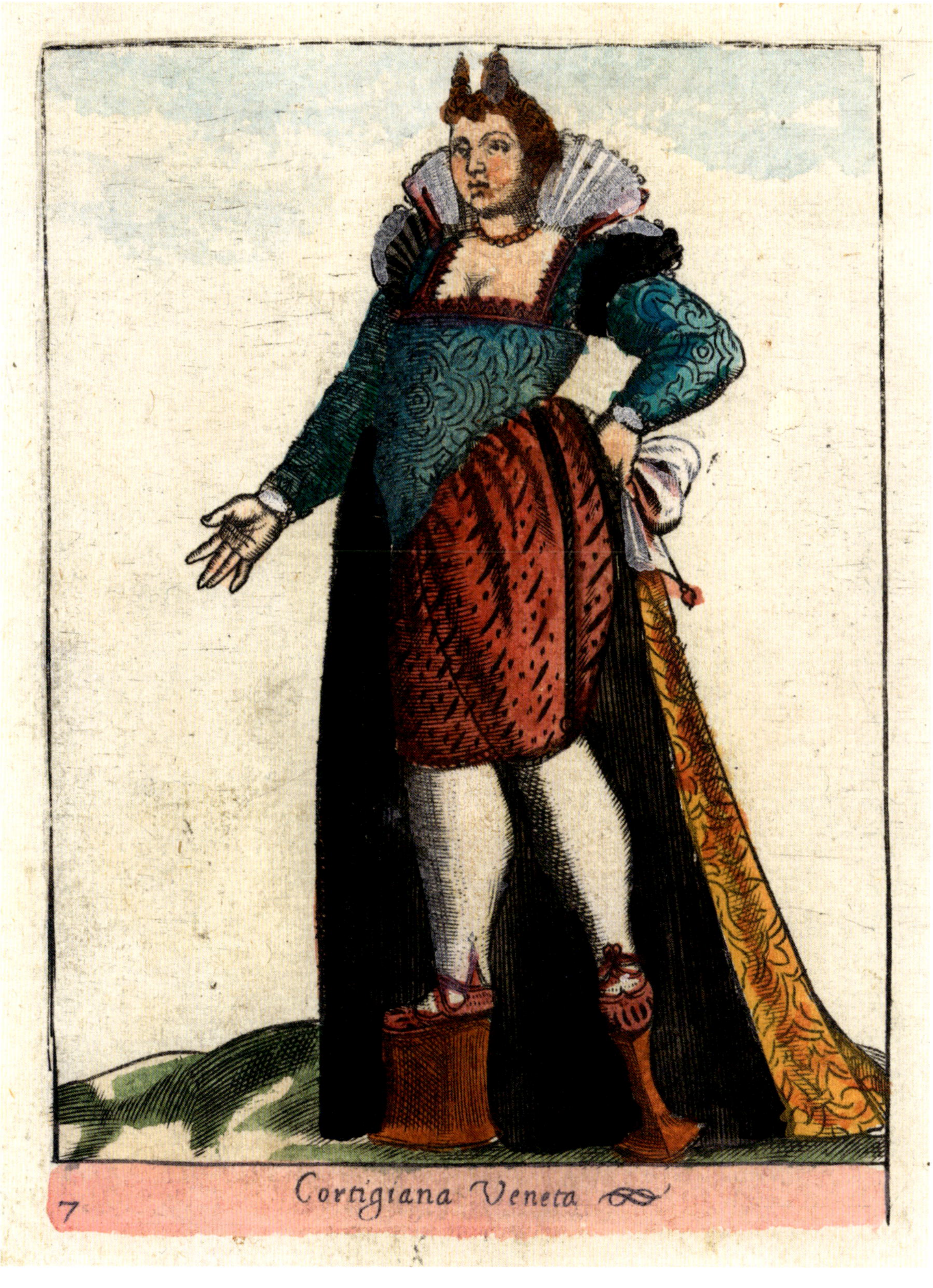

117 *Cortigiana Veneta* from Pietro Bertelli, *Diversarum nationum habitus*, Padua, 1589

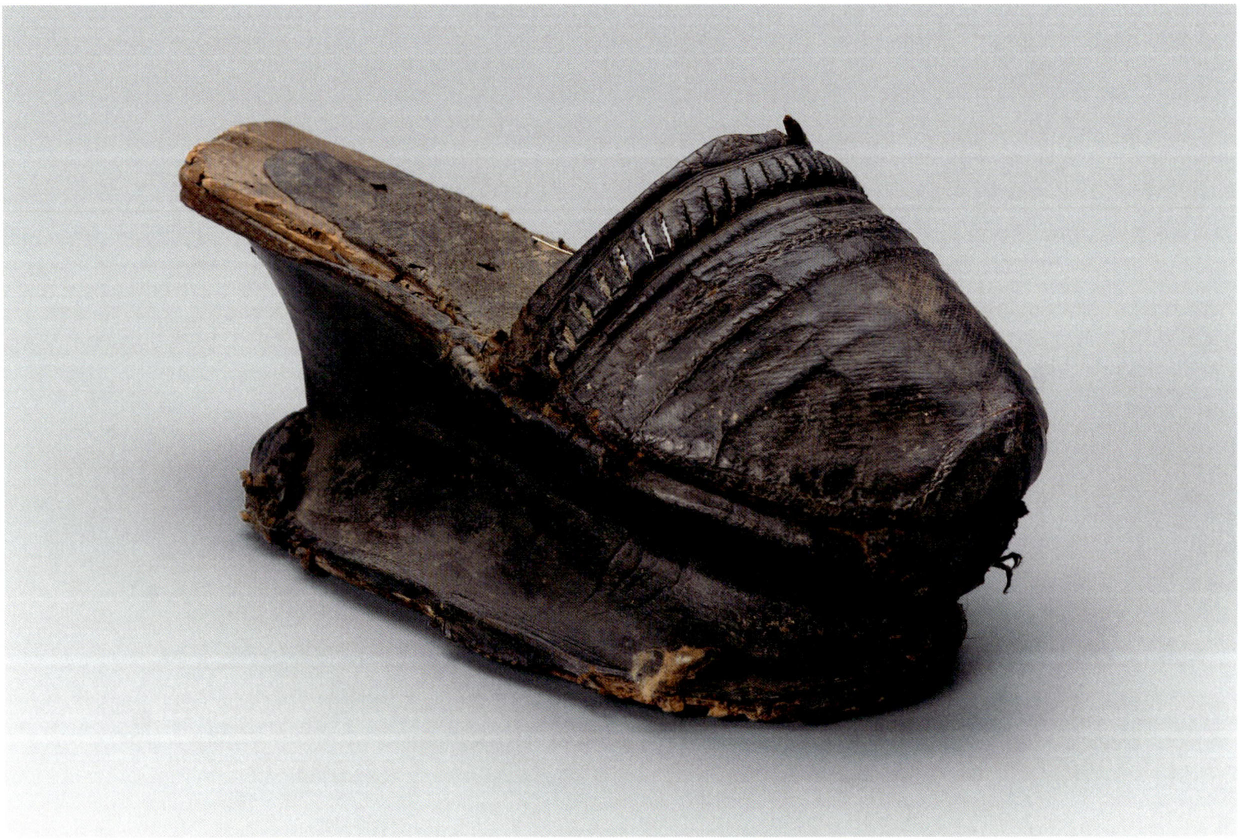

118 Chopine, 1580s

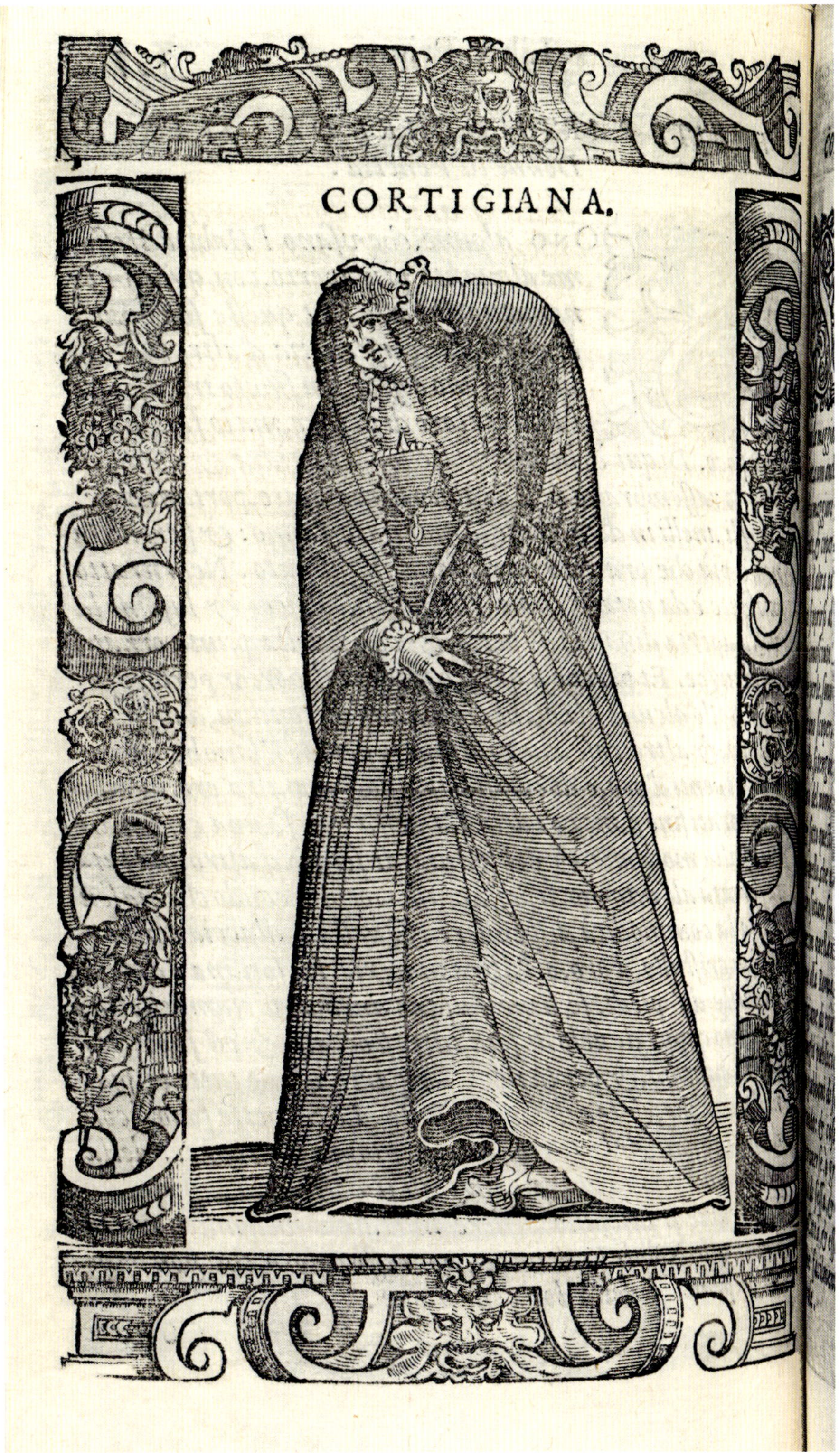

119 *Cortigiana* from Vecellio, *De gli habiti antichi et moderni di diverse parti del mondo*, 1590

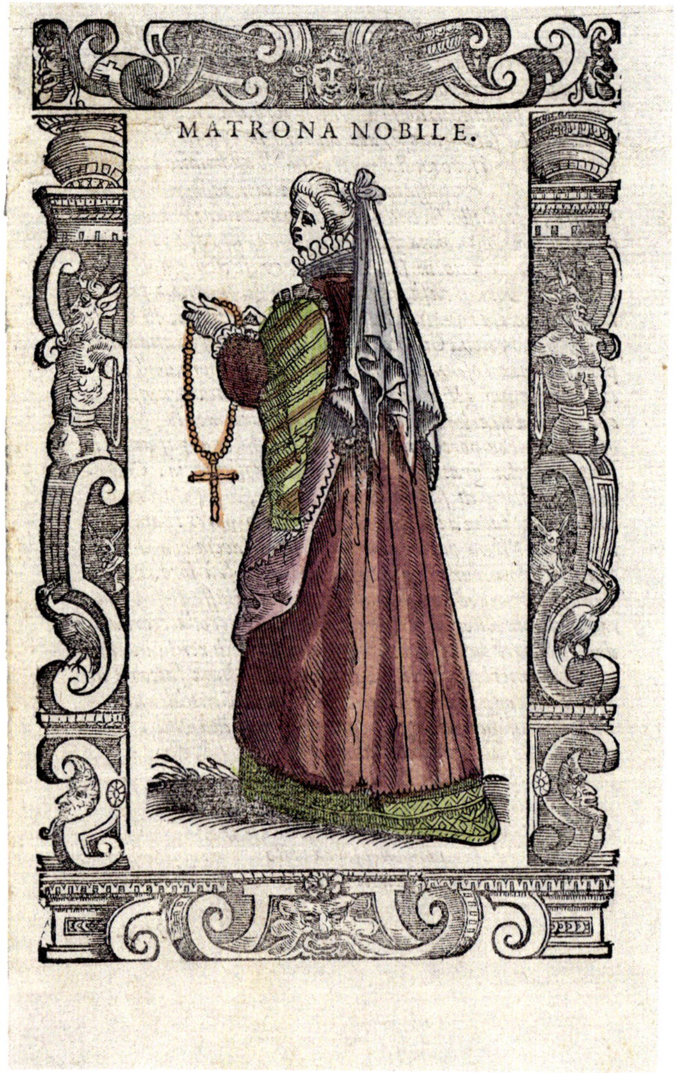

120

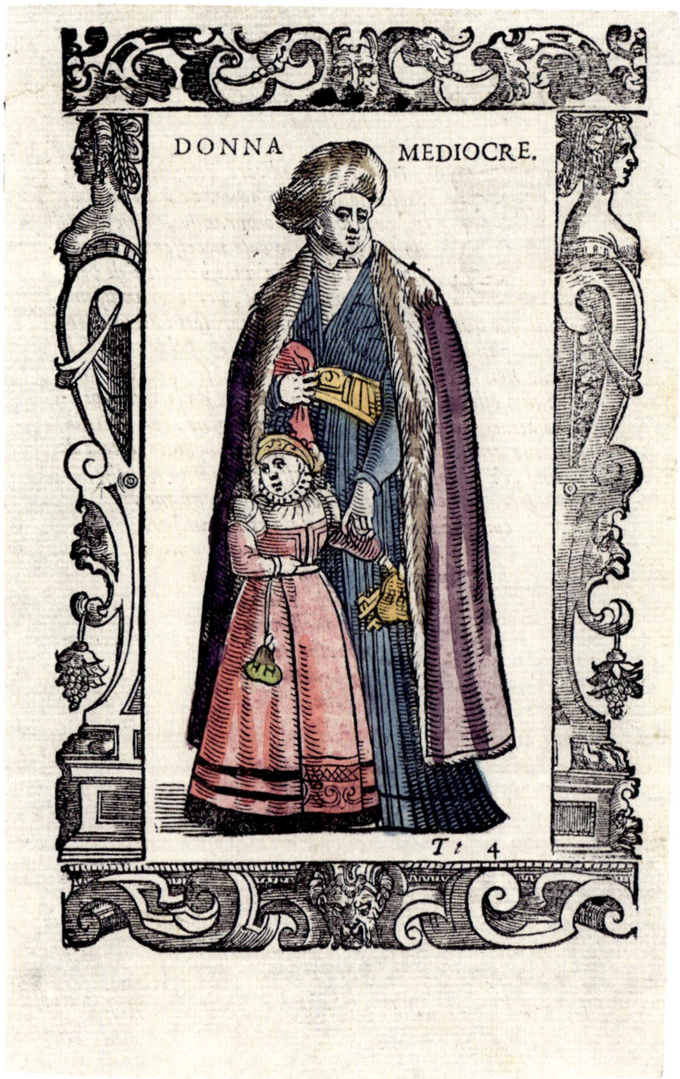

121

120 through 125 Woodcuts from Vecellio, *De gli habiti antichi et moderni di diversi parti del mondo*, 1590

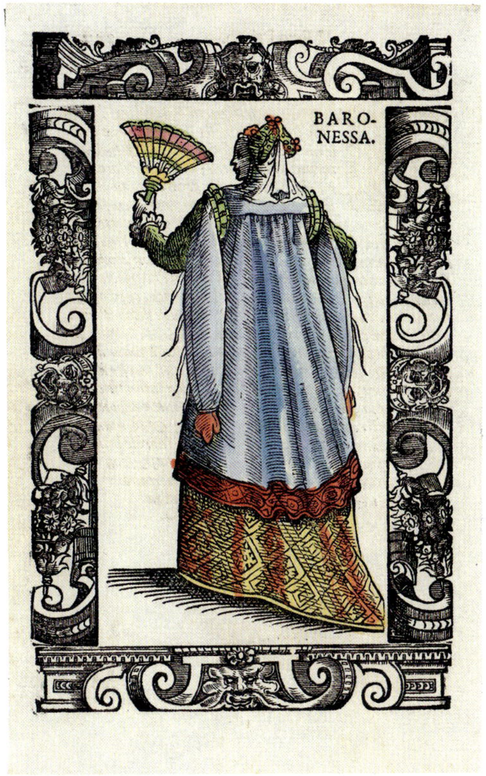

122

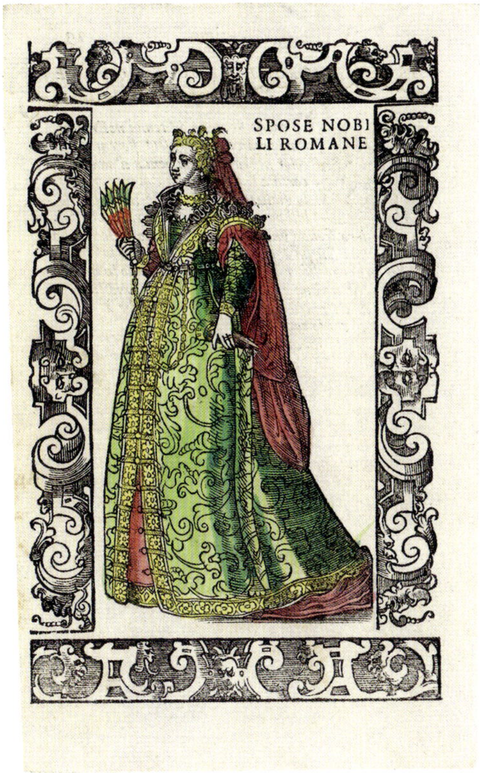

123

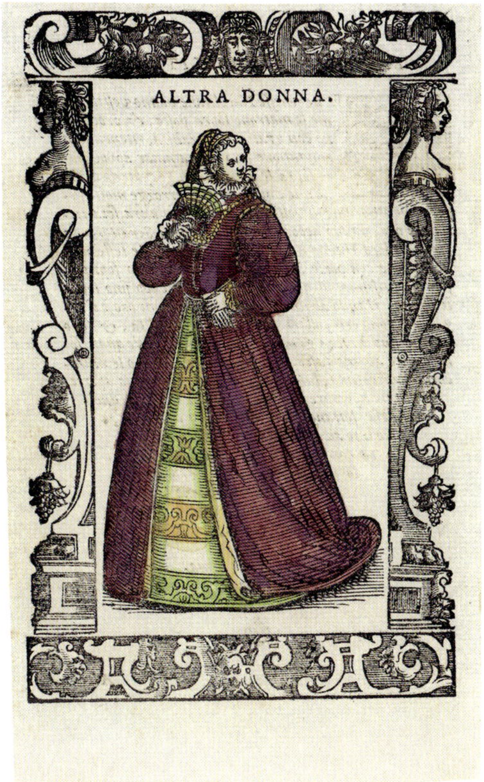

124

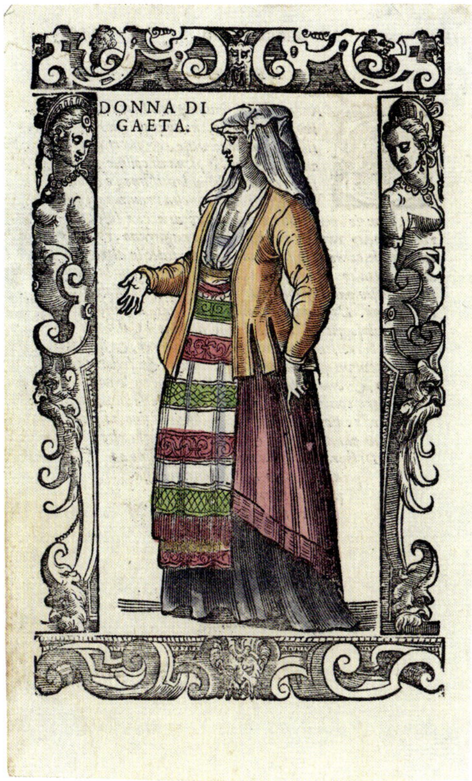

125

Notes

Hidden Gold

1. "L'oro che sta ne le miniere ascoso / non manca d'esser or, benche sepolto /E quando e tratta e sene se lavoro / e cosi ricco come l'altro oro." Quoted in Meredith K. Ray, *Daughters of Alchemy: Women and Scientific Culture in Early Modern Italy* (Cambridge, MA: Harvard University Press, 2015), 207n28. For Fonte, see Moderata Fonte (Modesta Pozzo), *The Worth of Women: Wherein Is Clearly Revealed Their Nobility and Their Superiority to Men*, ed. and trans. Virginia Cox (Chicago: University of Chicago Press, 1997); Moderata Fonte (Modesta Pozzo), *Floridoro: A Chivalric Romance*, ed. Valeria Finucci, trans. Julia Kisacky (Chicago: University of Chicago Press, 2006), 145; and Sarah Gwyneth Ross, *The Birth of Feminism: Woman as Intellect in Renaissance Italy and England* (Cambridge, MA: Harvard University Press, 2009).

2. Trailblazing work on women artists includes Linda Nochlin, "Why have there been no great women artists?" (1971), reprinted in Linda Nochlin and Catherine Grant, *Why Have There Been No Great Women Artists* (London: Thames and Hudson, 2021); *Women Artists: 1550–1950*, eds. Ann Sutherland Harris and Linda Nochlin (Los Angeles: Los Angeles County Museum of Arrt, 1976); Mary D. Garrard, *Artemisia Gentileschi: The Image of the Female Hero in Italian Baroque Art* (Princeton: Princeton University Press, 1989); Fredrika H. Jacobs, *Defining the Renaissance Virtuosa: Women Artists and the Language of Art History and Criticism* (Cambridge: Cambridge University Press, 1997); and Paola Tinagli, *Women in Italian Renaissance Art: Gender, Representation, Identity* (Manchester: Manchester University Press, 1997).

3. For women writers, see Margaret L. King and Albert Rabil Jr., "The Other Voice in Early Modern Europe: An Introduction to the Series," in *Lucrezia Tornabuoni de' Medici: Sacred Narratives*, ed. and trans. Jane Tylus (Chicago: University of Chicago Press, 2001).

4. Joan Kelly-Gadol, "Did Women Have a Renaissance" in *Becoming Visible: Women in European History,* ed. Renate Bridenthal and Claudia Koonz (Boston: Houghton Mifflin, 1977), 137–64. See also Anabel Thomas, "Moving on from Joan Kelly-Gadol," *Oxford Art Journal* 22, no. 2 (1999): 44–53.

5. Sheila Barker, "Introduction," in *Women Artists in Early Modern Italy: Careers, Fame, and Collectors* (Turnhout, Belgium: Brepols, 2016); Sheila Barker, "Art as Women's Work: The Professionalization of Women Artists, 1350–1800," in *By Her Hand*: *Artemisia Gentileschi and Women Artists in Italy, 1500–1800*, ed. Eve Straussman-Pflanzer and Oliver Tostmann (New Haven: Yale University Press, 2021), 43–51.

6. See Kate Lowe, *Nuns' Chronicles and Convent Culture in Renaissance and Counter-Reformation Italy* (Cambridge: Cambridge University Press, 2003); Anabel Thomas, *Art and Piety in the Female Religious Communities of Renaissance Florence: Iconography, Space, and the Religious Woman's Perspective* (Cambridge: Cambridge University Press, 2003); and Sharon T. Strocchia, *Nuns and Nunneries in Renaissance Florence* (Baltimore: Johns Hopkins University Press, 2009).

7. Sharon T. Strocchia, "The Nun-Apothecaries of Renaissance Florence: Marketing Medicines in the Convent," *Renaissance Studies* 25, no. 5 (November 2011): 627–47; Ray, *Daughters of Alchemy*; Sharon T. Strocchia, *Forgotten Healers: Women and the Pursuit of Health in Late Renaissance Italy* (Cambridge, MA: Harvard University Press, 2019); Sheila Barker and Sharon T. Strocchia, "Household Medicine for a Renaissance Court: Caterina Sforza's *Ricettario* Reconsidered," in *Gender, Health and Healing, 1250–1550*, ed. Sara Ritchey and Sheila Barker (Amsterdam: Amsterdam University Press, 2020).

8. Sharon T. Strocchia, "Knowing Hands: Nuns and the Needle Arts in Renaissance Italy," in *Artiste nel chiostro: Produzione artistica nei monasteri femminili in età moderna*, ed. Sheila Barker with Luciano Cinelli (Florence: Nerbini, 2015; *Memorie Domenicane* n.s. 46), 31–52.

9. Catherine E. King, *Renaissance Women Patrons: Wives and Widows in Italy, c. 1300–1550* (Manchester: Manchester University Press, 1998);

Allison Levy, ed., *Widowhood and Visual Culture in Early Modern Europe* (London: Routledge, 2016).
10. Sheryl E. Reiss and David G. Wilkins, *Beyond Isabella: Secular Women Patrons of Art in Renaissance Italy* (Kirksville, MD: Truman State University Press, 2001); Stefanie Solum, *Women, Patronage, and Salvation in Renaissance Florence: Lucrezia Tornabuoni and the Chapel of the Medici Palace* (Farnham, UK: Ashgate, 2015).
11. Christine de Pizan, *The Book of the City of Ladies and Other Writings*, ed. Sophie Bourgault and Rebecca Kingston, trans. Ineke Hardy (Indianapolis: Hackett, 2018), xxxv, 23.
12. Victor M. Schmidt, "Painting and Individual Devotion in Late Medieval Italy," in *Visions of Holiness: Art and Devotion in Renaissance Italy*, ed. Andrew Ladis and Shelley E. Zuraw (Athens: Georgia Museum of Art, 2001), 21–36.
13. Schmidt, "Painting and Individual Devotion," 22.
14. Donato d'Arezzo (Italian [Aretine], active 1315–about 1340) and Gregorio d'Arezzo (Italian [Aretine], active 1315–about 1340), *Saint Catherine of Alexandria and Twelve Scenes from Her Life*, about 1330. J. Paul Getty Museum, Los Angeles, 73.PB.69. In this version, Jesus, a baby in his mother's arms, places a ring on Catherine's finger.
15. Peter Thornton, *The Italian Renaissance Interior, 1400–1600* (New York: Harry N. Abrams, 1991), 149–53.
16. Katherine L. Jansen, "'Pro bono pacis': Crime, Conflict, and Dispute Resolution: The Evidence of Notarial Peace Contracts in Late Medieval Florence," *Speculum* 88, no. 2 (April 2013): 449–50; for the broader context, see Katherine L. Jansen, *Peace and Penance in Late Medieval Italy* (Princeton: Princeton University Press, 2018).
17. Lois Drewer, "Margaret of Antioch the Demon-Slayer, East and West: The Iconography of the Predella of the Boston Mystic Marriage of St. Catherine," *Gesta* 32, no. 1 (1993): 11–20.
18. Paroma Chatterjee, *The Living Icon in Byzantium and Italy, Eleventh to Thirteenth Centuries* (Cambridge: Cambridge University Press, 2014).
19. Laurence B. Kanter, *Italian Paintings in the Museum of Fine Arts, Boston: 13th–15th Century*, vol. 1 (Boston: Museum of Fine Arts, 1994), 91–95.
20. For a close comparison between lay marriage and the symbolic marriage of nuns to Jesus, see Kate Lowe, "Secular Brides and Convent Brides: Wedding Ceremonies in Italy during the Renaissance," in *Marriage in Italy, 1300–1600*, ed. Trevor Dean and Kate Lowe (Cambridge: Cambridge University Press, 1998), 41–65.
21. De Pizan, *The Book of the City of Ladies*, 135–37.

Exemplary Women

1. Giovanni Dominici, *Regola del governo di cura familiare*, ed. Donato Salvi (Florence: Angiolo Garinei, 1860); Jacqueline Marie Musacchio, *Art, Marriage, and Family in the Renaissance Palace* (New Haven: Yale University Press, 2008), 190–243.
2. John Pope-Hennessy, *Donatello Sculptor* (New York: Abbeville Press, 1993), 280–88; Francesco Caglioti, *Donatello ed i Medici: Storia del David e della Giuditta* (Florence: Leo S. Olschki Editore, 2000); Francesco Caglioti, *Donatello: The Renaissance* (Venice: Marsilio Editori, 2022), 93.
3. See Kevin R. Brine, Elena Ciletti, and Henrike Lähnemann, eds., *The Sword of Judith: Judith Studies across the Disciplines* (Cambridge: Open Book Publishers, 2010), for essays on the figure and image of Judith; see especially Roger J. Crum, "Judith between the Private and Public Realms in Renaissance Florence," 291–306; Sarah Blake McHam, "Donatello's *Judith* as the Emblem of God's Chosen People," 307–24; and Diane Apostolos-Cappadona, "Costuming Judith in Italian Art of the Sixteenth Century," 325–43.
4. Charles Seymour Jr., *Michelangelo's David: A Search for Identity* (Pittsburgh: University of Pittsburgh Press, 1967); McHam, "Donatello's *Judith*," 24.
5. Geraldine A. Johnson, "Idol or Ideal? The Power and Potency of Female Public Sculpture," in *Picturing Women in Renaissance and Baroque Italy*, ed. Geraldine A. Johnson and Sara F. Matthews Grieco (Cambridge: Cambridge University Press, 1997), 222–45; 231 for quotation.
6. W. Tschermak von Seysenegg, "Die Judith von Giovanni della Robbia," *Keramos* 114 (1986): 27–36; Musacchio, *Art, Marriage, and Family*, 237–43.
7. Adrian W. B. Randolph, "Renaissance Household Goddesses: Fertility, Politics, and the Gendering of Spectatorship," in *The Material Culture of Sex, Procreation, and Marriage in Premodern Europe*, ed. Anne L. McClanan and Karen Rosoff Encarnación (New York: Palgrave, 2002), 163–90; Jacqueline Marie Musacchio, in *Art and Love in Renaissance Italy*, ed. Andrea Bayer (New York: Metropolitan Museum of Art, 2008), 118–19.
8. Katherine Ludwig Jansen, *The Making of the Magdalen: Preaching and Devotion in the Later Middle Ages* (Princeton: Princeton University Press, 2000); Erin E. Benay and Lisa M. Rafanelli, *Faith, Gender and the Senses in Italian Renaissance and Baroque Art* (New York: Routledge, 2015).
9. For context on women's asceticism, see Caroline Walker Bynum, *Holy Feast and Holy Fast: The Religious Significance of Food to Medieval Women* (Berkeley: University of California Press,

1987); Susanna Elm, *Virgins of God: The Making of Asceticism in Late Antiquity* (Oxford: Clarendon Press, 1994); and Stefanie Solum, *Women, Patronage, and Salvation in Renaissance Florence: Lucrezia Tornabuoni and the Chapel of the Medici Palace* (Farnham, UK: Ashgate, 2015), 67–71.
10. Caglioti, *Donatello*, 76.
11. John Pope-Hennessy with Ronald Lightbown, *Catalogue of Italian Sculpture in the Victoria and Albert Museum* (London: Her Majesty's Stationery Office, 1964), 137, 194–95, fig. 184 also for a mention of other versions.
12. Solum, *Women, Patronage, and Salvation*, 186–95.
13. Holly Flora suggests persuasively that this painting may have been made for a Florentine convent in *Sanctity Pictured: The Art of the Dominican and Franciscan Orders in Renaissance Italy*, ed. Trinita Kennedy (Nashville: Frist Center for the Visual Arts, 2014), 197–98.
14. See Benay and Rafanelli, *Faith, Gender and the Senses*, 82–89, for a series of glazed terracotta altarpieces made for convent settings in Florence in the first half of the sixteenth century.
15. Sharon T. Strocchia, "Knowing Hands: Nuns and the Needle Arts in Renaissance Italy," in *Artiste nel chiostro: Produzione artistica nei monasteri femminili in età moderna*, ed. Sheila Barker with Luciano Cinelli (Florence: Nerbini, 2015; *Memorie Domenicane* n.s. 46), 31–52. Stacey Shimizu, "The Pattern of Perfect Womanhood," in *Women's Education in Early Modern Europe: A History, 1500–1800*, ed. Barbara J. Whitehead (New York: Garland, 1999), 75–76.
16. Ellen Callmann, *Apollonio di Giovanni* (Oxford: Oxford University Press, 1974), 64–66; see also Cristelle L. Baskins, *Cassone Painting, Humanism, and Gender in Early Modern Italy* (Cambridge: Cambridge University Press, 1998).
17. For marriage, its rituals, and the objects associated with these rituals, see Musacchio, *Art, Marriage, and Family*, 2–62. For the Meeting of Solomon and Sheba, see Musacchio, in *Art and Love in Renaissance Italy*, cat. no. 73, 159–61.
18. Marta Ajmar-Wollheim and Flora Dennis, eds., *At Home in Renaissance Italy* (London: V&A Publications, 2006), 120–21; Adrian W. B. Randolph, *Touching Objects: Intimate Experiences of Italian Fifteenth-Century Art* (New Haven: Yale University Press, 2014), 139–67.
19. Stephen K. Scher, ed., *The Currency of Fame: Portrait Medals of the Renaissance* (New York: Harry N. Abrams, 1994), 44–46. See also Musacchio in *Art and Love in Renaissance Italy*, cat. no. 73, 161, for such hats as signs of foreignness.
20. See Jillian Stinchcomb, "Race, Racism, and the Hebrew Bible: The Case of the Queen of Sheba," *Religions* 12, no. 10 (2021): 795, for a recent consideration and review of the premodern sources for the idea that the Queen of Sheba was Black.
21. See Kathleen Bickford Berzock, ed., *Caravans of Gold, Fragments in Time: Art, Culture and Exchange across Medieval Saharan Africa* (Princeton: Princeton University Press, 2019), for the trade in gold from Africa in the Middle Ages.
22. Jacqueline Marie Musacchio, *The Art and Ritual of Childbirth in Renaissance Italy* (New Haven: Yale University Press, 1999).
23. For European ideas about centralized churches taking inspiration from buildings in Jerusalem, especially the Church of the Holy Sepulchre, and the conflation of the Dome of the Rock with an idea of Solomon's Temple, see Pamela Berger, *The Crescent on the Temple* (Leiden: Brill, 2012), 149–58. Here the pediment of the building is inscribed "Templum Salamon."
24. Jacqueline Marie Musacchio, "Lambs, Coral, Teeth, and the Devotional Intersection of Religion and Magic in Renaissance Tuscany," in *Images, Relics, and Devotional Practice in Medieval and Renaissance Italy*, ed. Sally J. Cornelison and Scott B. Montgomery (Tempe, AZ: Arizona Center for Medieval and Renaissance Studies, 2005), 151–53.

The Materials of Marriage

1. Christiane Klapisch-Zuber, *Women, Family, and Ritual in Renaissance Italy*, trans. Lydia G. Cochrane (Chicago: University of Chicago Press, 1985); Trevor Dean and Kate Lowe, eds., *Marriage in Italy, 1300–1600* (Cambridge: Cambridge University Press, 1998); Andrea Bayer, ed., *Art and Love in Renaissance Italy* (New York: Metropolitan Museum of Art, 2008); and Jacqueline Marie Musacchio, *Art, Marriage, and Family in the Renaissance Palace* (New Haven: Yale University Press, 2008).
2. For the significance of pearls and other gems in portraits of women, see David Alan Brown, ed., *Virtue and Beauty: Leonardo's* Ginevra de' Benci *and Renaissance Portraits of Women* (Washington, D.C.: National Gallery of Art, 2001), 65–68.
3. Rebecca Zorach and Michael W. Phillips Jr., *Gold: Nature and Culture* (London: Reaktion Books, 2016), 114–38.
4. Strategic marriages for the many children of Giovanni II Bentivoglio and his wife Ginevra Strozzi at the very least illuminate the importance of marriage in the political life of Bologna in the period; see Elizabeth Louise Bernhardt, "Behind the Scenes of Fifteenth-Century Marriage Schemes: Forced Marriages,

Family Alliances and Power Politics in Bentivoglio Bologna" in *Bologna: Cultural Crossroads from the Medieval to the Baroque; Recent Anglo-American Scholarship*, ed. Gian Mario Anselmi, Angela De Benedictis, and Nicholas Terpstra (Bologna: Bononia University Press, 2013), 161–71.
5. For marriage diptychs, see Everett Fahy, "The Marriage Portrait in the Renaissance, or Some Women Named Ginevra," in Bayer, ed., *Art and Love in Renaissance Italy*, 18–21; see also Adrian W. B. Randolph, "Performing the Bridal Body in Fifteenth-Century Florence," *Art History* 21 (1998): 182–200.
6. In Italian: "Chi semina virtù, fama rechorlie."
7. Dora Thornton and Marta Ajmar, "When Is a Portrait Not a Portrait? *Belle Donne* on Maiolica and the Renaissance Praise of Local Beauties," in *The Image of the Individual: Portraits in the Renaissance*, ed. Luke Syson and Nicholas Mann (London: British Museum Press, 1998), 138–53.
8. See catalogue entries 9, 10, and 11 by Dora Thornton for similar luster-glazed bowls with women in the center, golden bands, and trophy decorations on the rims in Bayer, ed., *Art and Love in Renaissance Italy*, 76–77.
9. Jacqueline Marie Musacchio, "Lambs, Coral, Teeth, and the Devotional Intersection of Religion and Magic in Renaissance Tuscany," in *Images, Relics, and Devotional Practice in Medieval and Renaissance Italy*, eds. Sally J. Cornelison and Scott B. Montgomery (Tempe, AZ: Arizona Center for Medieval and Renaissance Studies, 2005), 151–53.
10. For Deruta lusterware, for example, see Michael Brody, "Religious Subjects on Sixteenth Century Deruta *Piatti da pompa*," in *Domestic Devotions in Early Modern Italy*, ed. Maya Corry, Marco Faini, and Alessia Meneghin (Leiden: Brill, 2019), 187–219, who cites Cipriano Piccolpasso, *Li tre libri dell'arte del vasaio* (The Three Books of the Potter's Art): "When the wares are good, they seem like gold," 189. For this kind of straw work, usually made by women, see Eve Borsook, Roberto Lunardi, Barbara Schleicher, and Gianni Guido Rosetti, eds., *L'oro dei poveri: La paglia nell'arredo liturgico e nelle immagini devozionali dell'Italia centrale fra il 1670 e il 1870* (Florence: Edizioni Polistampa, 2000).
11. For the value of artistic skill in relation to the value of the material of gold, see, for example, Roger Jones, "Mantegna and Materials," *I Tatti Studies in the Italian Renaissance* 2 (1987): 71–73; Luke Syson and Dora Thornton, *Objects of Virtue: Art in Renaissance Italy* (Los Angeles: Getty, 2001), 89; and for a survey of objects and their materials as related to marriage, 37–77.
12. For a survey of Renaissance textiles for use in the home, see Peter Thornton, *The Italian Renaissance Interior, 1400–1600* (New York: Harry N. Abrams, 1991), 69–84.
13. See catalogue entry 16 by Dora Thornton for the rituals signaled by the joined hands, the *fede* ring, and the profile portraits, all references to marriage and its rituals; Bayer, ed., *Art and Love in Renaissance Italy*, 83–84.
14. In Italian:"Io te do la mano. Dammi la fede."
15. For one example of clasped hands related to marriage on an ancient example, see Ring with clasped hands, Roman, 3rd century A.D., sardonyx and gold, width: 2.3 cm, Gift of Robert E. Hecht, Jr. in memory of Robert E. Hecht, Sr. and Julia K. Hecht, 63.1555, Museum of Fine Arts, Boston.
16. See Musacchio, "Lambs, Coral, Teeth," for these Agnus Dei pendants and their functions in the home in relation to marriage, birth, and child rearing. See also Irene Galandra Cooper, "Investigating the 'Case' of the Agnus Dei in Sixteenth-Century Italian Homes," in Corry, Faini, and Meneghin, ed. *Domestic Devotions in Early Modern Italy*, 220–43.
17. This discussion is drawn from Howard Tzvi Adelman, "The Venetian Identities of Beatrice and Brianda de Luna," *Nashim: A Journal of Jewish Women's Studies & Gender Issues* 25 (Fall 2013): 10–29, which pulls together many important sources to lay out the complex story of the Nasi family in Italy. Gracia the Younger is not the subject of the article, but a great deal about her emerges from the documents related to the lives of her mother and aunt.
18. Cecil Roth, *The House of Nasi: Doña Gracia* (Philadelphia: Jewish Publication Society of America, 1948); Andrée Aelion Brook, *The Woman Who Defied Kings: The Life and Times of Doña Gracia Nasi* (St. Paul, MN: Paragon House, 2002); Marianna D. Birnbaum, *The Long Journey of Gracia Nasi* (Budapest: Central European Press, 2003); and Robert Bonfil, "Business, Politics and Philanthropy: Doña Gracia Nasi as a Metaphor," *Italia* 21 (2012): 7–41.
19. Daniel M. Friedenberg, *Jewish Medals from the Renaissance to the Fall of Napoleon (1503–1815)* (New York: Clarkson N. Potter, 1970); Stephen K. Scher, ed., *The Currency of Fame: Portrait Medals of the Renaissance* (New York: Harry N. Abrams, 1994); Eleonora Luciano, "Medals of Women from the Italian Renaissance Courts" (Ph.D. diss., Indiana University, 1997); Christine Chiorian Wolken, "Beauty, Power, Propaganda, and Celebration: Profiling Women in Sixteenth-Century Italian Commemorative Medals" (Ph.D. diss. Case Western University, 2012).
20. Another cast is at the Jewish Museum, New York: Pastorino di Giovan

Michele de' Pastorini (about 1508–1592), Medal of Gracia Nasi the Younger, 1558. Gift of the Samuel and Daniel M. Friedenberg Collection, FB 77.
21. Adelman, "Venetian Identities," 17; see also Birnbaum, *The Long Journey*, 75–114.

Prayer and Practice
1. Catherine Lawless, "Sensing the Image: Gender, Piety, and Images in Late Medieval Tuscany," *Open Arts Journal* 4 (Winter 2014–15): 62–74; Abigail Brundin, Deborah Howard, and Mary Laven, *The Sacred Home in Renaissance Italy* (Oxford: Oxford University Press, 2018); Carolina Walker Bynum, *Dissimilar Similitudes: Devotional Objects in Late Medieval Europe* (Brooklyn: Zone Books, 2020); and Maya Corry, Deborah Howard, and Mary Laven, eds., *Madonnas and Miracles: The Holy Home in Renaissance Italy* (London: Philip Wilson, 2017).
2. Stefanie Solum, *Women, Patronage, and Salvation in Renaissance Florence: Lucrezia Tornabuoni and the Chapel of the Medici Palace* (Farnham, UK: Ashgate, 2015).
3. Adrian Randolph, "Regarding Women in Sacred Spaces," in *Picturing Women in Renaissance and Baroque Italy,* ed. Geraldine A. Johnson and Sara F. Matthews Grieco, (Cambridge: Cambridge University Press, 1997), 17–41; Mary D. Garrard, "The Cloister and the Square: Gender Dynamics in Renaissance Florence," *Early Modern Women: An Interdisciplinary Journal* 11, no. 1 (Fall 2016): 5–43.
4. For women's participation in confraternities, see Christopher F. Black, *Italian Confraternities in the Sixteenth Century* (Cambridge: Cambridge University Press, 1989), 34–38; Nicholas Terpstra, "Women in the Brotherhood: Gender, Class, and Politics in Renaissance Bolognese Confraternities," *Renaissance and Reformation* n.s., 14, no. 3 (Summer 1990): 193–212; and Barbara Wisch and Diane Cole Ahl, eds., *Confraternities and the Visual Arts in Renaissance Italy: Ritual, Spectacle, Image* (Cambridge: Cambridge University Press, 2000), 9–12. Women's consororites existed, but their history is still being pieced together; see Sharon T. Strocchia, "Sisters in Spirit: The Nuns of Sant'Ambrogio and Their Consorority in Early Sixteenth Century Florence," *The Sixteenth Century Journal* 33, no. 3 (Autumn 2002): 735–67.
5. Kate Lowe, *Nuns' Chronicles and Convent Culture in Renaissance and Counter-Reformation Italy* (Cambridge: Cambridge University Press, 2003); Anabel Thomas, *Art and Piety in the Female Religious Communities of Renaissance Florence: Iconography, Space, and the Religious Woman's Perspective* (Cambridge: Cambridge University Press, 2003); and Sharon T. Strocchia, *Nuns and Nunneries in Renaissance Florence* (Baltimore: Johns Hopkins University Press, 2009).
6. Isa Ragusa and Rosalie B. Green, eds., *Meditations on the Life of Christ: An Illustrated Manuscript of the Fourteenth Century,* trans. Isa Ragusa (Princeton: Princeton University Press, 1961); Sarah McNamer, *Affective Meditation and the Invention of Medieval Compassion* (Philadelphia: University of Pennsylvania Press, 2010).
7. Laurence B. Kanter, *Italian Paintings in the Museum of Fine Arts, Boston: 13th–15th Century,* vol. 1 (Boston: Museum of Fine Arts, 1994), 52–53; Catherine Lawless, "'Make Your House Like a Temple': Gender, Space, and Domestic Devotion in Medieval Florence," *Religions* 11, no. 120 (2020).
8. Frederick Ilchman, "Questioning Connoisseurship: The Other Late Titian in Boston" in *Venetian Painting Matters,* ed. Jodi Cranston, (Turnhout: Brepols, 2015), 91–112.
9. Paul Hills, *Veiled Presence: Body and Drapery from Giotto to Titian* (New Haven: Yale University Press, 2018), 173–97, especially 193–95.
10. Lisa Beaven, "Faith and Fetish: Objects and the Body in Catholic Devotional Practice," in *Emotion and the Seduction of the Senses, Baroque to Neo-Baroque*, ed. Lisa Beaven and Angela Ndalianis (Kalamazoo: Medieval Institute Publications, Western Michigan University, 2018), 235–56.
11. Catherine E. King, *Renaissance Women Patrons: Wives and Widows in Italy, c. 1300–1550* (Manchester: Manchester University Press, 1998); Allison Levy, ed., *Widowhood and Visual Culture in Early Modern Europe* (London: Routledge, 2016).
12. Giovanni Dominici, *Regola del governo di cura familiare*, ed. Donato Salvi (Florence: Angiolo Garinei, 1860); Jacqueline Marie Musacchio, *Art, Marriage, and Family in the Renaissance Palace* (New Haven: Yale University Press, 2008), 190–243; Brundin, Howard, and Laven, *Sacred Home*, 69–78.
13. Jacqueline Marie Musacchio, "Lambs, Coral, Teeth, and the Devotional Intersection of Religion and Magic in Renaissance Tuscany," in *Images, Relics, and Devotional Practice in Medieval and Renaissance Italy*, ed. Sally J. Cornelison and Scott B. Montgomery (Tempe, AZ: Arizona Center for Medieval and Renaissance Studies, 2005), 151–53.
14. Christiane Klapisch-Zuber, *Women, Family, and Ritual in Renaissance Italy*, trans. Lydia G. Cochrane (Chicago: University of Chicago Press, 1985), 310–29; Musacchio, *Art, Marriage, and Family*, 177–80; Maya Corry and Zuzanna Sarnecka, in Corry, Howard, Laven, eds., *Madonnas and Miracles*, 92–93.
15. Marietta Cambareri with Courtney Leigh Harris and Abigail Hykin,

Della Robbia: Sculpting with Color in Renaissance Florence (Boston: MFA Publications, 2016), 38–41.
16. Anne Winston-Allen, *Stories of the Rose: The Making of the Rosary in the Middle Ages*, (University Park: The Pennsylvania State University Press, 1997).
17. Sharon T. Strocchia, "Knowing Hands: Nuns and the Needle Arts in Renaissance Italy," in *Artiste nel chiostro: Produzione artistica nei monasteri femminili in età moderna*, ed. Sheila Barker with Luciano Cinelli (Florence: Nerbini, 2015; *Memorie Domenicane* n.s. 46), 31–52.
18. Strocchia, *Nuns and Nunneries*; Thomas, *Art and Piety*.
19. Alessandra Bartolomei Romagnoli, *Santità e mistica femminile nel Medioevo* (Spoleto: Fondazione Centro Italiano di Studi sull'Alto Medioevo, 2013); see "Le metamorfosi del testo: Il caso di Veronica di Binasco," 549–85; Alessandra Bartolomei Romagnoli, Emore Paoli, and Pierantonio Piatti, eds., *Angeliche visioni: Veronica di Binasco nella Milano del Rinascimento* (Florence: SISMEL Edizioni, 2016).
20. Lowe, *Nuns' Chronicles*.
21. Sharon T. Strocchia, "Learning the Virtues: Convent Schools and Female Culture in Renaissance Florence," in *Women's Education in Early Modern Europe: A History, 1500–1800*, ed. Barbara J. Whitehead (New York: Garland, 1999), 3–46.
22. Thomas, *Art and Piety*; Marietta Cambareri, "Della Robbia Sculptures for Florentine Renaissance Convents," in *The Materiality of Terracotta Sculpture in Early Modern Europe*, ed. Zuzanna Sarnecka and Agnieszka Dziki (New York: Routledge, 2023).
23. Garrard, "The Cloister and the Square," 23–26.
24. Sharon T. Strocchia, "Savonarolan Witnesses: The Nuns of San Jacopo and the Piagnone Movement in Sixteenth-Century Florence," *Sixteenth Century Journal* 38, no. 2 (2007): 393–418; Tamar Herzig, *Savonarola's Women: Visions and Reform in Renaissance Florence* (Chicago: University of Chicago Press, 2008).
25. Craig A. Monson, *Disembodied Voices: Music and Culture in an Early Modern Convent* (Berkeley: University of California Press, 1995); Robert L. Kendrick, *Celestial Sirens: Nuns and Their Music in Early Modern Milan* (Oxford: Clarendon Press, 1996); and Laurie Stras, *Women and Music in Renaissance Ferrara* (Cambridge: Cambridge University Press, 2018).
26. Elissa B. Weaver, *Convent Theatre in Early Modern Italy: Spiritual Fun and Learning for Women* (Cambridge: Cambridge University Press, 2002).
27. Strocchia, "Knowing Hands," 37–38.
28. Quoted in Lawless, "Sensing the Image," 64.
29. Giulio Busi and Silvana Greco, eds., *The Renaissance Speaks Hebrew* (Milan: Silvana Editoriale, 2019).
30. Cissy Grossman, "Womanly Arts: A Study of Italian Torah Binders in the New York Jewish Museum Collection," *Journal of Jewish Art* 7 (1980): 35–43; Howard Adelman, "Rabbis and Reality: Public Activities of Jewish Women in Italy during the Renaissance and Catholic Restoration," *Jewish History* 5, no. 1 (Spring 1991): 30–31.
31. Thanks to Simona Di Nepi for her help with these inscriptions.
32. Norman Kleeblatt and Vivian B. Mann, *Treasures of the Jewish* Museum (New York: Jewish Museum, 1986), 56.
33. Shalom Sabar, "Bride, Heroine and Courtesan: Images of Jewish Women in Hebrew Manuscripts of the Renaissance in Italy," in *Proceedings of the Tenth World Congress of Jewish Studies* (Jerusalem: World Congress of Jewish Studies, 1990), 63–70, especially 68.
34. Evelyn Cohen, "The Illustrations in Maraviglia's Prayer-Book," The Polonsky Foundation Catalogue of Digitised Hebrew Manuscripts, British Library, www.bl.uk.

Artists Known and Unknown

1. Mary D. Garrard, "Here's Looking at Me: Sofonisba Anguissola and the Problem of the Woman Artist," *Renaissance Quarterly* 47, no. 3 (Autumn 1994): 567–68, 573–74; Sheila Barker, ed., *Women Artists in Early Modern Italy: Careers, Fame, and Collectors* (Turnhout: Brepols, 2016), 7–8; Sarah Gwyneth Ross, *The Birth of Feminism: Woman as Intellect in Renaissance Italy and England* (Cambridge, MA: Harvard University Press, 2009), 92–94.
2. Barker, ed., *Women Artists*, 5–14; Sheila Barker, "Art as Women's Work: The Professionalization of Women Artists, 1350–1800," in *By Her Hand: Artemisia Gentileschi and Women Artists in Italy, 1500–1800*, ed. Eve Straussman-Pflanzer and Oliver Tostmann (New Haven: Yale University Press, 2021), 43–51.
3. Sheila Barker and Luciano Cinelli, eds., *Artiste nel chiostro: Produzione artistica nei monasteri femminili in età moderna* (Florence: Nerbini, 2015; *Memorie Domenicane* n.s. 46); Jonathan K. Nelson, *Plautilla Nelli (1524–1588): The Painter-Prioress of Renaissance Florence* (Florence: Syracuse University Press, 2008); and Sharon T. Strocchia, "Knowing Hands: Nuns and the Needle Arts in Renaissance Italy" in *Artiste nel Chiostro*, ed. Barker and Cinelli.
4. Sheila Barker, *Artemisia Gentileschi* (London: Lund Humphries, 2021), 53–55.
5. Babette Bohn, *Women Artists, Their Patrons, and Their Publics in Early Modern Bologna* (University Park: The Pennsylvania State University Press, 2021).

6. Sharon T. Strocchia, "Learning the Virtues: Convent Schools and Female Culture in Renaissance Florence," in *Women's Education in Early Modern Europe: A History, 1500–1800,* ed. Barbara J. Whitehead (New York: Garland, 1999); Howard Tzvi Adelman, "The Literacy of Jewish Women," in Whitehead, ed., *Women's Education*; Ross, *The Birth of Feminism*, 1–13; and Barker, "Art as Women's Work," 44.

7. Virginia Cox, "Women Writers and the Canon in Sixteenth-Century Italy: The Case of Vittoria Colonna," in *Strong Voices, Weak Histories: Early Women Writers and Canons in England, France, and Italy*, Pamela J. Benson and Victoria Kirkham, ed. (Ann Arbor: University of Michigan Press, 2005), 14–31; Ramie Targoff, *Renaissance Woman: The Life of Vittoria Colonna* (New York: Farrar, Straus and Giroux, 2018), especially 159–75 for the publication of her poems.

8. Recent work on Sofonisba Anguissola includes Leticia Ruiz Gómez, ed., *A Tale of Two Women Painters: Sofonisba Anguissola and Lavinia Fontana* (Madrid: Museo Nacional del Prado, 2019); and Michael W. Cole, *Sofonisba's Lesson: A Renaissance Artist and Her Work* (Princeton: Princeton University Press, 2019).

9. Garrard, "Here's Looking at Me," 556–622.

10. Garrard, "Here's Looking at Me," 566–68. The Italian phrase reads "per poter in un tempo mostrare due meraviglie insieme, l'una dell'opera, l'altra della Maestra." See also Fredrika H. Jacobs, *Defining the Renaissance Virtuosa: Women Artists and the Language of Art History and Criticism* (Cambridge: Cambridge University Press, 1997), 127–29.

11. Jacobs, *Defining the Renaissance Virtuosa*, 56–57; Cole, *Sofonisba's Lesson,* 98–113 and 16–47. For the importance of the support of fathers in their daughters' education and success, see Ross, *Birth of Feminism*, 1–13, 20–52.

12. Jacobs, *Defining the Renaissance Virtuosa*, 38–39, 51–55. See also Barker, "Art as Women's Work," 45.

13. Garrard, "Here's Looking at Me," 583–86; Cole, *Sofonisba's Lesson*, 50–64, 89–94.

14. For recent interpretations of the cipher, see Jorge Sebastiàn Lozano in Gomez, ed., *A Tale of Two Women Painters*, 95; Cole, *Sofonisba's Lesson*, 33–39; Oliver Tostmann in Straussman-Pflanzer and Tostmann, ed. *By Her Hand*, 56–57.

15. For Anguissola's use of the Latin word *virgo* to describe herself, see Garrard, "Here's Looking at Me," 582–83; Sheila Barker, "The First Biography of Artemisia Gentileschi: Self-Fashioning and Proto-Feminism in Cristofano Bronzini's Notes on Women Artists," *Mitteilungen des Kunsthistorischen Institutes in Florenz* 60, no. 3 (2018): 424–25.

16. Alejandro Vergara, in Gomez, ed., *A Tale of Two Women Painters*, 134–37. Cole, in *Sofonisba's Lesson*, stresses Anguissola's role as a teacher throughout her life; for Van Dyck, see 150.

17. For Lavinia Fontana, see Caroline Murphy, *Lavinia Fontana: A Painter and Her Patrons in Sixteenth-Century Bologna* (New Haven: Yale University Press, 2003); Gomez, ed., *A Tale of Two Women Painters*, 27–34; Bohn, *Women Artists, Their Patrons, and Their Publics*, 36–52; Aoife Brady, ed., *Lavinia Fontana: Trailblazer, Rule Breaker* (Dublin: National Gallery of Ireland, 2023).

18. Caroline P. Murphy, "Lavinia Fontana and Female Life Cycle Experience in Late Sixteenth-Century Bologna," in *Picturing Women in Renaissance and Baroque Italy*, ed. Geraldine A. Johnson and Sara F. Matthews Grieco (Cambridge: Cambridge University Press, 1997), 120–29.

19. For Barbara Longhi, see Giordano Vironi, "Barbara Longhi," *Dizionario Biografico degli Italiani* 65 (2005); Liana De Girolami Cheney, *Barbara Longhi* (London: Lund Humphries, 2023). For a related painting, see Serena Simoni, "Una nuova 'Madonna del Latte' di Barbara Longhi," *Romagna arte e storia* 24 (2004): 105–12.

20. Meghan Holmes, "Disrobing the Virgin: The *Madonna Lactans* in Fifteenth-Century Italian Art," in Johnson and Grieco, eds., *Picturing Women*, 167–95.

21. Holmes, "Disrobing the Virgin," 182.

22. Cecelia M. Dorger, "Studies in the Image of the *Madonna Lactans* in Late Medieval and Renaissance Art" (PhD diss., University of Louisville, 2012), 167–79, 181–202.

23. Recent work on Artemisia Gentileschi includes Barker, *Artemisia Gentleschi,* and Letizia Treves, ed., *Artemisia* (London: National Gallery, 2020); for this painting, see 226n5, and for other works on copper, 121. See also Mary D. Garrard, *Artemisia Gentileschi: The Image of the Female Hero in Italian Baroque Art* (Princeton: Princeton University Press, 1989), 173.

24. Oliver Tostmann, "The Advantages of Painting Small: Italian Women Artists and the Matter of Scale," in Straussman-Pflanzer and Tostmann, eds., *By Her Hand*, 31–41.

25. For her signature on *The Last Supper* with the words "Pray for the painter" (or *Orate pro pictora* in Latin), see Catherine Turrill, in *Plautilla Nelli, (1524–1588): The Painter-Prioress of Renaissance Florence*, ed. Jonathan K. Nelson (Florence: Syracuse University Press, 2008), 13.

26. Evelyn Lincoln, "Making a Good Impression: Diana Mantuana's Printmaking Career," *Renaissance Quarterly* 50, no. 4 (Winter 1997): 1101–47.

27. Quoted in Lincoln, "Making a Good Impression," 1105.
28. Lincoln, "Making a Good Impression," 1116–24.
29. Translated in Lincoln, "Making a Good Impression," 1128–29.
30. Christine Chiorian Wolken, "Beauty, Power, Propaganda, and Celebration: Profiling Women in Sixteenth-Century Italian Commemorative Medals" (PhD diss., Case Western University, 2012), 251–65. Diana Mantuana does not seem to have joined the Accademia di San Luca, nor the Compagnia di San Luca from which it developed.
31. Eve Borsook, Roberto Lunardi, Barbara Schleicher, and Gianni Guido Rosetti, eds., *L'oro dei poveri: La paglia nell'arredo liturgico e nelle immagini devozionali dell'Italia centrale fra il 1670 e il 1870* (Florence: Edizioni Polistampa, 2000).
32. Strocchia, "Knowing Hands," 31–33, 36; Barker, "Art as Women's Work," 48.
33. Ann Rosalind Jones, "Labor and Lace: The Crafts of Giacomo Franco's *Habiti delle donne venetiane*," *I Tatti Studies in the Italian Renaissance* 17, no. 2 (September 2014): 399–425, especially 406–12.
34. Margaret F. Rosenthal and Ann Rosalind Jones, *Cesare Vecellio's* Habiti Antichi et Moderni: *The Clothing of the Renaissance World; Europe, Asia, Africa, the Americas* (London: Thames and Hudson, 2008), 261.
35. Jacobs, *Defining the Renaissance Virtuosa*, 59–60, 105–107; Evelyn Lincoln, "Models for Science and Craft: Isabella Parasole's Botanical and Lace Illustrations," *Visual Resources* 17, no. 1 (2001): 1–35.
36. Jacobs, *Defining the Renaissance Virtuosa*, 59–60, 105–107; Evelyn Lincoln, "Models for Science and Craft."
37. Norman Kleeblatt and Vivian B. Mann, *Treasures of the Jewish Museum* (New York: Jewish Museum, 1986), 56.
38. Christine de Pizan, *The Book of the City of Ladies and Other Writings*, ed. Sophie Bourgault and Rebecca Kingston, trans. Ineke Hardy (Indianapolis: Hackett, 2018), 89–90.

Illustrious Women

1. Marietta Cambareri, in *Bonacolsi l'Antico: Uno scultore nella Mantova di Andrea Mantegna e di Isabella d'Este*, ed. Filippo Trevisani and Davide Gasparotto (Milan: Electa, 2008), 262–63.
2. Giovanni Boccaccio, *On Famous Women*, trans. Guido A. Guarino (New York: Italica Press, 2011), 192.
3. Brian Curran, *The Egyptian Renaissance: The Afterlife of Ancient Egypt in Early Modern Italy* (Chicago: University of Chicago Press, 2007), 172–76.
4. Nicholas Penny, "The History of the Plinth, Pedestal, and Socle," in *Collecting Sculpture in Early Modern Europe*, ed. Nicholas Penny and Eike D. Schmidt (New Haven: Yale University Press, 2008), 467.
5. Anne H. Allison, "The Bronzes of Pier Jacopo Alari-Bonacolsi, Called Antico," *Jahrbuch der Kunsthistorischen Sammlungen in Wien* 89–90 (1993–94): 55, 240–43; Wendy Stedman Sheard, in *Tiziano: Amor Sacro e Profano*, ed. Maria Grazia Bernardini (Milan: Electa, 1995), 271–74.
6. Allison, "Bronzes of Pier Jacopo Alari-Bonacolsi," 243.
7. Leonard Barkan, *Unearthing the Past: Archaeology and Aesthetics in the Making of Renaissance Culture* (New Haven: Yale University Press,1999), 233.
8. For Castiglione's poem, see Curran, *Egyptian Renaissance*, 172–73.
9. Stephen J. Campbell, *The Cabinet of Eros: The Studiolo of Isabella d'Este and the Rise of Renaissance Mythological Painting* (New Haven: Yale University Press, 2004), 92.
10. Barkan, *Unearthing the Past*, 246–47.
11. Stephen J. Campbell, "Mantegna's Triumphs: The Culural Politics of Imitation 'all'antica' at the Court of Mantua," in *Mantegna*, ed. Stephen J. Campbell and Jérémie Koering (Malden, MA: Wiley Blackwell, 2015), 91–105.
12. See Andrea Bayer, ed., *Art and Love in Renaissance Italy* (New York: Metropolitan Museum of Art, 2008), 321–23, for the association of wreaths with marriage poetry and celebrations.
13. Lisa Boutin, "Isabella d'Este and the Gender Neutrality of Renaissance Ceramics," *Women's Studies* 40, no. 1 (2011): 23–47, especially 29–34.
14. Boutin, "Isabella d'Este," 32; Campbell, *Cabinet of Eros*, 75–78; Tim Shephard, "Constructing Isabella d'Este's Musical Decorum in the Visual Sphere," *Renaissance Studies* 25, no. 5 (November 2011): 684–706, especially 699–703.
15. Shephard, "Constructing Isabella d'Este's Musical Decorum," 696–99; Campbell, *Cabinet of Eros*, 118, and, for Isabella as the "Tenth Muse," 199–200; William F. Prizer, "Isabella d'Este and Lucrezia Borgia as Patrons of Music: The *Frottole* at Mantua and Ferrara," *Journal of the American Musical Society* 38 (1985): 1–37.
16. Francis Fletcher, "Mantegna's Fictive Bronze *Judith* and *Dido*: Beyond Exemplarity," in Campbell and Koering, eds., *Mantegna*, 177–99.
17. Paul H. D. Kaplan, "Isabella d'Este and Black African Women," in *Black Africans in Renaissance Europe*, ed. T. F. Earle and K. J. P. Lowe (Cambridge: Cambridge University Press, 2005), 125–54.
18. Stephen Kolsky, *The Ghost of Boccaccio: Writings on Famous Women in Renaissance Italy* (Turnhout: Brepols, 2005). See also Babette Bohn, "The Antique Heroines of Elisabetta Sirani," *Renaissance Studies* 16, no. 1 (March 2002): 52–79.

19. Kolsky, *Ghost of Boccaccio*, 82.
20. Kolsky, *Ghost of Boccaccio*, 117.
21. Sarah Gwyneth Ross, *The Birth of Feminism: Woman as Intellect in Renaissance Italy and England* (Cambridge, MA: Harvard University Press, 2009), 30–40.
22. Kolsky, *Ghost of Boccaccio*, 148–58.
23. See Kolsky, *Ghost of Boccaccio*, for this quote, 157; for Isabella d'Este and Margherita and Cornelia Cantelmo, 156–58.
24. See Nathaniel Silver, *Botticelli: Heroines and Heroes* (Boston: Isabella Stewart Gardner Museum, 2019); see also Jill Burke, *The Italian Renaissance Nude* (New Haven: Yale University Press, 2019).
25. See Victoria S. Reed, "Don't Look Now: The Turning Figure of Perseus and Two Images of Renaissance Decapitation," *Iconografia* 16 (2017): 164–73, especially 168.
26. Geraldine A. Johnson, "Idol or Ideal? The Power and Potency of Female Public Sculpture," in *Picturing Women in Renaissance and Baroque Italy*, ed. Geraldine A. Johnson and Sara F. Matthews Grieco (Cambridge: Cambridge University Press, 1997), 222–45, especially 240–44.
27. Christine de Pizan, *The Book of the City of Ladies and Other Writings*, ed. Sophie Bourgault and Rebecca Kingston, trans. Ineke Hardy (Indianapolis: Hackett, 2018), 135–37.

Science and Sorcery

1. Meredith K. Ray, *Daughters of Alchemy: Women and Scientific Culture in Early Modern Italy* (Cambridge, MA: Harvard University Press, 2015); Sharon T. Strocchia, *Forgotten Healers: Women and the Pursuit of Health in Late Renaissance Italy* (Cambridge, MA: Harvard University Press, 2019); Sheila Barker and Sharon T. Strocchia, "Household Medicine for a Renaissance Court: Caterina Sforza's *Ricettario* Reconsidered," in *Gender, Health and Healing, 1250–1550*, ed. Sara Ritchey and Sheila Barker, (Amsterdam: Amsterdam University Press, 2020).
2. Ray, *Daughters of Alchemy*, 36.
3. Sharon T. Strocchia, "The Nun-Apothecaries of Renaissance Florence: Marketing Medicines in the Convent," *Renaissance Studies* 25, no. 5 (November 2011): 627–47.
4. For women in professional guilds, see Sheila Barker, "Art as Women's Work: The Professionalization of Women Artists, 1350–1800," in *By Her Hand: Artemisia Gentileschi and Women Artists in Italy, 1500–1800*, ed. Eve Straussman-Pflanzer and Oliver Tostmann (New Haven: Yale University Press, 2021), 45–47.
5. Evelyn Welch, "Space and Spectacle in the Renaissance Pharmacy," *Medicina e Storia* 8, no. 15 (2008): 127–58.
6. Serinity Young, *Women Who Fly: Goddesses, Witches, Mystics, and Other Airborne Females* (Oxford: Oxford University Press, 2018), 46–47, 154–55.
7. Christine de Pizan, *The Book of the City of Ladies and Other Writings*, ed. Sophie Bourgault and Rebecca Kingston, trans. Ineke Hardy (Indianapolis: Hackett, 2018), 73–74, for example, recounts only the positive aspects of Medea's knowledge and magic, and her vital assistance to Jason, which aligns with her representation here.
8. Mary D. Garrard, *Artemisia Gentileschi: The Image of the Female Hero in Italian Baroque Art* (Princeton: Princeton University Press, 1989), 141–79.
9. Lisa Boutin, "Isabella d'Este and the Gender Neutrality of Renaissance Ceramics," *Women's Studies* 40, no. 1 (2011): 23–47; for the Painter of the Apollo Basin, see John V. G. Mallet, "Il pittore del bacile di apollo," in *La maiolica italiana del Cinquecento: Il lustro eugubino e l'istoriato del ducato di Urbino*, ed. Gian Carlo Bojani (Florence: Centro Di, 2002), 85–112.
10. Guy Tal, "Disbelieving in Witchcraft: Allori's Melancholic Circe in the Palazzo Salviati," *Athanor* 22 (2004): 57–65.
11. Peter Humphrey and Mauro Lucco, *Dosso Dossi: Court Painter in Renaissance Ferrara* (New York: Metropolitan Museum of Art, 1998), 89–92.
12. Ray, *Daughters of Alchemy*, 82.
13. Cecilia Muratori, "Better Animal than Human: The Happy Animal and the Human Animal in the Renaissance Reception of Aristotle," *Freiburger Zeitschrift für Philosophie und Theologie* (2019): 491–94.
14. For a good summary of the argument that these prints represent Circella, see the online entry for Parmigianino's *Circella beve la pozione magica di fronte a degli uomini su una nave* (inv. 1972 Fr., The Uffizi, Florence), euploos.uffizi.it.
15. Elizabeth Cropper, "On Beautiful Women, Parmigianino, *Petrarchismo*, and the Vernacular Style," *The Art Bulletin* 58, no. 3 (1976): 374–94.
16. Ray, *Daughters of Alchemy*, 78–83.
17. Moderata Fonte (Modesta Pozzo), *Floridoro: A Chivalric Romance*, ed. Valeria Finucci, trans. Julia Kisacky (Chicago: University of Chicago Press, 2006), 236.
18. Guido Ruggiero, *Binding Passions: Tales of Magic, Marriage, and Power at the End of the Renaissance* (Oxford: Oxford University Press, 1993), 149–52.
19. On women, nature, and scientific culture, see Ray, *Daughters of Alchemy*, 51–52, 73–110.
20. See 151n7 for the statuette of *Dovizia*, which has analogous significance.
21. See, for example, De Pizan, *The Book of the City of Ladies*, 97–104, who presents several chapters about sibyls and female prophets.

Hands and Minds

1. Ann Rosalind Jones and Peter Stallybrass, *Renaissance Clothing and the Materials of Memory* (Cambridge: Cambridge University Press, 2000); Sharon T. Strocchia, "Knowing Hands: Nuns and the Needle Arts in Renaissance Italy," in *Artiste nel chiostro: Produzione artistica nei monastei femminili in età moderna,* ed. Sheila Barker with Luciano Cinelli (Florence: Nerbini, 2015; *Memorie Domenicane* n.s. 46), 31–52. Marta Ajmar-Wollheim and Flora Dennis, eds., *At Home in Renaissance Italy* (London: V&A Publications, 2006), 155–60.

2. Stacey Shimizu, "The Pattern of Perfect Womanhood," in *Women's Education in Early Modern Europe: A History, 1500–1800,* ed. Barbara J. Whitehead (New York: Garland, 1999).

3. Jones and Stallybrass, *Renaissance Clothing*, 105–33; Giancarlo Fiorenza, "Homer's *Odyssey* and the Image of Penelope in Renaissance Art," in *Homère à la Renaissance: Mythe et Transfigurations,* ed. Luisa Capodieci and Philip Ford (Rome: Académie de France à Rome, 2011), 223–40.

4. Shimizu, "Pattern of Perfect Womanhood"; Femke Speelberg, "Fashion and Virtue: Textile Patterns and the Print Revolution, 1520–1620," *The Metropolitan Museum of Art Bulletin* 73, no. 2 (Fall 2015); and Ann Rosalind Jones, "Labor and Lace: The Crafts of Giacomo Franco's *Habiti delle donne venetiane,*" *I Tatti Studies in the Italian Renaissance* 17, no. 2 (September 2014): 399–425.

5. Speelberg, "Fashion and Virtue," 19; Strocchia, "Knowing Hands," 32–33.

6. Strocchia, "Knowing Hands," 33–34.

7. See Sheila Barker and Sharon T. Strocchia, "Household Medicine for a Renaissance Court: Caterina Sforza's *Ricettario* Reconsidered," in *Gender, Health and Healing, 1250–1550,* ed. Sara Ritchey and Sheila Barker (Amsterdam: Amsterdam University Press, 2020), 139–65, for experiential knowledge as central to women's education and practice in the context of healing and medicinal practices.

8. Leatrice Mendelsohn, *Paragoni: Benedetto Varchi's* Due Lezzioni *and Cinquecento Art Theory* (Ann Arbor: UNI Research Press, 1982).

9. Speelberg, "Fashion and Virtue," 43.

10. Margaret F. Rosenthal and Ann Rosalind Jones, "Cesare Vecellio and His World," in *Cesare Vecellio's* Habiti Antichi et Moderni: *The Clothing of the Renaissance World. Europe, Asia, Africa, The Americas* (London: Thames and Hudson, 2008), 8–48.

11. Fredrika H. Jones, *Defining the Renaissance Virtuosa: Women Artists and the Language of Art History and Criticism* (Cambridge: Cambridge University Press, 1997), 59–60, 105–11; Evelyn Lincoln, "Models for Science and Craft: Isabella Parasole's Botanical and Lace Illustrations," *Visual Resources* 17, no. 1 (2001): 1–35; and Speelberg, "Fashion and Virtue," 39–47.

12. Speelberg, "Fashion and Virtue," 39, 44. Parasole sometimes made subtle changes to her name. Here, instead of Isabella, she uses Isabetta.

13. Lincoln, "Models for Science and Craft," 18–22; Jones, "Labor and Lace," 404.

14. William F. Prizer, in "Cardinals and Courtesans: Secular Music in Rome 1500–1520," in *Italy and the European Powers: The Impact of War, 1500–1530*, ed. Christine Shaw (Amsterdam: Brill, 2006), 253, cites and translates the letter in full; see also Sarah Gwyneth Ross, *The Birth of Feminism: Woman as Intellect in Renaissance Italy and England* (Cambridge, MA: Harvard University Press, 2009), 54–66, especially 62.

15. Strocchia, "Knowing Hands," 37–38.

16. Jones, "Labor and Lace," 412–15.

17. For Franco and Venice, see Jones, "Labor and Lace," 415–25.

18. Elizabeth Semmelhack, *On a Pedestal: From Renaissance Chopines to Baroque Heels* (Toronto: Bata Shoe Museum, 2009).

19. Rosenthal and Jones, "Cesare Vecellio and His World."

20. Katherine Bond, "Fashioned with Marvelous Skill: Veils and the Costume Books of Sixteenth-Century Europe" in *Materialized Identities in Early Modern Culture, 1450–1750,* ed. Susanna Burghartz, Lucas Burkart, Christine Göttler, and Ulinka Rublack (Amsterdam: Amsterdam University Press, 2021), 325–68.

Select Bibliography

Adelman, Howard Tzvi. "Rabbis and Reality: Public Activities of Jewish Women in Italy during the Renaissance and Catholic Restoration." *Jewish History* 5, no. 1 (Spring 1991): 27–40.

Adelman, Howard Tzvi. "The Venetian Identities of Beatrice and Brianda de Luna." *Nashim: A Journal of Jewish Women's Studies & Gender Issues* 25 (Fall 2013): 10–29.

Ajmar-Wollheim, Marta, and Flora Dennis, eds. *At Home in Renaissance Italy*. London: V&A Publications, 2006.

Barkan, Leonard. *Unearthing the Past: Archaeology and Aesthetics in the Making of Renaissance Culture*. New Haven: Yale University Press, 1999.

Barker, Sheila. *Artemisia Gentileschi*. London: Lund Humphries, 2021.

Barker, Sheila. "The First Biography of Artemisia Gentileschi: Self-Fashioning and Proto-Feminism in Cristofano Bronzini's Notes on Women Artists." *Mitteilungen des Kunsthistorischen Institutes in Florenz* 60, no. 3 (2018): 405–35.

Barker, Shelia, ed. *"The Immensity of the Universe" in the Art of Giovanna Garzoni*. Livorno: Casa Editrice Sillabe Editori, 2020.

Barker, Sheila, ed. *Women Artists in Early Modern Italy: Careers, Fame, and Collectors*. Turnhout, Belgium: Brepols, 2016.

Barker, Sheila, and Sharon T. Strocchia. "Household Medicine for a Renaissance Court: Caterina Sforza's *Ricettario* Reconsidered." In *Gender, Health and Healing, 1250–1550*, edited by Sara Ritchey and Sheila Barker, 139–65. Amsterdam: Amsterdam University Press, 2020.

Baskins, Cristelle L. *Cassone Painting, Humanism, and Gender in Early Modern Italy*. Cambridge: Cambridge University Press, 1998.

Baskins, Cristelle L., Adrian W. B. Randolph, Jacqueline Marie Musacchio, and Alan Chong. *The Triumph of Marriage: Painted Cassoni of the Renaissance*. Boston: Isabella Stewart Gardner Museum, 2008.

Bayer, Alexandra, ed. *Art and Love in Renaissance Italy*. New York: Metropolitan Museum of Art, 2008.

Benay, Erin E., and Lisa M. Rafanelli. *Faith, Gender and the Senses in Italian Renaissance and Baroque Art*. New York: Routledge, 2015.

Birnbaum, Marianna D. *The Long Journey of Gracia Nasi*. Budapest: Central European Press, 2003.

Boccaccio, Giovanni. *On Famous Women*. Translated by Guido A. Guarino. New York: Italica Press, 2011.

Bohn, Babette. *Women Artists, Their Patrons, and Their Publics in Early Modern Bologna*. University Park: Pennsylvania State University Press, 2021.

Borsook, Eve, Roberto Lunardi, Barbara Schleicher, and Gianni Guido Rosetti, eds. *L'oro dei poveri: La paglia nell'arredo liturgico e nelle immagini devozionali dell'Italia centrale fra il 1670 e il 1870*. Florence: Edizioni Polistampa, 2000.

Boutin, Lisa. "Isabella d'Este and the Gender Neutrality of Renaissance Ceramics." *Women's Studies* 40, no. 1 (2011): 23–47.

Brady, Aoife, ed. *Lavinia Fontana: Trailblazer, Rule Breaker*. Dublin: National Gallery of Ireland, 2023.

Brine, Kevin R., Elena Ciletti, and Henrike Lähnemann, eds. *The Sword of Judith: Judith Studies across the Disciplines*. Cambridge: Open Book Publishers, 2010.

Brown, David Alan, ed. *Virtue and Beauty: Leonardo's* Ginevra de' Benci *and Renaissance Portraits of Women*. Washington, D.C.: National Gallery of Art, 2001.

Brundin, Abigail, Deborah Howard, and Mary Laven. *The Sacred Home in Renaissance Italy*. Oxford: Oxford University Press, 2018.

Burke, Jill. *The Italian Renaissance Nude*. New Haven: Yale University Press, 2019.

Busi, Giulio, and Silvana Greco, eds. *The Renaissance Speaks Hebrew*. Milan: Silvana Editoriale, 2019.

Bynum, Caroline Walker. *Holy Feast and Holy Fast: The Religious Significance of Food to Medieval Women*. Berkeley: University of California Press, 1987.

Campbell, Stephen J. *The Cabinet of Eros: The Studiolo of Isabella d'Este and the Rise of Renaissance Mythological Painting*. New Haven: Yale University Press, 2004.

Campbell, Stephen J., and Jérémie Koering, eds. *Mantegna*. Malden, MA: Wiley Blackwell, 2015.

Cheney, Liana De Girolami. *Barbara Longhi*. London: Lund Humphries, 2023.

Cohen, Evelyn. "The Illustrations in Maraviglia's Prayer-Book." The Polonsky Foundation Catalogue of Digitised Hebrew Manuscripts, British Library. www.bl.uk.

Cole, Michael W. *Sofonisba's Lesson: A Renaissance Artist and Her Work*. Princeton: Princeton University Press, 2019.

Cornelison, Sally J., and Scott B. Montgomery, eds. *Images, Relics, and Devotional Practice in Medieval and Renaissance Italy*. Tempe, AZ: Arizona Center for Medieval and Renaissance Studies, 2005.

Corry, Maya, Deborah Howard, and Mary Laven, eds. *Madonnas and Miracles: The Holy Home in Renaissance Italy*. London: Philip Wilson, 2017.

Curran, Brian. *The Egyptian Renaissance: The Afterlife of Ancient Egypt in Early Modern Italy*. Chicago: University of Chicago Press, 2007.

De Pizan, Christine. *The Book of the City of Ladies and Other Writings*. Translated by Ineke Hardy. Edited by Sophie Bourgault and Rebecca Kingston. Indianapolis: Hackett, 2018.

Dean, Trevor, and Kate Lowe, eds. *Marriage in Italy, 1300–1600*. Cambridge: Cambridge University Press, 1998.

Dominici, Giovanni. *Regola del governo di cura familiare*. Edited by Donato Salvi. Florence: Angiolo Garinei, 1860.

Fonte, Moderata (Modesta Pozzo). *Floridoro: A Chivalric Romance*. Edited by Valeria Finucci. Translated by Julia Kisacky. Chicago: University of Chicago Press, 2006.

Fonte, Moderata (Modesta Pozzo). *The Worth of Women: Wherein Is Clearly Revealed Their Nobility and Their Superiority to Men*. Edited and translated by Virginia Cox. Chicago: University of Chicago Press, 1997.

Friedenberg, Daniel M. *Jewish Medals from the Renaissance to the Fall of Napoleon (1503–1815)*. New York: Clarkson N. Potter, 1970.

Garrard, Mary D. *Artemisia Gentileschi: The Image of the Female Hero in Italian Baroque Art*. Princeton: Princeton University Press, 1989.

Garrard, Mary D. "Here's Looking at Me: Sofonisba Anguissola and the Problem of the Woman Artist." *Renaissance Quarterly* 47, no. 3 (Autumn 1994): 556–622.

Grossman, Cissy. "Womanly Arts: A Study of Italian Torah Binders in the New York Jewish Museum Collection." *Journal of Jewish Art* 7 (1980): 35–43.

Harris, Ann Sutherland, and Linda Nochlin, eds. *Women Artists, 1550–1950*. Los Angeles: Los Angeles County Museum of Art, 1976.

Herzig, Tamar. *Savonarola's Women: Visions and Reform in Renaissance Florence*. Chicago: University of Chicago Press, 2008.

Hills, Paul. *Veiled Presence: Body and Drapery from Giotto to Titian*. New Haven: Yale University Press, 2018.

Ilchman, Frederick. "Questioning Connoisseurship: The Other Late Titian in Boston." In *Venetian Painting Matters*, ed. Jodi Cranston, 91–112. Turnhout: Brepols, 2015.

Jacobs, Fredrika H. *Defining the Renaissance Virtuosa: Women Artists and the Language of Art History and Criticism*. Cambridge: Cambridge University Press, 1997.

Jansen, Katherine Ludwig. *The Making of the Magdalen: Preaching and Devotion in the Later Middle Ages*. Princeton: Princeton University Press, 2000.

Johnson, Geraldine A., and Sara F. Matthews Grieco, eds. *Picturing Women in Renaissance and Baroque Italy*. Cambridge: Cambridge University Press, 1997.

Jones, Ann Rosalind. "Labor and Lace: The Crafts of Giacomo Franco's *Habiti delle donne venetiane*." *I Tatti Studies in the Italian Renaissance* 17, no. 2 (September 2014): 399–425.

Jones, Ann Rosalind, and Peter Stallybrass. *Renaissance Clothing and the Materials of Memory*. Cambridge: Cambridge University Press, 2000.

Kanter, Laurence B. *Italian Paintings in the Museum of Fine Arts, Boston: 13th–15th Century*. Vol 1. Boston: Museum of Fine Arts, 1994.

Kelly-Gadol, Joan. "Did Women Have a Renaissance?" In *Becoming Visible: Women in European History*, ed. Renate Bridenthal and Claudia Koonz, 137–64. Boston: Houghton Mifflin, 1977.

Kennedy, Trinita, ed. *Sanctity Pictured: The Art of the Dominican and Franciscan Orders in Renaissance Italy*. Nashville: Frist Center for the Visual Arts, 2014.

King, Catherine E. *Renaissance Women Patrons: Wives and Widows in Italy, c. 1300–1550*. Manchester: Manchester University Press, 1998.

Klapisch-Zuber, Christiane. *Women, Family, and Ritual in Renaissance Italy*. Translated by Lydia G. Cochrane. Chicago: University of Chicago Press, 1985.

Kolsky, Stephen. *The Ghost of Boccaccio: Writings on Famous Women in Renaissance Italy*. Turnhout: Brepols, 2005.

Lawless, Catherine. "'Make Your House Like a Temple': Gender, Space, and Domestic Devotion in Medieval Florence." *Religions* 11, no. 120 (2020).

Lawless, Catherine. "Sensing the Image: Gender, Piety, and Images in Late Medieval Tuscany." *Open Arts Journal* 4 (Winter 2014–15): 62–74.

Levy, Allison, ed. *Widowhood and Visual Culture in Early Modern Europe*. London: Routledge, 2016.

Lincoln, Evelyn. "Making a Good Impression: Diana Mantuana's Printmaking Career." *Renaissance Quarterly* 50, no. 4 (Winter 1997): 1101–47.

Lincoln, Evelyn. "Models for Science and Craft: Isabella Parasole's Botanical and Lace Illustrations." *Visual Resources* 17, no. 1 (2001): 1–35.

Lowe, Kate. *Nuns' Chronicles and Convent Culture in Renaissance and Counter-Reformation Italy*. Cambridge: Cambridge University Press, 2003.

Luciano, Eleonora. "Medals of Women from the Italian Renaissance Courts." PhD diss., Indiana University, 1997.

McNamer, Sarah. *Affective Meditation and the Invention of Medieval Compassion*. Philadelphia: University of Pennsylvania Press, 2010.

Murphy, Caroline P. *Lavinia Fontana: A Painter and Her Patrons in Sixteenth-Century Bologna*. New Haven: Yale University Press, 2003.

Musacchio, Jacqueline Marie. *The Art and Ritual of Childbirth in Renaissance Italy*. New Haven: Yale University Press, 1999.

Musacchio, Jacqueline Marie. *Art, Marriage, and Family in the Renaissance Palace*. New Haven: Yale University Press, 2008.

Nelson, Jonathan K., ed. *Plautilla Nelli (1524–1588): The Painter-Prioress of Renaissance Florence*. Florence: Syracuse University Press, 2008.

Nochlin, Linda. *Why Have There Been No Great Women Artists*. London: Thames and Hudson, 2021.

Prizer, William F. "Isabella d'Este and Lucrezia Borgia as Patrons of Music: The *Frottole* at Mantua and Ferrara." *Journal of the American Musical Society* 38 (1985): 1–37.

Randolph, Adrian W. B. "Performing the Bridal Body in Fifteenth-Century Florence." *Art History* 21 (1998): 182–200.

Randolph, Adrian W. B. *Touching Objects: Intimate Experiences of Italian Fifteenth-Century Art*. New Haven: Yale University Press, 2014.

Ragusa, Isa, and Rosalie B. Green, eds. *Meditations on the Life of Christ: An Illustrated Manuscript of the Fourteenth Century*. Translated by Isa Ragusa. Princeton: Princeton University Press, 1961.

Ray, Meredith K. *Daughters of Alchemy: Women and Scientific Culture in Early Modern Italy*. Cambridge, MA: Harvard University Press, 2015.

Reiss, Sheryl E., and David G. Wilkins. *Beyond Isabella: Secular Women Patrons of Art in Renaissance Italy*. Kirksville, MD: Truman State University Press, 2001.

Rosenthal, Margaret F., and Ann Rosalind Jones. *Cesare Vecellio's* Habiti Antichi et Moderni: *The Clothing of the Renaissance World; Europe, Asia, Africa, the Americas*. London: Thames and Hudson, 2008.

Ross, Sarah Gwyneth. *The Birth of Feminism: Woman as Intellect in Renaissance Italy and England*. Cambridge, MA: Harvard University Press, 2009.

Roth, Cecil. *The House of Nasi: Doña Gracia*. Philadelphia: Jewish Publication Society of America, 1948.

Ruggiero, Guido. *Blinding Passions: Tales of Magic, Marriage, and Power at the End of the Renaissance*. Oxford: Oxford University Press, 1993.

Ruiz Gómez, Leticia, ed. *A Tale of Two Women Painters: Sofonisba Anguissola and Lavinia Fontana*. Madrid: Museo Nacional del Prado, 2019.

Sabar, Shalom. "Bride, Heroine and Courtesan: Images of Jewish Women in Hebrew Manuscripts of the Renaissance in Italy." In *Proceedings of the Tenth World Congress of Jewish Studies*, 63–70. Jerusalem: World Congress of Jewish Studies, 1990.

Scher, Stephen K., ed. *The Currency of Fame: Portrait Medals of the Renaissance*. New York: Harry N. Abrams, 1994.

Semmelhack, Elizabeth. *On a Pedestal: From Renaissance Chopines to Baroque Heels*. Toronto: Bata Shoe Museum, 2009.

Shephard, Tim. "Constructing Isabella d'Este's Musical Decorum in the Visual Sphere." *Renaissance Studies* 25, no. 5 (November 2011): 684–706.

Silver, Nathaniel. *Botticelli: Heroines and Heroes*. Boston: Isabella Stewart Gardner Museum, 2019.

Solum, Stefanie. *Women, Patronage, and Salvation in Renaissance Florence: Lucrezia Tornabuoni and the Chapel of the Medici Palace*. Farnham, UK: Ashgate, 2015.

Speelberg, Femke. "Fashion and Virtue: Textile Patterns and the Print Revolution, 1520–1620." *The Metropolitan Museum of Art Bulletin* 73, no. 2 (Fall 2015).

Stras, Laurie. *Women and Music in Renaissance Ferrara*. Cambridge: Cambridge University Press, 2018.

Straussman-Pflanzer, Eve, and Oliver Tostmann, eds. *By Her Hand: Artemisia Gentileschi and Women Artists in Italy, 1500–1800*. New Haven: Yale University Press, 2021.

Strocchia, Sharon T. *Forgotten Healers: Women and the Pursuit of Health in Late Renaissance Italy*. Cambridge, MA: Harvard University Press, 2019.

Strocchia, Sharon T. "Knowing Hands: Nuns and the Needle Arts in Renaissance Italy." In *Artiste nel chiostro: Produzione artistica nei monasteri femminili in età moderna*, edited by Sheila Barker with Luciano Cinelli, 31–52. Florence: Nerbini, 2015; *Memorie Domenicane* n.s. 46.

Strocchia, Sharon T. "The Nun-Apothecaries of Renaissance Florence: Marketing Medicines in the Convent." *Renaissance Studies* 25, no. 5 (November 2011): 627–47.

Strocchia, Sharon T. "Savonarolan Witnesses: The Nuns of San Jacopo and the Piagnone Movement in Sixteenth-Century Florence." *Sixteenth Century Journal* 38, no. 2 (2007): 393–418.

Strocchia, Sharon T. "Sisters in Spirit: The Nuns of Sant'Ambrogio and Their Consorority in Early Sixteenth Century Florence." *The Sixteenth Century Journal* 33, no. 3 (Autumn 2002): 735–67.

Syson, Luke, and Dora Thornton. *Objects of Virtue: Art in Renaissance Italy*. Los Angeles: Getty, 2001.

Targoff, Ramie. *Renaissance Woman: The Life of Vittoria Colonna*. New York: Farrar, Straus and Giroux, 2018.

Thomas, Anabel. *Art and Piety in the Female Religious Communities of Renaissance Florence: Iconography, Space, and the Religious Woman's Perspective*. Cambridge: Cambridge University Press, 2003.

Thornton, Peter. *The Italian Renaissance Interior, 1400–1600*. New York: Harry N. Abrams, 1991.

Tinagli, Paola. *Women in Italian Renaissance Art: Gender, Representation, Identity*. Manchester: Manchester University Press, 1997.

Treves, Letizia, ed. *Artemisia*. London: National Gallery Company, 2020.

Trevisani, Filippo, and Davide Gasparotto, eds. *Bonacolsi l'Antico: Uno scultore nella Mantova di Andrea Mantegna e di Isabella d'Este*. Milan: Electa, 2008.

Weaver, Elissa B. *Convent Theatre in Early Modern Italy: Spiritual Fun and Learning for Women*. Cambridge: Cambridge University Press, 2002.

Whitehead, Barbara J. ed. *Women's Education in Early Modern Europe: A History, 1500–1800*. New York: Garland, 1999.

Zorach, Rebecca, and Michael W. Phillips Jr. *Gold: Nature and Culture*. London: Reaktion Books, 2016.

List of Illustrations

Unless otherwise noted, all works are in the collection of the Museum of Fine Arts, Boston. Dimensions are given as height × width × depth.

Hidden Gold

1 & 3
Barna da Siena
Italian (Sienese), active about 1330–1350
The Mystic Marriage of Saint Catherine, about 1340
Tempera on panel
138.7 × 111.1 cm (54⅝ × 43¾ in.)
Sarah Wyman Whitman Fund, 15.1145

2
Jacopo di Cione
Italian (active in Florence), first documented 1365, died 1398/1400
The Mystic Marriage of Saint Catherine of Alexandria, with Saint Louis of Toulouse and a Franciscan Nun Donor, about 1375–80
Tempera and tooled gold on panel
81.1 × 62.2 cm (31⅞ × 24½ in.)
The John G. Johnson Collection, Philadelphia Museum of Art, cat. 6.

Exemplary Women

4
Donatello
Italian (Florentine), 1386–1466
Judith and Holofernes, 1457–64
Bronze
H. 236 cm (93 in.)
Palazzo Vecchio, Florence

5
Giovanni della Robbia
Italian (Florentine), 1469–1529 (?)
Judith, about 1520
Glazed terracotta
H. 71.1 cm (28 in.)
Gift of Mrs. Albert J. Beveridge in memory of Delia Spencer Field, 46.839

6
Giovanni della Robbia
Abundance, about 1520
Glazed terracotta
H. 65.8 cm (25⅞ in.)
Gift of Mrs. Albert J. Beveridge in memory of Delia Spencer Field, 46.840

7
Donatello
Penitent Magdalen, about 1453–55
Painted wood with traces of gilding
H. 188 cm (74 in.)
Museo dell'Opera del Duomo, Florence

8
Mary Magdalen Surrounded by Angels, about 1480–1500
Italian (Florence)
Terracotta with traces of polychromy
64.5 × 40 cm (25⅜ × 15¾ in.)
Gift of Mrs. C. C. Perkins, 95.1377

9
Gherardo del Fora
Italian, 1445–1497
Saint Mary Magdalen between Saint Peter Martyr and Saint Catherine of Siena, about 1475
Tempera on panel
42.5 × 28.5 cm (16¾ × 11¼ in.)
Bowdoin College Museum of Art, Brunswick, Maine, Gift of the Samuel H. Kress Foundation

10
Monte delle Oratione, 1496
Italian (Florence)
Illustrated book with two woodcuts
20 × 13.8 × 1 cm (7⅞ × 5⅜ × ⅜ in.)
Fund in memory of Horatio Greenough Curtis, 39.589

11
Fragment of a textile with the Noli Me Tangere, 14th–15th century
Italian
Silk compound weave with satin foundation and patterning wefts of silk and gilded animal membrane wrapped around linen
32.1 × 24 cm (10½ × 14⅛ in.)
Denman Waldo Ross Collection, 04.1640

12
Apollonio di Giovanni di Tomaso
Italian (Florentine), about 1416–1465
Journey of the Queen of Sheba
Tempera on panel
39.1 × 133.4 cm (15⅜ × 52½ in.)
Herbert James Pratt Fund, 23.252

13 & 14
Francesco del Cossa
Italian (Ferrarese), about 1436–about 1478
The Meeting of the Queen of Sheba and Solomon and *Cherub Holding Cornucopias of Cherries*, third quarter of the 15th century
Tempera and oil on panel
61 × 61 cm (24 × 24 in.)
Gift of Mrs. Walter Scott Fitz, 17.198

Materials of Marriage

15
Lorenzo Costa
Italian (Ferrarese), about 1460–1535
Portrait of a Woman with a Pearl Necklace, probably 1485–95
Oil on panel
44.1 × 33.9 cm (17⅜ × 13⅜ in.)
Bequest of Mrs. Thomas O. Richardson, 25.227

16
Plate with woman's profile, early 16th century
Italian (Deruta)
Tin-glaze earthenware (maiolica) with metallic luster decoration
Diam. 40.5 cm (16 in.)
Boston Athenaeum

17
Probably by Maestro Giorgio Andreoli
Italian, born in 1465–70, died in 1555
Plate with female head and border with trophies, 1524
Tin-glazed earthenware (maiolica) with metallic luster decoration
Diam. 20.4 cm (8 in.)
Anita M. Linzee Fund, 46.460

18
Casket, 16th century
Italian (Venice)
Straw marquetry on colored paper and pine
20.3 × 43.2 × 17.8 cm (8 × 17 × 7 in.)
Museum purchase with funds donated by Mrs. Charles Gaston Smith's Group, 40.234

19
Table cover, 17th century
Italian
Linen plain weave embroidered with silk and metal threads (gilt silver and silver strips wrapped around silk)
109 × 224.5 cm (43½ × 88⅜ in.)
Mary L. Smith Fund, 58.1016

20
Towel, 16th–18th century
Italian
Linen twill weave with complementary and supplementary cotton patterning wefts
191.7 × 50.8 cm (75½ × 20 in.)
Denman Waldo Ross Collection, 20.917

21
Lace, 17th century
Italian
Linen, needle lace
13.7 × 93 cm (5⅜ × 36⅝ in.)
Bequest of James William Paige, 95.916

22
Length of velvet, 15th century
Italian (possibly Venice)
Silk velvet brocade with silk and gold-colored metallic thread
236 × 60.5 cm (92⅞ × 23⅞ in.)
Mary L. Smith Fund, 58.22

23
Inkwell, about 1500
Italian (Faenza)
Tin-glazed earthenware (maiolica)
8.2 × 20 × 27.9 cm (3¼ × 7⅞ × 11 in.)
John H. and Ernestine A. Payne Fund, 56.310

24
Betrothal ring, 15th–16th century
Italian
Silver
¼ × ½ in. (0.7 × 1.2 cm)
William D. Boardman Collection—Gift of Mrs. Alice L. Boardman, 01.5974

25 & 26
Marriage pendant, about 1455–65
Italian (Florence)
Silver-gilt and niello
4.1 × 1.2 cm (1⅝ × ½ in.)
H. E. Bolles Fund, 69.74

27
Pastorino di Giovan Michele de' Pastorini
Italian, 1508–1592
Gracia Nasi the Younger, 1558
Bronze
Diam. 6.5 cm (2½ in.)
Theodora Wilbour Fund in memory of Zoë Wilbour, 2021.113

Prayer and Practice

28
Meditationi sopra la Passione, about 1495
Italian (Florence)
Illustrated book with 12 woodcuts
19.3 × 14 × 1.5 cm (7⅝ × 5½ × ⅝ in.)
Bequest of W. G. Russell Allen, 64.390

29
Bernardo Daddi
Italian (Florentine), active about 1320–1348
The Crucifixion, before 1328
Tempera on panel
40.3 × 32.1 cm (15⅞ × 12⅝ in.)
Helen Collamore Fund, 23.211

30
Titian (Tiziano Vecellio)
Italian (Venetian), about 1488–1576
Saint Catherine of Alexandria,
about 1567
Oil on canvas
119.1 × 100 cm (46⅞ × 39⅜ in.)
1948 Fund and Otis Norcross Fund,
48.499

31
Ludovico Carracci
Italian (Bolognese), 1555–1619
Portrait of a Widow, about 1585
Oil on canvas
99.7 × 77.5 cm (39¼ × 30½ in.)
Dayton Art Institute
Museum purchase with funds provided
by Dr. and Mrs. E.R. Arn and the Junior
League of Dayton, Ohio, Inc., 1958.15

32
Andrea della Robbia
Italian (Florentine), 1435–1525
Virgin and Child, about 1500
Glazed terracotta
52.1 × 36.2 × 12.7 cm (20½ × 14¼ × 5 in.)
Gift of Charles C. Perkins, 76.700

33
Mariano D'Angelo Romanelli
Italian (Sienese), active 1376–1410
*The Christ Child Wrapped in
Swaddling Clothes*, about 1375–1400
Polychromed and gilded wood
H. 46 cm (18½ in.)
Private Collection

34
Cap and cushion, late 16th–
early 17th century
Italian
Silk satin embroidered with gold
metallic yarns
Cap: 20.3 × 15.2 × 7.6 cm (8 × 6 × 3 in.)
Cushion: 21 × 19 cm (8¼ × 7½ in.)
Gift of Philip Lehman in memory of his
wife Carrie L. Lehman, 38.1278, 38.1280

35
The Annunciation, late 15th century
Italian (Faenza)
Tin-glazed earthenware (maiolica)
50.8 × 39.4 cm (20 × 15½ in.)
Kiyi and Edward M. Pflueger Collection.
Bequest of Edward M. Pflueger and Gift
of Kiyi Powers Pflueger, 2006.1106.1

36
The Visitation, late 15th century
Italian (Faenza)
Tin-glazed earthenware (maiolica)
50.8 × 39.4 cm (20 × 15½ in.)
Kiyi and Edward M. Pflueger Collection.
Bequest of Edward M. Pflueger and Gift
of Kiyi Powers Pflueger, 2006.1106.2

37
Fragment of a textile with the
Annunciation, 14th–15th century
Italian (Florence)
Silk compound weave with patterning
wefts of silk and linen core wrapped
with gilded animal membrane
15.3 × 84.5 cm (6 × 33¼ in.)
1931 Purchase Fund, 35.86

38
Fragment of a textile with the
Annunciation,
15th century–16th century
Italian
Silk brocaded with silk and
metallic threads
16.5 × 59.5 cm (6½ × 23⅜ in.)
Denman Waldo Ross Collection, 96.471

39
Embroidery with the Pietà, 16th century
Probably Italian
Silk satin embroidered with silk,
metal wrapped silk thread, and
coiled metal thread
31.4 × 29.5 cm (12⅜ × 11⅝ in.)
William E. Nickerson Fund, No. 2, 64.62

40 through 48
Isodor Isolani
Italian, about 1480–1428
*Inexplicabilis mysteriis gesta beatae
Veronicae virginis*, Milan, 1518
Illustrated book with 10 woodcuts
20.3 × 15.2 × 2.4 cm (8 × 6 × 1 in.)
William A. Sargent Fund, 63.137

49
Girolamo Savonarola
Italian (Ferrarese), 1452–1498
Predicha e revelationi, Florence, 1495
Illustrated book with one woodcut
20.7 × 14.5 × 1.2 cm (8⅛ × 5¾ × ½ in.)
William A. Sargent Fund, 46.1197

50
*La rappresentatione di S. Apollonia
vergine, & martire*, Florence,
16th century
Italian
Illustrated book with 12 woodcuts
20.6 × 14.6 × 0.7 cm (8⅛ × 5¾ × ¼ in.)
William A. Sargent Fund, 40.742

51
Lace, 17th century
Italian
Linen needle lace
21.4 × 39.6 cm (8⅜ × 15⅝ in.)
Gift of Henry W. Bliss, 23.651

52
Torah binder, 17th century
Italian
Linen plain weave with drawn-work
and linen embroidery; needle lace inserts
and bobbin lace trim
20.3 × 372.1 cm (8 × 146½ in.)
Bequest of James William Paige, 95.992

53 through 55
Joel ben Simeon
German, active about 1445–after 1509
Prayer book (*Siddur*), Florence, 1469
Illuminated manuscript
14 × 9.5 cm (5½ × 3¾ in.)
British Library, Add MS 26957

Artists Known and Unknown

56
Vittoria Colonna
Italian, 1492–1547
Rime, Venice, 1542
Illustrated book with two woodcuts
15.8 × 11 × 1.1 cm (6¼ × 4⁵⁄₁₆ × ⁷⁄₁₆ in.)
Gift of Miss Anna C. Hoyt, 27.1316

57
Sofonisba Anguissola
Italian (Cremonese), about 1532–1625
Self-Portrait, about 1556
Oil (?) on parchment
8.3 × 6.4 cm (3¼ × 2½ in.)
Beth Monroe Fund—Bequest of
Emma F. Monroe, 60.155

58
Lavinia Fontana
Italian (Bolognese), 1552–1614
Virgin Adoring the Sleeping Christ Child,
about 1605–10
Oil on panel
15.2 × 25.4 cm (6 × 10 in.)
Beth Monroe Fund—Bequest of
Emma F. Monroe, 1986.514

59
Barbara Longhi
Italian (Ravennate), 1552–about 1638
Virgin and Child
Oil on canvas
36.2 × 29.5 cm (14¼ × 11⅝ in.)
Charles Potter Kling Fund, 2022.187

60
Artemisia Gentileschi
Italian, 1593–after 1654
The Sleeping Christ Child, 1630–32
Oil on copper
12.4 × 17.5 cm (4⅞ × 6⅞ in.)
Charles Potter Kling Fund and Beth
Munroe Fund—Bequest of
Emma F. Monroe, 2022.102

61
Diana Mantuana
Italian (Mantuan), about 1535–after 1587
After Giulio Romano
Italian, about 1499–1546
Latona Giving Birth to Apollo and Diana on the Island of Delos, 1561–65
Engraving
26.3 × 38.7 cm (10⅜ × 15¼ in.)
George Peabody Gardner Fund, 58.426

62
Diana Mantuana after Giulio Romano
Christ and the Woman Taken in Adultery, 1575
Engraving
42.5 × 58.4 cm (16¾ × 23 in.)
Harvey D. Parker Collection—
Harvey Drury Parker Fund, P1542

63
Diana Mantuana
After Francesco Salviati
Italian, 1510–1563
The Holy Family Receiving a Basket of Fruit from a Young Woman, 1575–76
Engraving
24.7 × 17.5 cm (9¾ × 6⅞ in.)
Gift of Amory Coolidge, 43.1368

64
Diana Mantuana after Francesco Salviati
The Virgin and Child, 1576
Engraving
31.2 × 23.8 cm (12¼ × 9⅜ in.)
Bequest of William Perkins Babcock,
B1653

65
Diana Mantuana
After Cornelis Cort
Netherlandish, 1533–1578
The Thorn-Puller, 1581
Engraving
31.8 × 21.5 cm (12½ × 8½ in.)
Sumner Bequest, M5890

66 & 67
Medal of Diana Manutana, 16th century
Italian (Rome)
Bronze
Diam. 4 cm (1⅝ in.)
The British Museum, G3, IP.688
© The Trustees of the British Museum

68
Lace, 16th century
Italian
Linen drawn with bobbin lace trim
220 × 24 cm (86⅝ × 9½ in.)
Gift of Miss Harriet G. Hamlin, in
memory of her sister Jane Hamlin,
43.237

69
Cesare Vecellio
Italian (Venetian), 1521–1601
Donna dell'Ischia from *De gli Habiti Antichi et Moderni di Diversi Parti del Mondo*, Venice, 1590
Woodcut with hand-applied color on
cream laid paper
17.5 × 10.7 cm (7 × 4¼ in.)
Gift of L. Aaron Lebowich, 50.2585

70
Isabella Catanea Parasole
Italian (Roman), about 1575–about 1625
Gemma pretiosa delle virtuose donne,
Rome, 1625
Illustrated book with 38 woodcuts
13.5 × 18.8 × 0.8 cm (5⅜ × 7⅜ × ⅜ in.)
William A. Sargent Fund, 42.496

71
Lace, 17th century
Italian
Linen, needle lace
10.2 × 325.1 cm (4 × 128 in.)
Gift of Mrs. Paul G. Pennoyer in memory
of her mother Jane Norton Morgan,
41.931

72
Honorata Foa
Italian, 16th century
Torah binder, 1582–83
Linen embroidered with silk thread
19.1 × 386.1 cm (7½ × 152 in.)
The Jewish Museum
Gift of Dr. Harry G. Friedman, F 4927

Illustrious Women

73
Pier Jacopo Alari Bonacolsi
Italian (Mantuan), about 1460–1528
Cleopatra, about 1519–22
Bronze with traces of gilding
H. 64.5 cm (25⅜ in.)
William Francis Warden Fund, 64.2174

74
Sleeping Ariadne, early 2nd century A.D.
Marble
161.5 × 195 cm (63⅝ × 76¾ in.)
Vatican Museums, MV.548.0.0
Photograph: PHAS/UIG /
Bridgeman Images

75
Andrea Andreani
Italian, 1558/59–1629
After Andrea Mantegna
Italian, Paduan, active in Mantua,
1431–1506
Julius Caesar on His Chariot, 1599
Chiaroscuro woodcut
37.7 × 37.8 cm (14⅞ × 14⅞ in.)
Bequest of W. G. Russell Allen,
2004.611.9

76
Andrea Andreani after Andrea Mantegna
Captives, 1599
Chiaroscuro woodcut
37 × 37.9 cm (14⅝ × 14⅞ in.)
Bequest of W. G. Russell Allen,
2004.611.7

77
Andrea Andreani after Andrea Mantegna
Musicians and Standard-Bearers, 1599
Chiaroscuro woodcut
37.2 × 37.8 cm (14⅝ × 14⅞ in.)
Bequest of W. G. Russell Allen,
2004.611.8

78 & 79
Francesco Xanto Avelli da Rovigo
Italian, born about 1486–87, possibly
died in 1542
Plate with Cleopatra and Marc Antony,
1542
Tin-glazed earthenware (maiolica)
Diam. 26.4 (10⅜ in.)
Gift of Mr. and Mrs. George Washington
Wales, 95.371

80
Nicola da Urbino
Italian, active by 1520, died in 1537–38
Plate with Perseus and Andromeda,
about 1524
Tin-glazed earthenware (maiolica)
Diam. 26.8 cm (10½ in.)
Otis Norcross Fund, 41.105

81
After Andrea Mantegna
The Four Muses, about 1497–1505
Engraving
23.2 × 32.9 cm (9⅛ × 12⅞ in.)
Fund in memory of Horatio Greenough
Curtis, 25.688

82
Attributed to Giovanni Antonio da
Brescia
Italian, active about 1490–1520
After Andrea Mantegna
Judith with the Head of Holofernes,
about 1490–1507
Engraving
31.1 × 22.6 cm (12¼ × 8⅞ in.)
Gift of Gustav Mayer, M28145

83
Girolamo Mocetto
Italian (Venetian), about 1458–1531
After Andrea Mantegna
Judith with the Head of Holofernes,
about 1500–1510
Engraving
29.5 × 20.2 cm (11⅝ × 8 in.)
Gift of William Norton Bullard, 23.954

84
Giovanni Boccaccio
Italian, 1313–1375
De Claris Mulieribus, Ulm (Germany),
1473
Illustrated book with 81 woodcuts
30.5 × 21.7 × 3 cm (12 × 8½ × 1⅛ in.)
Maria Antoinette Evans Fund, 31.1401

85 & 86
Jacopo Filippo Foresti
Italian, 1434–1520
De plurimus claris sceletisque mulieribus, Ferrara, 1497
Illustrated book with 172 woodcuts
31.6 × 22.1 × 5.3 cm (12½ × 8¾ × 2⅛ in.)
William A. Sargent Fund, 41.2

87
Marcantonio Raimondi
Italian, 1480–1527/34
After Raphael (Raffaello Sanzio)
Italian (Urbinate), 1483–1520
The Death of Lucretia, about 1511–12
Engraving
21.6 × 13.4 cm (8½ × 5¼ in.)
Gift of Mrs. T. Jefferson Coolidge,
21.10894

88
Antonio Minello de' Bardi
Italian, about 1465–1529
Bust of a classical heroine,
early 16th century
Marble
H. 34.9 cm (13¾ in.)
Private Collection

89
Bernardino Luini
Italian (Milanese), active in 1512, died in 1532
Salome with the Head of Saint John the Baptist, 1515–25
Oil on panel
62.2 × 51.4 cm (24½ × 20¼ in.)
Gift of Mrs. Walter Scott Fitz, 21.2287

90
After Raphael
The Martyrdom of Saint Cecilia, early to mid-16th century
Italian
Engraving
23.5 × 39.2 cm (9¼ × 15⅜ in.)
Harvey D. Parker Collection—Harvey Drury Parker Fund, P1085

91
Andrea Andreani
After Giambologna
Flemish (active in Italy), 1529–1608
The Rape of a Sabine, about 1584
Chiaroscuro woodcut
45.4 × 20.2 cm (17⅞ × 8 in.)
Gift of W. G. Russell Allen, 27.1278

92
Alfonso Patanazzi
Italian (Urbinate), active early 17th century
Plate with the reconciliation of the Romans and the Sabines, 1610
Tin-glazed earthenware (maiolica)
Diam. 49.2 cm (19⅜ in.)
Gift of Henry S. Hall, Jr., RES.56.52

Science and Sorcery

93
Albarello, early 16th century
Italian (Deruta)
Tin-glazed earthenware (maiolica)
H. 21.6 cm (8½ in.)
Bequest of George Washington Wales, 03.209

94
Albarello, about 1600
Italian (Sicily)
Tin-glazed earthenware (maiolica)
H. 24.5 cm (9⅝ in.)
Bequest of George Washington Wales, 03.205

95
Plate depicting Medea and Aeson, about 1530
Italian (Urbino)
Tin-glazed earthenware
Diam. 26 cm (10¼ in.)
Boston Athenaeum

96
Dosso Dossi
Italian (Ferrarese), active 1512–42
Circe and Her Lovers in a Landscape, about 1525
Oil on canvas
100.8 × 136.1 cm (39⅝ × 53⅝ in.)
National Gallery of Art, Samuel H. Kress Collection, 1943.4.49
Photograph: Courtesy National Gallery of Art, Washington

97
Antonio da Trento
After Parmigiano (Girolamo Francesco Maria Mazzola)
Italian (Parmenese), 1503–1540
Circella Drinking with the Companions of Ulysses, mid-16th century
Chiaroscuro woodcut
21.5 × 19.1 cm (8½ × 7½ in.)
Harvey D. Parker Collection—Harvey Drury Parker Fund, P1691

98
Antonio da Trento after Parmigiano
Circella Giving Drink to the Companions of Ulysses, mid-16th century
Chiaroscuro woodcut
23.7 × 21 cm (9⅜ × 8¼ in.)
Bequest of W. G. Russell Allen, 64.1094

99
Giovanni della Robbia
Italian (Florentine), 1469–1529 (?)
Flora, about 1500
Glazed terracotta
17.5 × 13.5 × 14 cm (6⅞ × 5⅜ × 5½ in.)
Zoe Oliver Sherman Collection, 22.658

100
Il Robetta (Cristofano di Michele Martini)
Italian, 1462–after 1534
Allegory of Abundance, about 1510–1520
Engraving
24.8 × 18.4 cm (9¾ × 7¼ in)
Harvey D. Parker Collection—Harvey Drury Parker Fund, P1017

101
Ugo da Carpi
Italian, active about 1502–1532
Sibyl Reading, early 16th century
Chiaroscuro woodcut
28.2 × 22.7 cm (11⅛ × 8⅞ in.)
Bequest of W. G. Russell Allen. 64.1076

102
Andrea Andreani
Italian, 1558/59–1629
Woman Contemplating a Skull, 1591
Chiaroscuro woodcut
39.3 × 26.9 cm (15½ × 10⅝ in.)
Bequest of W. G. Russell Allen, 1975.467

Hands and Minds

103 & 104
Domenico da Sera
French (active in Italy), 16th century
Ornamento de le belle e virtudiose donne, Venice, 1543
Illustrated book with 45 woodcuts
20.7 × 15.3 × 1.3 cm (8⅛ × 6 × ½ in.)
George Nixon Black Fund, 34.707

105 & 106
Matteo Pagano
Italian, 1515–1588
La gloria e l'honore di ponti tagliati a fogliami, Venice, 1555
Illustrated book with 29 woodcuts
20.7 × 15.6 × 1 cm (8⅛ × 6⅛ × ⅜ in.)
William A. Sargent Fund, 41.487

107 & 108
Cesare Vecellio
Italian (Venetian), 1521–1601
Corona delle nobili et virtuose donne libro primo, Venice, 1591
Illustrated book with 79 woodcuts
14 × 20.8 × 1.6 cm (5½ × 8¼ × ⅝ in.)
William A. Sargent Fund, 42.495

109
Isabella Cattaneo Parasole
Gemma pretiosa della virtuose donne, 1625
See fig. 70

110
Chopines, 1610–1620
Italian (Venice)
Tooled alum tanned leather over wood, silk tassels, and silk woven tape
10.9 × 13.7 × 21.7 cm (4⁵⁄₁₆ × 5⅜ × 8½ in.)
The Elizabeth Day McCormick Collection, 44.522a-b

111
Découpé folding fan, about 1590–1600
Italian or French
Carved ivory sticks and cut skin leaf with silk plain weave and mica inserts
44 cm (17⁵⁄₁₆ in.)
Oldham Collection, 1976.182

112
Towel, 17th century
Italian
Linen plain weave with needle lace inserts and trim
72 × 162 cm (28⅜ × 63¾ in.)
Gift of Mrs. George Linder, 07.855

113
Giacomo Franco
Italian, 1550–1620
Habiti d'houmeni et donne venetiane, Venice, 1610
Illustrated book with 26 engravings and etchings
30.2 × 21.3 × 1.2 cm (11⅞ × 8⅜ × ½ in.)
William A. Sargent Fund, 44.826

114
Chopines, about 1590–1610
Italian (Venice)
Tooled leather over wood with metallic braid
30.2 × 16.2 × 24 cm (11⅞ × 6⅜ × 9½ in.)
The Elizabeth Day McCormick Collection, 44.556a-b

115, 116 & 119
Cesare Vecellio
De gli habiti antichi et moderni di diverse parti del mondo, Venice, 1590
Illustrated book with 420 woodcuts
19 × 12.6 × 4.6 cm (7½ × 5 × 1¾ in.)
Museum purchase with funds by exchange from the William Sturgis Bigelow Collection, 42.685

117
Pietro Bertelli
Italian (Paduan), active late 16th–early 17th century
Diversarum nationum habitus, Padua, 1589
Unbound engravings with hand-applied color
11.2 × 8.2 cm (4⅜ × 3¼ in.)
The Elizabeth Day McCormick Collection, 44.870.1-53

118
Chopine, 1580s
Italian (Venice)
Tooled leather over wood
7 × 10 × 21.6 cm (2¾ × 3⅞ × 8½ in.)
The Elizabeth Day McCormick Collection, 44.551

120 through 125
Cesare Vecellio
Woodcuts from *De gli habiti antichi et moderni di diversi parti del mondo*, Venice, 1590
Woodcut with hand-applied color on cream laid paper
Approximately 17.4 × 10.8 cm (7 × 4¼ in.)

120
Matrona Nobile
Gift of L. Aaron Lebowich, 50.2593

121
Donna Mediocre
Gift of L. Aaron Lebowich, 50.2608

122
Baronessa
Gift of L. Aaron Lebowich, 50.2605

123
Altra Donna
Gift of L. Aaron Lebowich, 50.2601

124
Sposa Nobili Romane
Gift of L. Aaron Lebowich, 50.2597

125
Donna di Gaeta
Gift of L. Aaron Lebowich, 50.2600

Acknowledgments

I thank Matthew Teitelbaum, Ann and Graham Gund Director, for his support of this project. Thanks to Christina Yu Yu, Matsutaro Shoriki Chair, Art of Asia, for her commitment to the exhibition through a series of unforeseen delays. I am especially grateful to Edward Saywell, who was enthusiastic about the show from the beginning, and instrumental in supporting this publication. Frederick Ilchman, Chair and Mrs. Russell W. Baker Curator of Paintings, Art of Europe, was unwavering in his commitment to the exhibition and supportive as I worked on this book.

I thank the lenders to the exhibition, for their enthusiasm for the project and for their patience as we worked out the timing. At the British Library, I thank Liz Jolly, Ilana Tahan, Lucy Scanlon, and Momo Sekido. At the Bowdoin College Museum of Art, I thank Anne Collins Goodwin, Frank H. Goodwin, and Laura Latman. At the Dayton Art Institute, I thank Michael Roediger, Jerry N. Smith, and Sally Kurz. At the Jewish Museum, I thank Claudia Gould, Claudia Nahson, Julie Maguire, and Jannette Reichel. At the Boston Athenaeum, I thank Lily Sterling. Special thanks to Barbara and Jon Landau for once again sharing the Italian Renaissance sculptures in their collection with us, and with our visitors. I also thank Alison Oscar for all her help.

I thank Tamara Petrosian Davis for her support of this project, and express my gratitude for her generosity and encouragement of my work and the work of the Art of Europe at the MFA for so many years. I thank Dr. Susanna I. Lee for her support of the exhibition, and for her encouragement in stressing the role of women as healers and scientists across time. Generous support for this publication provided by the Andrew W. Mellon Publications Fund. Additional support from Tamara Petrosian Davis and Charles Howard Davis II.

I would like to thank the scholars whose work provided the basis for this project: so much innovative, painstaking research has gone into the uncovering of Italian Renaissance women's history, and while notes in the text acknowledge their contributions, these cannot convey my gratitude for the inspiration that their work has provided. Many generously shared thoughts and ideas with me directly as well, either in conversation or at a roundtable held in 2019: thanks to Sheila Barker, Cristelle Baskins, Danielle Carrabino, Evelyn Cohen, Anne-Marie Eze, Theresa Flanigan, Meredith Fluke, Gilbert Jones, Stephanie Leone, Allison Levy, Kate Lowe, Shannon McHugh, Jacqueline Marie Musacchio, Roberta Olson, Catherine O'Reilly, Chiara Piadatella, Sarah G. Ross, Nathaniel Silver, and Ramie Targoff.

Because this is a project primarily based in the collections of the MFA, my deepest gratitude goes to the many colleagues across the Museum who have contributed to this book and the exhibition it accompanies. Many thanks to Hope Stockton, editor and collaborator on the publication; she shaped the text into a book, pushed me at every turn, and was a patient and good companion on a long journey: I cannot thank her enough. I also thank Jennifer Snodgrass for believing in the book project from the start. MFA Publications worked with Anjali Pala, who designed a book that highlights the allure of so many objects that have long remained in the shadows. Thanks to Maggie Loh for facilitating new photography, and to our brilliant photographers, Michael Gould, Saravuth Neou, and Damon Beale. Thanks to Debra Lakind, who helped assure that the book's visual impact would be strong. I am grateful to Hee Jung Lee, Jordan Barnes, and Paul McAlpine in the MFA library for their support of my research.

I happily thank current and former curatorial colleagues who have contributed to this project: Meghan Melvin, Jean S. and Frederic A. Sharf Curator of Design; Ben Weiss, Leonard A. Lauder Senior Curator of Visual Culture, Department of Prints and Drawings; especially, Patrick Murphy, Lia and William Poorvu Associate Curator of Prints and Drawings; Pamela Parmal, Chair and David and Roberta Logie Curator of Textiles; Lauren Whitley; Jennifer Swope, David and Roberta Logie Curator of Textiles; Bobby Giglio; Nancy Berliner, Wu Tung Senior Curator of Chinese Art; and Laura Weinstein, Ananda Coomaraswamy Curator of South Asian and Islamic Art. A special word of remembrance and gratitude for the late David Becker, who first introduced me to the MFA's rich collection of Italian Renaissance printed books. My colleagues in Conservation have been true partners in this work: Abigail Hykin, Robert P. and Carol T. Henderson Head of Objects Conservation, has been a constant companion and instrumental in the conservation of so many works of Renaissance sculpture and decorative arts over the last two decades, including many in this show. Pamela Hatchfield, Robert P. and Carol T. Henderson Head of Objects Conservation Emerita; William Mastandrea, Gale R. Guild and Henry R. Guild Fellow for Advanced Training; Flavia Perugini; Marie Stewart; Gerri Strickler; and Emilie Trehu have all contributed to the conservation of works for this project. Allison Luxner, paper conservator, has been a font of knowledge, care, and enthusiasm, and a partner in the selection of books and openings. Annette Mannick, head of Paper Conservation, has supported the project from its earliest days. Meredith Montague in Textiles Conservation has been an inspiring teacher as I looked closely at Renaissance textiles for the first time. Her meticulous attention to their care, display, and photography, and her deep enthusiasm for them has been a true gift. Joel Stephenson's attention to and admiration for the Renaissance shoes in the show is much appreciated. Christine Storti's research into the technique of cut straw has been a revelation. All my gratitude to Rhona MacBeth, Director of Conservation and Scientific Research, Eijk and Rose-Marie van Otterloo Conservator of Paintings and Head of Paintings Conservation, for supporting a project that has involved members of most of the labs that she supervises, but most of all for the privilege and pleasure of looking at paintings with her to consider their condition, treatment, and presentation. Lydia Vagts; Sarah Mastrangelo, Cunningham Associate Conservator of Paintings; and Rachel Childers in Paintings Conservation have all worked on paintings for the project. Richard Newman and Erin Mysak in Research Science helped us all understand the works through analysis and investigation. Brett Angell, Kimberly McPartland, Neal Johnson, Ales Hlousek, Gregory Porter, Andrew Haines, John Carleton, and Melissa Krok-Horton were central to the presentation of these objects to our audiences.

I am grateful to my colleagues in Exhibitions and Design including Patrick McMahon, Kat Bossi, and Angie Morrow. It is my greatest pleasure to thank our project manager Mary Nelson for her attention to detail, her support and enthusiasm, and her warm spirit of friendship that makes challenges so much easier to face. Keith Crippen has overseen the project through several iterations. I am grateful to him and to Chelsea Garunay for her early work on the exhibition. I thank my partner in shaping the presentation of the objects, designer Luisa Respondek. Luisa has been an inspiration: her ideas, her beautiful working drawings that deserve a place next to the Renaissance objects in the exhibition, her enthusiasm, creativity, and focus have pushed me in new directions. I thank Tatiana Klusak for her work on integrating words and images, something central to Renaissance creativity. Thanks to Head Registrar Jill Kennedy-Kernohan for her work on bringing the loans to the MFA.

Catherine Johnson-Roehr has been a partner on the show from the beginning, helping to shape the ideas and the message, and calmly steering the interpretation goals. I am so grateful for her contributions, support, and good counsel. I thank Adam Tessier for his early support for the project. I am grateful to Dalia Habib Linssen for organizing our academic roundtable and for all her efforts to connect with the academic community. George Sharoun, Michael Roper, and Sarah Cowan have been generous with ideas for presenting the show to our public. Sean Halpert has made sure that the Italian Renaissance is well represented in our bookstore. I am sincerely grateful to current and former colleagues in Development, especially Stephanie Heinbeck, Lucia Marconi, and Emma Rose Rainville for their efforts on behalf of the project and publication.

In Art of Europe, I thank Frederick Ilchman and Cara Wolahan for their help with the paintings in the book and show, and Cara in particular with her help with the loans to the show; Courtney Harris and Thomas Michie, Russell B. and Andrée Beauchamp Stearns Senior Curator of Decorative Arts and Sculpture Emeritus, Art of Europe, for support, advice, and research on the decorative arts objects; and Katie Hanson, Antien Knapp, and Julia Welch for their support. Special thanks to Simona Di Nepi, Charles and Lynn Schusterman Curator of Judaica, whose work on Judaica, Jewish history and experience as well as Italian Renaissance art has been inspiring for this project. Thanks to Victoria Reed, Sadler Senior Curator for Provenance, who has worked on so many objects in the show across time, as both a Renaissance scholar and a provenance curator.

I am so proud to work with these brilliant, dedicated professionals: each made important contributions to this project. A personal note of thanks to Nancy Berliner; Lawrence Berman, Norma Jean Calderwood Senior Curator of Ancient Egyptian, Nubian, and Near Eastern Art; Nonie Gadsden, Katharine Lane Weems Senior Curator of American Decorative Arts and Sculpture; Kristen Gresh, Estrellita and Yousuf Karsh Senior Curator of Photographs; Karen Haas, Lane Senior Curator of Photographs; Erica Hirschler, Croll Senior Curator of American Paintings; Thomas Michie; Anne Nishimura Morse, William and Helen Pounds Senior Curator of Japanese Art; Ben Weiss; and Lauren Whitley for friendship and support in difficult times.

Outside the Museum, I thank Denise Allen, Jo Ann Cambareri, Richard and Jonel Cambareri, Claude Cernuschi, Mary Di Matteo, Susan Forster, Kathy McGuinn, Gregory Molinari, Lucio Riccetti, Martha Richardson, Barbara Ross, and Sheila Sawyer, for their love, friendship, and support. I honor the memory of my parents, Marie and Richard Cambareri, and my grandmothers, Mary Serritella and Carmella Cambareri, who remain with me in spirit every day.

Marietta Cambareri
Senior Curator of European Sculpture and
Jetskalina H. Phillips Curator of Judaica

Index

MFA Boston

MFA Publications
Museum of Fine Arts, Boston
465 Huntington Avenue
Boston, Massachusetts 02115
www.mfa.org/publications

Published in conjunction with the exhibition *Strong Women in Renaissance Italy*, organized by the Museum of Fine Arts, Boston, September 9, 2023–January 7, 2024.

Exhibition generously supported by Tamara Petrosian Davis and Charles Howard Davis II. Additional support from Dr. Susanna I. Lee, the Cordover Exhibition Fund, the Patricia B. Jacoby Exhibition Fund, and The Bruce and Laura Monrad Fund for Exhibitions.

Generous support for this publication provided by the Andrew W. Mellon Publications Fund. Additional support from Tamara Petrosian Davis and Charles Howard Davis II.

ISBN 978-0-87846-892-8
Library of Congress Control Number: 2023933902

Details: p. 2, fig 9; p. 4, fig. 11; p. 6, fig. 19; p. 8, fig 16; p. 10, fig. 1; p. 18, fig. 2; p. 20, fig. 13; p. 36, fig. 22; p. 50, fig. 40; p. 78, fig. 63; p. 98, fig. 73; p. 116, fig. 92; p. 118, fig. 95; p. 130, fig. 103.

Front cover: Lorenzo Costa, *Portrait of a Woman with a Pearl Necklace* (detail, fig. 15).
Back cover: Pier Jacopo Alari Bonacolsi, *Cleopatra* (detail, fig. 73).
Endpapers: Patterns from Isabella Catanea Parasole, *Gemma pretiosa delle virtuose donne*, 1625 (fig. 70).

Illustrations in this book were photographed by the Imaging Studios, Museum of Fine Arts, Boston, except where otherwise noted.

Edited by Hope Stockton
Proofread by Dalia Geffen
Design and production by Anjali Pala
Typeset in Heldane Text and National
Printed on 150 gsm GardaPat Kiara
Printed and bound at Verona Libri, Verona, Italy

Distributed by
ARTBOOK | D.A.P.
75 Broad Street, Suite 630
New York, New York 10004
www.artbook.com

FIRST EDITION

Printed and bound in Italy
This book was printed on acid-free paper.

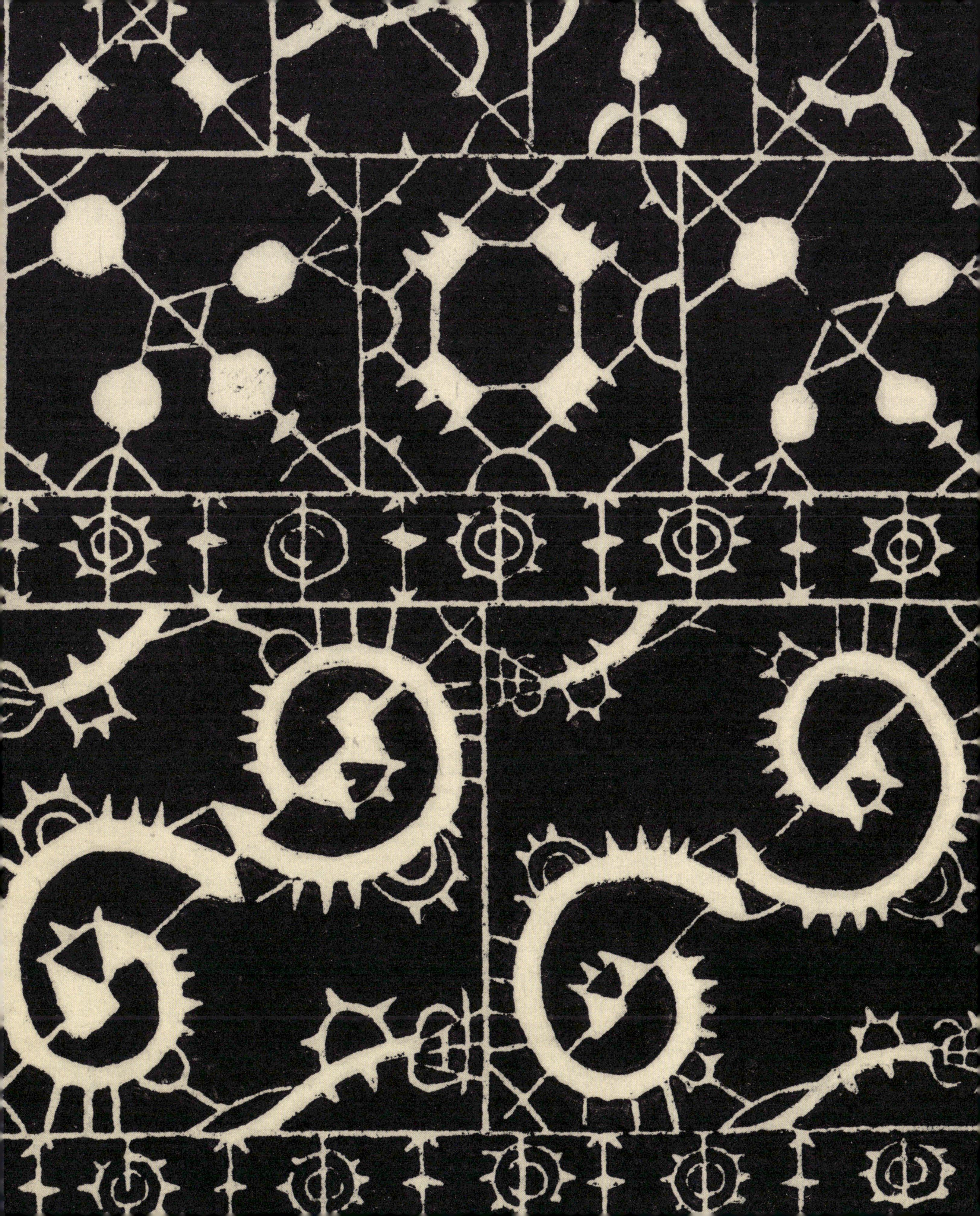

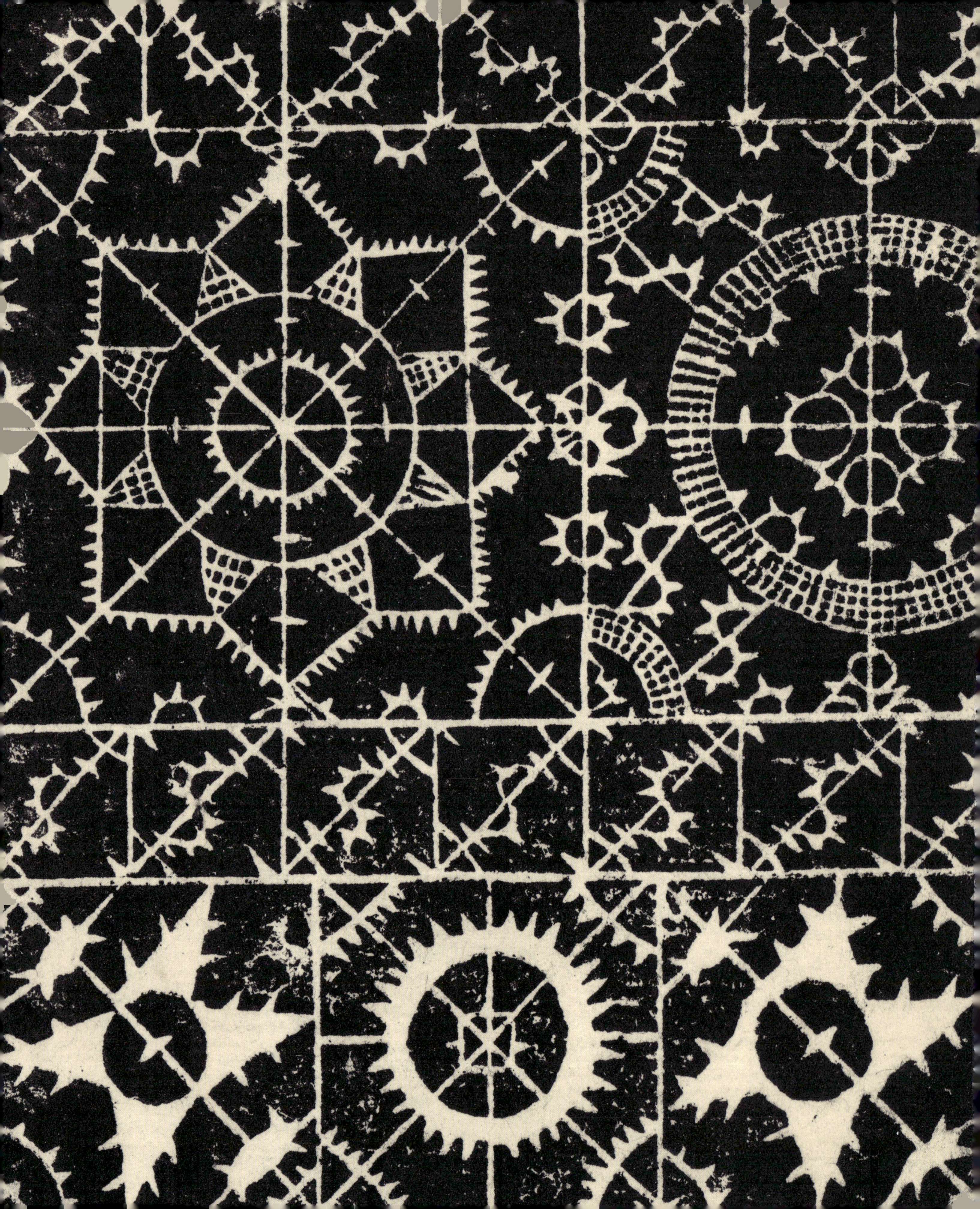